TRUE

$10.95

DATE			

90

98

• Mrs. Fearnow's Delicious Brunsw   Maunsel White's
• Panola Pepper Sauce • Amber Br   gdon's Happy Hollo
y Hams • Colonel Bill Newsom's Ke   snort Smoked Rainb
• Callaway Gardens Speckled Heart Grits • White Lily Flour • Bailey's Homemade Ho
• Jelly Sherardiz   ansel's Rice • Garber
Yams • Warrento   ssinger's Flying Pig B
Arrow Ranch Ax   ory-Smoked Sausage
• Golden Mill So   ms Sweet Vidalia Oni
f Luck Scottish S   ker Deluxe Moon Pies
Kitchen Derb   otato Chips • Charlie
Rendezvous   Barq's Root Beer • L
vine • Crickle   ens Cut Leaf Poke Sa
• Mrs. Fear   • Maunsel White's
• Panola Pep   Higdon's Happy Hollo
y Hams • Co   ksnort Smoked Rainb
• Garber Farr   nions • Callaway Gardens
ed Heart Grit   Pepper Jelly • Mayhaw J
dized Pecans   • Ledford Mill Borrowed
en Arrow Ra   s Hickory-Smoked Sausag
• Golden Mi   f Luck Scottish Shortbre
hoes and   s Kitchen Derby Pie • Lis
Orchard   Zapp's Potato Chips • C
Rendezv   e • Barq's Root Beer • L
vine • Cr   Allens Cut Leaf Poke Sa
• Mrs.   ard • Maunsel White's
• Panola   lly Higdon's Happy Hollo
y Hams   Bucksnort Smoked Rainb
• Garber   nions • Callaway Garden
ed Heart   Pepper Jelly • Mayhaw J
dized Pe   • Ledford Mill Borrowed
en Arrow   Hickory-Smoked Sausag
• Golden   f Luck Scottish Short'

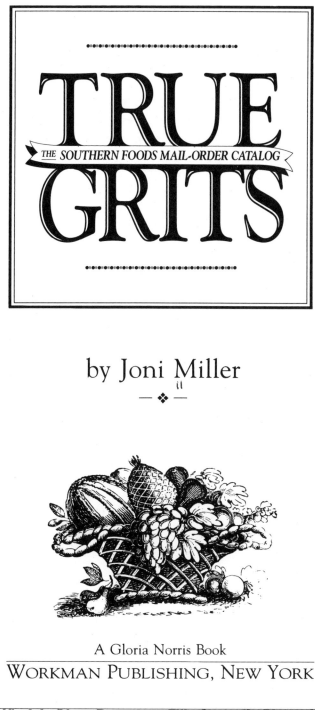

TRUE GRITS

THE SOUTHERN FOODS MAIL-ORDER CATALOG

by Joni Miller

A Gloria Norris Book

WORKMAN PUBLISHING, NEW YORK

Library of Congress Cataloging-in-Publication Data

Miller, Joni K.
          True grits : The southern foods mail-order
          catalog / Joni Miller.
               p.   cm.
          Includes index.
          ISBN 0-89480-344-1
1. Food—Catalogs.
2. Cookery, American—Southern style.
3. Grocery trade—Southern States—Directories.
I. Title. TX354.5.M55   1989
664′.029′473—dc20
                                        88-51583
                                           CIP

Product photography: Walt Chrynwski
Cover illustration: Joseph Scrofani
Cover design: Charles Kreloff

Workman Publishing Company, Inc.
708 Broadway
New York, New York 10003

Manufactured in the United States of America

First printing August 1990
10   9   8   7   6   5   4   3   2   1

For Gammie.
She fed me.

Acknowledgments

True Grits started out to be a modest-size mail-order guide to Southern foods, but along the way the page count began to rival *Gone with the Wind*. This is another way of saying the manuscript was late. Thus it is with the deepest appreciation that I thank for their patience, kindness, and graciousness at every turn: my associate Gloria Norris, who suggested the idea of this book; my publisher, Peter Workman, whom I admire for his vision of publishing; my editor, Suzanne Rafer, whose deft skills and generous spirit are unrivaled.

Photographer Walt Chrynwski made the fine products look their best, gave them a home in his studio, and was an enthusiastic taster.

I appreciate as well the efforts of others at Workman, among them Bert Snyder and his sales force, art director Charles Kreloff and designer Judy Doud Lewis, Steve Garvan (for ham help), Beth Pearson, Mary Wilkinson, and Shannon Ryan.

There would be no book without the special help provided by my dear friends Cathy O'Haire and Judy Langer. I am grateful to the other friends who made the long haul with me, as tasters and supporters: Jane Bosveld, Gerdi Eller, Wade McCann, John McCormack, Len Redican, Michael and Maria Volpe, Janet Ziff and Len Berman, and Albert Volk and Danny Saltiel (who hope they never see another peanut).

Representatives of state departments of agriculture were most cooperative: Lanny Williams and Suellen Stokes (Georgia); Elizabeth Smith (Kentucky); Roy L. Johnson and Chris Walters (Louisiana); Theresa Hamby (North Carolina); Becky Walton (South Carolina); Joe Gaines, Kevin Hosey, Lou Pitts (Tennessee); Carol Guthrie, Danny Presnal, Paulette Schwartz (Texas); also Pat Robbins of the Arkansas State Plant Board and Pamela Brady of the University of Arkansas Cooperative Extension Service. For information they shared, I am grateful to the Georgia Peanut Commission; Louisiana Yam Commission; National Sweet Sorghum Producers and Processors Association; Betsy Owens, Director of Growers Peanut Food Promotions; Sweet Potato Council of the U.S.; Texas Fresh Promotional Board. Toombs-Montgomery Vidalia Onion Growers; Betty Bazemore at the Vidalia Chamber of Commerce; Vidalia Onion Growers & Distributors Association; Carol Wells of the French Market Corporation; Joseph Ball of the Florida Gift Fruit Shippers Association; Virgil Culver and Daniel E. McGee of the Mississippi Specialty Foods Association; Lisa Lafoon of FLAVA.

Among the food professionals who shared their time and information, I'm grateful to: Harriet Aldridge of the *Arkansas Gazette*; Helen Austin of the *Arkansas Democrat*; Lee Bailey; Sally Belk of *Bon Appetit*;

Nathalie Dupree, author of *The New Southern Cooking*; Camille Glenn, author of *The Heritage of Southern Cooking*; Heather McPherson of *The Orlando Sentinel*; Charles Patteson, author of *Kentucky Cooking*; Frank Stitt of the Highlands Bar & Grill in Birmingham, Alabama; Nach Waxman of Kitchen Arts & Letters.

Thanks as well to: Joy Angel of Angel Craft, Inc.; Nelson Bangs at the Dr Pepper Company; Pam Barefoot of the Blue Crab Bay Company; Shane Bett of the Prospect Store in Prospect, Kentucky; Lawrence Bloemer, Jr., of Bloemer Food Sales, Louisville, Kentucky; Sharon Burress of Miller's Country Hams, Dresden, Kentucky; Christine Cahn of White Lily Foods; Rita Calvert; Debbie Dean of Indianola Pecan House, Indianola, Mississippi; Stanley Demos of The Stanley Demos Coach House, Lexington, Kentucky; Crescent Dragonwagon of Dairy Hollow House in Eureka Springs, Arkansas; Dottie Eckman of Basket Occasions, Brentwood, Tennessee; Sandy and Steve Forrest of Mountain Mercantile, Moravian Falls, North Carolina; Mrs. Avie Lou Frye of Danville, Kentucky; Francis Hunter of Hill Country Foods, Dallas, Texas; Liz Johnson of Cobble & Mickle Books; Patrick Keenan of Pioneer Flour Mills, San Antonio, Texas; Philip Kovats of Maker's Mark Bourbon Products, Louisville, Kentucky; Louis Lamb, owner of Lamb's Grist Mill, Hillsboro, Texas;

Pamela Ann Melton of Ruthie's Chip Corporation in Dallas; Pat Mitchamore of Jack Daniel's; Courtney Parker of Natchez, Mississippi; Fred T. Parker of Parker's Peanuts, Courtland, Virginia; John Penn of Penn's Country Hams, Mannsville, Kentucky; Kitty Peterson and Hooker Rhodes of the Louisiana Pecan Festival; Sam and Diane Rushing of The Winery Rushing in Merigold, Mississippi; Carolyn Sharp of Schwegmann Giant Supermarkets in New Orleans; Margie Spurlock of Royal Crown Cola Company; Betty Wright of Siddens Country Hams in Bowling Green, Kentucky; Carol Yancey of Admore Cheese.

Extra special thanks to my friend Paula Perlis who pitched in when the going got tough; designer Kathy Herlihy-Paoli, an early friend of the project; longtime Kermit resident Lee G. "Bull Plug" McWorkman for verifying my memories of Jett's Diner; Juanita Ledet and her late husband, Harold, for hospitality in Louisiana; J.J., as always; and to Lewis Shuckman of Louisville, Kentucky, for his enthusiastic checkup calls.

Contents

Greetings from Jett's Diner

Folks who write about food are often asked, "What's the best thing you ever ate?" I really get a kick out of being asked that because I know my answer always comes as a surprise. It was—and always will be—the chicken fried steak I ate as a kid at Jett's Diner in Kermit, Texas.

You've probably never heard of Kermit (you're not alone, even lots of Texans haven't). It was a dusty little backwater town where the tumbleweeds and oil derricks outnumbered the people, and the movie theater opened only on weekends. Back in the mid-1950s little towns like Kermit didn't have apartments; most everyone lived in a house or maybe a house trailer. Transients like the oil field workers bunked down in rooming houses or took advantage of residential rates at hotels like the Reneau. So when my grandmother, an adventurous Auntie Mame–type character, took a job as a reporter at *The Winkler County News*, we wound up living at the Reneau. And taking our meals at Jett's Diner a few blocks away.

Looking back on those suppertimes at Jett's, I realize our daily presence must have struck the other diners as a bit surreal, though probably they wouldn't have used that word. We were exotic by small-town standards—a small, chic, aggressive middle-aged woman in an expensively tailored big-city suit and a polite, impeccably groomed, slightly owlish little girl in a flowered dress who used a lot of big words. Jett, a round little woman with thick, chore-roughened hands, presided over the table. On either side of her sat oil field workers, rugged sunburned characters in plaid flannel shirts, smelling and looking squeaky-clean from washing up with Lava soap. They had names like Boomer and Cecil and Harlan and Petey. Like gentlemen, they left their Stetsons hanging on wooden pegs near Jett's front door.

These were big men with big appetites. My grandmother and I were not intimidated. We were little women with big appetites. And each night, set out before us all, on a brilliantly white tablecloth starched so stiff and smooth you could have skated on it if you'd had a mind to, were the foods that united us. Platters heaped with golden fried chicken, tender pot roast, smothered pork chops, maybe some thick-cut fried ham slices with their translucent edges barely curling up, and that memorable crunchy-crusted chicken fried steak with loads of peppery cream gravy. There were so many side dishes that their back-and-forth traffic pattern almost prevented you from actually eating.

No sooner would you grab onto a piece of chicken and aim for your mouth than some fellow at the other end of the table would wave his hand toward his plate and say, "Lem, pass them beans on down here to this end." (If you got impatient waiting on the pickled beets or the iced-tea pitcher, you'd just half rise out of your chair and stretch for them. It was considered good manners to murmur "Pardon my boarding-house reach" as you did this.) Mountains of slightly lumpy mashed potatoes with gravy, string beans flecked with bacon and onion, fried green tomatoes encrusted in a light coating of crushed saltines, black-eyed peas in their own likker, little nuggets of cornmeal-dusted fried okra, red beans, roasted ears, maybe a dish of baked corn and tomatoes. Always plenty of hot-from-the-oven rolls and big hunks of cornbread. You had to pace yourself some so there was room for dessert. During peach season there might be half-moon-shaped fried peach pies with crimped edges or a Pyrex dish of syrupy peach cobbler with a doughy bottom crust and pretty twisted crisscrosses of dough across the top. The butterscotch and rice puddings were highly regarded but no match for the pecan pie, according to some.

Nobody ever pushed their chair back from Jett's table unfulfilled. It was a physical—and mental—impossibility. The same was also true of the meals I ate at my grand-mother's table—the thick, rich stews with clouds of cornmeal dumplings dotting the surface, the tart Key lime pies with towering meringues, the smothered chicken, the early morning bowls of grits swimming with butter. Jett's cooking and my grandmother's each filled the void with the simple goodness that is the hallmark of Southern home cooking.

We are what we eat is certainly true enough, but I've always thought that idea doesn't cover quite enough territory. It seems to leave by the wayside the foods we grew up eating, the meals from our past, the treasured taste treats of childhood. We are also what we *ate*. I like to think of this as a sort of gastronomic gene-alogy. I am the fluffy biscuits and smoked pork chops and corn fritters and black-eyed peas and crispy cornsticks and cooked custards and towering strawberry shortcakes that I grew up on. My own appetite descends in a direct line from the luscious home cooking of my grand-mother and from those communal meals I ate at Jett's. To this day those flavors speak to my tastebuds in a very special way. They remind me that when warmth and hospitality and simple goodness share a table, your inner being is just as satisified as your hunger. Bite by bite my food memories made me the eater—and the cook—that I am today.

Now, don't get me wrong. I'd never shun a sun-dried tomato and I'm no stranger to fast food, but if I were stranded on a desert island, I'd rather have true grits for company. And my search for the true grits I grew up on is how this book came to be.

Grits have always been my comfort food. Now I know that when the going gets tough some people turn to chocolate or bagels or macaroni and cheese or Jell-O, but the cure for what ails me has always been a big, restorative, creamy bowl of grits. One day as I stood patiently stirring a mess of snowy white supermarket grits at my stove, I realized they were really very different from the grits I grew up with—they were paler, they tasted less like corn. It set me thinking: Did anybody still grind grits the old-fashioned way? I found the answer (Adams Mill in Alabama) and along the way I discovered that countless other traditional Southern foods and ingredients were still available by mail. It was just a question of finding them.

I asked my displaced Southern friends around the country what they missed most, and then I tracked down their favorites. I asked Southern newspaper food editors, cookbook authors, and chefs what foods they felt they couldn't live without if they moved, and then I tried to locate sources. I'd always known that Southern baked goods were lighter and more tender than Northern ones, but I had never understood that the reason lay in the White Lily flour that's on practically every

Southern grocery store shelf but never found on a shelf in the North. And I discovered new things to eat that are every bit as tasty as some of the old ones (Rowena Japp's Almond Pound Cake, for example). I found slick mail-order setups and tiny businesses run out of people's homes. I found farmers and artisans and small-town entrepreneurs. I found a lot of good things to eat.

Jett's Diner is long gone and my grandmother passed away a few Thanksgivings ago, but knowing about the mail-order sources in the following pages means you and I can recreate some of the magic of their memorable meals. *True Grits* is a Southern grocery store between book covers. True grits are just a phone call away. Now let's go shopping.

A WORD OR TWO ON
HOW TO USE THIS BOOK
— ❖ —

Mail-ordering foods and ingredients is a relatively simple process these days, but even so there are a few points worth making about these Southern sources. For example, while some of the companies are pretty big and have a slick catalog, an official mail-order department, and an 800-number, others are quite small—perhaps operating from someone's home, mill, or farm—and therefore operate on a less sophisticated scale. They may not have a catalog, brochure, or even an order form. Smaller sources in particular often don't accept credit cards, and many request prepayment (often you can just call and find out how much to send). A few trusting souls ship on "the honor system" (they send you the goodies with a bill payable upon receipt of your order). Postage and han-

dling costs vary, as you'd expect. Most orders are shipped via either UPS or Federal Express at charges based on weight and shipping zones. However, be aware that in some cases (i.e., ordering meat and/or fish products) the cost of air shipping may equal or even exceed the cost of what you're actually ordering.

MOST IMPORTANT OF ALL: Always write or call ahead for current prices and availability (crops do occasionally fail, droughts do occur, and sometimes people just plain sell out early). Prices fluctuate. The figures quoted were accurate at press time, but are intended as guidelines only.

Wine • Crickle • Evelyn's Pralines • Goo Goo Clusters • The Allens Cut Leaf Poke
s • Mrs. Fearnow's Delicious Brunswick Stew • Fuller's Mustard • Maunsel White's
e • Panola Pepper Sauce • Amber Brand Smithfield Ham • Billy Higdon's Happy Hol
try Hams • Colonel Bill Newsom's Kentucky Country Hams • Bucksnort Smoked Rain
• Callaway Gardens Speckled Heart Grits • White Lily Flour • Bailey's Homemade H
er Jelly   Sherardiz   ansel's Rice • Garbe
Yams • Warrento   ssinger's Flying Pig
en Arrow Ranch Ax   ory-Smoked Sausag
n • Golden Mill So   ms Sweet Vidalia O
of Luck Scottish S   ker Deluxe Moon Pi
s Kitchen Derby Pi   otato Chips • Char
s Rendezvous Ribs   Barq's Root Beer •
rwine • Crickle • E   ens Cut Leaf Poke S
s • Mrs. Fearnow   • Maunsel White's
e • Panola Pepper   Higdon's Happy Hol
try Hams • Colone   ksnort Smoked Rain
• Garber Farms Cajun Yams • Bland Farms Sweet Vidalia Onions • Callaway Garde
kled Heart Grits • White Lily Flour • Bailey's Homemade Hot Pepper Jelly • Mayhaw
ardized Pecans • Virginia Diner Peanuts • Ellis Stansel's Rice • Ledford Mill Borrowe
ken Arrow Ranch Axis Venison • Comeaux's Boudin • Mayo's Hickory-Smoked Sausa
n • Golden Mill Sorghum • Steen's Pure Cane Syrup • Best of Luck Scottish Shortbr
eshoes and Nails • Double Decker Deluxe Moon Pies • Kern's Kitchen Derby Pie • L
n Orchard Cake • Warrenton Original Nashville Rum Cakes • Zapp's Potato Chips •
s Rendezvous Ribs • Maurice Bessinger's Flying Pig Barbeque • Barq's Root Beer •
rwine • Crickle • Evelyn's Pralines • Goo Goo Clusters • The Allens Cut Leaf Poke S
s • Mrs. Fearnow's Delicious Brunswick Stew • Fuller's Mustard • Maunsel White's
e • Panola Pepper Sauce • Amber Brand Smithfield Ham • Billy Higdon's Happy Hol
try Hams • Colonel Bill Newsom's Kentucky Country Hams • Bucksnort Smoked Rain
t • Garber Farms Cajun Yams • Bland Farms Sweet Vidalia Onions • Callaway Garde
kled Heart Grits • White Lily Flour • Bailey's Homemade Hot Pepper Jelly • Mayhaw
ardized Pecans • Virginia Diner Peanuts • Ellis Stansel's Rice • Ledford Mill Borrow
ken Arrow Ranch Axis Venison • Comeaux's Boudin • Mayo's Hickory-Smoked Sausa
n • Golden Mill Sorghum • Steen's Pure Cane Syrup • Best of Luck Scottish Shortb

"We North Carolinians, of course, know—we are not taught, we are born knowing—that barbecue consists of pork cooked over hickory coals and seasoned with vinegar and red-pepper pods."
—Tom Wicker
The New York Times

"I was raised in Arkansas on tomato-sauce barbeque and to me there's no other kind."
—Jim Turner
Super Swine Sizzlers, 1989 Grand Champions, Memphis in May International Barbeque Contest

Describe the best barbecue you ever ate to another barbecue fan and *maybe* he'll agree with you. Or maybe there'll be a lot of finger jabbing and hollering. What we can all agree on is this: Barbecue is the art of cooking meat slowly over smoky heat until it's scrumptiously tender and soaked with wood-smoke flavor that satisfies as no other food can.

Barbecue experts are a world unto themselves. Some will ship their actual barbecue while others will share only their secret sauce through the mail, leaving the rest up to you. The two sections that follow honor these different points of view.

Barbecue from the Best Pits in the South

"There may be religious, political, athletic, or sexual images that stir deeper emotions—may be—but nothing in the realm of Southern food is regarded with more passionate enthusiasm by the faithful than a perfectly cooked and seasoned pork shoulder or slab of ribs."

—John Egerton, Southern Food

You don't need to roast a pig yourself in order to give a great barbecue. Thanks to the wonders of modern transport, some of the South's most famous barbecue places send shipments direct from their kitchens to your premises by Federal Express or UPS. So invite a few friends over, spread out that plastic tablecloth, lay in a supply of Wet-Naps, and get ready to "eat till it ouches you." All you have to add is the stuff on the side—coleslaw, white loaf bread, and definitely plenty of beer, iced tea, and the *vin de pays*, Coca-Cola.

Brazos River Bar-B-Qued Beef Brisket and 2-Pot Bar-B-Que Sauce

When you're talking barbecue in Texas, you're talking beef, and brisket is the cut of choice. This barbecued beef comes out of the Brazos Valley in east-central Texas, just a few miles from the area around the banks of the Brazos River, which attracted some of the first Texas settlers. Owner Craig Conlee's family came to the area in the 1800s and got involved in everything from ranching to restau-

Brazos Beef Emporium
700 South Bryan Street
Bryan, Texas 77803-3928
(800) 8SAUCES; (409)
776-0298 (Monday to Friday,
8:30 A.M. to 5:30 P.M., CST)

Free color brochure (Note: Second-day air charges are added for meat products sent to climates warmer than 60 degrees.)
VISA, MasterCard, American Express

rants. His granddaddy, a rancher, was also the county sheriff, and his grandmother's cooking was known throughout the valley (coincidentally, she fixed meals for the jailbirds). Craig imagines that her home cooking might have reformed a few outlaws.

At Brazos they take nice lean cuts of brisket, rub them with some spices, and patiently pit-cook them over mesquite and oak for six to eight hours. The result is a plump, flavorful rendition of Texas barbecue that's moist and tender, and lets your tastebuds know the meat was kissed by mesquite smoke. Each 4-to-6-pound cut is flash-frozen and vacuum-packed, and shipped in an insulated, reusable cooler. It'll arrive accompanied by a 12-ounce bottle of Brazos's famous 2-Pot Bar-B-Que Sauce.

Heating the brisket is easy as pie—just wrap the meat in foil and warm it for about 40 minutes at 350°F or—you boil-in-bag devotees are going to love this—leave it in the bag and place the whole shebang in boiling water for 35 minutes. It'll cost you $39.65, plus $5 shipping, to feed 10 to 15 hungry barbecue fans.

The 2-Pot Bar-B-Que Sauce, once described in *Texas Monthly* magazine as "a powerful henna-colored liquid that's so good you could drink it with a straw," is tomatoey-tasting with a hearty, smoky flavor and no added sugar. And how about that name? The ingredients are simmered in two pots—one with spices, ketchup, etc., the other with vinegar—and their contents are not combined until just the right moment. Warmed over low heat, the sauce enhances barbecue, fajitas, chicken, and even plain old burgers. A case of twelve 12-ounce bottles costs $41, including shipping.

Craig Conlee likes to say his Brazos products are based on "150 years of barn raisings, square dances, and Sunday dinners." Now there you go!

Charlie Vergos Rendezvous Ribs and Famous Barbecue Sauce

**Charlie Vergos Rendezvous
52 South Second Street
Memphis, Tennessee 38103**

**(800) 524-5554, at tone dial
BBCUE; (901) 523-2746
(Tuesday to Friday, 10 A.M. to
4 P.M., CST)**

**Free order form
VISA, MasterCard, American
Express**

Years ago Memphis, Tennessee, pronounced itself the "Pork Barbecue Capital of the World," and no one's ever dared dispute the claim. Memphians are just plain barbecue crazy, as opinionated as can be about their taste in swine dining. There's a barbecue spot on practically every corner in this city where barbecue is more than just a favorite food. Some say barbecue is "the element that binds Memphis into a community."

In this town, Charlie Vergos Rendezvous is a living legend. Since 1948, his pork ribs have been packing them in at his picturesque cellar restaurant tucked in an alley across from the luxurious old Peabody Hotel. The walls are plastered with old newspapers, signs, and calling cards from practically everyone who's ever visited. Charlie is the acknowledged master of "dry" ribs, seasoning his with a vinegar-paprika-spice mixture that seals in the flavor. Dark brown, crusty, lean, and moist, these ribs boast a deep-rooted smoky flavor that lasts right down to the bone. Dry ribs are even kind of dainty in an oddball way—your fingers don't come away all sticky. (The "wets" in town prefer their ribs basted with a rich, gooey tomato-based sauce that's messier to eat.) In researching their first-rate guide, *Real Barbecue*, Greg Johnson and Vince Staten traveled all over the nation to nail down the best barbecue. At the Rendezvous, they found the ribs they were looking for: "There is nothing like them anywhere," they rhapsodized. A lot of Memphians agree because they eat up to three tons of ribs a week at Vergos's 400-seat restaurant.

Charlie's son John, who gave up a law practice to join the family business, says that the shipped-ribs business started when the Vergoses ran a tiny ad in *The Wall Street Journal* and found themselves overwhelmed with orders. Bill Cosby and Frank Sinatra are numbered among their mail-order customers.

Rendezvous's ribs live up to their promise . . . and more. They arrive in a bright red box that announces, "You're Getting Ribbed." Inside is a black-and-white paper soda-jerk hat for you to don as you heat and serve up the ribs. For those who insist on adding sauce at the table, the shipment includes a 4.5-ounce plastic bottle of Charlie Vergos Rendezvous Famous Barbecue Sauce, which is thick, dark red, and contains vinegar, along with some chili powder and garlic. But if you're like me, you'll find that adding the sauce is like gilding the lily.

The Rendezvous packaging is tops. Besides the goofy hat, shipments come with clear instructions for heating the frozen ribs or storing them (they have a refrigerator life of 5 to 7 days). The minimum consists of five orders of ribs (usually there are 6 bones per order, so we're talking 30 ribs here). This is more than ample to feed five barbecue fiends, six if people restrain themselves (but they won't want to), and costs $85, including shipping. On the side, you'll want to serve cole slaw, white bread (some of us like Wonder Bread), baked beans, and plenty to drink.

VISITING THE SOURCE
— ❖ —

Charlie Vergos Rendezvous restaurant's official street address is 52 South Second Street (phone 523-2746), but it's really on General Washburn Alley, which is right across the street from the Peabody Hotel. Hours are Tuesday through Thursday from 4:30 P.M. to midnight; Friday and Saturday from noon to 1 A.M.; closed Sunday.

BARBECUE:
UP FROM THE PITS
— ❖ —

Here's a peculiar thing about barbecue: Almost all the cooks are men. Maybe it's because barbecue began outdoors in Colonial America. Strong men dug a pit, fired up a pile of hardwood, slung a 100-pound pig on a spit over the smoking coals, and stayed up all night turning the pig, basting it, and keeping the coals going. All of this took place in a primal male atmosphere created out of the enjoyment of strong drink and the telling of tall tales. Even if a man nowadays has only a boring old technologically advanced gas cooker, the scent of barbecuing still wafts a blood-tingling aroma of adventure along with the smoke.

Barbecue hooks into two passions of the Southern heart: religion and politics. Churches found the smell of roasting pig a foolproof way of attracting potential converts. Southern politicians discovered the barbecue as a means of attracting voters. You got a free meal; he got you to listen to his speech. By the turn of the century the political barbecue became a necessary political act akin to reaching a TV audience on *Face the Nation*. Even today, Tennessee and North Carolina both claim that no man has ever been elected governor of the state without throwing a barbecue.

There's truth to the notion that the best barbecue often hides behind the tackiest exterior. Look for the cement-block building painted lime green or pink. Does the place look as though it started as a grocery store or service station? All to the good—especially if little additions have been added on. That means the barbecuer's morsels have attracted one round of customer after another. Another rule of thumb is to examine the place's parking lot. The barbecue parking lot proclaims that good food is a great leveler. As Gary D. Ford advised in *Southern Living* magazine, "If pickup trucks are parked beside expensive imports, the barbecue addict knows the barbecue is good because everyone in town eats there."

Like no other food of the South, barbecue has a mystique that lifts it above the mere chewing, gnawing, and savoring of good food, above the notion that barbecue is a culinary tribal rite of men, meat, and secret sauces. It is commonly acknowledged that the South is going to go on cooking like this—slow and easy and over smoke—because this is the best way to do it.

Gridley's Pork Bar-B-Q Ribs, and Sauce

**Gridley's Fine Bar-B-Q
8571 Cordes Circle
Germantown, Tennessee 38139
(901) 757-9867 (Monday to
Friday, 8:30 A.M. to 4:30 P.M.,
CST)**

**Free order form
VISA, MasterCard, American
Express**

Gridley's is the home of the ultimate Memphis "wet" barbecue, the kind where the sweetish sauce is lavished on the ribs as they're cooking so the flavor seeps way, way down into the meat (and even the bones). What Charlie Vergos Rendezvous is to dry ribs, Gridley's is to wet ones: state of the art. Elvis liked to dine on Gridley's barbecue, and food authority Craig Claiborne, who grew up in Sunflower, Mississippi, has been known to launch himself directly from the Memphis airport to Gridley's for a barbecue fix.

The late Clyde Gridley founded the original restaurant in 1975 with his wife, Celeste, and their five daughters. It's always been a family affair and still is, with innumerable Gridley aunts, uncles, and cousins pitching in. Today there are three locations presided over by gold-jacketed, high-energy waiters, and it's said the restaurants serve more than 30 *tons* of barbecue in just one week!

The chopped pork shoulder barbecue is a country treat—richly porky in flavor, smoky and tender, with succulent fatty undertones. For $50 (plus Federal Express next-day air charges of around $40) you can order the Bar-B-Q Box with 5 pounds of barbecue, enough to feed sandwiches to 15 to 20 guests. The meat, which arrives frozen, is shipped with an 8-ounce bottle of the Gridley sauce of your choice, which comes in mild, spicy, and hot (my favorite). This is a sweetish, vinegarish sauce, and you can see tomato seeds floating at the bottom of the bottle. Also included are six small loaves of Gridley's homemade bread for sopping up sauce.

The chopped pork is tasty, but lights will go off for the ribs, which make their appearance drenched in a thick tomato-based sauce that has penetrated deep into the meat while forming a delectable crust on the surface. They're messy, as

THE TASTE OF MEMPHIS GRIDLEY'S

good wets are supposed to be, so have plenty of napkins on hand. The Rib Box, which also comes with a bottle of sauce and six homemade loaves of white bread, has three full slabs of ribs (13 to 14 bones per slab), enough to feed six people. It costs $60, plus Federal Express next-day air charges of around $40. Gridley's does not ship Celeste's famous pecan pie, which is served for dessert at the restaurants, but your favorite local version should do just fine—assuming you have the stamina to eat anything after the ribs. Gridley's shipping is smoothly professional. Just remember that there are no Sunday or Monday barbecue shipments; if you want Saturday delivery there is an additional $10 charge.

Gridley's sauces can be ordered by the case, mixed or all one flavor. A case of fifteen 8-ounce bottles costs $26, including shipping; a case of twelve 37-ounce bottles costs $40, including shipping. Gridley's is just plain hard to beat.

VISITING THE SOURCE

— ❖ —

There are three Gridley's restaurants in Memphis: 6065 Old Macon Road, 5339 Elvis Presley Blvd., and 6430 Winchester Road. Hours are Monday through Friday, 11 A.M. to 10:30 P.M.; Saturday and Sunday, 11 A.M. to 11 P.M.

— ❖ —

John Wills Bar-B-Que Pork Shoulder, Ribs, and Brisket

John Wills burst onto the Memphis barbecue scene in 1980 when he and a group of friends calling themselves John Wills and His Tennessee Playboys beat out a field of 250 contestants to win the coveted Grand Championship at the Memphis in May World Championship Barbecue Cooking Contest. The next year he walked off with the Grand Championship again, and spurred by success, he opened his own restaurant in the competitive world of Memphis barbecue. Only two months later, *Memphis* mag-

**John Wills Bar-B-Que Pit
2450 Central Avenue
Memphis, Tennessee 38104
(901) 274-8000 (Monday to
Thursday, 11 A.M. to 8 P.M.;
Friday and Saturday, 11 A.M.
to 9 P.M.; Sunday, noon to 8
P.M., CST)**

**Free price list and reheating
instructions
VISA, MasterCard, American
Express**

*Memphis barbecue champ,
John Wills.*

azine conducted an intense four-month-long series of tastings to determine once and for all who
made the best barbecue sandwich served in
Memphis. And—you guessed it!—Wills captured
the coveted Best Barbecue Sandwich award. One
judge was overheard murmuring, "Hickory-
smoked ambrosia on a bun." Now Wills is sharing that pork sandwich via mail order with barbecue lovers who live outside Memphis.

Don't let "sandwich" fool you. The 10-pound
pork shoulder he ships is food for a feast—16 to
20 of your closest friends can dine well on it once
it's heated, pulled, chopped, and set atop a bun.
Wills slowly cooks each shoulder over hickory
coals for around five hours, basting it every 45
minutes with a "secret" sauce. The shoulder arrives semi-frozen, and the meat will take at least
two days to thaw in the refrigerator, or six to
eight hours to thaw at room temperature. Then
all you do is heat it all the way through in a
250°F oven for approximately two hours. To be
authentic, warns Wills sternly, the pork must be
pulled from the bone, not chopped or sliced from
it. Once it's pulled, take a cleaver and chop the
meat into small chunks. Now put your nose
down near the meat and sniff—the smokiness
that wafts up will make you think you're
right there at the pit. And the outside crust!
That's what Wills is most famous for. It's
those crispy, smoky-brown pieces that are
the bits most barbecue lovers try to hog, so
be fair about it and mix them up democrati-
cally with the succulent, tender interior meat.

This is advanced barbecue, several degrees
more sophisticated than the classic, and it is
subtle, superb, and infinitely satisfying. To
duplicate the meal that Wills's restaurant customers line up for, serve the pork on toasted
hamburger buns with coleslaw and sweet baked
beans on the side. And for dessert, you could

JOHN WILLS'S WATERMELON ICE

— ❖ —

Peel a large, ripe, sweet watermelon and cut into chunks. Remove the seeds and purée or finely chop in batches in a food processor. You will need 2 quarts of purée. Add 1 cup of confectioner's sugar and pour the purée into an ice cream freezer. Freeze according to manufacturer's instructions.

VISITING THE SOURCE

— ❖ —

make the watermelon ice served in the restaurant (see box).

The shoulder costs $100, including shipping ($10 extra for Saturday delivery). But it's not as expensive as it sounds when you realize that it only figures out to around $5 per person. Wills's own sweet yet tangy sauce comes with the order; you specify whether they should send the mild or hot one.

Wills also ships a 6-pound whole barbecued brisket (a cut from the chest of the steer that is more often served in Texas than in Tennessee) for $85, postpaid (includes sauce; takes six to eight hours at room temperature to thaw). Ribs—either pork or beef—cost $90 for three slabs.

This barbecue is addicting. "We handle a lot of customers in Washington and New York who order every week," says John Wills. It's not hard to taste why.

If you want to pig out at John Wills's in person, the original Central Avenue restaurant is open Monday through Thursday from 11 A.M. to 10 P.M.; Friday and Saturday until 11 P.M.; and Sunday, noon until 10 P.M. A newer location at 5101 Sanderlin (phone, 761-5101) stays open a little later.

— ❖ —

Maurice Bessinger's Flying Pig Barbeque Service and Gourmet Barbeque Sauce

Maurice Bessinger's Piggie Park is a roadside barbecue shrine, a mecca that fans from all over the country have been known to travel to from stunning distances in order to indulge in the famous pork ribs and chopped ham barbecue. Topped by a huge American flag, Piggie Park is a curb-service drive-in where waitresses in red, white, and blue scurry to give service in three minutes (it's guaranteed—right there in print on the menu!).

HOG HEAVEN:
A GUIDE TO
SOUTH CAROLINA
BARBECUE
— ❖ —

"On any given Thursday over 80,000 pounds of pork . . . hit pits, grills, ovens, and cookers around South Carolina."

A few years back, Allie Patricia Wall, a South Carolina English teacher, was sitting in her favorite barbecue haunt—the renowned "Bub" Sweatman's farmhouse near Eutawville—when a doubt hit her: Could there be barbecue even greater than Bub's in South Carolina? She and a writer friend, Ron Layne, traveled 5,000 miles and ate at more than 100 places, comparing pork in all its incarnations and talking with "the people of the pits." *Hog Heaven* is their *inside* insider's guide to the best barbecue places in South Carolina, a state whose six distinct barbecue regions produce an amazing variety of sauces, ranging from the mustard bastes held holy in the central area to the tomato sauces of the red-clay country.

Wall and Layne make your mouth water with their knowledgeable descriptions of each meal, and their dead-on descriptions practically put you right on the premises of pale green cement-block joints, service stations turned barbecue cafés, and other humble fronts behind which this high art is practiced. The book's summary of barbecue traditions and lore is particularly good, including the tale of one supposed namer of barbecue— Bernard Quayle, a Colonial party-giver whose popular and lavish outdoor country feasts and pit cooking took place at his ranch, known as "the—[bar]BQ."

The book was published a few years ago but remains surprisingly up-to-date, no doubt because most barbecue joints are timeless—they rarely seem to close down or change addresses. In addition to location and hours, each entry provides a full description of the barbecue style, preparation, and ambiance.

Hog Heaven (121 pages, paperback) may be ordered for $4.95, postpaid, from the publisher: Sandlapper Publishing, Inc., P.O. Box 1932, Orangeburg, South Carolina 29116-1932.

Maurice's Gourmet Barbeque
P.O. Box 6847
West Columbia,
South Carolina 29171

800-MAURICE;
(803) 791-5887 (Monday to
Friday, 8 A.M. to 5 P.M., EST)

Free order form
VISA, MasterCard, certified
check

Inside the sit-down restaurant, where the meat is pit-cooked over hickory coals for 18 hours and basted with Maurice's mustard-based "heirloom recipe secret sauce," the smell is intoxicating.

Maurice's operation is no mere restaurant; we're talking about a massive barbecue preparation and cooking complex equipped with a fancy high-tech, mechanical blast freezer for mail-order barbecue and so on. The surprise, of course, is that none of this bigness has affected the quality and flavor of Maurice's barbecue specialties, whether you're eating right at the source or phoning an order from Maine or California.

The Flying Pig has barbecue shipping down to an art. Entrées are flash-frozen, then packed in insulated containers for two-day shipping. All prices include packaging, handling, and air express. You can choose from a wide variety of offerings, starting with three 1-pound packages of chopped ham barbecue ($45.50), moving up to seven racks of "Lean & Spicy" barbecued ribs ($169, enough to serve 21 guests), or splurging on a whole barbecued ham ($99).

Your best bet for a first-time order is the "Get Acquainted Special," which costs $79.99. It's a movable feast that lets you sample each Bessinger specialty: a whole rack of the slightly sweet, smoky barbecued pork ribs, 2 pounds of chopped ham barbecue (heat and serve on buns), and a large order of hash over rice (a South Carolina barbecue side dish made with hog jowls and liver) are shipped along with the "Dinner for Two," a microwave-ready container with smaller servings of the same items to use for a separate meal later. If you serve it all at one time, it will probably feed six hungry people. (And don't forget—you'll want to set out coleslaw and white bread as accompaniments.) A caution: There are no reheating instructions. Don't worry, though; you can pop the food right in the microwave for seven minutes or a conventional oven set at around 350°F until it's hot.

Everything is well sauced, but you should order a bottle of Maurice's famed Gourmet Barbeque Sauce for extra splashing around. This tangy, sweetish mustard-based sauce is kind of an unnerving yellowish-green color and comes in three versions. The regular—the most popular— is made with apple cider, herbs, spices, soy sauce, mustard, vinegar, and ketchup; the hickory is the same but with hickory flavoring; and the spicy takes on extra voltage from peppers and additional spices. A 16-ounce plastic bottle costs $6, or you can get a 3-pack (mixed or all the same) for $14.75.

This enlightening map of South Carolina's barbecue sauce regions first appeared in South Carolina: A Geography, *by Charles Kovacik and John J. Winberry.*

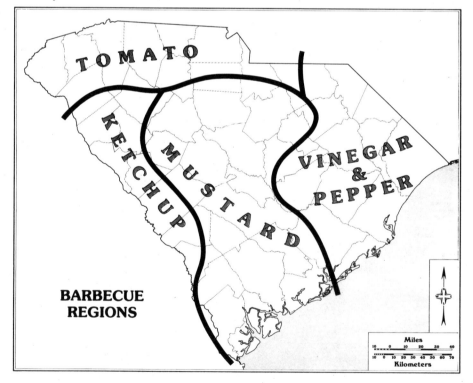

BARBECUE REGIONS

VISITING THE SOURCE
— ❖ —

Maurice's Piggie Park restaurant is located at 1600 Charleston Highway and is open Monday through Friday from 10 A.M. to 11 P.M.

— ❖ —

Moonlite Bar-B-Q Inn Bar-B-Q Sauces and Chopped BBQ Mutton

Owensboro, Kentucky, was proud when one of this country's foremost barbecue connoisseurs, Calvin Trillin, devoted a now-famous *New Yorker* article some years ago to western Kentucky's contribution to barbecue: mutton. But then, they were already proud. They say the first barbecue on record here in Daviess County was on July 4, 1834. It's hard to beat that! Owensboro, which lies smack in the heart of mutton-barbecue territory, is said to be a town where you can drive from one end to the other without ever losing the smell of hickory smoke from barbecue places. The most famous of these is the Moonlite Bar-B-Q Inn.

Since the 1960s, Hugh and Catherine Bosley have been serving up a staggeringly generous buffet to the Moonlite's crowds. As many as a thousand customers a night fill up on barbecued mutton, pork, ribs, chicken, ham, and beef—a smorgasbord of barbecue. Three generations of Bosleys now run the business, which includes a catering division that can whip up picnics for 4,000 and a mail-order division that ships Moonlite's barbecue sauces, barbecued mutton, and other delectables such as honey, sorghum, baked hams, and even its own cookbook.

The Moonlite sauces wear their hearts on their sleeves—no pretensions. Their healthy, bright red color proclaims a tomato base, sweetened by a stiff dose of brown sugar, and both the regular Bar-B-Q Sauce and the Thick & Spicy Bar-B-Q Sauce are appetizingly thick. The Thick & Spicy has a bit more tartness and sass, but neither will make a guest gasp for a beer to put

Moonlite Bar-B-Q Inn
2708 Parrish Avenue
Owensboro, Kentucky 42301
(502) 684-8143

Free brochure and order form
VISA, MasterCard, American
Express

BURGOO AND BARBECUE
— ❖ —

Eat barbecue in Kentucky and most likely the dish on the side is burgoo, a Southern stew that's along the lines of a thick, peppery soup. Like its kissing cousin Brunswick stew, found in Georgia and the Carolinas, it's a dish that draws on a long history and an almost equally long list of ingredients (vegetables like corn, potatoes, cabbage, and tomatoes, and meaty thickeners like fat hens, squirrels "in season," hogs, and mutton). This is one of the great "public" dishes of the South. Time was, you couldn't attend a horse sale, church supper, political rally, Derby Day, or barbecue in Kentucky without the reassuring sight of the burgoo chef, huge wooden paddle in hand, presiding over gigantic iron caldrons of his tasty specialty burbling over a wood fire. James T. Looney is said to have served a crowd of up to 10,000 and his fame was such that horse-owner E. R. Bradley's 1932 Kentucky Derby winner, Burgoo King, was named after him. These chefs were not shy about showing off, but they looked to a higher authority before pronouncing a burgoo ready for eating: a preacher blessed the mess by waving a rabbit's foot over it.

out the fire. Spooned on your own barbecue, the sauces add a sweet, tomatoey blanket of flavor that appeals to classic-barbecue fans. A pint bottle of the Bar-B-Q Sauce costs $1.65, a half-gallon, $4.60, plus shipping charges of $2.95 on orders under $10; a pint of the Thick & Spicy costs $2.10, plus shipping. (Above $10, shipping prices go up accordingly.) The sauces are also included in several very nicely done-up and modestly priced gift baskets that range from $15.95 to $39.95, postpaid.

If you want to try western Kentucky barbecued mutton—they churn out an average of 10,000 pounds a *week* of it here, pit-cooked over hickory for 16 hours—the Moonlite ships an excellent, earthy-tasting chopped mutton for $3.75

Moonlite Bar B-Q Inn, Inc.

per pound and sliced mutton for $6.95. Both come frozen in plastic pouches and are shipped next-day air for $11 plus $1 per pound. The classic side dish to serve along with this barbecue is a peppery dish of burgoo (see box). And, oh, yes, if you're going to serve the chopped mutton as a sandwich, forget the bun and heap the meat on cornbread and top with slices of dill pickle, just like they do in Owensboro, the self-styled "Bar-B-Q Capital of the World."

VISITING THE SOURCE
— ❖ —

The Moonlite Bar-B-Q Inn is located off the Parrish Avenue exit of the Wendell Ford Expressway. Hours are Monday through Saturday from 9 A.M. to 9 P.M., Sunday from 10 A.M. to 3 P.M. The famous lunch buffet is served from 11 A.M. to 2 P.M., the evening buffet from 4 P.M. to 9 P.M. (except on Sunday).

— ❖ —

Willingham's World Champion "Karanuff" Bar-B-Que Ribs, WHAM Sauce, and Dry-Rub Seasoning

Willingham's
P.O. Box 17312
Memphis, Tennessee
38187-0312
(800) 227-RIBS; (901)
324-7787; (901) 682-0100
(7 days, 10 A.M. to 9 P.M., CST)

Free order form
VISA, MasterCard, American Express, Discover

John Willingham was running a highly regarded barbecue place in Collierville, Tennessee, when he entered the 1983 Memphis in May World Championship Barbecue Cooking Contest and won not only first place in the ribs category, but the Grand Championship as well. He repeated this feat the following year, and then went on to win as Grand Champion in that northern outpost, the American Royal Barbecue Contest in Kansas City. So he decided to open up a barbecue restaurant in highly competitive, Memphis, where he's been a big success.

Willingham's style of ribs lies somewhere in between the two traditional Memphis rib styles known as "wet" and "dry." They are lean and incredibly flavorful with a deep, rich taste from the sophisticated spices they've been rubbed with before being hung on a carousel in Willingham's W'HAM Turbo Cooker. The pork ribs are dry

and nongreasy outside and juicy on the inside.

John Willingham ships his Karanuff (as in "Send it overnite to show U KARANUFF") World Champion Rib Pacs by the overnight courier of your choice (average shipping charge is $20). Order for yourself, or as the name suggests, have ribs sent to anyone to whom you want to say "I love you," "I'm sorry," "Thank you," or whatever. I've tried the pork ribs (four racks of six bones each, $29.95, plus shipping), but you can also order beef ribs (four racks of four bones each, $29.95, plus shipping), lamb ribs (six racks of six bones each, $34.95, plus shipping), or 1½-inch thick lamb chops (eight chops, $49.95, plus shipping). Just heat 'em and eat 'em. Each shipment comes with a little plastic bottle of a wet sauce called Sweet 'n' Sassy and a packet of Hot Stuff, a powerful dry seasoning that can be combined with the sauce for extra power.

WHAM sauces and dry seasonings, which are as tasty as the ribs themselves, can also be ordered; there is a six-bottles-of-one-flavor minimum per order. The wet sauces, meant to be used as a marinade or at the table over cooked meat, come in 20-ounce plastic bottles (six for $20, plus shipping); the dry-rub seasonings, which come in 14-ounce plastic bottles (six for $25, plus shipping), are massaged into meats before they're cooked. Flavors include Mild, Hot, or Cajun Hot (20 percent hotter than the mild in terms of spice heat and the one that hit my tastebuds just right.) Then there's Hot Stuff ("For Big Kids Only"), a hang-onto-your-tonsils dry rub (six 3.5-ounce containers, $20, plus shipping).

VISITING THE SOURCE
— ❖ —

Willingham's World Champion Bar-B-Que restaurant is located in Memphis at 54 South Holmes, across the street from East High School; phone, 324-7787. It's open seven days a week from 11 A.M. to 9 P.M.

Sauce Sources

"Start a sauce collection. To do that properly you've either got to do a lot of traveling, or else you've got to start licking a few stamps in with the spareribs. . . . There is absolutely nothing like the sight of row upon row of secret sauces . . . ."
—Greg Johnson and Vince Staten,
Real Barbecue

Once you've tasted great mail-order barbecue you may be inspired to branch out on your own. As any barbecue master will tell you, a "secret" sauce or dry-rub is the backbone of barbecuing. Barbecue sauce is a very personal thing—ask a master what's in his sauce and he'll squint vaguely in your direction and mutter "Things . . . [long pause] secret things." You're never going to pry out more information than that, but it may not matter so much once you realize that some of the tastiest "secret" sauces can be ordered direct from the sorcerer. Just be aware: None of these guys thinks of barbecue in terms of a single, dinky little backyard cookout, and they mostly ship sauces by the *case*. They can't imagine that anyone might need a *small* supply. So maybe you'll use it all, maybe you won't. Maybe you'll give away a bottle to everyone you know. Maybe you'll wind up using it in un-heard of ways. Who knows, perhaps after you've tasted all the great sauces in this section you'll haul off and perfect your own.

Craig's Original Barbecue Sauce

Cache River Enterprises
P.O. Box 272
Brinkley, Arkansas 72021
(501) 734-2633 (no phone orders)

Free order form
Prepaid orders only

Lawrence Craig was working as a riverboat cook for the Army Corps of Engineers on the Mississippi River when he developed a barbecue sauce that pleased the men on board mightily. He took it ashore in the 1940s and opened a barbecue place in DeValls Bluff, Arkansas, where the sauce became a regional favorite. Locals weren't the only ones who approved; game hunters visiting the area from all over began buying a bottle or two of Craig's special sauce to take back home. But it's only in the last couple of years that anyone outside east Arkansas could get their hands on a bottle of Craig's through mail order.

Craig's is a pour-on, or "table," sauce, meaning it's not for basting but for pouring on your barbecue right at the table. As soon as you screw off the top of the bottle, a rich aroma rushes up. The dark orangey-brown sauce has a vinegar-tomato base; Craig's "perfected" recipe omits sugar, relying on the apples and oranges the sauce is cooked with to soften the taste. It's blended with soy sauce, "secret" spices, some undisclosed fresh vegetables (onions and bell pepper definitely), and hickory flavor, which all meld together into a full, expertly balanced, mildish sauce that's in a taste niche all its own. Thick, with a lingering hickory undercurrent, Craig's Original Barbecue Sauce is terrific on just about anything you put on the table except the cutlery and dessert.

Faithful to the original formula, the sauce is now made in an old schoolhouse on the farm of Bobby Fuller, a family friend to whom Craig turned over the tasks of marketing and production. The sauce comes in mild, medium, and a tongue-scorching hot. You can order a three-bottle sampler with one of each for $6, plus shipping, or a case of twelve 12.7-ounce bottles (all one variety or mixed) for $16.20, plus shipping.

Now in his seventies, with the secret formula in good hands, Lawrence Craig spends most of his time fishing. But his wife still drops by the old schoolhouse each day, says Fuller, and is the company's best taste-tester.

— ❖ —

Johnny Harris' Famous Bar-B-Cue Sauce

**Johnny Harris' Famous Bar-B-Cue Sauce Co.
2801 Wicklow Street
Savannah, Georgia 31404
(912) 354-8828**

Free order form
VISA, MasterCard, American Express, Discover

Now here's an inspiring bit of news for barbecue fanatics: You can actually order the famed thick, tangy sauce that in 1985 won the Patron's Choice award at the second annual Diddy-Wa-Diddy barbecue sauce contest held in Olathe, Kansas. It was also the favorite in the "vinegary-sauce" category at a blind tasting conducted by *Food & Wine* magazine.

Before the sauce, of course, there was a small roadside barbecue stand started by Virginian Johnny Harris back in 1924. The colorful Harris, who used to keep a menagerie of exotic animals out behind the barbecue shed and got a kick out of cruising around Savannah in his Rolls-Royce, later moved to the present larger, more elegant quarters, where he casually poured the sauce into old whisky and soft-drink bottles for locals to take home with them. After Harris died in 1942, the business was carried on by the late Red Donaldson, a longtime employee (whose son Phillip now runs things), and it was their idea to start bottling the sauce about 40 years ago.

The sauce recipe was a collaboration between Harris and his cook, John Moore, and to this day no preservatives or thickeners interfere with its concentrated goodness. Open a bottle, take a whiff, and the back of your mouth immediately starts to pucker up—that's because the predominant ingredients are vinegar and mustard, plus ketchup, Worcestershire sauce, lemon, and a few spices, with only the barest smidgen of sugar. It tastes best when heated before using (you'll get

SMOKIN' CHIPS

— ❖ —

Great barbecue chefs choose their wood carefully and so should you. But home chefs don't always have an easy time locating the chunks and chips of wood needed for small-scale barbecuing and smoking. That's why it's good to know about the *Grill Lovers Grill Book*, a mail-order catalog from W. C. Bradley in Columbus, Georgia, one of the world's largest manufacturers of gas barbecue grills under the name Char-Broil. The colorful 32-page catalog features grills along with a wide assortment of barbecuing paraphernalia.

You can order Jack Daniel's Barrel Chips cut right from 25-year-old barrels once used at the distillery. These chips perfume the cooking area and meat at hand with the aroma of bourbon and aged hardwood (2-pound bag, $6.95, plus shipping). Alder Chips and Chunks add subtle flavor to fish (especially trout) and poultry (2-pound bag of chips, $4.50; 7½-pound bag of chunks, $7.50); or for a sweet, mild taste, try using Pecan Chips

with pork or beef (3-pound bag, $4.95). Long-burning mesquite is available in chips (2-pound bag, $4.50) or chunks (5-pound bag, $7.50). And, of course, Char-Broil also ships Hickory Chips or Chunks, the classic barbecue wood (2-pound bag of chips, $4.50; 5-pound bag of chunks, $7.50), as well as more difficult to find woods such as peach and apple.

A heavy, cast-iron grill smoker box that fits on the fire grate of any gas grill ($19.95) and 10-ounce bottles of Charlie Vergos Rendezvous Barbecue Sauce and Seasoning (the pair, $9.95) are also available. Shipping charges are extra and run about $3.95 on orders up to $20.

For a free catalog, contact Char-Broil, P.O. Box 1300, Columbus, Georgia 31993; phone (800) 241-8981. Ordering hours are Monday through Friday, 8 A.M. to 8 P.M., EST; Saturday, 8:30 A.M. to 5:30 P.M.; Sunday, noon to 5 P.M. VISA and MasterCard accepted.

"double the flavor," says Phillip Donaldson) and should be used as a dunking or dipping sauce or even as a marinade, rather than for basting. For grilled foods, for instance, you'd just liberally slather a bunch of heated sauce over the surface right before serving. Tasty over virtually all meats, the sauce can also be used as an all-around flavor enhancer.

The stubby 12-ounce glass bottles bear a bright yellow, painted-on label and are shipped six at a time in sturdy gift cartons for $14, post-paid, east of the Mississippi ($16, west of the Mississippi). Although a hickory-smoke version is available, the regular one is the most popular.

VISITING THE SOURCE
— ❖ —

The Johnny Harris Restaurant is located at 1651 East Victory Drive, about a 12-minute drive from downtown Savannah. There's an informal dining area with high-backed red booths known as the Kitchen where you can watch the barbecue being cooked in a huge open pit, or you can opt for the posher knotty-pine main dining room complete with a painted frieze of the countryside and an 80-foot domed sky-blue ceiling atwinkle with stars overhead. The legendary hickory- and oak-smoked barbecue (especially the leg of spring lamb or spare ribs) is the most popular thing to eat here, but the batterless ("nude") fried chicken also has a lot of fans. Hours are Monday through Thursday, 11:30 A.M. to 11 P.M.; Friday and Saturday, 11:30 A.M. to 1 A.M.; closed Sunday.

— ❖ —

Lucious "The King's" Barbecue Seasoning

Luscious is a high food compliment peculiar to the South (as in "Honey, I'm telling you, it was *luscious*!!") And Lucious Newsom, The King, a self-proclaimed "entertainer with food," makes seasonings that are a whole lot

SHRINES TO SWINE:
THE BARBECUE FESTIVAL
— ❖ —

Barbecue festivals are divine madness. Think of them as the public altars of swine worship. No matter which school of barbecue you favor or grew up with, a festival is fun and educational for your palate. The biggest of all the festivals is held, appropriately, in Memphis, the "Pork Barbecue Capital of the World." Each year on the third weekend in May, the Memphis in May World Championship Barbecue Cooking Contest draws more than 200 barbecue chefs and their pit teams along with a crowd of some 80,000 "tasters" to Tom Lee Park alongside the majestically flowing Mississippi River. At stake are the highly vied-for titles of World Champion in pork ribs, pork barbecue, whole hog, and the World Grand Championship. Winning this last title launched the careers of two of Memphis's more recent barbecue legends, John Wills and John Willingham (and both ship their specialties via mail order; see pages 23 and 31). The judges are guided to their final choices by fine barbecuing skills and newly invented sauces containing "secret" ingredients that range from Jack Daniel's to cinnamon, but showmanship is a major part of the game, too. Why else would those grown-ups on the teams dress in outfits like Elizabethan doublets or don riverboat gambler duds? The team names are a hoot—Swine Lake Ballet, the Best Little Boarhouse in Texas, ZZ Chop, the Pit and the Pigulum, Serious Waist (a team from a local garbage-disposal service), the Senate Sizzlers (a noncompeting Washington group led by Tennessee senator Albert Gore, Jr.). And yes, at last, the first women's team, the Pork Matrons Society, launched in 1989!

Modestly priced barbecue is prepared and sold from stands representing some of Memphis's most famed barbecue spots. As a visitor, you don't have to do anything more strenuous than take in the live music and savor your barbecue while watching the teams cavort.

Memphis doesn't have a monopoly on barbecue festivals; they're all over the place, from Clarksdale, Mississippi, to Nacogdoches, Texas. Another smaller festival of note is held a week before the Memphis one: the International Bar-B-Q Festival in Owensboro, Kentucky. Owensboro calls itself the "Bar-B-Q Capital of the World." Contact: Owensboro-Davis County Tourist Commission, 326 Elizabeth Street, Owensboro, Kentucky 42301; phone (502) 926-1100.

c/o Southern Seasonings, Inc.
428 McCallie Avenue
Chattanooga, Tennessee
37402

(615) 756-5880 (no phone orders)

Free order form
Prepaid orders only

better than good—they're luscious.

Lucious learned his barbecue skills in Memphis but then moved to Chattanooga, where he became a popular barbecue caterer. A few years ago, after 38 years of barbecuing, Lucious found himself short of money and decided to convert his closely guarded cooking secret into a seasoning to be sold in stores. So he hitchhiked down to Birmingham to sell his idea to a distributor. Hesitant at first, the distributor quickly came around to Lucious's way of thinking after sampling his ribs. Next thing you know, Lucious had started his own company.

The King is of the dry-rub school of barbecue, which means the meat is rubbed with a dry seasoning mixture before cooking, and sauce, if any, is served on the side. "If it's cooked right you don't need no sauce," says Lucious. His product is definitely a seasoning rather than a sauce, and it comes in a largish packet. "You don't add *any* water," he emphasizes. To fix ribs, sprinkle about a tablespoon of Lucious "The King's" Barbecue Seasoning on the meat side of the ribs and rub it in, then flip over to the bone side and do the same. Rub it in real good, then grill or oven-cook. And the seasoning is good on chicken, too.

When you chomp down on your first bite of ribs prepared the King's way, your first thought is "Why, it's like country sausage!" Sage, the chief herb in sausage, must be part of Lucious's "special blend of salt, spices, and herbs" that make a distinctive, down-home crust unlike any other you may have tasted. Guests who tasted ribs prepared with The King's dry-rub declared them . . . luscious. And, although I haven't tried it yet, one of his satisfied customers says basting the dry-rub ribs with Jamaican Pickapepper Sauce (available in most large supermarkets) just before they've finished cooking is "awesome."

Lucious "The King's" Barbecue Seasoning

comes in 2½-ounce packages, enough to rub approximately 9 pounds of meat. You can order a single packet for $1.75, but since the standard shipping and handling charge is $2.50, you might as well order a dozen for $17.88 and pay the same shipping. The King also makes a Southern Meatloaf Seasoning (with MSG), which lifts that old standby above the ordinary. You can mix the two seasonings in a shipment.

— ❖ —

Wilber's Barbecue Sauce

**c/o WWW Associates, Inc.
P.O. Box 1155
Goldsboro, North Carolina
27530
No phone orders**

**Free order form
Prepaid orders only**

A great chasm divides North Carolina barbecue fans. "Down East" they roast a whole pig without basting and then dress it with a thin vinegar and pepper sauce. Folks in western North Carolina—roughly west of Raleigh—scorn this sauce that puckers your mouth and serve their barbecue basted with a tomato-based sauce.

Wilber's is a fine example of Down East sauce. It comes from Wilber's Barbecue in Goldsboro, which is admired far and wide for its classic barbecue. Owner Wilbur Shirley still cooks hogs over live-oak coals—no gas cookers allowed on the premises. The sauce he deems worthy to serve on it is a thin, terra-cotta–colored vinegar spiced with red and black pepper. At first bite, Wilber's adds deeply satisfying flavor to the meat, then about halfway through you feel the heat move up your tongue. It's not hot enough to make you feel World War III is going off in your mouth—just a warm, attention-getting spike of taste. As Wilber's label states, "It's spicy good."

WWW Associates, which distributes Wilber's Barbecue Sauce, takes the flattering attitude that if you're discerning enough to order Wilber's, you couldn't possibly want fewer than twelve bottles. The case of twelve 10-ounce, shaker-type bottles costs $24, including shipping and handling, east of the Mississippi, and $27 west of the Mississippi. If you can't see yourself using that many, you can earn the undying gratitude of a Down East enthusiast with a gift bottle or two. Or—who knows?—maybe you can even convert a die-hard tomato-based-sauce type.

VISITING THE SOURCE

— ❖ —

Wilber's Barbecue restaurant itself is located on Highway 70, four miles east of Goldsboro, and is open Monday through Saturday from 6 A.M. to 9 P.M., Sundays from 6 A.M. to 2:30 P.M. and from 5 P.M. to 9 P.M. Don't forget to save room for the banana pudding!

THIRST-QUENCHERS

Y ou haven't truly experienced thirst until you've lived in the South, where most of the time it's as hot as the hub of hell. Of course, all that hot, humid weather accounts for Southerners' legendary "unquenchable thirst." When it's too hot to breathe, you can count on that endless glass of iced tea at every meal, paralyzingly potent frosty Mint Juleps served elegantly out on verandas, and long-neck bottles of RC and Coke to guzzle thankfully by the side of a dusty road.

Southerners just seem to be born with a taste for carbonation. Maybe it's part of their native high spirits. In this section you'll discover Cheerwine and Barq's, two fine regional soft drink brands that are *not* carried at every convenience store in America. A tall, cool drink of good fresh water is also highly prized and there's none better than Texas's Artesia Water drawn from artesian wells deep underground.

You can order the only tea grown in America direct from a plantation on an island off the South Carolina coast or the exact same coffee served at New Orleans's famous Café Du Monde. And there are deliciously refreshing contemporary versions of old-time colonial cider and muscadine grape juice, two old-time favorites.

Alpenglow Sparkling Ciders

Linden Beverage Co., Inc.
Route 1, Box 35
Linden, Virginia 22642
(703) 635-2118

Free order form
Prepaid orders only

Orchardist Ben Lacy III and his family have updated cider, the colonists' favorite beverage, creating a truly delightful line of sparkling ciders called Alpenglow. Named after the rosy aura of refracted light that can be seen on the Shenandoah mountains at sunrise and sunset, they're as fresh-tasting as can be.

The Lacy family has been growing apples at Freezeland Orchards on 450 mountaintop acres near Manassas Gap since 1906. As a child, Ben heard his father extoll the delights of a sparkling apple cider he had drunk in his youth while traveling in Europe as a Rhodes Scholar. The elder Lacy, head of a theological seminary, always thought it would make a festive alternative to liquor at parties. In 1979 Ben and his stepdaughter Betsy McIntyre Quarles began figuring out a carbonation process to add zip to cider without adding alcohol. They succeeded—how is a closely guarded secret—and today, at Linden Beverage Co., four Alpenglow sparkling ciders are bottled right next door to the family's retail farm market, The Apple House.

The all-natural, nonalcoholic ciders come in champagne bottles with fancy-looking foil-covered caps; the label assures imbibers there are no preservatives and no added sugar. Alpenglow has been served at the White House and dining establishments in Williamsburg, where it's offered as an alternative to wine (some Virginia wineries keep it on hand for visiting children).

The champagne-colored Virginia Sparkling Cider, made from a blend of Red Delicious and Winesap apples, has a clean, crisp, full-bodied apple taste that's lovely. You know you're drinking something special. Like beer, the cider develops a foamy head when poured into a glass. It is made by crushing whole apples into a pulp, which is then pressed to extract pure juice. After overnight refrigeration, the juice is filtered and

Alpenglow *Sparkling Cider*

carbonated (the secret), and bottled while still icy cold. Delicate pale yellow Sparkling Scuppernong Cider, my favorite, is a subtle blend of North Carolina white muscadine grapes and Virginia apples. Mulled Sparkling Cider, which has a full, mellow taste from "secret" spices, is reminiscent of a dessert wine. The newest Alpenglow is Sparkling Classic Blush, a garnet-colored cider spiked with French-hybrid Virginia-grown red grapes that add a full, fruity bouquet and aroma. The ciders, at their best well chilled, tingle the palate pleasantly and maintain their carbonation for up to three days after opening.

Alpenglow Sparkling Ciders in 25.4-ounce bottles are available postpaid. A single bottle costs $7; a 3-pack of one flavor costs $17; a case of 12 (one flavor) costs $35. All prices include shipping.

VISITING THE SOURCE
— ❖ —

At The Apple House, the Lacy family's roadside store (located on Route 55 off the Linden/Skyline Drive exit of Interstate 66), you can get gas, buy a country ham, or load up on apples from the orchard, bottles of Alpenglow, and homemade apple-butter donuts or apple pie. Open seven days a week from 7 A.M. to 6 P.M.

— ❖ —

American Classic Tea

On a tiny barrier island only 20 miles from historic Charleston, partners Mack Fleming, a native South Carolinian who is a tea researcher and horticulturist, and William Barclay Hall, Jr., a Canadian-born third-generation tea taster who apprenticed in England, are making history. At the 130-acre Charleston Tea Plantation, they've set out to prove that tea can be grown commercially—and successfully—in America, something that hasn't happened for nearly a hundred years. The part-

**Charleston Tea Plantation
P.O. Box 12810
Charleston, South Carolina
29412
(803) 559-0383**

**Free order form
Prepaid orders only**

ners' plantation was once an experimental research station opened by the Thomas J. Lipton Company in the 1960s. In 1986, Lipton decided to suspend its American tea-growing efforts and Fleming, the site's last manager, purchased it. The partners' tea is called American Classic, and it comes, at least for now, only in teabags, so it's easy to use for the South's favorite thirst-quencher, the endless glass of iced tea.

Hall, one of only eight tea tasters in America, believes the real reason American-grown tea has not succeeded is due to the costly, labor-intensive nature of tea harvesting—the leaves must be picked by hand. Mack Fleming agrees. And he believes he's solved that problem with a special hybrid machine he developed while working for Lipton. Part tobacco harvester, part cotton picker, Fleming's invention is, as he describes it, "lots of hydraulics and American technology." Other elements of tea processing are still done by hand at the Charleston Tea Plantation, however, including the all-important final sorting of leaves by size.

Wadmalaw Island's climate and soil—high

GROWING TEA IN AMERICA
— ❖ —

Mack Fleming and William Barclay Hall, Jr., were not the first to grow tea in America. In 1795 French botanist André Michaux planted tea outside Charleston, and although the plants thrived, his work was not carried on after his death. In the late 1900s the Department of Agriculture subsidized tea growing in several states but eventually withdrew support due to high labor and production costs. A South Carolina chemist named Charles Shepard was the last brave soul who pursued growing and marketing tea in America. From 1888 until his death in 1915, his Pinehurst tea was grown in Summerville, South Carolina. It even won first place at the Louisiana Purchase Exposition in St. Louis, but the business did not survive its owner's death.

temperatures and humidity combined with very sandy soil—would seem ideal for tea growing, though some tea industry doubters feel it lacks the necessary elevation. Nevertheless, Fleming and Hall have successfully harvested, cured, packaged, and shipped their new tea for several years now. American Classic is a blend of the more than 200 teas grown on the plantation, and it makes a brisk, clear, clean-tasting cup of tea. An advantage over imported teas is freshness— while it may take some imported leaves as long as a year to reach store shelves in America, American Classic can make the transition from plantation field to your teapot and then to your teacup in less than two weeks.

American Classic Tea is shipped in two sizes: a box of 20 teabags costs $3.50, postpaid; a case of six boxes (120 teabags) can be ordered for $13.50, postpaid.

VISITING THE SOURCE
— ❖ —

A visit to the Charleston Tea Plantation is a charming, educational outing. Reservations are required; tours are conducted on Tuesdays and Thursdays, during the harvest season from May through October. You'll observe the tea fields (one-acre plots of tea plants bordered by century-old cedars) as well as the processing of the tea leaves. The tour concludes with a gracious afternoon tea served on the veranda. Ann Fleming, Mack's wife, is in charge of tea, making sure there are delicious traditional Low Country teatime treats to savor, like shrimp-paste sandwiches, Huguenot torte, and Sally Lunn bread and scones served with locally made jellies. About a 30-minute drive from Charleston, the plantation is on Wadmalaw Island at 6617 Maybank Highway. (From Charleston: cross the Ashley River, follow Highway 700 to the island, and look for the plantation's unmarked entrance. It's on the left-hand side of the main road.)

THE ENDLESS GLASS
OF ICED TEA
— ❖ —

In the Southern home or restaurant there is no such thing as *a* glass of iced tea. Between the scorching weather and the rich food, most diners need more than a stingy single glass of tea to quench their thirst during a meal. Even in the most modest Southern café, the waitress pops up at your elbow several times to refill your glass—without charge. (When a Southerner visits a Northern restaurant and orders iced tea, the first shock comes when the menu says a glass is $1.50, or even more. The second comes when the bill arrives with a *charge* for refills.)

The best iced tea, without acidy taste, is "sun tea." Get yourself a quart jar and fill it with clear, fresh water. Tap water will do just fine, but the most delicious tea—the tea that Southerners remember from home meals and dinner-on-the-ground—is made from artesian-well water, drawn from an old-fashioned well bored more than a thousand feet underground to where the water is purest. Now add two teabags per quart of water, screw on the lid of the jar, and set it out in the sun to steep naturally. A half hour to an hour usually turns the brew the dark golden-amber that most folks favor.

Pour the tea into tall tumblers over, if possible, crystal-clear ice—the kind you used to buy at the icehouse and now get at the deli or convenience store. (Somehow ice clear enough to see through always tastes better than the gray, oxygen-filled chunks your own refrigerator turns out.) Lemon and sugar should be offered on the side (though many Southern eateries insist on serving it presweetened, which is a real abomination), to be stirred in with long iced-tea spoons. And as your guests stir, you'll all hear the ritual dinner music that is ground deep into Southern memories. As novelist Joan Williams describes: "The quiet was broken by a sound like the tinkling of many small bells. Grace having been said, everyone at once stirred sugar into his iced tea."

And don't forget to set that big, backup pitcher of tea on the table for keeping the endless glasses refilled.

Artesia Water

Artesia Waters, Inc.
4671 Walzem Road
San Antonio, Texas 78218
(512) 654-0293

Free order form
Prepaid orders only

Deep in the heart of Texas hill country they're sinking wells not for oil but for a fantastic-tasting brand of mineral water called Artesia Water. It's so popular in Texas these days that it outsells Perrier and tourists buy it at airports as souvenirs. In France, where bottled water is a matter of connoisseurship, Artesia is served at Paris's Bar à Eaux. It also consistently comes out on top in U.S.-held blind taste tests.

It all began with 15 hand-bottled samples and Rick Scoville's desire to "kick Perrier in the derrier." Back in 1981 Rick, a former industrial glue sales rep, turned his sights to the Edwards Aquifer, an area where surface water from the Frio River northwest of San Antonio descends underground and flows east over 176 miles of limestone, absorbing rich minerals along the way until it reemerges in San Marcos. Today a well on the grounds of Scoville's production facility taps into this source.

Artesia Water (named after artesian, or underground, wells) is a mineral water with tons of character but no salt, sugar, sodium, or calories. One thing that sets it apart from others is the light touch used in adding carbon dioxide (that's what makes it bubbly). Many other waters practically explode in your mouth, but Artesia is gently effervescent. Sipping it is like having your palate tickled just a little. As a result, "you taste the water, not the explosion," Scoville notes. And you *do* want to appreciate the taste, because although you can drink plain Artesian Water (which is zingy and refreshing), it also comes in flavors that are pure-tasting and subtle from "a kiss of natural extracts." (Flavored ones have less than 2 calories per 7 ounces.) Scoville has gone to remarkable lengths to obtain eight zesty yet subtle flavorings. He rounded up the best extracts from every manufacturer in America and then let wine experts pick the best. The flavors,

spelled the cute way, include the best-selling Cranberi, followed by Razpberi, Lyme, Peech, Mandrin Orange, Lemin, Almund, and Cherry.

Although distribution of Artesia Water is expanding outside the South and West, it can still be difficult to find, so the Scoville family is willing to ship it mail order. The Tesia Pack comes in a carton of eight 7-ounce bottles (one of each flavor). Minimum order is three cartons for $10, plus shipping. Cases of twenty-four 7-ounce bottles—plain or one flavor—cost $9.40, plus shipping.

— ❖ —

Barq's Root Beer

Barq's, Inc.
P.O. Box 1278
Biloxi, Mississippi 39533
(601) 432-7001

Free price list
Prepaid orders only

It's pronounced "Barks." Once it was mixed in backyard tubs in Biloxi by Edward Barq, who learned the art of flavor chemistry in the vineyards of France. On the market for over 90 years, Barq's is now one of the two top-selling bottled root beers in America. Southern soft-drink consumers are passionately devoted to it—one out of every five soft drinks consumed along the Mississippi Gulf Coast is a Barq's Root Beer.

Edward and his brother Gaston established Barq Brothers Bottling Company in the scenic French Quarter of New Orleans in 1890. Gaston died two short years later, but Edward, carrying on alone, won a gold medal for a concoction called Orangine at the 1893 Chicago World's Fair. A few years later he moved to Biloxi, a booming beachfront resort that attracted a rich New Orleans crowd. The sweating socialites worked up a fierce thirst in the heat, and Edward was right there to slake it with his Barq's Biloxi Pop, a soft-drink line he created in 1898 that included the root beer and creme soda soft drinks that are still so popular today. It was, forgive the pun, a Mom and Pop operation—during the day Edward delivered soft drinks to the general stores

Edward Barq, Sr. (far right), in a 1901 photograph taken in front of his first plant.

in a horse-drawn wagon, stopping along the way to sell individual bottles to parched sunbathers; at night he and his wife, Elodie, washed bottles and mixed up the next day's drinks.

By the time Edward died in 1943, Barq's was a household word in the South and Barq's metal advertising signs dotted the premises of practically every eating joint and gas station, as well as countless rural fenceposts. These days Barq's is owned by a pair of businessmen who bought it from the family in the late 1970s, but the founder's great-grandson "Sonny" remains involved in the business. In fact, every can of Barq's Root Beer bears a note from Sonny. "I'd like to know what you think," Sonny says to consumers. The result is a steady flow of fan mail.

Sonny gets a lot of letters because Barq's Root Beer is truly delicious. It's a strong-flavored, creamy brew that is not as sickly sweet or syrupy-

tasting as other root beers, and it's made using an elaborate formula based on 20 aromatic ingredients. The root beer is available by mail in attractive silver-colored 12-ounce cans (in grocery stores it's also sold in fabulous-looking long-necked amber bottles known as Amberjacks, but these, alas, are not available for shipping). You can order a case of 24 cans of Barq's Root Beer in either the regular or diet version for $17, postpaid. (I would suggest going for the regular since, like most artificially sweetened products, the diet version is overly sweet.)

— ❖ —

Café Du Monde Coffee

**The Company Store
1039 Decatur Street
New Orleans, Louisiana 70116
(504) 581-2914**

**Free order form
VISA, MasterCard, Discover**

"Coffee, doughnuts, and romance, all for a dime"—that's how locals used to describe New Orleans's scenic, bustling French Market, which was once dotted with coffee stalls. Each stall drew a specific clientele—business types cut deals at Maspero's Exchange, while at Café des Exiles aristocratic survivors of the French Revolution compared notes about previous lives of privilege. Today's prices for a thick white cup of steaming, restorative café au lait and a trinity of piping hot French Market doughnuts known as beignets are higher, but the romance lingers. At Café Du Monde, the last remaining "stall," visitors and residents alike pop in and out 24 hours a day to dreamily contemplate life and love under the gentle whir of overhead fans.

Since the 1860s, Café Du Monde has served New Orleans's legendary blend of strong coffee with chicory (usually one part ground white endive root to three parts blended beans) at its original French Market stand facing Jackson Square, where horse-drawn carriages line up to tempt visitors to view the Vieux Carré from the slow lane. The custom of mixing coffee with chic-

Café Du Monde
ORIGINAL FRENCH MARKET COFFEE STAND

ory, basically an extender or filler that adds a bitter, somewhat peppery taste, is said to have developed in France during the Napoleonic era when coffee shipments from England were blocked. Deprived coffee lovers concocted a bland barley liquid but soon discovered that adding chicory provided a fuller taste, and the habit of adding chicory stuck even after shipments of real coffee resumed.

Authentic New Orleans café au lait should start with coffee made in a drip coffee maker. Pour equal parts coffee and scalded milk *simultaneously* into a cup. If your early morning motor skills are in operation, put the liquids in pots with long spouts and pour from an impressive height to achieve café au lait's characteristic layer of foam on top.

Beignets are a traditional morning (and late night) accompaniment to café au lait. Usually served in threes, these small rectangular pillows of fried yeast dough, cousins of the American doughnut and the Mexican sopapilla, are served under an avalanche of powdered sugar. The secret to homemade beignets is canned evaporated milk. The easy way out is to use Café Du Monde's own powdered beignet mix, available in 28-ounce boxes (enough for about five dozen). All you do is add water, roll out the dough, cut it into 2¼-inch squares, and fry until puffy and light golden. A 15-ounce vacuum-packed can of the stand's special coffee and chicory blend along with a box of beignet mix will cost under $10, postpaid.

— ❖ —

Cheerwine

Carolina Beverage
Corporation
P.O. Box 697
Salisbury, North Carolina
28145-0697
(704) 637-5881

Form letter with ordering
information
Prepaid orders only

Since 1917, four generations of the Peeler family have bottled Cheerwine, one of the South's most delightful soft drinks. It's cheery and it's cherry. Octogenarian C. A. Peeler, president and son of the founder, claims that's exactly how it got its name. "Somebody suggested it was a cheerful drink," he recalls, and it does look something like a burgundy. It's been called "the Coors of the soft-drink set."

In 1913, founder L. D. Peeler was a franchise bottler of MintCola, a now-defunct brand. This was the era when America was dotted with small, regional soft-drink brands, each with a colorful name, many featuring oddball flavorings. Back then L.D. bottled his cola in the morning using a foot-pedal filling machine located in a farm-supply store and then made afternoon deliveries in a horse and buggy. In 1917 a persuasive flavor salesman talked L.D. into blending a cherry flavor derived from oil of almond with the MintCola base and some citrus flavors. Only minor adjustments have been made to Cheerwine's formula since then.

Cheerwine's complex flavor is hard to pinpoint. It's not as syrupy sweet as most Southern soft drinks. The obvious comparison to Cherry Coke simply doesn't do justice to its tangy, kind of peppery, wild-cherry flavor. But once you've tasted it, you can't live without it. For this reason, it's become something of a cult item. And although Cheerwine's distribution network is inching purposefully into areas beyond the Pied-

CHEERWINE CAROLINA COOLER
— ❖ —

½ cup superfine sugar
4 cups fresh orange juice
½ cup fresh lemon juice
1 cup Southern Comfort
¼ cup cherry brandy
3 cans (12 ounces each)
  Cheerwine, chilled

An adaptation of the traditional Orange-Blossom Punch and Plantation Punch, this recipe can also be made without alcohol and using a sugar substitute.

Stir the sugar and orange juice together. Add the lemon juice, Southern Comfort, and cherry brandy. Refrigerate to blend flavors a minimum of 12 hours. Just before serving, place the juice mixture in your favorite punch bowl and slowly add the Cheerwine. *Serves 20*

mont, the company does a brisk mail-order business. Both the regular version and the caffeine-free diet version made with NutraSweet are shipped in cases of twenty-four 12-ounce cans for $10.70 plus UPS charges (a case weighs 23 pounds and to Chicago, for instance, would cost an additional $5).

Carolinians like to have fun with their Cheerwine. At holidays it surfaces as an ingredient in everything from a festive punch, bourbon balls, and ham glaze to a good homemade ice cream. (Recipes sent on request with orders.)

— ❖ —

Community Coffee

In the French-speaking parts of south Louisiana the most popular brand of grocery-store coffee, which comes in brilliant red-orange bags, is called *Pacquet Rouge*. That's because there's no easy French pronunciation of Community, the brand's official name. They don't drink wimp coffee blends in Louisiana, and a cup of Pacquet Rouge will surely make your tastebuds sit up straight—by local definition the coffee in

Community Kitchens
P.O. Box 2311
Baton Rouge, Louisiana
70821-2311

(800) 535-9901 (Monday to
Friday, 7 A.M. to 7 P.M.;
Saturday, 7 A.M. to 6:30 P.M.;
Sunday, 12 P.M. to 6 P.M., CST)
Fax (504) 381-7940

Free 51-page illustrated color
catalog
VISA, MasterCard, American
Express

Louisiana is dark, potent, and rich-tasting.

The Community Coffee Company of Baton Rouge, the largest family-owned coffee processing company in the world, began in 1919 as Henry "Cap" Saurage's small Full Weight Grocery. Back then most families roasted and ground their own beans, so it was regarded as a welcome convenience when Cap started buying beans in New Orleans, which he roasted and ground to order. Then a good deed turned into good business when Cap hired his brother-in-law (the father of 13 children), sending him out in a horse-drawn wagon to try selling coffee to other stores. It worked better than anyone imagined. Pretty soon Cap realized he was selling more coffee than groceries, and by 1924 he had changed the name of his business to the Community Coffee Company. Cap Saurage never actually retired; when he died in 1966 at the age of 81 he was still hauling open the company gates at six in the morning. Today one of his sons, H. Norman Saurage, Jr., runs the coffee plant, and his grandchildren are part of the company, too.

Community Coffee has filled mail orders through its Community Kitchens catalog for the past eight years. (Long before that, though, the Saurages had always responded when expatriate Louisianans wrote them begging for shipments of "dark" Louisiana coffee.)

The two most popular blends of Pacquet Rouge, all-purpose grind or whole bean, are the Dark Roast (8.5-ounce bag, $3.95, plus shipping) and the slightly sweet Coffee & Chicory (New Orleans Blend; 13-ounce bag, $3.95, plus shipping). Decaffeinated versions are also available. For those who wish to concoct their own New Orleans-style coffee, pure, imported French chicory is sold in 16-ounce bags ($2.45). Community recommends one part chicory to three parts coffee with hot scalded milk.

CAFE BRULOT

— ❖ —

⅔ cups sugar
Zest of 1 orange
Zest of 1 lemon
2 sticks cinnamon
1 teaspoon cloves
1 cup bourbon, rum, or
 brandy
6 cups strongly brewed
 Community Dark
 Roast or New Orleans
 Blend Coffee

Place all the ingredients except the coffee in a saucepan or chafing dish. Heat gently, stirring to dissolve the sugar; mash the citrus zests, and combine the cinnamon and cloves. When the mixture is warm, carefully flame some of it in a long-handled metal ladle and return it to the pan. Add the coffee slowly. Serve immediately, or for more flavor, let stand over very low heat for a few minutes. *Serves 6*

A line of Private Reserve Select Coffees in silver bags are Community's fancier ones, and these can be ordered alone or as part of the Gourmet Coffee Club explained in the catalog.

One other item for coffee lovers is worth mentioning. The heavy-gauge aluminum canister called the Fresh-O-Lator ($11) stores up to 2 pounds of coffee (or flour, sugar, cereal, etc.) and keeps moisture and insects at bay. It's manufactured exclusively for Community Coffee Company, and they say many of the original Fresh-O-Lators are still in use after 30 years.

The catalog is upscale and sophisticated, loaded with a wide selection of Louisiana food products especially packaged for Community (spices, hot sauce, andouille), as well as kitchenware and home accessories.

— ❖ —

Kentucky Mint Julep Syrup

You know Kentucky Derby time is drawing near when Kentucky hostesses start polishing their mint-julep cups and eyeing the tulip and azalea beds. The Derby is actu-

ally run at Churchill Downs on the first Saturday in May, but the orgy of fine food, gracious hospitality, and mint-julep consumption begins about a week before.

Derby breakfasts served around 11:30 are a social highlight—big, festive, rather formal parties featuring elaborate groaning boards of traditional favorites such as slivers of country ham with beaten biscuits, scrambled eggs with fried apples or baked cheese grits, salads made of tender Bibb lettuce, luscious wedges of Kern's Kitchen Derby-Pie, and . . . plenty of frosty mint juleps.

There are as many theories on how to make a proper mint julep as there are opinions about the perfect way to fry chicken. The basic elements—fresh mint, water, sugar, and a fine Kentucky bourbon over finely crushed ice—are not in dispute, but how they are handled is hotly debated. Some believe a julep only tastes right in a frosted silver cup, while others argue that glass is fine. Kentucky and Virginia both claim its initial creation. Whether or not the julep should be sipped through a straw is another touchy area, as is whether the mint should be bruised or crushed.

Kentucky Mint Julep Syrup is the foolproof way for a lazybones to make a potent mint julep without actually confronting one of those famous, elaborately detailed, and lyrical recipes that begin with advice such as "Take from the cold spring some water pure as angels . . .". Actually, this syrup is made with Kentucky Highbridge springwater, sugar, and oil of mint, plus the barest hint of coloring, which gives it an almost imperceptible pale green color. One bottle, used according to the miniature recipe folder that comes attached to the bottle's neck, is enough to make 20 to 30 "stiff drinks," says Tillie Moore, who began marketing the syrup several years ago. The syrup can also be used to sweeten fruit punches and iced tea. A 12.4-ounce green bottle of Kentucky Mint Julep Syrup, with a pretty pink label, costs $3.95 (plus shipping). High shipping charges ($4.50 postage is the minimum) make it sensible to order other things, such as silver-plate mint-julep cups ($18.95), at the same time. (See the box below for more Derby items.) Jars of Tillie Moore's two other products, Hot Dang and Hot Damn Old Kentucky Beer Cheese (see page 364) are also featured in this catalog.

KENTUCKY DERBY PARTY SUPPLIES

— ❖ —

Everything you need to throw an authentic-in-every-detail Kentucky Derby bash is available direct from the Derby's home-town of Louisville. Betty Biesel, the daughter of a Kentucky breeder of Tennessee walking horses, is the owner of Party Kits Unlimited, a retail shop that produces a mail-order catalog crammed with Derby-theme goodies.

Two types of complete Derby-motif party kits are available that include everything from cups, plates, and napkins printed with the official Derby logo to party invitations, tote tickets, and decorations (Party Kit #8191 sells for $35.40; Homestretch Party Kit, $32.70). Party favors include Derby derbies for the host to wear ($5), lucky brass horseshoes ($2.50 each), and Styrofoam "straw" hats ($1.50 each). And, of course, you'll want a cassette of "Call to the Post" and "My Old Kentucky Home" ($5) as well as the absolutely essential silver-plate mint-julep cup ($18.95) and straws (package of 100, $2). Shipping charges are extra. To order, see the information on page 59.

Watering Trough

MINT JULEP
— ❖ —

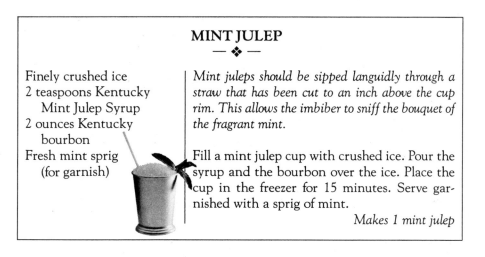

Finely crushed ice
2 teaspoons Kentucky
   Mint Julep Syrup
2 ounces Kentucky
   bourbon
Fresh mint sprig
   (for garnish)

Mint juleps should be sipped languidly through a straw that has been cut to an inch above the cup rim. This allows the imbiber to sniff the bouquet of the fragrant mint.

Fill a mint julep cup with crushed ice. Pour the syrup and the bourbon over the ice. Place the cup in the freezer for 15 minutes. Serve garnished with a sprig of mint.

Makes 1 mint julep

— ❖ —

Peychaud's Aromatic Cocktail Bitters

Sazerac Co., Inc.
P.O. Box 52821
New Orleans, Louisiana
70152-2821

(504) 831-9450
Fax (504) 831-9450 (Att: ext. 47)

Free order form
Prepaid orders only

The cocktail was invented in New Orleans, but by whom is a matter of debate. Some people say it was invented around 1850 by a bartender at New Orleans's famed Sazerac Coffeehouse. Another theory says it originated around 1800 and its creator may have been Antoine Amedie Peychaud. An apothecary by trade, Peychaud brought with him from Santo Domingo the secret formula for a liquid tonic with restorative properties called bitters. Around New Orleans, where the food was rich and business affairs were discussed languidly and at length over drinks, it was thought a shot of bitters could pretty much cure anything that ailed you. A splash of curative bitters, it was discovered, also added zest to a glass of brandy. At his Vieux Carré shop Peychaud served a concoction of brandy with a dash of his bitters to customers in a double-end china egg cup known as a *coquetier* (probably the precursor of the jigger). Mispronunciation ("cock-tay") and Americanization took their toll and the term *cocktail* was the result. Over the years, cooks discovered that the

piquancy of Peychaud's Bitters also added flavor to pork, poultry, and rice dishes.

The spicy red liquid known as Peychaud's Aromatic Cocktail Bitters is a secret, highly aromatic blend of herbs, spices, and alcohol (there's also a touch of food coloring). Peychaud's Bitters are traditional and essential in making a famous New Orleans mixed drink called the Sazerac, which is sugar-sweetened rye whiskey or bourbon combined with a little anise-flavored liqueur and a few drops of the bitters. According to John Mariani's *Dictionary of American Food and Drink*, most likely the herbs in bitters include gentian, orange, quinine, and ginger. The bitters come in a bottle with a marvelous old-fashioned curlicue-covered label (5-ounce bottle, $3; 10-ounce bottle, $4; both postpaid).

MARTINEZ
— ❖ —

4 ounces gin
1 dash dry vermouth, or more to taste
3 drops Peychaud's Aromatic Cocktail Bitters
Lemon twist

Place an ice cube in a cocktail shaker and pour the gin over it. Add the vermouth and bitters. Stir and serve in a chilled glass with a lemon twist.

Serves 1

— ❖ —

Southern Touch Muscadine Juice

Muscadine grapes might be called a new "old" Southern fruit. For generations scuppernongs and other varieties of muscadines grew wild along creek banks and woods in the sandy soil of the coastal plains region from southeastern Virginia to Texas.

**Southern Touch Foods
Corporation**
P.O. Box 2853
Meridian, Mississippi
39302-2853

(800) 233-1736 (Monday to
Friday, 8 A.M. to 5 P.M., CST)
Fax (601) 483-1864

Free 24-page color catalog
VISA, MasterCard, American
Express, Discover

Uniquely flavorful, the wild grapes have always been informally harvested in the South for use in homemade preserves and wine. But they've never been what you'd call a commercial crop. The last time anybody tried to make a commercial go of the grapes was back in the 1800s when Colonel Paul Garrett produced a bestselling wine in North Carolina called Virginia Dare scuppernong wine. But with the advent of Prohibition, his carefully cultivated vineyards pretty much bit the dust and nobody paid attention to the muscadine's commercial possibilities again until the mid-1960s.

Now there's a renewal of interest in this Southern classic and today the world's largest cultivated muscadine vineyard is located on 770 acres in Clarke County, Mississippi, a joint effort of entrepreneur Paul Broadhead's Southern Touch Foods Corporation and the folks at Mississippi State University. Here scuppernongs and other muscadine varieties are flourishing once again. The large, round fruits vary in color from a pale, golden-russet to a deep purple and may grow as large as an inch in diameter. Thick-skinned yet tender, they have a sweet, rich taste with a hint of agreeable tartness that makes them just right for juice, jams, and jellies. A combination of grapes from this vineyard supplemented by those purchased from smaller growers in Florida, Alabama, Georgia, the Carolinas, Louisiana, and Arkansas are used in Southern Touch's line of naturally sweet muscadine specialties made from both golden and red grapes.

There is a truly delicious 100 percent natural Muscadine Juice with a tart, fruity aroma that wafts up the instant a bottle is opened. The juice contains no added sugar, water, color, or flavorings (it is vitamin C enriched). It comes in two versions, golden (the color of Champagne) made from the scuppernong variety of muscadine, and .

red, which is a blend of scuppernongs and other muscadines. Aside from their colors, the two taste quite similar, though the golden may be just a tiny bit sweeter. With either type, the clean, crisp flavor comes through best when it's drunk plain, though the juices can also be used in place of cider in hot spiced drinks, or to make healthy frozen-juice bars. Both juices are available in 32- and 10-ounce bottles. Three 32-ounce bottles of one kind will cost $14.95; four 10-ounce bottles cost $7.50 (both include postage). Or you may want to sample both by ordering a selection that includes two 10-ounce bottles of each juice for $7.50, postpaid.

Southern Touch makes good use of the muscadine in a number of other products including jelly, jams, and preserves. The preserves, which are particularly good, contain whole muscadine skins, which add a pleasant, almost musky bit of extra flavor. "The Little Red Taster," with a 10-ounce jar each of jelly, jam, and preserves costs $8.95, postpaid. These jams and preserves are particularly compatible with white meats such as chicken or pork (think of them as alternatives to the usual old cranberry sauce). The two syrups, a red and a golden one for pouring over pancakes, waffles, or ice cream, cost $7.50, postpaid, for two 12-ounce bottles of the same color. Southern Touch's muscadine bounty is also available in various gift boxes and baskets ranging in price from $7.50 to $59.95.

As a special introduction for folks who have never savored the muscadine, the company will send a "free" sample package containing one 10-ounce Muscadine Juice and a 10-ounce jelly; you pay only $2.50 to cover packing and delivery, which is credited toward your first order.

THREE SOUTHERN FAVORITES

— ❖ —

THE REAL THING

"You know, the South is really not dependent on the Coca-Cola Company financially; it's just that without Coke a lot of us wouldn't know what to drink for breakfast."
—Nathalie Dupree
Cooking of the South

According to the folks at the Coca-Cola Company, "if all the Coke ever produced were placed in traditional 6½-ounce bottles, there would be 2.4 trillion bottles, which laid end to end would wrap around the earth 11,863 times, reach the moon 1,237 times, or stretch one third of the way to Saturn." There's no telling how many of those Cokes were consumed in the South, but you can bet your bottom dollar it's an astounding amount.

While Coke is the premier Southern thirst-quencher, don't think for a minute it's just for drinking on a hot day. Every time you turn around there's a recipe staring up at you that calls for Coke—everything from cakes and congealed salads to barbecue sauces and ham glazes use Coke as an ingredient (I'm talking "classic " Coke, here, of course).

Like hundreds of other soft drinks around the turn of the century, Coca-Cola was invented by a pharmacist. According to legend, on May 8, 1886, Atlanta pharmacist John Styth Pemberton produced the first syrup in a brass pot in his backyard. He took a jug of it down the street to Jacobs' Pharmacy, where, fizzed with carbonated water, it went on sale for a nickel a glass. Dr. Pemberton's partner and bookkeeper, Frank M. Robinson, who thought "the two C's would look well in advertising," suggested the name and in his own handwriting penned Coca-Cola's famous script trademark. First-year sales of the new beverage averaged nine drinks a day, and it was promoted with hand-painted oilcloth signs hung on store awnings. Dr. Pemberton sold kegs of the syrup to other fountains for a while but eventually began selling out to various partners. In 1891, entrepreneur Asa Candler became the sole owner.

Bottled Coke was the brainchild of a Mississippi candy merchant looking for a way to serve the beverage at picnics. Soon he was sending bottles of Coke up and down the Mississippi River to plantations and lumber

(continued)

camps. By 1916, Coke's distinctive hobble-skirt contour bottle design was established and Coca-Cola was a symbol of the American way of life. Coke is synonymous with hospitality in the South, as in "You sit down right there and cool off and I'll get us a Coke."

ME AND MY RC

Any Southerner over a certain age—say, 45 or so—remembers the after-school pleasure of searching for the big 12-ounce RC in the soft-drink ice chest. By the laws of gravity the big RCs sank to the bottom of the frigid water, hidden deep under the rolling stacks of smaller Nehi Oranges, Dr Peppers, and NuGrapes. Ignoring the numbing of your hand, you persisted until—at last!—your

fingers closed on the long, tall bottle that gave you more cola for your money than any other drink. If your reddened hand still possessed flexibility, you probably then purchased the second item of after-school feasting—a bag of peanuts—and fed the salty peanuts into the icy sweetness of the RC. Drinking this concoction was a slow, sweet escape from duty. And tomorrow's homework seemed a long way away.

Actually, the first Royal Crown was a ginger-ale fizz water. Around the turn of the century a young pharmacist, Claud A. Hatcher, was experimenting in creating soft drinks in the basement of the wholesale grocery business he ran with his father in Columbus, Georgia, and hit on a pleasant ginger-ale formula he called Royal Crown. This was an era when countless soda drinks were peddled by pharmacies all over America, but unlike many long-forgotten small brands, Hatcher's prospered. However, it wasn't until the low times of the Depression, after Hatcher's death in 1933, that the company came up with a brilliantly tasty new sparkling cola, and the management marketed it under the name of Hatcher's old ginger ale: Royal Crown. Twelve ounces for a nickel was a great buy in Depression times, and RC, as it quickly became known, emerged as one of the great soft drinks of the South. A hillbilly song immortalized it and another of its snacktime companions: "I Want an RC and a Moon Pie."

While corporate changes have swept much of the company headquarters up to Illinois, the syrup division stays right on in Columbus, Georgia. That news kind of makes you yearn for an RC and a Moon Pie.

DR PEPPER: HAVE A BITE TO DRINK AT 10, 2, AND 4!

It seems that Texans won't bother to claim a thing unless it's the biggest, richest, or first. With Dr Pepper—one of your old-time great soft drinks—they've got a big Texas first. Concocted in 1885 by Waco pharmacist Charles Alderton, Dr Pepper is the oldest of all the major brand soft drinks in America. (Take that, you-know-who!)

For decades the old script "Dr. Pepper" logo (with the period) on bottles was a signal of refreshment. The famous Dr. Pepper outdoor thermometer, the ice chests, and bottles are collector's items. And the clock face and accompanying jingle that Dr. Pepper introduced in the 1940s became part of Southern humor. The clock, with an illogical three hands, pointed simultaneously to 10, 2, and 4, while the jingle advised you to have one at those hours every day. Having one at "10, 2, and 4" became a wisecrack for all kinds of services the wisecracker needed three times a day, ranging from the whimsical to the vulgar.

Dr. Pepper burst on the scene at Wade Morrison's Old Corner Drug Store in Waco, Texas, where customers gathered of a morning to chat over such news as the latest wagon-train arrival on the banks of the nearby Brazos River. Charles Alderton, the owner's assistant, had already made a hit with the locals by mixing his own flea powder for Waco's canines, and he now noticed the soda fountain's customers were tired of the sarsaparilla- and fruit-flavored carbonated drinks he served. He whipped up a new blend so popular it required a name. Wade Morrison, the owner, still pined for the teenage daughter of a pharmacist he'd worked for back in Virginia. The girl's father, Dr. Charles Pepper, had discouraged marriage plans. Supposedly hoping to win the father's goodwill, Morrison named the drink "Dr. Pepper" after him. The ploy didn't work—he ended up marrying a local girl—but "Dr. Pepper," with its non-cola, cherrylike flavor, went on to become a fabulous success—even though some purists still miss the old script logo (and the period after Dr that went with it).

s • Mrs. Fearnow's Delicious Brunswick Stew • Fuller's Mustard • Maunsel White's
• Panola Pepper Sauce • Amber Brand Smithfield Ham • Billy Higdon's Happy Holl
ry Hams • Colonel Bill Newsom's Kentucky Country Hams • Bucksnort Smoked Rain
• Callaway Gardens Speckled Heart Grits • White Lily Flour • Bailey's Homemade H
r Jelly   Sherardiz...   ...nsel's Rice • Garber
Yams • Warrento...   ...singer's Flying Pig I
n Arrow Ranch Ax...   ...ory-Smoked Sausage
• Golden Mill So...   ...ms Sweet Vidalia On
of Luck Scottish S...   ...ker Deluxe Moon Pie
s Kitchen Derby Pi...   ...otato Chips • Charl
s Rendezvous Ribs...   ...Barq's Root Beer •
wine • Crickle • E...   ...ens Cut Leaf Poke S

FOR THE SWEET TOOTH

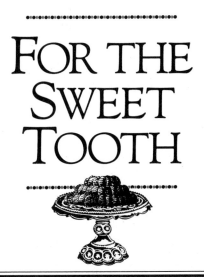

s • Mrs. Fearnow'...   ... • Maunsel White's
• Panola Pepper...   ...Higdon's Happy Holl
ry Hams • Colone...   ...ksnort Smoked Rain

• Garber Farms Cajun Yams • Bland Farms Sweet Vidalia Onions • Callaway Garde
kled Heart Grits • White Lily Flour • Bailey's Homemade Hot Pepper Jelly • Mayhaw
rdized Pecans • Virginia Diner Peanuts • Ellis Stansel's Rice • Ledford Mill Borrow
ken Arrow Ranch Axis Venison • Comeaux's Boudin • Mayo's Hickory-Smoked Sausa
n • Golden Mill Sorghum • Steen's Pure Cane Syrup • Best of Luck Scottish Shortb
shoes and Nails • Double Decker Deluxe Moon Pies • Kern's Kitchen Derby Pie • Li
n Orchard Cake • Warrenton Original Nashville Rum Cakes • Zapp's Potato Chips •
s Rendezvous Ribs • Maurice Bessinger's Flying Pig Barbeque • Barq's Root Beer •
wine • Crickle • Evelyn's Pralines • Goo Goo Clusters • The Allens Cut Leaf Poke S
s • Mrs. Fearnow's Delicious Brunswick Stew • Fuller's Mustard • Maunsel White's
e • Panola Pepper Sauce • Amber Brand Smithfield Ham • Billy Higdon's Happy Hol
try Hams • Colonel Bill Newsom's Kentucky Country Hams • Bucksnort Smoked Rain
• Garber Farms Cajun Yams • Bland Farms Sweet Vidalia Onions • Callaway Garde
kled Heart Grits • White Lily Flour • Bailey's Homemade Hot Pepper Jelly • Mayhaw
rdized Pecans • Virginia Diner Peanuts • Ellis Stansel's Rice • Ledford Mill Borrow
ken Arrow Ranch Axis Venison • Comeaux's Boudin • Mayo's Hickory-Smoked Sausa
n • Golden Mill Sorghum • Steen's Pure Cane Syrup • Best of Luck Scottish Shortb

When the notorious Southern sweet tooth isn't focusing on cakes and pies, you can bet it's pursuing candy. The legacy of the country store candy counter, grandmother's candy bowl, and the coveted recipes of the ladies' church circle cookbook remain in safe hands because lots of old-time treats like Goo Goo Clusters are still produced by their original makers. From Louisiana there are Evelyn LeBlanc's hand-made pralines (the best in the world, not just the South), from Georgia there's a positively addicting peanut brittle known as Crickle, and from Kentucky there's a bourbon candy so good it's sinful.

How important is candy in the South? Well, for years the label on a Goo Goo Cluster pointed out it was "a nourishing lunch." That pretty much sums up the candy issue.

Buckley's Original English Toffee and Pecan Butter Brittle

Buckley's Fancy Foods & Confections, Ltd.
P.O. Box 14119
Baton Rouge, Louisiana 70898-4119

(504) 642-8381 (Monday to Friday, 8 A.M. to P.M., CST)

Free order form
VISA, MasterCard

Customer loyalty is a good indicator of just how delicious some things are. So it's worth noting that M. S. "Papa" Buckley's very first mail-order customer from 31 years ago is still placing orders for Buckley's scrumptious morsels of Original English Toffee.

Back in the late 1950s in Mississippi, Papa Buckley perfected a special recipe for a hand-made toffee made from almonds, sugar, and butter that he made once a year for a local church bazaar and sent at Christmastime to friends and relatives in Georgia. Word got out, as it tends to when something good to eat is involved, and pretty soon people were trying to place orders for more. Eventually Buckley converted his back-yard greenhouse into a candy kitchen and began a small mail-order business (early on, orders from strangers were mailed care of the church, simply addressed "Toffeemaker"). The candy was made in 5-pound batches and stirred with a bizarre-looking contraption Buckley invented because his arms got so tired (imagine a drill press converted into a beater and propelled by an old clothes-dryer motor). Once the candy reached the proper consistency it was poured onto marble slabs, spread by hand with a spatula, and cut into bite-size pieces with a pizza cutter.

It's a pleasure to report that very little about Papa Buckley's toffee has changed over the years. When he retired in 1979, the business was taken over by his daughter, Beverly Buckley Stern, who eventually moved the candy making from the greenhouse into a factory in the small rural community of Sunshine, Louisiana, outside Baton Rouge. But the candy is still made in small batches, carefully spread, cut, and packaged by hand. Only the freshest ingredients are used, there are no preservatives, and the candies are vacuum-packed in tins to ensure freshness. In the past year or so, many specialty food shops

have begun stocking these candies, but you can still order them from the original maker.

Buckley's Original English Toffee is a thin, crunchy, pale tan-colored confection made from sugar, butter, margarine, and ground almonds. The toasty, buttery-tasting candies are cut into bite-size squares and come in 2-pound tins with a very distinguished-looking label ($13, postpaid). I'm partial to the award-winning Pecan Butter Brittle, which Beverly began making several years ago. Made from the same ingredients as the toffee but with pecans bits (Sunshine is pecan-growing territory) instead of almonds, pieces of this candy are a darker caramel color with a deeper mellow flavor (12-ounce tin, $9.50, postpaid). The toffee and brittle are most fun to savor when you're stretched out on the bed with a good book.

Also available are Sunshine Pecans, small roasted pecan halves with a praline coating ($9.50 for a 12-ounce tin, postpaid), and three flavors of medium-roast, whole bean "Dessert Coffees" (Pecan Praline, Almond Toffee, Chocolate Mist, 8-ounce tin, $8.50, postpaid). A Gift Pack with 1 pound of the toffee, a 12-ounce tin of the brittle, and an 8-ounce tin of the coffee of your choice ($25, postpaid) is a nice way to acquaint yourself with Papa Buckley's sweet legacy.

— ❖ —

Crickle®

Crickle is a registered trademark of DeSoto Confectionery & Nut Company.

If Jimmy Carter hadn't become president, A. B. Carlan might still be farming peanuts and running a supply store. And Nancy Carlan's incredible nut brittle might still be the best-kept secret of Sumter County, Georgia. But tiny DeSoto is just a stone's throw from Plains, situated along U.S. Highway 280, and that bit of road was so clogged with tourists back in the 1970s that local farmers were having a hard time bring-

DeSoto Confectionery & Nut Company
P.O. Box 72
DeSoto, Georgia 31743
(800) 237-8689; (912) 874-1200 (Monday to Friday, 8 A.M. to 6 P.M., EST)

Free illustrated color brochure
VISA, MasterCard

ing their crops into town. In an effort to both "entertain" and sidetrack tourists, the Carlans converted a little frame house on their property into a roadside candy kitchen, hired two local women as candy cooks, and set out to break "the brittle barrier" with Nancy's unique twist on a favorite Southern confection.

Nancy Carlan makes the best peanut and pecan brittle you're ever likely to taste. (A. B.'s business associates used to look forward to his visits because he always brought along a batch in a Tupperware tub.) Most brittles glom onto your teeth, but Nancy's melts in your mouth. It's light, delicate, and crispy rather than rock hard. That's why the Carlans patented the name Crickle for it. Each golden-brown slab of Crickle is laden with Georgia peanuts or pecans. And there are no additives or preservatives. "It's not the recipe," Nancy Carlan says firmly, "it's how it's made." Though the company is not so small anymore (sales are almost $1 million and there's a large concrete candy factory) Crickle is still mixed in ordinary hand-held pots and poured onto marble slabs by a person, not a machine.

Peanut Crickle comes in cellophane bags (six ½-pound bags, $23.95, postpaid), plastic pails (1 pound, $8.95, postpaid) and tins (2 pounds, $22.95). Pecan Crickle costs a few dollars more. A combination gift box is a good way to taste both (box with a 1-pound bag of each, $18.95).

Other tasty DeSoto specialties include Popcrickle, a combination of popcorn, pecans, almonds, and peanuts drenched in a honey-vanilla glaze (14-ounce plastic pail, $7.95, postpaid) and Teejays, crunchy candy-coated peanuts (24-ounce plastic pail, $12.95, postpaid). DeSoto giftbox selections are available year round, shipped in a sturdy mailing carton. Prices are postpaid to the East Coast; add $2 per order for Rocky Mountain and West Coast shipments.

Davidson of Dundee Natural Citrus Juice Candies, Marmalades, Jellies, and Butters

Davidson of Dundee
P.O. Box 800
Dundee, Florida 33838

(813) 439-1698 (Monday to Friday, 8 A.M. to 5 P.M., EST)

Free 12-page color catalog
VISA, MasterCard

Chances are if you've traveled what is jokingly known by locals as Florida's "tourist trail" (places like Cypress Gardens, EPCOT Center and Busch Gardens), you've seen boxes of these unusual, jewel-like fruit candies at every turn.

When Glen Davidson was a little kid in Winter Haven, Florida, his mother made a delicious confection from fresh citrus fruit juice. Glen grew up and left Florida, becoming, among other things, vice-president and director of marketing at the Sheaffer Pen Company. But in the mid-1960s he decided there was more to life than spending it in the corporate fast lane. Missing his home state, Davidson began to think of ways to return to Florida and still make a living. Remembering his mother's unique candy, he perfected a similar recipe and opened a small candy shop located on heavily traveled U.S. 27 just north of the Dundee Road intersection (hence the name—it's got nothing to do with Scotland).

In the early days, it was just Davidson and two helpers working crazy hours. From that first day of business with sales of $17.50, Davidson's candy store has grown into a classic small-business-makes-good success story. During the peak tourist season, the kitchen staff ("We sorta work like a family group") makes about one and a half tons of Florida confections *daily*, all of it by hand, in kitchens famed for their sparkling cleanliness.

These natural citrus juice candies, which look like small rectangular jewels, have an amazingly true, clear flavor and a delicate, soft-yet-firm texture a little like a gumdrop though definitely not as rubbery. The flavors—lemon, orange, grapefruit, lime, and tangerine (my favorite)—taste precisely as they would if you were eating the fruit itself; there's no monkey business with extraneous ingredients.

The standard assortment of flavors—lemon, orange, and lime—comes in two sizes: a 12-ounce box costs $6.50, and a 24-ounce box, $10.50, plus additional shipping charges to selected states. For an additional 50 cents you can choose your own combination. I recommend trying the special assortments that include all of the juice candy flavors along with something known as Pecan Orangettes, which are soft citrus candies sprinkled with bits of pecan (12-ounce box, $6.75; 24-ounce box, $10.95). Combination boxes of very nice old-fashioned crystallized Florida orange and grapefruit peels that I remember as a special treat from childhood are sold in 12-ounce boxes ($7.25). Gift assortments look touristy in a fun way—for example, there's a Florida-shaped tray packed with an assortment of the candies nestled around a solid white chocolate . . . alligator ($10.95)!

Besides the candies, 52 or so different marmalades, jellies, and butters in uncommon flavors are sold in pudgy jars. Davidson likes to joke

that "we use everything but the seed," and many of the fruits come from his own citrus groves. In tastings, coconut butter and the tangerine and tangelo marmalades stood out from the pack. Various assortments are available at prices that run from $5.95 for three 3-ounce jars to $12.95 for six 8-ounce jars (prices include shipping to most states).

VISITING THE SOURCE
— ❖ —

Davidson of Dundee Citrus Candy Factory is located on U.S. Highway 27 between Cypress Gardens and Disney World. Glen Davidson and his staff extend a genuinely warm welcome to everyone. You might call the factory tourist-friendly. Visitors can peer through large glass windows and observe the candy and jelly making. Because "customers ought to be able to taste before they buy," samples of all products are available in the display room. The factory is open seven days a week, generally from 8 A.M. to 6 P.M., with extended hours during the peak season of June through August.

— ❖ —

Elmer's Gold Brick Chocolate Nut Topping

Chocolate greed is a serious condition that attacks millions of Americans every day, producing anxiety and even headaches if not "treated." For decades one of the most meltingly delicious treatments has been Southern-made Elmer's Gold Brick, a heavy square of smooth chocolate laced with pecan bits and wrapped in distinctive gold foil. The candy was launched in the late 1930s, in the teeth, you might say, of the Depression, by the New Orleans–based Elmer's Candy Company. (Elmer's was already famous for its Heavenly Hash, an addictive blend of marshmallow, chocolate, and pecans tucked in a star-studded blue foil box.) Other candy manufacturers were sell-

c/o Rodgers & Rhoads
P.O. Box 3138
Covington, Louisiana 70434
No phone orders

Free order form
Prepaid orders only

ing bigger 3- and 4-ounce candies for a nickel, but Elmers boldly launched its much smaller 1-ounce Gold Brick for a nickel, too, labeling it "The Candy Bar with the Million-Dollar Taste." About this time Americans were relieving their fears of bankruptcy at the movies, where every other film was a screwball comedy about millionaires. Apparently Elmer's Gold Brick tapped into that same need to feel rich, and the candy sold like crazy.

A short while later Elmer's came up with another brilliant idea: a unique secret-recipe ice-cream topping made with the same ingredients found in Gold Brick candy. But this was a topping with a difference—you heated it first, and when the pale brown, pecan-studded sauce was poured over a nice big cold mound of ice cream, it immediately hardened into a brittle shell that kids of all ages then and now loved cracking into with a spoon.

Unless you live around New Orleans, the topping is pretty hard to find these days except by mail from Rodgers & Rhoads, which ships it postpaid only in the following quantities: 3-jar pack, $14; 6-jar pack, $24.50.

Elmer's Gold Brick Chocolate Nut Topping is best served over old-fashioned ice cream made in a hand-turned freezer packed with ice.

— ❖ —

Evelyn's Pralines

They call her the "Praline Lady." Hands-down, no fooling around, Evelyn LeBlanc makes the best pralines on earth—creamy, sumptuously rich, mega-size pralines so magnificent you'll probably want to remember me in your will because I introduced you to them. Actually, there's a whole cult of Evelyn's Pralines fans who are probably going to be a little put out that I'm sharing her with you, but

**Mrs. Edward LeBlanc
209 Chevis Street
Abbeville, Louisiana 70510
No phone orders**

**No order form; send
self-addressed, stamped card
or letter to confirm current
prices
Prepaid orders only**

that's just too bad.

Pralines (pronounced "PRAH-leans") are a classic Creole confection with a romantic past. It is said that Cesar du Plessis-Praslin, a French diplomat with an eye for the ladies, wooed potential conquests with bonbons. But one day, at a critical moment in an amorous campaign, he ran out of candy. Hastily, he sent his chef into the kitchen to contrive an emergency delicacy using whatever ingredients were on hand. The chef, no slouch, worked a little quick magic with some sugar and almonds, creating a new candy that was soon so popular that Praslin's friends were begging for the recipe and calling the new candies by his name. Much later Ursuline nuns brought the recipe with them from France to New Orleans, where native pecans were substituted for the almonds.

Evelyn LeBlanc made her pralines as family gifts for many years before going into business— quite by accident. Her cousin Marie LaCasse's birthday celebration at Black's Oyster Bar was the turning point. Evelyn had set a gift basket of her pralines on the table. And because people in Abbeville, Louisiana, are friendly, when curious tourists at the next table leaned over and asked what they were and if they might have a taste, Evelyn said sure. Naturally, the tourists asked where to buy some to take home. The next day Evelyn started delivering baskets of her pralines for local restaurants to sell.

Evelyn makes her pralines completely by hand in small batches (about 24 candies at a time) in the government-inspected candy kitchen attached to the back of her little white house (the C. S. Steen Syrup Mill is just a mile or so away). She calls the praline-making process "pouring." It's time-consuming and there are no shortcuts. "Pralines are a temperamental kind of candy and the recipe is a tricky one," she says. The ingredi-

EVELYN'S

ents are hand-measured, and Evelyn roasts the pecans fresh for each batch. Except for the busy Christmas season, when her cousins and siblings help with the wrapping, Evelyn works alone.

Sugary-style New Orleans pralines are made with canned milk or light cream. Evelyn LeBlanc's pralines, adapted from a classic Acadian recipe handed down in her family, are made with whipping cream (with no additives), which gives them extra depth of flavor. The only other ingredients are pure Louisiana ribbon cane sugar, real butter, and big, luscious papershell pecan halves (not mingy little pieces). Each creamy praline measures about three inches across and almost an inch high. They are astonishingly rich—try as I might, I've never been able to eat a whole one by myself. The pralines are shipped individually wrapped in a very classy doily-lined square red box tied with gold cord. A 1-pound box costs $9.95, postpaid; the 2-pound box costs $19.95, postpaid. Evelyn, who gets lots of fan mail, says the best compliment is that her customers keep reordering.

— ❖ —

Goo Goo Clusters, Goo Goo Supremes, and King Leo Stick Candy

Standard Candy Company
Mail Order Department
P.O. Box 101025
Nashville, Tennessee 37210
(615) 889-6360 (Monday to Friday, 8 A.M. to 5 P.M., CST)

Free order form
VISA, MasterCard

When the name is whimsical and the calories are serious, you're talking about a Goo Goo Cluster, the South's favorite candy.

Standard Candy Company founder Howell H. Campbell created the first cluster in 1912 in his own kitchen, supposedly naming it after the noise his infant son made during taste tests. The round Goo Goo Cluster, one of America's pioneer multiple ingredient candy bars, is a combination of milk chocolate, roasted peanuts, caramel, and marshmallow packaged in a silvery gray wrapper—a truly satisfying chewy blob that grows on you. The gold-wrapped Goo Goo Clus-

ter Supreme, loaded with pecans instead of peanuts, is a more recent concoction masterminded by Standard's young president, James Spradley, Jr.

The nostalgic pull of the Goo Goo is no trifling matter. Tennesseeans grew up munching on them during school recess and Goo Goos have always been heavily advertised on Nashville's famous *Grand Ole Opry* show. Like the Moon Pie, the Goo Goo enjoys cult status, and boxes of Goo Goos are shipped around the world. The *Today* show's Willard Scott took a bunch of Goo Goos with him to China. Tennessee-born Dinah Shore regularly receives shipments from her cousins, politician Howard Baker passed his supply around the Capitol, and actor James Garner sees to it he's always got some on hand.

Though distribution to stores is still strongest in Tennessee and parts of Mississippi, Alabama, and Kentucky, the company is making a big push to go national. Meanwhile, Standard Candy receives up to a hundred weekly fan letters and orders from those who want their Goo Goos *now*.

Ideally, Goo Goo Clusters should be eaten at room temperature so they're soft and chewy, but they can be stored in the refrigerator for several months with no flavor loss. A 6-pack of Goo Goo Clusters or Supremes costs $3.50, postpaid; a box of 24, $11.25; or a case of twenty-four 6-packs, $43.20. Goo Goos are not shipped between April 15 and October 15.

KING LEO
— ❖ —

King Leo stick candy, less well known, was Standard Candy's first product back in 1901. These striped candy sticks are like the ones your grandmother always kept on hand in the candy jar. Peppermint is the most popular flavor, but the little 3½-inch-long sticks are also made in clove, lemon, and vanilla. The flavors are pleasantly strong and true—when you take the

lid off a tin, their scent rushes up at you. They're packaged in an old-fashioned red, white, and blue tin that's a graphic flash from the past: a magnificently maned lion posing with his front paws resting on a stack of the sticks. Each 2-pound tin is lined with corrugated paper to prevent breakage, and the candy lasts indefinitely if kept in a cool, dry place. One tin costs $5.25 postpaid; or a case of 12 tins costs $45.95, postpaid.

— ❖ —

Lammes "Texas Chewie" Pecan Pralines

Lammes Candies
P.O. Box 1885
Austin, Texas 78767
(512) 835-6794

Free color brochure
Prepaid orders only

In 1878 William Wirt Lamme, a chronic gambler, opened the Red Front Candy Shop on Congress Avenue near the State Capitol in Austin. Never a man to withstand temptation, he lost the business in 1885 in a poker game. Two weeks later, his son D. T. Lamme bought the store back for $250 (the elder Lamme moved on, irresistibly lured by the next poker game).

Hardworking D. T., who chose a lamb logo to help people pronounce the family name correctly, dispensed rock candy and taffy up front while testing family candy recipes in back. By 1892 he had perfected his now world-famous "Texas Chewie" Pecan Praline, a toothsome, soft, chewy mass of buttery rich caramel laden with local pecans. The pralines were made only to order, so those in the know placed requests with D. T. and exercised patience. Once enough requests piled up, he'd make up a 25-pound batch, sending customers a handwritten notification. Visitors to Austin tried and tried to get D. T. to supply some of those molar-menacing morsels to take home. Finally in 1920 the pralines went public when D. T. relented and established a mail-order department, which now accounts for 30 percent of the firm's business.

D. T. operated his business with flair (Lamme's was the first in Austin to have one of

those newfangled neon signs) and resiliency (when the Depression hit the candy business hard, D. T. produced tamales!) before selling it to his three children in 1945. Lammes Candies has prospered since then. Currently the family looks after four Austin-area retail stores and a manufacturing facility that produces an extensive line of confections and nurtures a booming mail-order division. D. T.'s original "Texas Chewie" Pecan Pralines remain the star attraction (a 1-pound box containing 15 individually wrapped cookie-size candies costs $10.45, postpaid). Also memorable are Lammes Longhorns, caramel-pecan clusters coated in rich milk chocolate (a 10-ounce box housing 15 clusters costs $9.45, postpaid in the continental U. S. only). Due to hot weather, chocolate products such as the Longhorns are shipped only October 1 through May 15.

VISITING THE SOURCE
— ❖ —

Austin residents savor a Lammes Candies secret specialty not available to mail-order customers—hand-dipped, chocolate-covered fresh strawberries that are sold for only three days each year. The production schedule is confiden-

tial, but word always leaks out, especially if you've got a friendly clerk who'll call when the sale is about to begin. There are four Lamme's shops: Northcross Mall at Anderson Lane and Burnet Road; Barton Creek Square Mall at Loop 1 and 360; 5330 Airport Boulevard; and One American Center at 6th and Congress.

— ❖ —

Maker's Mark® Bourbon Chocolates

**Ehrler's Candies
1370 Belmar Drive
Louisville, Kentucky 40213
(502) 459-1070**

**Free order form
VISA, MasterCard**

Maker's Mark Bourbon Chocolates is a registered trademark of Ehrler's Candies. Maker's Mark is a trademark of Maker's Mark Distillery Inc.

Combine rich, dark chocolate with the South's finest, limited-edition, hand-crafted bourbon, and what do you get? Candy with a kick!

The tiny Maker's Mark distillery in Loretto, Kentucky, makes a sought-after sipping-whiskey that's been called "the Rolls-Royce of bourbon." Ehrler's Candies is a small, well-known Louisville company that still makes candy the old-fashioned way. A few years ago, the specialties of these two old-line Kentucky firms converged, and the result is a thoroughly sublime confection that absolutely should not be missed. To give you an idea of just how good sublime is, almost everyone who sampled candies from the first box I received asked for a Xerox of the order form and turned right around and got some for themselves.

Bourbon chocolates are a Kentucky tradition, and there's no doubt the flavors of bourbon and chocolate have a special affinity for each other. Maker's Mark president Bill Samuels, Jr., used to travel with a batch of his wife Nancy's home-made ones as a treat for business associates. But Nancy doesn't bother making them anymore; she and Bill agree that Ehrler's makes better ones. And even though it's Samuels's bourbon that makes the candies so special, the recipe, developed by master candy makers John Boles and David Lindsey, is an Ehrler's secret.

At the center of each premium, hand-

Maker's Mark.

fashioned Maker's Mark Bourbon Chocolate is a cream filling laced with this fine bourbon. The taste is pleasantly—even amazingly—potent, though there is actually less than 5 percent bourbon by volume used in the candies. Somehow, without resorting to artificial shenanigans, Ehrler's has mastered maintaining the essence of bourbon while using a very small amount of the liquor. Whatever it is they do, it works like a charm, because the flavor is true and practically melodic. The candies are covered with dark chocolate and crowned, by hand, with a decorative Southern pecan half. They come in a rather elegant-looking dark brown box embossed in gold with the Maker's Mark logo; inside are 32 delicious candies that will disappear in no time. A 13½-ounce box costs $14.95, plus $2.50 per box shipping to each address (add 50 cents for each additional box mailed to the same address). Treat yourself to a box at Derby time or just because they're luxurious to have on hand.

— ❖ —

Peach Leather

Harold's Cabin, the name of a special nook located in a huge Piggly Wiggly supermarket near the Charleston docks, sells Charleston-area food specialties to take home or mail order, and among these is old-fashioned peach leather.

Long before fruit leathers were a mainstay of health-food confection sections, peach leather was a sweet treat homemade on plantations. Making the leather was a fairly involved process. Sweetened, sliced peaches were slowly cooked until tender, puréed through a sieve, and the mixture was poured into shallow pans, covered with netting, and set out to dry in the brilliant, hot sun. In later years, the purée was spread to dry on panes of glass or even on door and win-

c/o Harold's Cabin
Piggly Wiggly
445 Meeting Street
Charleston, South Carolina
29403

(803) 722-2766 (Monday to
Friday, 8 A.M. to 5 P.M., EST)

Free brochure
VISA, MasterCard

dow screens. While still flexible, the sheets were sprinkled with a light dusting of sugar, cut into strips, and rolled into little cylinders.

The Harold's Cabin version of the leather is pleasantly chewy and the sugary coating nicely offsets the tart peach flavor. The chubby, cigarette-size rolls may be called leather, but they're light and refreshing. A roll or two is particularly tasty accompanied by after-dinner coffee. A 4-ounce box of peach leather will run a somewhat pricey $3.69, plus shipping.

Harold's ships a variety of other Charleston foods (see page 92) that you may want to try at the same time.

— ❖ —

Priester's Southern Colonels Butter Pecan Crunch, and Pecan Divinity

Priester's Pecans
227 Old Fort Drive
Fort Deposit, Alabama 36032

(800) 633-5725 (Monday to
Friday, 8 A.M. to 4:30 P.M., CST)
Fax (205) 227-4294

Free 20-page color catalog
VISA, MasterCard, American
Express, Diners Club, Carte
Blanche, Discover

While this 54-year-old company does indeed sell delicious pecans, what they're most famous for is a wide range of homemade candies incorporating pecans. "Everything is made from scratch," according to Jewel Cook, who runs the candy kitchen. She ought to know—she's worked at Priester's for more than 30 years.

Perhaps Priester's best-known goody is Southern Colonels. Made of soft (but not sticky) whole cream caramel poured over pecan pieces, each square candy is hand-dipped in dark or milk chocolate (20-ounce box of 28 all dark chocolate candies, $15.75; all milk chocolate, $15.50, both postpaid).

Then there's owner Ned Ellis's favorite, Butter Pecan Crunch. These thin, very crispy pieces of pecan-dotted butter crunch are hand-dipped in milk chocolate (1-pound tin, $17.25, postpaid).

Then there's Pecan Divinity. Now, when I was a little girl I used to beg my grandmother to make divinity, that special confection that looks like clouds and tastes sort of like powdered sugar

JUST PECANS

— ❖ —

would if it were solid enough to bite into. Priester's is one of the very few places still making this old-fashioned treat (probably because it's tricky to make). Their divinity is creamy-tasting mounds containing pecan bits (1-pound tin, $13.25; 26-ounce bag, $14.50, both postpaid).

Priester's was founded by the late Lee C. Priester, who started out selling pecans off the back of a pickup out in front of a local filling station and then expanded into mail order. Ned Ellis, son of the late H. R. Ellis, who was Priester's longtime business associate and partner, now owns the company. Ned knows his pecans—he started out as a pecan buyer for the company in the 1960s. Priester's processes more than 2 million pounds of pecans annually, many grown locally. Pecans (shelled or unshelled) and pecan halves (natural or roasted and salted) are sold in a variety of sizes and packaging (the average price is around $9 per pound). The decorative gift tins are unusually tasteful and low-key in contrast to the pretty tacky ones that show up in lots of other mail-order food catalogs. Priester's ships everything in the catalog year round, but remember that a new crop of pecans is harvested around the end of October or first week of November, so that's when they're freshest. Priester's mails out over a million catalogs each year, a large one in September (that includes an aged pecan fruitcake) and a smaller one in the spring. Items marked with a half-pecan symbol in the catalog are also sold in no-frills polyethylene bags and plain cartons at lower prices.

VISITING THE SOURCE

— ❖ —

The Kernel's Store, Priester's rustic-looking retail outlet, is located about 30 miles south of Montgomery at the intersection of Interstate 65 and Highway 185. Managed by May Ellis, Ned's wife, and their daughter Ellen, it's housed in the same building as the big candy kitchen. A gallery built through the kitchen allows visitors to watch brittle-pulling and chocolates being hand-dipped. Sample jars of candies are on hand for tasting. And for especially weary travelers, there are rocking chairs on the front porch, and the Ellises will even provide you with a cool tumbler of water to sip. The store is open Monday through Saturday from 9 A.M. to 5 P.M.; Sunday from 1 P.M. to 5 P.M.

— ❖ —

Rebecca-Ruth's Original 100-Proof Bourbon Whiskey Cremes and Kentucky Colonels

Rebecca-Ruth Candies
P.O. Box 64
Frankfort, Kentucky
40602-0064

(800) 444-3766; (502)
223-7475 (Monday to Friday,
9 A.M. to 5 P.M., CST)

Free 16-page black-and-white
illustrated catalog
VISA, MasterCard, American
Express, Discover, Diners
Club, Carte Blanche

Rebecca-Ruth is the first company to have produced candy made with 100-proof bourbon. Back in 1919 Rebecca Gooch and Ruth Hanly, a couple of restless young schoolteachers, decided they were better at candy making than at teaching. Since Prohibition had canceled the action in the barroom of the Old Frankfort Hotel, they got the manager to allow them to turn the curved rose-marble bar into a candy counter. Sales were brisk from the beginning and the zany, hardworking duo were inventive and persistent promoters. They careened around the central Kentucky countryside in a used car mounted with sandwich-board-style advertising, a startling sight for local farmers and tourists swimming in the Kentucky River. They were not above standing in front of their own shop window enthusiastically exclaiming over the display until they'd drawn a crowd.

Ruth's marriage and move to a new town ended the partnership, but by the time Rebecca married in 1929, Ruth, now Mrs. Booe with a small son named John, had returned to Frankfort and missed candy making. Ruth bought back the business she had cofounded and began developing new candies. One was the now-famous Mint Kentucky Colonel, a mild-flavored

Ruth Hanly Booe, co-founder of Rebecca-Ruth Candies.

Cream is the main ingredient in Kentucky Creamed Pull Candy.

minty cream center nestled between two sautéed pecan halves and coated in thin dark chocolate (13-ounce box, $13.75, postpaid).

In 1936 a friend casually remarked that the two best tastes in the world were a sip of bourbon and Ruth's Mint Kentucky Colonels. It set Ruth thinking. The result was a candy with character: 100-Proof Bourbon Whiskey Cremes, a soft bourbon-laced cream center coated in chocolate and jauntily topped with a small pecan half (13-ounce box, $13.45, postpaid).

Ruth died in 1973 at the age of 82, but her original recipes are still followed by her son John Booe, his wife, Carolyn, and their son Charles, who oversee five retail candy shops. The Booes make and sell a range of other candies, including creams laced with rum, cognac, or scotch (13-ounce box, $13.75, postpaid); elegant vanilla-flavored Opera Creams (13-ounce box, $11.45, postpaid); and unusual melt-in-your-mouth Kentucky Creamed Pull Candy made with cream (13-ounce box, $12.00, postpaid). The assortment called Americana Chocolates is extra-special because of the extraordinary person who makes them. The centers of these candies are handmade by longtime friend and employee Edna Robbins, who has been with the firm for 60 years! The 14 delicious centers include brown-sugar pecan fudge, vanilla butter cream, maple cream, and chocolate fudge nut, each dipped in your choice of milk or dark chocolate (13-ounce box, $13.75, postpaid).

Note: To ensure freshness, summer shipments (June 1 through September 30) are shipped via UPS Air packed with a "Blue Ice" bag at an additional charge of $8 for each shipment.

The candies are made by 10 employees in a facility behind the charming main Rebecca-Ruth store (112 East Second Street). The original marble bar top is in the factory.

CANNED GOODS

s • Mrs. Fearnow's Delicious Brunswick Stew • Fuller's Mustard • Maunsel White's
• Panola Pepper Sauce • Amber Brand Smithfield Ham • Billy Higdon's Happy Holl
ry Hams • Colonel Bill Newsom's Kentucky Country Hams • Bucksnort Smoked Rain
• Callaway Gardens Speckled Heart Grits • White Lily Flour • Bailey's Homemade H
r Jelly   Sherardiz   nsel's Rice • Garber
Yams • Warrento   ssinger's Flying Pig
n Arrow Ranch Axi   ory-Smoked Sausage
• Golden Mill So   ms Sweet Vidalia On
f Luck Scottish Sl   er Deluxe Moon Pie
Kitchen Derby Pi   otato Chips • Charli
Rendezvous Ribs   Barq's Root Beer •
wine • Crickle • B   ns Cut Leaf Poke S
s • Mrs. Fearnow'   • Maunsel White's
• Panola Pepper   Higdon's Happy Holl
ry Hams • Colone   ksnort Smoked Rainl
• Garber Farms Cajun Yams • Bland Farms Sweet Vidalia Onions • Callaway Garden
led Heart Grits • White Lily Flour • Bailey's Homemade Hot Pepper Jelly • Mayhaw
dized Pecans • Virginia Diner Peanuts • Ellis Stansel's Rice • Ledford Mill Borrowe
en Arrow Ranch Axis Venison • Comeaux's Boudin • Mayo's Hickory-Smoked Sausa
• Golden Mill Sorghum • Steen's Pure Cane Syrup • Best of Luck Scottish Shortbr
hoes and Nails • Double Decker Deluxe Moon Pies • Kern's Kitchen Derby Pie • Lis
Orchard Cake • Warrenton Original Nashville Rum Cakes • Zapp's Potato Chips •
Rendezvous Ribs • Maurice Bessinger's Flying Pig Barbeque • Barq's Root Beer •
wine • Crickle • Evelyn's Pralines • Goo Goo Clusters • The Allens Cut Leaf Poke Sa
s • Mrs. Fearnow's Delicious Brunswick Stew • Fuller's Mustard • Maunsel White's
• Panola Pepper Sauce • Amber Brand Smithfield Ham • Billy Higdon's Happy Holle
ry Hams • Colonel Bill Newsom's Kentucky Country Hams • Bucksnort Smoked Rainl
• Garber Farms Cajun Yams • Bland Farms Sweet Vidalia Onions • Callaway Garde
led Heart Grits • White Lily Flour • Bailey's Homemade Hot Pepper Jelly • Mayhaw
dized Pecans • Virginia Diner Peanuts • Ellis Stansel's Rice • Ledford Mill Borrowe
en Arrow Ranch Axis Venison • Comeaux's Boudin • Mayo's Hickory-Smoked Sausa
• Golden Mill Sorghum • Steen's Pure Cane Syrup • Best of Luck Scottish Shortbr

"Canning gives the American family—especially in cities and factory towns—a kitchen garden where all good things grow, and where it is always harvest time."
> —James H. Collins
> *The Story of Canned Foods*

Canned goods have been the cook's friend ever since Gail Borden patented condensed milk in cans and it became standard issue to Civil War troops. On grocery store shelves in the South today you'll find quite an array of regional brands of canned fruits and vegetables. Most of them aren't very different from the ones you'd find up North. But there are a handful that are truly special—so special, in fact, that Southerners who move to other parts of the country literally feel they can't live without them.

One of these is Mrs. Fearnow's Delicious Brunswick Stew, an unexpectedly tasty version of a great Southern dish that's traditionally served up at political rallies, family reunions, and as an accompaniment to barbecue. Another is Ro★Tel Tomatoes and Green Chilies, a zestier-than-usual version of canned tomatoes that's so popular Southern cookbooks even specify it by name in recipes. And if you've always wondered what that almost mythical Southern green, poke salet, tastes like, this is your chance to order a can and find out.

The Allens Cut Leaf Poke Salet Greens

Allen Canning Company
General Offices
P.O. Box 250
Siloam Springs, Arkansas 72761

No phone orders
No order form or brochure; send letter of inquiry for current case price plus UPS charges
Prepaid orders only

In the spring pokeweed, or poke salet, grows abundant and wild throughout the South, particularly in Arkansas. For two or three weeks, usually in May, lucky rural cooks gather these greens from their own backyards, along-side fence rows or roads near wooded areas. Young, tender green leaves (a little paler in color than spinach) are plucked before the plants mature. Leaves are stripped from the stalk (the berries and stems are poisonous), parboiled about 10 minutes, then boiled again in a change of water seasoned with a dash of salt and perhaps a smallish chunk of fatback for flavoring. That's what some cooks do. Others just head for the grocery store to buy a can of Allen Canning Company's hand-picked poke salet greens, which are canned in water with a little salt mere hours after they've been hand-harvested in Arkansas, Mississippi, and Oklahoma.

The flavor of poke salet is strong, earthy, and a little bitter. (Like sorghum or grits, this is one of those Southern treats not everyone acquires a taste for.) Heated through with a sprinkle of vinegar to cut the greens' natural bitterness, this canned version is pretty close to the fresh thing, especially if you serve it with a big hunk of corn-bread. Some folks mix the greens with spinach to tone the flavor down a bit; others add a dash of hot sauce or vinegar for zip.

Allen Canning is the country's largest independent canner, the leader of the pack when it comes to canned Southern specialty vegetables such as okra, rutabagas, kale, collard greens, yams, purple-hull peas, and white and gold hominy. Earl Allen's first cannery, in 1926, was housed in an abandoned distillery. That year Earl packed 4,000 cases of tomatoes—fewer than one of Allen's plants today can pack in an hour! Allen products are on supermarket shelves throughout the South under a variety of brand

Allen

CANNING COMPANY

names, including Brown Beauty, East Texas Fair, Pride of Louisiana, Sunshine, Uncle William, Georgia Belle, and Butterfield. Even Yankees have probably seen their colorful Popeye brand curly leaf or chopped spinach adding a touch of nutritional high camp to grocery shelves.

Today the company is still in the family, run by Earl's son and two grandsons. Drop them a line; they'll be happy to direct you to the nearest store selling their poke salet greens. (Thousands of older-generation relocated Southerners now living in the Midwest, Southwest, and Pacific Northwest still pine for poke.) Allen Canning doesn't have an official mail-order setup, but as a courtesy to doggedly persistent fans the company will ship a case of twenty-four 15-ounce cans for around $11 plus UPS charges (you must write to confirm shipping charges).

— ❖ —

Harris Atlantic She-Crab Soup

Harris Atlantic She-Crab Soup has to be one of the best condensed canned soups imaginable. It's a fine rendition of a celebrated Charleston specialty that draws on the famous blue crabs of the Southeastern coastal waters. Poetically called "beautiful swimmers," by the Indians, they are the basis for some extraordinary dishes. "Blue crabs," writes Bill Neal in *Bill Neal's Southern Cooking*, "find immortality in the dishes of the coastal cities."

Why does it have to be she-crab? Because the she-crabs contain orange eggs, or roe, in their bellies, which add an extra richness to the soup. So prized was the she-crab among Charlestonians that black street vendors of the past filled the morning air with boasts of their precious wares: "She-crab! She-crab!" Since he-crabs outnumber she-crabs five to one, she-crabs cost more and are harder to find.

c/o Harold's Cabin
Piggly Wiggly
445 Meeting Street
Charleston, South Carolina
29403
(803) 722-2766 (Monday to
Friday, 8 A.M. to 5 P.M., EST)

Free brochure
VISA, MasterCard

A milky, rose-colored soup, Harris Atlantic She-Crab Soup offers surprisingly generous clumps of crabmeat. Add a splash of sherry and you'll have a splendid taste of one of the South's most elegant soups. It looks nicest garnished with a few thin slices of scallions or with sieved hard-cooked egg yolks (used by Southern cooks to imitate the precious roe). Homemade she-crab soup is primarily a summer dish, served from late April through June (when the spawning season is at its height), but this canned version knows no season. The soup can be ordered by the individual can (10½ ounces, $1.39, plus shipping) or by the case (12 cans, $16.68, plus shipping).

VISITING THE SOURCE
— ❖ —

Harold's Cabin is a specialty-foods "boutique" with mail-order facilities located in a gigantic Charleston Piggly Wiggly near the waterfront. This is the place most Charleston visitors drop by to pick up edible souvenirs to take home. The store, which takes up a whole city block, is known locally as "Big Pig."

— ❖ —

House of Webster
Happy New Year
Meal Fixins

The House of Webster
P.O. Box 488
Rogers, Arkansas
72757-0488
(501) 636-4640

Free 34-page color catalog
Prepaid orders only (you will
be billed later at parcel-post
rates for exact amount of
postage, insurance, and sales
tax where applicable)

Any self-respecting Southerner knows that if you don't eat black-eyed peas and a mess of greens on New Year's Day, you'll be dogged by bad luck all year. This New Year's gift box should ensure there's good luck in the future, plus you'll hardly have to lift a hand to honor the tradition. It's so inexpensive and fun you should just haul off and order one for each of your relatives (an especially clever idea if you didn't get those Christmas presents mailed in time!). The House of Webster catalog identifies this gift box as "Happy New Year," and it includes two 15-ounce cans of the requisite black-eyed peas (seasoned with heavily smoked pork-jowl pieces, sugar, and spices; just heat), a

15-ounce can of Wild Poke Salad Greens (rural folkore suggests that eating greens guarantees money in the year to come), along with 1-pound bags of Old Mill Stream Stone-Ground Cornmeal and Flaky Buttermilk Biscuit Mix. Just open up those cans and heat the contents. Then all you have to do is make the biscuits and cornbread for sopping up the rich pot-liquor juices from the peas and greens. (Feeling energetic? Whip up a delicious cobbler for dessert using the recipe on the back of the biscuit mix sack). A lot of luck, a little work, and the whole shooting match, packed in an attractive, colorfully printed gift box depicting a scene of rural life, costs a modest $8.50, plus shipping. It'll feed three people and there'll probably be enough cornmeal to make some muffins the next day, too. A fancier version that also includes a slab of bacon as well as wild honey and sorghum costs $26.95, plus shipping.

The House of Webster, in the Arkansas Ozarks, is one of the South's oldest and largest mail-order firms. Roy Webster and his wife, Evelyn, started the business more than 50 years ago when Roy drove a rugged 125-mile daily newspaper route over winding Ozark roads. The enterprising Roy soon added two-crust pies (four

HOUSE OF
WEBSTER

cents!), bread, and chocolate milk to his small town delivery route. Nowadays, the Websters specialize primarily in very handsomely packaged business food gifts (many of America's largest corporations are longtime customers).

All of the House of Webster delectables radiate a cozy old-timeyness. They've been created, say the Websters, "to rekindle a warm image of a big, warm, friendly kitchen." Their jellies and preserves, for instance, come in Mason jars, and when you twist off the lid, there's a thick layer of paraffin just like your grandmother used. The jars of strawberry, peach, plum, huckleberry, wild crabapple, and more, are available in an almost infinite variety of combinations and may be ordered in gift packs accompanied by flower-splashed ceramic reproductions of the gravy boats, biscuit platters, teapots, and other wares in Evelyn Webster's own collection of antique American and European porcelain. Each such gift package comes with a little booklet of Roy Webster's memories of country life—from his parents' pride in their first strawberry harvest to the peppery fried chicken served when the preacher came to supper. The most wonderful replica in the collection, though, is of the Weir ceramic jar developed in the late 17th century for home food preserving ($14.50, filled with muscadine preserves). Four Mason jars of "tame" preserves or jelly cost $9.75, plus shipping; four "wild" ones like huckleberry cost slightly more.

— ❖ —

Mrs. Fearnow's Delicious Brunswick Stew

There's nothing she can't cook," agreed Lillie Pearl Fearnow's friends and kin. In the 1930s, Lillie had won 40 state fair ribbons to prove it, but it was her Brunswick stew, a great Southern dish, they favored.

So, in an attempt to raise cash during the De-

Fearnow Company
8691 Shady Grove Road
Mechanicsville, Virginia
23111
(804) 746-1928

Free form letter with prices
and shipping costs
Prepaid orders only

pression, it made sense for Mrs. Fearnow to place six pint jars of this savory, delicious hearty chicken and vegetable stew on consignment at the Richmond Women's Exchange, where it sold out in a flash. Demand grew steadily, with reorders pouring in at such a clip that Lillie couldn't keep up with them in her small farm kitchen. So she taught daughters-in-law Norma and Finnella the recipe, and soon their kitchens were overrun with pressure cookers and canning jars. By now it had an official name: Mrs. Fearnow's Delicious Brunswick Stew.

In 1946, Lillie's sons Clyde and Nelson bought 154 acres near their parents' truck farm. They planted vegetables for the stew and moved production out of their homes into the newly built Fearnow Brothers' Cannery. The site was named Hope Farm in tribute to the earth that had sustained the family through hard times.

The business grew, and the cannery expanded many times, but Lillie Pearl Fearnow, an indefatigable worker, always showed up at the crack of dawn, right up to the day she died in 1970 at age 88. It's still a hands-on family affair—Lillie's daughter-in-law Finnella and grandson George run things with assistance from cousin Raymond and brother-in-law William Kidd—though producing almost two million cans of stew a year in the warm, fragrant-smelling cannery is big business. The product remains pretty true to Lillie's original, though it's been adapted somewhat for canning (the traditional celery, which is bitter, and okra, which discolored the stew, are omitted). This is a genuinely superior canned product, a sturdy stew containing chicken and broth with tomatoes, carrots, potatoes, small lima beans, onions, parsley, and astonishingly crunchy little kernels of white shoe-peg corn.

The vivid yellow cans dot grocery store shelves in Virginia, North Carolina, and Maryland. (It's

BRUNSWICK STEW:
A GREAT SOUTHERN "PUBLIC" DISH
— ❖ —

Brunswick stew, burgoo, gumbo—all are traditional Southern communal fare. The stew is a hearty, highly seasoned, soupy mixture that *must* contain chicken, corn, and lima beans; *probably* celery, potatoes, a ham-bone, and some beef or veal; and *perhaps* rabbit or squirrel meat (in the beginning it was *always* made with squirrel). And of course, it must be liberally seasoned with plenty of red and black pepper.

The origins of Brunswick stew are a matter of dispute. Virginians will tell you it originated in Brunswick County and takes its name from Caroline of Brunswick, wife of King George IV. But Georgians, pointing to their city of Brunswick, also claim it. And you'll almost always find it served in Georgia as a side dish with barbecue (as in a pork platter with a bowl of the stew alongside). Then there's the theory that it was invented in 1828 at a political rally. In any event, homemade Brunswick stew turns up most often in the coastal areas of Virginia, North Carolina, and Georgia, and usually there'll be a hundred or so hungry people lined up ready to eat it.

with the stews, not the soups; Lillie whacked people on the shins with her cane if they called it soup). As a courtesy to folks who've moved out of the area, Kay Fearnow, who's married to George, ships cases all over the world (Supreme Court Justice Lewis F. Powell, Jr., is a fan). The stew comes in 20-ounce cans, which will serve 2 people (6 cost $12.80, 12 cost $23.95, and 24 cost $44.55), and hefty 29-ounce cans, which serve 3 or 4 people (6 cost $18.25 and 12 cost $34.10). UPS charges are extra and based on zip-code zone (shipping charges to California for twelve 20-ounce cans cost around $9). If you call for information, keep in mind that there is no answering machine, so you may have to keep trying.

SEE YOU AT THE
PIGGLY WIGGLY
— ❖ —

To many Southerners, a supermarket isn't just a supermarket, it's the good old Piggly Wiggly, a self-service grocery that for years had a quaint wooden turnstile for customers to pass through after paying. The Piggly Wiggly was also a social arena—a place to see and be seen, exchange snippets of gossip, or, if nothing else, nosily see what somebody else was buying for dinner. Founded by a country boy turned millionaire, self-made Clarence Saunders (not to be confused with Colonel Sanders of Kentucky Fried Chicken fame), the Piggly Wiggly caused a food-buying revolution.

There are numerous tall tales regarding the choice of the silly name (including the obvious "this little piggy went to market" theory), and Saunders liked to keep it a mystery—though once, when asked about it, he responded, "So people will ask just what you have asked!"

When Saunders opened his first Piggly Wiggly in downtown Memphis in 1916, he literally invented self-service merchandising, abolishing the cumbersome system of shopping through clerks. Customers were astonished. They were handed baskets, ushered into aisles arrayed with shelves of goods, and told to just shop away. At the front, only a couple of cashiers were needed to check them out, saving on overhead costs and helping to lower grocery prices. The flamboyant Saunders opened the little store with promotional style: the *de rigueur* beauty queen—Miss Piggly Wiggly—was chosen by impartial representatives of Memphis's three newspapers; patrons arriving in the first half hour were promised they'd be seen in the "moving-picture" being made of the occasion; and prizes were handed out.

Other grocers scoffed, but customers loved Piggly Wiggly.

Within a few years there were 1,200 Piggly Wigglys in 40 states. Saunders began building a mansion of Georgia pink marble called the Pink Palace, complete with its own golf course. (Rumor had it that Saunders wasn't welcome at country-club courses because he'd corrupted the caddies with his extravagant tips.) Unfortunately, Wall Street speculators began a raid on the Piggly Wiggly stock, and a giant public fight began that headline writers dubbed "the Piggly crisis." By the 1940s Saunders had lost his shirt, his chain, and his Pink Palace.

In later years Saunders tried to stage a comeback, inaugurating the "Keedozzle," a kind of grocery-store Automat, and the "Foodelectric" store, in which customers added up their own purchases. He lived until 1953, when the full impact of his idea

for merchandising was spreading and changing the landscape of America. Today Piggly Wiggly's corporate owner is Malone & Hyde, Inc., and there are more than 950 stores.

The majestic Pink Palace, now a museum run by the city of Memphis, contains a delightful, faithful reproduction of the first Piggly Wiggly, complete with turnstile and overhead platforms (from which clerks watched for theft). And for little kids, the museum features a dinosaur model that moves and scrapes its paws, a planetarium, a nature walk, and a miniature three-ring circus. Memphis Pink Palace Museum & Planetarium, 3050 Central Avenue, Memphis, Tennessee 38111; phone (901) 320-6320. Open Tuesday to Friday, 9:30 A.M. to 4 P.M.; Saturday, 9:30 A.M. to 5 P.M.; Sunday, 1 P.M. to 5 P.M.

"MAKING GROCERIES" AT SCHWEGMANN'S

❖

Most visitors to New Orleans hit the usual attractions such as Bourbon Street and the French Market, but rarely does anyone tell them that the ultimate local attraction—a genuine living legend, folklore in full swing—is a 15-store grocery chain called Schwegmann Bros. Giant Supermarkets. (Locals pronounce it "SHWEH-gah-muns," by the way.)

The first store opened in 1946, and the name of the game has remained the same ever since—providing mountains of goods to consumers at the lowest possible prices and relying on enormous volume sales for a profit. The phrase "making groceries" is a literal translation of how French-speaking residents of New Orleans once described going shopping: *faire le marché*. Everything about Schwegmann's is bigger than life. You've got to see 'em to believe 'em.

The Schwegmanns to visit is the one near the Industrial Canal on the Chef

Menteur Highway. Here the selling space is the size of three football fields, shopping carts are the size of most big-city apartment bathrooms, and the number of shoppers is breathtaking. You name it, Schwegmann's sells it—appliances, shoes (there's a Shoe Town), bicycles, pig lips, and beauty aids. Even the brown-paper grocery bags at Schwegmann's are unique—in a tradition begun by founder John Schwegmann, Jr., who was an opinionated politician and relentless crusader for his own ideals, the bags are printed with a constantly changing variety of civic-minded messages. The bags are so famous some people even cavort in Mardi Gras parades costumed as . . . you guessed it! A bag of groceries from Schwegmann's.

Ro★Tel Tomatoes and Green Chilies

Knapp-Sherrill Co.
P.O. Drawer E
Donna, Texas 78537
(512) 464-7843

Free color brochure
No shipments to Hawaii,
Alaska, or Canada
VISA, MasterCard

"They'll flat open your eyes. Clear your head. Jump-start your heart. And make you glad you're hungry." That's Crazy Sam Higgins, outlandish and irreverent expert on Texas victuals, describing what Ro★Tel Tomatoes and Green Chilies can do for your life, to say nothing of your cooking.

The lower Rio Grande Valley of Texas, lush, rich, and fertile, is famous for its garden vegetables, cotton, and superb grapefruit. It was about 40 years ago in the little South Texas town of Elsa that Carl Roettele first opened a small plant to can the area's vegetable bounty, including its fat, juicy tomatoes. (Figuring that folks might have a hard time pronouncing his German name, Carl shortened it to Ro★Tel on the labels.) What inspired him to toss some chilies in with the tomatoes we'll never know, but his product became a legend in the South and Southwest. National notoriety came to Ro★Tel back in 1963 when the wife of a Washington politician revealed in a national magazine that it was the secret ingredient in her fabulous chili.

Ro★Tel Tomatoes come diced or whole, seasoned with chopped green chili peppers, salt, cilantro, and spices. The brand name is frequently specified in numerous cookbooks since the flavor is so much zestier than that of ordinary old canned tomatoes. The diced version is just terrific for pot roast, and then of course, there's

FAMOUS RO★TEL CHEESE DIP
— ❖ —

1 pound pasteurized
   American cheese
1 can (10 ounces) Ro★Tel
   Tomatoes and Green
   Chilies

Melt the cheese in the top of a double boiler over simmering water. In a bowl, mix the Ro★Tel Tomatoes and Green Chilies with the cheese. Serve warm as a dip with corn chips, tortilla chips, or crackers.

that famous Ro★Tel Cheese Dip recipe printed on the back of every can (see page 101). When LBJ was president, White House executive chef Henry Haller made the dip with unprocessed cheese, serving it at receptions as Chili Con Queso.

Owners Knapp-Sherrill Co. are sympathetic to unfortunates who can't find Ro★Tel at the grocery store; each year they ship more than 10,000 cases to individuals. A case of twelve 10-ounce cans (six whole, six diced) accompanied by a recipe folder is shipped in a colorful mailing carton ($11.95, postpaid). Crazy Sam Higgins, a.k.a. "the King of Texas Soul Food," is the author of a zany, anecdotal collection of Ro★Tel recipes called *Snake, Rattle & Ro★Tel* ($9.35, postpaid). A more extensive gift pack contains two cans of each of the tomatoes and two 8-ounce jars of Ro★Tel Picante Sauce, plus a copy of Higgins's cookbook ($13.95 postpaid).

— ❖ —

Trappey's Golden Yams and Cajun-Style Gumbos

Trappey's Fine Foods, Inc.
P.O. Box 13610
New Iberia, Louisiana
70562-3610

(800) 365-8727;
(318) 365-8281 (Monday to Friday, 9 A.M. to 4:30 P.M., CST; ask to speak with gift shop)

Free color brochure of gift packs; nonillustrated order form of all Trappey's products (specify you want both when writing)
VISA, MasterCard

Trappey's (pronounced "trap-āys") is famous for more than those colorful bottles of Trappey's Red Devil Louisiana Hot Sauce and Pepper Sauce. Residents of the Southeast know Trappey's also produces a line of canned goods—including yams, beans, and okra—that are standard Southern supermarket items. The Acadian region of Louisiana that's Trappey's home is a prime growing area for the rich, orange-colored Louisiana yams, whose sweet, moist flesh is said to make them infinitely tastier than those grown anywhere else. Whatever it is that makes Louisiana yams extra special, founder B. F. Trappey, Sr., understood it—and he opened the world's first yam-canning plant in Lafayette back in the 1930s. The grocery trade said, "They'll never sell," but they were wrong, and today 70 percent of

Louisiana's yam harvest is canned.

Trappey's cans whole local yams in heavy syrup (17-ounce can, $1.05) and in syrup with pineapple added (17-ounce can, $1.15). Yams sold under the name Trappey's Sugary Sam come cut and packed in syrup (16-ounce can, $.90) or mashed without added sugar or salt (15½-ounce can, $.80). Both versions of yams in heavy syrup come in a gift-pack assortment with four other Trappey's products including Red Kidney Beans with Chili Gravy and Cut Okra with Tomatoes ($7.70, plus shipping).

The firm's newest canned products are three Cajun-style canned gumbos that are surprisingly flavorful and authentic-tasting. Gumbo is a hearty, spicy Louisiana specialty that's somewhere between a soup and a stew.

Trappey's Cajun-style canned gumbos include

TRAPPEY'S SWEET POTATO PECAN PIE
— ❖ —

1 can Trappey's Sugary
  Sam Mashed Yams
1½ cups milk, hot
1 cup brown sugar
1 tablespoon butter
1 teaspoon ground ginger
1 teaspoon ground
  cinnamon
1 teaspoon ground
  nutmeg
1 teaspoon salt
3 eggs, beaten
1 unbaked 9-inch piecrust
  shell, with a standing
  rim
½ cup finely chopped
  pecans

In a large bowl, mix together the yams, milk, sugar, butter, and seasonings. Gradually add the eggs. Pour the filling into the piecrust shell. Sprinkle with the pecans. Bake in a 425°F oven until the filling is set, about 35 minutes.

Makes one 9-inch pie

Visitors get a hearty welcome at the company store, located next to Trappey's Pepper Plant.

Okra (made with tender Clemson pods grown in Louisiana and south Texas), Chicken Sausage (spicy and thickened with okra), and Seafood Okra (dotted with bits of shrimp and crab). A 15-ounce can of each is sold in a gift pack for $7, plus shipping (individual cans run between $1.50 and $2 apiece). The rich, dark roux is flavorful, and though adding a little extra chicken or andouille of your own makes them even better, these gumbos are nothing to be ashamed about—the authentic Cajun flavor is there. A can of Trappey's gumbo, served piping hot over rice with a green salad and crusty New Orleans–style French bread on the side, will feed two or three people.

In addition to a whole series of gift packs, Trappey's will also ship any combination and quantity of their 60 or so canned and bottled individual products, including the yams and gumbos. The minimum order is $15, plus $4.50 for shipping and handling. Perusing the order form is a little like walking down a Louisiana supermarket aisle.

PANTRY PRIDE

MUSTARD

Crickle • Evelyn's Pralines • Goo Goo Clusters • The Allens Cut Leaf Poke Sa
• Mrs. Fearnow's Delicious Brunswick Stew • Fuller's Mustard • Maunsel White's
• Panola Pepper Sauce • Amber Brand Smithfield Ham • Billy Higdon's Happy Hollo
y Hams • Colonel Bill Newsom's Kentucky Country Hams • Bucksnort Smoked Rainb
• Callaway Gardens Speckled Heart Grits • White Lily Flour • Bailey's Homemade Ho
Jelly   Sherardiz   nsel's Rice • Garber
Yams • Warrento   ssinger's Flying Pig B
Arrow Ranch Ax   ory-Smoked Sausage
• Golden Mill So   ms Sweet Vidalia Oni
Luck Scottish S   ker Deluxe Moon Pies
Kitchen Derby P   otato Chips • Charli
Rendezvous Rib   Barq's Root Beer • L
ine • Crickle •   ens Cut Leaf Poke Sa
• Mrs. Fearnow   • Maunsel White's 1
• Panola Pepper   Higdon's Happy Hollo
Hams • Colone   ksnort Smoked Rainb

Garber Farms Cajun Yams • Bland Farms Sweet Vidalia Onions • Callaway Gardens
d Heart Grits • White Lily Flour • Bailey's Homemade Hot Pepper Jelly • Mayhaw J
ized Pecans • Virginia Diner Peanuts • Ellis Stansel's Rice • Ledford Mill Borrowed
n Arrow Ranch Axis Venison • Comeaux's Boudin • Mayo's Hickory-Smoked Sausag
• Golden Mill Sorghum • Steen's Pure Cane Syrup • Best of Luck Scottish Shortbrea
oes and Nails • Double Decker Deluxe Moon Pies • Kern's Kitchen Derby Pie • Lis
Orchard Cake • Warrenton Original Nashville Rum Cakes • Zapp's Potato Chips • C
Rendezvous Ribs • Maurice Bessinger's Flying Pig Barbeque • Barq's Root Beer • L
ne • Crickle • Evelyn's Pralines • Goo Goo Clusters • The Allens Cut Leaf Poke Sa
• Mrs. Fearnow's Delicious Brunswick Stew • Fuller's Mustard • Maunsel White's 1
Panola Pepper Sauce • Amber Brand Smithfield Ham • Billy Higdon's Happy Hollow
Hams • Colonel Bill Newsom's Kentucky Country Hams • Bucksnort Smoked Rainb
Garber Farms Cajun Yams • Bland Farms Sweet Vidalia Onions • Callaway Gardens
d Heart Grits • White Lily Flour • Bailey's Homemade Hot Pepper Jelly • Mayhaw Je
ized Pecans • Virginia Diner Peanuts • Ellis Stansel's Rice • Ledford Mill Borrowed
n Arrow Ranch Axis Venison • Comeaux's Boudin • Mayo's Hickory-Smoked Sausage
Golden Mill Sorghum • Steen's Pure Cane Syrup • Best of Luck Scottish Shortbrea

Once no Southern larder was complete unless it was stocked with comforting rows of hand-canned relishes and pickles. Cherished family recipes (like Aunt Flo's artichoke pickle recipe that took a blue ribbon at the Pittsfield County Fair and went so well with roast pork) were used to preserve the bounty of the summer harvest as a hedge against the dreary winter months ahead. Those jars of colorful chow-chow, stubby pickles, corn relish, and other good side dishes added variety at the table. A bottle of hot sauce usually kept company alongside the relishes just in case the beans needed a little shot of heat or the greens some livening up.

Even now you can still count on a Southern supper table being set with a bottle of hot sauce from Tabasco or Trappey's and at least two pretty little glass relish dishes filled with morsels to add an extra something sweet or tangy or sharp to go along with the food. A few sweet nuggets of Old South Honey Dew Cubes are tasty with cold sliced chicken, and some of their pickled watermelon alongside ham adds just the right touch. Everything from weekday cold-cuts to fried fish tastes better if you've got some Upside-Down Cajun Chow Chow or Talk O'Texas Crisp Okra Pickles on hand.

Condiments

Braswell's Artichoke Relish

A. M. Braswell Jr. Food Company, Inc.
P.O. Box 485
Statesboro, Georgia 30458
No phone orders

Free catalog at Christmas only; free nondescriptive brochure listing Braswell's products available year-round (Note: Braswell's does not provide product information or quote prices on the phone; all inquiries must be sent by mail.)
Prepaid orders only

I n the South, the sweet, crisp, ivory-colored flesh of the Jerusalem artichoke is the basis for an unusually tasty relish. Despite the name, a Jerusalem artichoke is not what you may think. Unlike the globe artichoke from California, these are slender, lumpy, tan-colored tubers that look very much like fresh ginger and are sometimes called sunchokes. The flesh, however, does indeed have an enticing taste somewhat similar to that of a globe artichoke heart.

Making a truly good artichoke relish is not easy; some I've tasted were overly sweet, limp-textured, and utterly uninspiring. But this version, from a Georgia producer of a line of more than 90 jellies, jams, pickles, and relishes, is really outstanding.

Braswell's Artichoke Relish is tangy and slightly chewy, with a pleasantly spiced, subtle flavor that makes it an excellent accompaniment to ham and pork as well as chicken, lamb, and game. In fact, this one tastes so homemade you could probably get away with claiming it came from your great-aunt Molly's closely guarded heirloom recipe.

A. M. Braswell, Jr., founded his business in his hometown of Statesboro after returning from service as a naval officer in World War II. Although Braswell's condiments are highly regarded, his sweet preserves shouldn't be ignored. Pear preserves, made from his mother Lillian's recipe using South Georgia fruits, were his first product, and people say they're as delicious now as they were back then. Still made mostly from local fruit, the preserves taste sweetly like the pears' essence; crisp, thin pear slices are dotted throughout. All in all, a splendid morning treat for a muffin. Braswell's Fig Preserves are good, too. Their flavor reminds me of the big glass jars of Kadota figs my grandmother used to buy for me as a special treat.

Braswell's does most of its business through specialty gourmet and grocery stores and only prints a mail-order gift catalog at Christmas. But you can order two sizes of gift boxes any time of the year, and the prices are extraordinarily reasonable for a vast selection that also includes such temptations as Artichoke Pickle, Green Tomato Relish, and Damson Plum Jam. A box of any four items chosen from Braswell's product list in 10½-ounce jars costs $8.95, postpaid; a box of eight 10½-ounce jars costs $14.95, postpaid.

— ❖ —

Fuller's Mustard

Virginia Mustard Corp.
P.O. Box 1068
Seapines Station
Virginia Beach, Virginia
23451
No phone orders

Free order form
Prepaid orders only

Fuller's Hotel and Restaurant was a downtown Phoebus, Virginia, landmark for most of this century. It was a genuine time warp with a pressed-tin ceiling, faded green booths, dozens of old signs, and food so plentiful and cheap you thought you were in an old movie. In recent years, it was impossible to tell which had the most character, the eatery itself (motto: "Eat Dirt Cheap"), irrepressible co-owner Nelson Fuller, or the place's revered family secret, a zippy, sweet mustard that regulars automatically reached for as they ordered a hamburger or hot dog and a brew.

Fuller's Mustard sat right there on the long mahogany bar pretending to be ordinary mustard in a yellow plastic squeeze bottle. The recently retired Nelson, who owned the place with his brother, Philip, until they closed it last year, remembers when their grandfather used to whip

Fuller's Mustard

Hot ★ Sweet ★ All Natural

NET WT. 5.25 OZ

up batches of the mustard at night after the restaurant closed. He used a recipe that had been in the family for more than a century. Nelson carried on the tradition, making small batches every day by "eyeballing it," for use in the restaurant only, though from time to time he'd break down and make a few jars to send as gifts to military customers who missed it. (Fuller's used to draw quite a crowd from nearby Fort Monroe and Langley Air Force Base.) A few years ago Philip's son and daughter-in-law decided to bottle the stuff in their basement and sell it. Months of Fuller family conferences, experimenting, and tastings were required before the clan reached a consensus on a formula adapted to bottling. The recipe had never really been written down. "It was always a little bit different each time," Nelson points out.

The mustard is a thick, butterscotch-colored paste made of deceptively innocent ingredients: mustard flour, cane sugar, distilled vinegar, and salt. This is sneaky stuff. First you'll experience a deep sweetness. Tasty. Nothing to sit down and write home about, but nice. Wait a few seconds. Now the heat hits like a bat out of hell. It'll reroute those clogged sinuses. It's sweet. It's mean. And a little goes a long way. The attractive black and white label on each little bottle has a drawing of Fuller's Hotel and Restaurant on it and some recipe suggestions (yes, there is hope for ordinary canned pork and beans). Fuller's Mustard has gotten so popular that the production outgrew the basement and now you can order it by mail. It comes in 5-ounce bottles ($2 each) and 10-ounce ones ($4 each). There is a minimum order of four bottles, but you may mix sizes to meet the minimum; postage and handling are extra. A 1-gallon plastic jar of the mustard (take it to your high school reunion picnic) costs $40, plus shipping.

Southern food is not just food cooked south of the Mason-Dixon line. It is a product of time and people as well as place.

—Bill Neal's
   Southern Cooking

Old South Sweet Pickled Watermelon, Cantaloupe, and Honey Dew Melon Cubes

Bryant Preserving Company
P.O. Box 367
Alma, Arkansas 72921

(800) 634-2413 (Monday to Friday, 9 A.M. to 5 P.M., CST)

Free price list
Prepaid orders only

Southern cooks have always delighted in bringing out home-preserved pickles and relishes from their own pantries to spice up a meal. Typically, a procession of little cut-glass dishes are proudly passed offering piccalilli, peach pickles, and colorful relishes made from everything from baby green tomatoes to okra. Given the dearth of time most of us have for peeling and pickling these days, it's good to know that Bryant Preserving Company can help fill the pantry with its jars of Old South Sweet Pickled Watermelon Rind Cubes, Sweet Pickled Cantaloupe Cubes, and Sweet Pickled Honey Dew Melon Cubes.

When it comes to making watermelon-rind pickles, John Egerton warns in his book *Southern Food*, the most tedious task is extracting the delicate white portion between green rind and red flesh. Bryant's handling of this laborious task staggers the imagination. Processing about 2,000 tons of watermelons a year, the workers peel each watermelon *by hand*, slice each thinly, and cut away the red meat. Then, reversing our usual method of watermelon eating—in which the red meat is gobbled down and the rinds are thrown to the chickens—the red meat is hauled off in dump trucks and fed to cattle. It's the tender white part of the rind that is chopped, sweetened, and pickled to be transformed into lime-green cubes that are simultaneously sweet and tart. The crunchiness of sweet pickled watermelon rind makes it an excellent foil for many soft Southern dishes. It's nice on an appetizer tray and it can be chopped up and added to tuna or chicken salad. A bottle tucked into the bottom of the picnic basket is a good idea, too.

When Bryant pickles its cantaloupe and honeydew melon cubes, it's the meat that's kept and turned into fruity, bright-colored relishes. These can be served either hot or cold, and the syrup they're packed in is good for glazing ham or poultry. Skewer a morsel of ham and one of these melon chunks and you've got a nice little tidbit.

Each of these three products can be ordered by the case. A case of twelve 10-ounce jars of one product costs $15.95, postpaid. For more variety—and fewer jars to store in the larder— you might try Bryant's new Arkansas Gift Pack containing a jar each of the Pickled Watermelon Rind, Cantaloupe, and Honey Dew Melon, plus a jar each of three newer products: Sweet Pickled Golden Cucumber Nuggets, Tomolives (pickled green baby tomatoes), and Candied Miniature Pickle Stix. It's packaged in a box shaped like the state of Arkansas and costs only $12.95, postpaid. While you might not pass the Bryant relishes off as having come from your own kitchen, you can serve them without shame in little cutglass dishes, or present them on one of those Lazy Susans so beloved by Southern hostesses.

— ❖ —

Talk O' Texas Crisp Okra Pickles

Talk O'Texas Brands, Inc.
1610 Roosevelt Street
San Angelo, Texas 76905

(800) 323-5641 (Monday to
Friday; 8 A.M. to 5 P.M., CST)

Free order form
VISA, MasterCard

Lots of people claim they don't like okra— it's one of those love 'em or loathe 'em vegetables. But I'm willing to bet those people who say they wouldn't touch okra with a 10-foot pole haven't experienced Talk O'Texas's Crisp Okra Pickles, which are totally different from the slimy cooked okra that has a bad reputation. Pickles aren't always cucumbers, you know, and okra's interesting flavor—somewhere between asparagus, artichoke hearts, and eggplant—lends itself superbly to pickling.

Okra is a culinary legacy from the black slaves who brought the vegetable with them from Africa to the Southeast. Cooked okra—the version many people love to hate—does indeed turn slimy and mucilaginous, but that's precisely what makes it a good natural thickening agent (Louisi-

OKRA STRUT: IRMO, SOUTH CAROLINA

— ❖ —

If it's October and you've got a craving for fried okra, you're in luck, because the Okra Strut is held each year on the first Saturday of October. The Strut began back in the mid-1970s as an event organized by the Lake Murray–Irmo Woman's Club to raise money for a badly needed local library. It worked—Irmo has its library—and now the town itself sponsors the event, which draws about 35,000 visitors annually. The ladies from the Woman's Club still have the most popular food booth; you have to line up for a dish of their perfect fried okra. A huge parade with floats winds up at the grounds of Irmo High School, where there are arts and crafts booths and lots of good things to eat, including barbecue sandwiches. The high point is the Shoot-out at the OKra Corral, in which brave souls confront bowls of plain boiled okra and see how much of the stuff they can eat in five minutes. For information, contact Town of Irmo, P.O. Box 406, Irmo, South Carolina 29063; (803) 781-7050.

ana gumbo is thickened with either okra or filé powder). It's also delicious sliced, dusted with cornmeal, and fried up nice and crispy.

A jar of Talk O'Texas Crisp Okra Pickles is a thing of beauty to an okra lover like myself. At Talk O'Texas's small semiautomated factory, a couple of million jars are shipped annually, mostly to grocery and specialty stores in the Southwest and Southeast and to diehard fans who get insecure without a few backup jars in the cupboard. Each fresh pod is hand-packed (workers wear gloves) into a large, stout glass jar that's filled to the brim with a mixture of vinegar, brine, and spices and herbs that include salt, pepper, and sage. Then the jars are sealed, cooked, and pasteurized. The resulting pickled okra is so crispy-crunchy it practically makes a snapping sound when you bite into a pod. There

are two versions: the "hot" (more accurately described as spicy than hot), which contains slim little red peppers that are visible nestled alongside the pods, and the "mild" (without peppers), which is simply a little less spicy. Stage your own taste test by ordering a mixed shipment of six 16-ounce jars (three jars of each type) for $14.95, postpaid; or Talk O'Texas will ship six jars of one kind for the same price. The pickles are best for plain old munching, especially with an ice-cold beer, or alongside a sandwich.

— ❖ —

Upside-Down Cajun Chow Chow and Pickles

Louisiana General Store
The Jackson Brewery
620 Decatur Street
New Orleans, Louisiana
70130

(800) 237-4841; (504)
947-0293 (Monday to Friday,
8 A.M. to 4 P.M., CST)

Free color catalog
VISA, MasterCard, American
Express

The first thing you notice about Lynne O'Leary's pickles is that the label on the jar is upside down. It's that way on purpose, designed so you'll store the jar with the lid end down instead of up. "The spices tend to settle to the bottom," she points out, so "by keeping them on their lids you always get a spicy pickle when you open the jar."

When Lynne was a little girl growing up in Louisiana, her grandmother made delicious spicy pickles from an old family recipe that had been handed down "forever." On special occasions the pickles emerged from the larder and appeared on the family relish tray. When Lynne grew up and had children of her own, she carried on the tradition, making the pickles for her family and as gifts for friends. Word got out in New Orleans about Lynne's pickles, and soon people were pulling up into her driveway to buy a case at a time. In 1988 Lynne made the official switch from giving her pickles away to selling them and moved into commercial production. Although she does not sell mail-order from her small production facility, you can place orders through the Louisiana General Store catalog, which contains hundreds of high-quality Louisiana specialties.

Upside-Down Cajun Pickles are thick-cut, crunchy rounds that are sweet (but not cloying) and spicy, with a hot punch of flavor from garlic and a bit of red pepper. You can see hefty slivers of fresh garlic floating around in the sugar-sweetened brine. Overall the taste is sweetly subtle, with a not-too-hot zing that hits after you've chewed a bit. Eat them with sandwich classics such as a hamburger or grilled cheese. The pickles are sold in 10-ounce ($4.00) and 20-ounce glass jars ($6.00).

Lynne also makes Upside-Down Cajun Chow Chow, which is so tasty you'll be tempted to eat it from the jar with a spoon. This is an untraditional chow-chow (no vegetables) that combines small diced bits of her Cajun pickles in a spicy mustard-based sauce flavored with onions, garlic, and spices. Thick and chunky, the chow-chow is absolutely delicious on a ham sandwich, served alongside sliced roast beef, or glorifying an ordinary hot dog. Upside-Down Cajun Chow Chow is sold in 10-ounce ($4.00) and 20-ounce glass jars ($6.00). A small wooden gift crate containing a 20-ounce jar of each costs $14.00. (Shipping is not included in any of the prices noted.) After you've developed a taste for Lynne's pickles and chow-chow, you may want to buy enough to last a while. Each is also available by the gallon for $35, plus shipping.

Zatarain's Creole Mustard

When it comes to Creole mustard, Zatarain's is the brand of preference in Louisiana and throughout the South. Zatarain's is to ordinary bright yellow ball-park mustard what pâté is to Vienna sausages. This 90-year-old New Orleans mustard is tangy and full-bodied, highly spiced, and flecked with coarse brown bits of dark spices and mustard

Louisiana General Store
The Jackson Brewery
620 Decatur Street
New Orleans, Louisiana 70130
(800) 237-4841; (504)
947-0293 (Monday to Friday,
8 A.M. to 4 P.M., CST)

Free color catalog
VISA, MasterCard, American
Express

seed. It imparts zing to everything from a rémoulade sauce served with shrimp to po'boys, the New Orleans version of a submarine sandwich.

Zatarain's Creole Mustard has a long, proud history as one of the first products put out by the famous New Orleans food manufacturer Emile A. Zatarain. Today the company name is synonymous not only with mustard but with crab boil, horseradish, filé powder, and countless seasonings and condiments relied on by generations of Louisiana cooks.

While it is increasingly easy to find Zatarain's Creole Mustard in grocery stores outside Louisiana, it can still be hard to get sometimes. So it's good news that it can be ordered from the mail-order department of the Louisiana General Store in three sizes of jars (note that shipping costs warrant combining an order for the mustard with other food items from this catalog). The 5½-ounce size is $.90, the 16-ounce is $1.75, and a giant economy-size gallon weighing 11 pounds costs $11.00 (shipping on this, for example, runs about $6).

Sauces

La Martinique Original Poppy Seed Dressing

As a little girl in Dallas I eagerly looked forward to shopping trips with my grandmother at Neiman-Marcus. I was only around 10 years old, and I can tell you it wasn't the prospect of a day of shopping that caused me any excitement; it was anticipating the wonderful lunch I knew I was going to eat in Neiman's famous restaurant, the Zodiac Room. Specifically, it was a fruit salad with a very spe-

Pace Foods, Inc.
Attn: Direct Shipment
Department
P.O. Box 12636
San Antonio, Texas 78212

(512) 224-2211 (no phone orders)

Free order form
Prepaid orders only

cial poppy-seed dressing that made my mouth water. I was surprised to find out not long ago that this dressing is now made commercially by the La Martinique Dressing Company.

La Martinique's creator was Esther Allidi, a Frenchwoman who came to Austin many years ago. Allidi opened the Liberty Bell restaurant in the mid-1930s and first created a French vinaigrette that she later marketed under the name La Martinique.

In the 1940s, she introduced the Original Poppy Seed Dressing later made famous by Helen Corbitt, the culinary genius at Neiman's. Actually, Corbitt never claimed to have invented the dressing, but she did figure out it was perfect dribbled over "the best grapefruit in the world," and naturally she meant Texas grapefruit. This version is very close to the one I remember; it's a creamy, sweet dressing made with diced onions and dotted with Dutch Blue poppy seeds. Wonderful sprinkled over sliced grapefruit, it's even tastier on mixed fresh fruit salad, which is the way I used to have it at the Zodiac Room.

Some years later a third dressing, Blue Cheese Vinaigrette, was added to the line. Unlike most blue-cheese dressings, however, it's thin and clear rather than thick and creamy, with crumbled bits of Wisconsin blue cheese. You can make a very good, fast French-style potato salad with this by pouring it over hot, cooked new potatoes and adding a sprinkling of cracked black pepper.

Though owned by big Pace Foods, the dressings are made in a small Austin factory where many of the ingredients are chopped and mixed by hand. Mostly as a favor to former Texas residents who can't buy the dressings readily elsewhere, Pace will ship them by the case to individuals. A case of twelve 8-ounce bottles of the poppy-seed dressing or vinaigrette costs $21, postpaid; the blue cheese is $24, postpaid.

Lusco's Salad Dressing, Broiled Shrimp Sauce, and Fish Sauce

Lusco's, Inc.
P.O. Box 79
Greenwood, Mississippi
38930
(601) 453-5365 (answering machine takes orders before 5 P.M., CST)

Free order form
VISA, MasterCard

To understand what makes these sauces special, first you have to know something about the place they come from. Though Lusco's is one of Mississippi's most famous restaurants it doesn't look the part. Set on an old street in Greenwood among a row of fading storefronts, it looks more like an old-fashioned grocery store overhung with a Coca-Cola sign. In fact, it did begin that way, as a grocery store opened by Italian immigrants Charles and Marie Lusco in 1933. The Luscos built private dining cubicles in the back a few years later and started serving pasta and chow mein, along with Papa Lusco's home brew, to Prohibition-era diners that included everyone who was anyone in the Delta plantation set.

During World War II soldiers stationed nearby discovered Lusco's (it was right across from the railroad), and carried memories of its fine meals across America. Lusco's is still in the family, now run by the fourth generation, Andy Pinkston and his wife, Karen. Karen greets the customers and Andy, who learned the Luscos' secret family recipes cooking alongside his aunts, is chef.

The ingredients in Lusco's famous vinaigrette and sauces are still a family secret, but anyone who has ever eaten at Lusco's will be happy to know that several years ago the Pinkstons began bottling and selling them for shipment. Lusco's Salad Dressing (12-ounce bottle, $5, plus shipping), which originated with Andy's great-aunt, is a tasty oil and vinegar mixture that's served on the restaurant's special salad. Creamy and full-flavored, it can also be used as an overnight marinade for sliced tomatoes, cucumbers, and hot peppers. Lusco's Broiled Shrimp Sauce (12-ounce bottle, $5.75, plus shipping) made with lemon juice, Worcestershire sauce, and molasses is the same one used for Lusco's famous broiled shrimp and is based on a recipe from Andy's grand-

Lusco's

mother. Available in hot and mild versions, it's zippy and good on other broiled seafood as well as on broiled chicken, quail, dove, and cornish hens. Lusco's Fish Sauce (12-ounce bottle, $5.25, plus shipping) is the same one that's served with the restaurant's signature dish of crispy broiled pompano. All you do is bring the sauce to a boil, combine with an equal amount of margarine, and pour over your favorite seafood.

VISITING THE SOURCE
— ❖ —

In the 1930s, the local gentry flocked to Lusco's and it became one of the most fashionable places in the Mississippi Delta, famed for the tenderest steaks and most succulent seafood north of New Orleans. To this day, diners are met in the front room (where aged canned goods are still displayed on shelves) and ushered to private booths behind chintz curtains for a cloistered eating experience that seems deliciously mysterious and almost sinful. Diners use a buzzer in the booth to summon their waiter, who lyrically chants the menu (the recitation is part of the tradition; only party poops ask for a printed menu). Nothing has changed at Lusco's . . . and no one wants it to.

Lusco's is located at 722 Carrollton Avenue; ask anyone in town and they'll tell you how to get there. Only dinner is served and the restaurant is open Tuesday through Saturday from 5 P.M. to 10 P.M.

— ❖ —

Maker's Mark® Bourbon Gourmet Sauce

Maker's Mark is a trademark of Maker's Mark Distillery Inc.

Almost a century ago, Henry Baines, popular chef of a private men's club in Louisville, perfected a sauce recipe that included among its ingredients a healthy snort of Kentucky bourbon. The fruity, spicy sauce was judged quite tasty by club members, one of whom happened to be L. B. Samuels, the father

Mousetrap Cheese
P.O. Box 43307
Middletown, Kentucky 40243
(502) 245-9197 (24 hours, 7 days a week)

Free 14-page color catalog
VISA, MasterCard

of the founder of Maker's Mark Bourbon. The recipe was Henry Baines's secret. Or so everyone thought until a few years back, when the recipe was found among L. B.'s papers by his grandson, Bill Samuels, Jr. Seems Henry had passed the recipe along to his friend. Bill Samuels, Jr., and fellow Kentuckian John Anson believe they've re-created the original. It's a thick, mahogany-colored sauce made from a litany of ingredients, including tomato paste, molasses, lime juice, orange peel, and mangos, and spiked with Maker's Mark Bourbon. Henry Baines would certainly approve. The sauce is sweet and tangy, with the flavor of mangos in the foreground. Use it as a flavor enhancer, baste, or sauce for everything from beef and spring lamb to vegetables.

Maker's Mark Bourbon Gourmet Sauce comes in a suitably distinguished-looking bottle with a red-wax-sealed cap that replicates the look of the bourbon bottle. It is available by mail through Mousetrap Cheese, a Kentucky catalog that specializes in gifts of mail-order foods from all over. A 16-ounce bottle is shipped with several recipes and costs $12.75, postpaid.

— ❖ —

Maunsel White's "1812" Wine Sauce

Irish-born Louisiana sugar plantation owner Maunsel White was a colorful philanthropic bon vivant with a taste for luxurious, refined clothes such as silk hose and Florentine vests, the choicest wines, and superb food. At Deer Range Plantation in Plaquemines Parish he took pride in setting a fine, abundant table for guests, including his good friends Andrew Jackson and Zachary Taylor.

Colonel White created two sauces for his own use. One was a unique, palate-stinging hot sauce made from his own homegrown chili peppers and created to sprinkle on oysters. Maunsel carried a

Gazin's
P.O. Box 19221
New Orleans, Louisiana
70179-0221

(800) 262-6410; (504)
482-0302 (Monday to Friday,
9:30 A.M. to 4:30 P.M., CST)

34-page color catalog, $1
(applied to first order)
VISA, MasterCard, American
Express

bottle of this with him at all times. According to John Tobin White, Maunsel's great-grandson, the sauce became so popular that "everybody started making it; it was as common as ketchup." (In 1868 a family on Avery Island, Louisiana, began commercially producing a similar sauce. We know it today as Tabasco.)

The colonel's other sauce, more delicate and subtle, consisted of spices and peppers blended with wines (including a unique orange wine Maunsel made on the plantation) and aged in wooden barrels. According to White family legend the sauce was first served at a special dinner in honor of General Andrew Jackson to commemorate the Battle of New Orleans, which was fought and won in 1815.

Maunsel White's grandson Sidney John White hit on the idea of making a commercial version from the secret recipe during the Depression, adopting the trademark name "1812" Wine Sauce. Today John Tobin White oversees production of the secret formula that "improves the taste of anything." The current sauce no longer contains Louisiana orange wine (no one makes it these days, though attempts have been made over the years to do so), and it's aged in stainless-steel tanks rather than wooden barrels. The pale brown liquid is truly mysterious, with a winey foretaste (some people have guessed quinine and tamarind are also there). The best way to try out the flavor, says White, is to put a dollop of Blue Plate mayonnaise on a saltine and sprinkle on a couple of drops of "1812." A drop or two will wake up mayo, cut commercial ketchup's sweetness, enhance heated canned soups, and add interest to melted butter for seafood. It can be sprinkled on chicken or fish before cooking and splashed in a Bloody Mary. In fact, White recommends using piquant "1812" in practically everything except your morning café au lait. Gazin's ships two 5-ounce bottles for $6.49, or a case of 12 for $35.95 (plus shipping).

— ❖ —

Panola Hot Pepper Sauce and Panola Jalapeño Pepper Sauce

**Louisiana General Store
The Jackson Brewery
620 Decatur Street
New Orleans, Louisiana 70130**

**(800) 237-4841; (504)
947-0293 (Monday to Friday 8
A.M. to 4 P.M., CST)**

**Free color catalog
VISA, MasterCard, American
Express**

When it comes to favorite Louisiana hot sauces, there are honest differences of opinion. And those differences are as fierily argued as the tongue-tingling sauces themselves. Panola Pepper Sauce ranks high both with native-born hot-sauce aficionados and out-of-state journalists who've rated it at tastings. Panola is relatively mild compared to other sauces, and unlike nearly all others made of fresh chopped peppers, Panola sauce is cooked (for seven to eight hours) and then aged for several months before bottling. The result is a russety red sauce more thickly textured than most, rich and full-bodied. Its maker Grady "Bubber" Brown says a splash of his Panola Pepper Sauce will wake up everything from steak to red beans, to say nothing of gumbos, soups, stews, Mexican dishes, sandwiches, any meat or seafood, party dips, eggs, and barbecue. I like to glob some on black-eyed peas or a plain omelet to give my taste buds a little bouncing around, but catfish fillets marinated in Panola Pepper Sauce before frying are nice and spicy, too.

Grady makes Panola Pepper Sauce from a 50-year-old recipe of his mother's that was ritually made up at Christmas as gifts for friends and became locally famous as "Mama's Pepper Sauce." When Grady returned from the navy, he took over the farm and the making of the family hot sauce, which became prized among his hunting camp buddies as "Bubber's Hot Sauce." While the exact recipe is guarded, he will say it's made from both cayenne and jalapeño peppers (more cayenne than jalapeño), along with vinegar, onions, sugar, salt, and "spices."

Grady Brown farms a 4,000-acre plantation near the Mississippi River in Louisiana's East Carroll Parish, raising cotton, soybeans, and crawfish. That's a lot of work, so it wasn't until 1983 that he and his wife and three children branched out into making Bubber's Hot Sauce and selling it from an old plantation house on the property. Within only a few years, he's seen his business double and redouble to the point where shipments are going to grocery stores as far away as Denver.

Grady has also forged ahead to perfect a Panola Jalapeño Pepper Sauce which represents the other major branch of hot sauces: a green sauce. Made of jalapeño peppers and aged for four months prior to bottling, it's quite a few degrees hotter than the original red sauce.

The sauces are available in small 3-ounce bottles ($1.50 each, plus shipping) or 5-ounce bottles ($2.25). Then again, you could think about eternity and order a whole gallon of each version ($30, plus shipping). *Panola*, by the way, is Choctaw for "land of cotton."

BUBBER'S BLOODYS
— ❖ —

46 ounces V-8 juice
4 tablespoons lemon juice
3 tablespoons
   Worcestershire sauce
½ teaspoon celery salt
1 teaspoon salt
2 teaspoons black pepper
2 to 3 tablespoons Panola
   Pepper Sauce, or to
   taste
Vodka
Celery sticks

These may also be made without the vodka.

Mix the first seven ingredients and chill. When ready to serve, pour some of the mixture over ice in a highball glass. Add a jigger of vodka and a piece of celery to each glass. Stir and serve.

Serves 8

Personalized Tabasco Brand Pepper Sauce

**Tabasco Country Store
McIlhenny Company
Avery Island, Louisiana
70513-5002**

**(800) 634-9599 (Monday to
Friday, 8 A.M. to 5 P.M., CST)**

**Free 16-page color catalog
VISA, MasterCard, American
Express**

Tabasco Brand Pepper Sauce is the grand-daddy of all Louisiana hot sauces. It's said that there's a bottle in over half of the households in America; in the South it's a staple "no good cook *would* do without and no poor cook *could* do without." A few drops on your morning eggs wakes up tastebuds; a couple of good squirts on black-eyed peas is essential. Some folks, like Mississippi-born food writer Craig Claiborne (who once said, "Tabasco sauce is like mother's milk to me"), just can't live without it.

Tabasco was invented in one of the most romantic spots in the South: Avery Island, a large salt deposit covered with topsoil that rises in the Gulf of Mexico just off the coast of South Louisiana a few miles from New Iberia. A land of bayous and marshes, South Louisiana is the heartland of Cajun culture and cooking.

Around 1850 a soldier returning to New Orleans gave Edmund McIlhenny some dried peppers, and he planted the seeds in his wife's kitchen garden on Avery Island. During the Civil War, McIlhenny and his family supplied salt from Avery Island at low prices to the Confederacy and as a result were driven from their land by Union forces. On their return from Texas, where they had taken refuge, they found their plantation ruined. However, a few of the pepper bushes survived. McIlhenny began experimenting with the hot peppers, creating a formula for the hot sauce—said to have been named after the Tabasco River in Mexico—that is still followed today by fourth-generation McIlhennys.

The bright red, blisteringly hot peppers (known as *Capiscum frutescens* and grown in this country only on Avery Island) are hand-harvested, crushed into a mash, and aged for three years in Arkansas white-oak barrels. The barrels are capped with wooden covers with holes drilled in them and then a layer of Avery Island salt is spread over the tops. After aging, the mash is mixed together with distilled vinegar and allowed to sit for a month. The result: a thin, red-hot sauce that is sold around the world. Sherpas on Himalayan climbing expeditions and NASA Skylab astronauts have scaled the heights with Tabasco, and it's an ingredient in the favorite lobster sauce of England's Queen Mother.

You can buy a regular bottle of Tabasco at just about any store, but the company's fun mail-order catalog offers some unusual variations on the old standby that can't be found elsewhere. This one, for instance, may be the ultimate gift for a hot-sauce lover: a personalized 12-ounce ("chef-size") bottle of Tabasco bearing a special fancy label that reads "from the private stock of . . ." The Tabasco calligrapher fills in your name (or that of the lucky recipient). It's shipped along with a 28-page illustrated cookbook by Paul Prudhomme featuring recipes from his Cajun childhood, many using Tabasco. Plus there's an extremely clever Authentic Cajun Certificate

THE HEIGHTS OF HOT SAUCE
— ❖ —

Once you discover how good Tabasco, Trappey's, and other hot sauces make food taste, you'll find yourself using them more and more. As a matter of fact, hot sauces are actually kind of addicting, producing euphoria among happy eaters. Serious scientists are studying how food that scorches your mouth can end up making you feel so good. One theory is that you know the pain is not dangerous, and this somehow—the details are still being studied, you understand— induces your brain to secrete endorphins, those substances that are also said to produce the "runner's high." Of course, it's also possible that hot sauce euphoria is being confused with relief— as in, once your mouth returns to normal, you're just plain relieved you didn't die.

PERSONALIZED TABASCO SAUCE
FROM
PAUL PRUDHOMME
— ❖ —

My grandfather, who splashed Tabasco sauce on everything except ice cream, would have adored this attractive gift version of his favorite sauce. Those clever people who run Paul Prudhomme's mail-order catalog offer a slightly fancier version of a personalized 12-ounce jumbo-size bottle of Tabasco. Their calligrapher will inscribe any name (up to eight letters) on a very special label decorated with a lovely color painting of Louisiana bayou country. It is a thing of beauty. Accompanying this bottle, too, is *Authentic Cajun Cooking*, the 28-page recipe booklet written by Chef Paul for Tabasco. The Personalized Tabasco Sauce Package costs $12.95, plus $2.50 postage, from K-Paul's Louisiana Mail-Order Catalog, (800) 654-6017; VISA, Master-Card, and American Express accepted.

that declares the recipient fit to claim himself a Cajun for any number of hilarious reasons. All three items can be yours for $15, plus modest shipping charges.

And, for those who like their Tabasco always within reach on the table, there's a very spiffy white ceramic sauce bottle holder stamped with the famous diamond logo ($6.50; you supply the 5-ounce bottle to put in it); globetrotters can order sets of four infinitessimal ⅛-ounce miniature bottles of Tabasco sauce packed in a little cardboard suitcase (three "suitcases" of sauce, $4.50, plus shipping). And there's lots more, including many handsome items with Tabasco's famous logo, such as an apron ($8.50, plus shipping), a towel and pot-holder set ($14.50, plus shipping), and decks of cards for bridge or poker (two decks, $16, plus shipping). Shipping charges are reason-

GRITS AND GRILLADES

— ❖ —

2 pounds veal or beef
   round, thinly sliced
6 tablespoons bacon
   drippings or salad oil
4 tablespoons all-purpose
   flour
1 medium onion, chopped
1 cup peeled and cubed
   tomatoes
1½ cups water
1 green bell pepper, cored,
   seeded, and chopped
1 clove garlic, chopped
1 bay leaf
1 tablespoon chopped
   fresh parsley
2 teaspoons salt
1 teaspoon Tabasco Pepper
   Sauce
½ teaspoon dried thyme
3 cups hot cooked grits

Brown the meat in the drippings in a deep skillet over medium-high heat. Remove the meat. Add the flour and brown, stirring constantly. Add the onion and tomatoes. Simmer a few minutes. Add the meat, water, pepper, garlic, bay leaf, parsley, salt, Tabasco, and thyme. Lower the heat, cover, and simmer until the meat is very tender, about 1½ hours. Add water during the cooking, if necessary, to make the sauce the consistency of thick gravy. Serve the grillades with a portion of hot grits on the side.

Serves 4 to 6

able; $2.85 on orders up to $10.00; $3.75 on orders up to $25.00.

VISITING THE SOURCE

— ❖ —

When the founder's son, Edward Avery McIlhenny, took over the business, he added another chapter to the colorful Tabasco history. Around the turn of the century, the beautiful white feathers of the snowy egret became all the rage in ladies' hats, and the bird was hunted to the point of extermination. McIlhenny rescued a few chicks and set up a sanctuary on Avery Island that successfully attracted migrating birds and saved the species. Today the refuge, known as Bird City, hosts descendants of the snowy egret and other water birds. It coexists with Jungle Gardens, 200 acres of stunning camellias, azaleas, and other flowers that delight visitors from 9 A.M. to 5 P.M. every day (including holidays) for a small admission fee.

Visitors are also invited to tour the nearby Tabasco Pepper Sauce Factory. You'll know you're there because the smell of the pepper sauce literally drifts out the door. Free tours are conducted Monday through Friday from 9 A.M. to 11:45 A.M. and 1 P.M. to 3:45 P.M.; Saturday, 9 P.M. to 11:45 P.M.

— ❖ —

Thomas Steak & Barbeque Sauce

Thomas Sauce Company
P.O. Box 8822
Greensboro, North Carolina 27419
(919) 299-7665

Free order form
Prepaid orders only

When Dwight Thomas was a little kid delivering newspapers in his hometown, he used to drop by a small hole-in-the-wall restaurant where they served terrific sandwiches. No matter which sandwich he chose, it came topped with a special cinnamon-colored sauce that made everything taste better. After Dwight grew up, he'd pick up jugs of the sauce to use at home. Naturally, when the restaurant closed down, he got kind of nervous about the idea of life without that sauce. Using his last gallon of the original mixture, he set about duplicating its flavor and began sharing it with friends. A few years ago Thomas, who owns a company that specializes in industrial signs, decided to produce it commercially.

Thomas Sauce is a sweetish, kind of tangy tomato-based mixture flecked with black pepper and made with enough vinegar and spices for it to have some bite but not a lot of spicy heat. In the best possible sense, it's a flavor enhancer, because although it's very flavorful it never "takes over." It can be used as a table or pouring sauce (as in "Skip the ketchup and use Thomas Sauce"), splashed on top of hot dogs, fries, or any

A BOOK
FOR
HOT SAUCE FANS
— ❖ —

*"Hot peppers are habit-forming . . . .
When people begin to use hot peppers in their food, they soon reach a
point when they cannot enjoy a meal
without them. Food seems dull,
bland, and monotonous."*
—Richard Schweid
Hot Peppers

In the autumn of 1978, jour-
nalist Richard Schweid
bought four new tires for his
Toyota and set out toward hot-
sauce country: New Iberia, Louisiana. His book, *Hot Peppers* (209
pages, paperback), is filled with
the fascinating history of hot peppers, their origins, folklore, and
uses, and an explanation of how

various hot sauces—including Tabasco and Trappey's—are made.
New Iberia lies in the heart of
Cajun country, and Schweid's in-
sights into Cajun culture are colorful, highly detailed, and sensitive.

Hot Peppers was out of print
when Joe Cahn, co-owner of The
New Orleans School of Cooking
and Louisiana General Store, ran
across a copy a few years ago. He
decided the book was "so incredibly good and important" that he
helped arrange for the publica-
tion of an updated version. The
book costs $7.95, plus postage,
and may be ordered through the
Louisiana General Store catalog,
620 Decatur Street, The Jackson
Brewery, New Orleans, Louisiana
70130; (800) 237-4841. VISA,
MasterCard, and American Express are accepted.

Special Sauces

kind of meat sandwiches. But it's equally tasty to have on hand to marinate or baste foods such as chicken, steak, ribs, chops, shrimp, turkey, and fish. It'll make baked beans taste like barbecued beans, and it does wonders for coleslaw. In this part of North Carolina, people spice Brunswick stew with it, and the local country club uses it for their annual pig picking.

The sauce is shipped only by the case, but you'll probably find it goes fast. A case of twelve 5-ounce bottles costs $13.50, plus UPS charges of around $5.00. Larger, 14-ounce bottles run around $24 per case of twelve, plus UPS charges of around $7.00. My guess is that Dwight Thomas was probably only half joking when he told me, "We *drink* it here at home."

— ❖ —

Trappey's Pepper Sauce and Red Devil Louisiana Hot Sauce

Trappey's Fine Foods, Inc.
P.O. Box 13610
New Iberia, Louisiana
70562-3610
(800) 365-8727;
(318) 365-8281 (Monday to Friday, 9 A.M. to 4:30 P.M., CST; ask to speak with gift shop)

Free color brochure of gift packs; nonillustrated order form of all Trappey's products (specify you want both when writing)
VISA, MasterCard

A few miles from Avery Island, where the McIlhenny family produces Tabasco sauce, lies New Iberia, Louisiana, the home of Trappey's, a source for two other famed Louisiana hot sauces.

In the late 1800s, blacksmith and farmer B. F. Trappey became interested in the spicy red tabasco peppers that thrived in South Louisiana. Taking a lesson from the pickle industry, he gathered together some secondhand whiskey and wine barrels and began preserving peppers in a brine solution. A short time later, he and his sons began producing a stingingly hot sauce sold in little glass bottles. Until recently Trappey's remained a family firm, with W. J. Trappey, B. F.'s grandson, on the board. The elfin 93-year-old is chairman of the board emeritus and the last Trappey family member involved in the business.

Today the company bottles 12 sauces, including two especially fine hot ones. Bright orange Trappey's Pepper Sauce is still made from B.F.'s original formula. In blind professional taste tests conducted by Jenifer Harvey Lang for her book *Tastings* (which identifies the best pantry basics), this sauce was chosen number one in its category because of its good pepper flavor and moderate heat. Trappey's Pepper Sauce is a classic, no-nonsense formulation that enhances the flavor of foods it's sprinkled on. It's made exclusively from locally grown tabasco peppers that have been mashed to a pulp, deseeded, aged for three to four years in oak casks, and mixed with distilled vinegar. Pungent, with robust hot pepper flavor and no metallic aftertaste, it's hot enough to sting a little but won't paralyze your tastebuds, and it has a slightly pulpy consistency that's desirable in hot sauces.

Trappey's Red Devil Louisiana Hot Sauce, a deep orangey-red sauce with milder flavor and heat than the pepper sauce, is made from purée of hand-picked cayenne peppers, and it's Trappey's number-one seller. The peppers used are a special strain developed by Trappey's to grow extra long (8 to 12 inches) and meaty. Unlike the pepper sauce, this formula does contain a stabilizer in addition to the traditional peppers, distilled vinegar, and salt, but again, there's no undesirable aftertaste.

A bottle of each sauce comes as part of a giftpack that also contains jars of other Trappey's products: Hot Pickled Cocktail Okra and Torrido Chili Peppers, New Orleans Style Steak Sauce, and Chef Magic Worcestershire Sauce ($9.65). They may also be ordered individually or by the case; there is a $15 order minimum and a $4.50 shipping and handling charge. The Pepper Sauce costs $1.10 per 2-ounce bottle, the Red Devil Sauce $.80 per 6-ounce bottle. For other Trappey's products, see page 102.

VISITING THE SOURCE
— ❖ —

Visitors are welcome to tour Trappey's Pepper Sauce Plant, which is located in New Iberia, Louisiana, at 900 East Main Street. Brief free tours are conducted Monday through Friday about every 45 minutes from approximately 9 A.M. until 2:30 P.M. Next door to the plant is bright, airy Trappey's Cajun store, which is open Monday through Saturday from 9 A.M. to 4:30 P.M. Gift packs of Trappey's products are on sale here along with local crafts; free coffee and tasting samples are usually available.

HOW HOT IS HOT?
— ❖ —

It's no big surprise that the main appeal of that fiery hot sauce is the heat. Manufacturers of hot sauce calculate this heat based on a rating system known as Scoville Heat Units; hotter sauces have higher numbers. According to Jenifer Harvey Lang's book *Tastings*, Tabasco sauce has a palpitating 9,500 "heat rating." (It's no wonder some bartenders will tell you that the way to ace out a cold is to put a few drops of Tabasco sauce in a glass of soda water.) Trappey's Pepper Sauce is ranked at a more modest 2,400 units (and Trappey's Red Devil Louisiana Hot Sauce a relatively calm 1,000 units). This by no means suggests they're not hot, but your toes probably won't curl up if you use a few drops.

COUNTRY HAMS

"Eternity: a ham and two people."
—Conventional wisdom
attributed to various
insightful sources

*" . . . as long as the smell of fried ham in the
skillet or the taste of boiled ham on a biscuit
survives in memory, there will be traditionalists
at work in country smokehouses, carefully
crafting this gem of Southern foods."*
—John Egerton,
Southern Food

If you're a Northerner, you've probably never
tasted a country ham, let alone attempted to
prepare one. If you're a Southerner, you will
probably go to your grave believing there is no
greater delicacy on earth than a country ham. A
Southern-style country ham is an uncured pig's hind
leg transformed into a monumentally salty, complex-
tasting, richly colored meat. If you are ordering a
country ham for the first time, remember, the meat
is meant to be eaten in paper-thin slivers. Some
ham men sell sliced country ham
in packages, and you may
want to try the taste
out this way first
before ordering
an entire ham.

Amber Brand Smithfield Ham and Joyner's Red Eye Country Style Ham

**The Smithfield Companies
P.O. Box 487
Smithfield, Virginia 23430
(800) 628-2242; (804)
357-2121 (Monday to Friday,
8 A.M. to 5 P.M., EST)**

**Free 11-page color catalog
VISA, MasterCard, American
Express**

VISITING THE SOURCE
— ❖ —

This company is a blending of two formerly independent Virginia ham producers, each well known for a distinctive ham. The Smithfield Ham and Products Company, in business since 1925, produces Amber Brand Smithfield Hams, which have been smoked over a combination of oak, hickory, and apple woods and aged an average of 9 to 11 months. Uncooked Ambers weigh between 13 and 15 pounds and cost $39.95, plus $5.75 shipping. A fully cooked, ready to serve Amber (9 to 11 pounds) costs $49.95, plus $5.75 shipping.

The W. W. Joyner Company, established in 1889, was purchased several years ago by Smithfield Ham. Joyner's Red Eye Country Style Hams have been quite popular over the years, and a great many ham lovers swear by them. Many people find them easier to eat than a Smithfield because, although they are smoked in the same fashion, they are aged for a shorter time (between 70 and 90 days) and thus are milder-tasting and not as dry. An uncooked Red Eye weighs between 12 and 14 pounds and costs $35.95, plus $5.50 shipping. A fully cooked one (9 to 11 pounds) costs $45, plus $5.50 shipping.

Also sold through the catalog are copies of *The Smithfield Cookbook*, a spiral-bound volume of excellent recipes put out by the Junior Woman's Club of Smithfield. There is a chapter of recipes using Smithfield ham, as well as scores of others for local favorites such as Thirteen Day Pickles, the Joyner family's version of white fruitcake, and Essie's Barbequed Rabbit. It sells for $11.95, plus $1.75 shipping.

This company is the only large-scale Smithfield ham producer to maintain a retail store. Joyner's Genuine Smithfield Ham Shop is located at 301 Main Street in Smithfield. Hours are Monday to Friday, 9 A.M. to 5 P.M.

Billy Higdon's Happy Hollow Country Hams

**Higdon's Foodtown
507 West Main Street
Lebanon, Kentucky 40033
(502) 692-3274 or 692-3881**

**Free brochure
VISA, MasterCard**

In the central Kentucky town of Lebanon (population 6,600) Billy Higdon's Foodtown store has grown famous for two things, neither of which you'd necessarily expect to find on your way to the detergent aisle in a 21,000-square-foot supermarket: Hotpoint appliances and Billy's own home-cured country hams.

For almost 40 years (about as long as he and his wife, Rita, have been in the grocery business), Billy cured hams more or less as a hobby. He'd do maybe a hundred a year, and what he and his family didn't eat or give to friends he sold in his store. Sales were so good, a few years ago he decided to expand his curing. Billy uses Kentucky-grown pigs and cures the hams in two smokehouses on his 350-acre dairy farm a few miles

MARION COUNTY COUNTRY HAM DAYS
LEBANON, KENTUCKY
— ❖ —

Ham Days just gets "pigger and pigger" each year. The festival takes place in the Victorian-style downtown area of Lebanon, in the heart of Kentucky ham country. In the crisp fall morning 50,000 visitors feast on a country ham breakfast featuring sizzling slices of local ham (Billy Higdon's hams are among those served), scrambled eggs, fried apples, and homemade biscuits with local honey; later on there's barbecue, ham sandwiches, bean soup with homemade cornbread, and apple cider pressed right before your eyes.

There are more contests than you can shake a stick at: hog calling, tobacco spitting, pipe smoking, nail driving, hot-pepper eating, and hay-bale tossing. The Pigasus Parade is just as silly as you might imagine. But the award for the finest home-cured ham (after judging, it's auctioned off for charity) is serious business, as it should be. Ham Days are held the last weekend of September each year. For information, contact: Lebanon/Marion County Chamber of Commerce, 107A West Main Street, Lebanon, Kentucky 40033; phone (502) 692-2661.

east of town. Billy's curing process involves rubbing the hams "real good with a mixture of red and black pepper" (sometimes, though not always, he may add a pinch of sodium nitrate to encourage good color) and brief smoking over hickory wood cut from his own trees to turn them that nice pecan color that's characteristic of country hams. Like the best ham men, he "lets nature take its course," and the hams hang aging in the smokehouse through the winter and summer and the all-important "June sweats."

Higdon Happy Hollow Country Hams cost $2.69 per pound, with the average ham weighing about 16 pounds. This is the same price they're sold at in the store. The price has not gone up in years, primarily, says Billy, "because we *want* people to try our hams." Shipping is extra and depends on where you live, but it runs less than $10. The best way to place an order is by just calling the store and giving them your credit card number. The hams range in age from 8 to 12 months or so; the super-dry and salty two-year-old hams preferred by old-timers are sometimes available by special request. If you want a ham for the Christmas holidays, be sure to order early. Billy only cures around 1,200 hams yearly and usually sells out before Christmas.

Ham man Billy Higdon.

THE REAL TRUTH ABOUT FIXING A COUNTRY HAM

— ❖ —

"The proper boiling of a proper ham reaches the level of high art."
—Martha McCulloch-Williams
*Dishes & Beverages of
the Old South*

If you grew up in the North and have never tasted a Southern-style country ham, you have also never prepared one.

If you're a Southerner, you've probably eaten country ham, but for one reason or another it's likely you never prepared a ham yourself. In this instance, ignorance may well be bliss.

FOREWARNED IS FOREARMED

I'm going to level with you right off the bat: Preparing a country ham can be an unmitigated pain in the neck. It is hard, greasy, muscle-challenging work. Nobody ever admits this, especially not in print, but it's true. If you are given the choice between ordering an uncooked country ham and an already prepared one, don't be proud; pay the extra money and let the purveyor do the preparation for you. It's worth every extra dollar it costs. This is especially true if you live in an average-size apartment in a big city, where kitchens and stoves tend to be on the small side. If you cannot be swayed and want to fix the ham yourself, the first thing to bear in mind is that the preparation time involved is roughly two days from soaking to the final, brief baking.

Virtually all individuals and companies that sell country hams include their own preparation instructions. Even so, the basics as outlined below are pretty much the same for most hams. Before beginning, be sure to take note of how much your ham weighs (some purveyors mark the weight on the cloth sack the ham arrives wrapped in; others make a notation on the invoice or preparation instructions).

EQUIPMENT

Make certain you have on hand a hacksaw, a stiff-bristled brush, and—this is most important and the thing you're least likely to have—a container such as a gigantic (and I mean huge) stockpot or a lard can with soldered seams. Make sure the pot is large enough to accommodate the entire ham plus an inch or so of water above the ham plus some space at the top. If you have trouble finding one, you can order a big copper boiler through S. Wallace Edwards (see page 149).

MEETING MOLD

Unwrap the ham. The ham is perhaps not the most appetizing-looking sight. Edna Lewis, author of *In Pursuit of Flavor* and a country-ham lover if ever there was one, has stated in no uncertain terms that her favorite, the Smithfield, looks "like it's been buried." There may be a patina of visible mold (some ham men scrub this off before they ship to you). Do not panic and throw the ham out—that mold is the venerable sign of a good, properly aged ham, a badge of authenticity. So take the stiff-bristled brush and scrub the ham under lukewarm running water until the mold disappears. (Whether or not there is mold on the exterior, the ham should always be scrubbed.)

DEALING WITH THE HOCK

Remember the hacksaw? Take it and saw off the hock. You don't *have* to do this, but it's customary and makes the ham a more manageable size. If you don't think you can handle this, you might try taking the ham to your local butcher and asking him to saw it off; however many butchers (especially in the North) don't want to be bothered, and they may require proof from you that the ham has been cured to federal specifications. Save the hock to season beans, greens, and what have you. John Egerton, author of *Southern Food*, recommends sawing the hock into rounds about an inch thick, then wrapping and freezing them for future use, which is a sensible, excellent idea.

SOAKING

Regardless of the type and age, all country hams should be soaked before they are cooked *unless you plan to slice the ham and use it for frying.* Take another close look at your ham and literally size it up. It's big, so it must be put to soak in something big, too. Big, as in your bathtub, kitchen sink (if it's a very large one and you don't think you'll do dishes for a day), a plastic or aluminum washtub, a picnic cooler, or the lard can or stockpot you'll boil it in later. The purpose of soaking the ham is to remove some of the salt. Older hams are the saltiest and need to soak the longest. Regardless of the ham's age, the longer it soaks (within reason, of course), the less salty the meat will be. Place the ham inside the container and cover it with cool water. As a rule of thumb, any ham 6 months or older should be soaked for a minimum of 12 hours and no more than 24 hours (Smithfields, the saltiest hams, require the longest soaking time).

Change the water every couple

(continued)

of hours; otherwise all you're doing is rebrining the ham, a reversal of the desired effect. This is a rather nasty task. The water can get high-smelling and quite greasy. You will probably need assistance to dump the old water out unless you are an Olympic shot put contender or an avid weightlifter. A 15-to-20-pound ham covered with water weighs a lot—a heck of a lot more than most people can possibly lift alone. So don't. Make sure there's someone around to help.

BOILING

Once the ham has soaked sufficiently, remove it from the water. At this point, it looks (and smells) especially piggy-like. Most, though not all, instructions will tell you to place the ham in a large container (the lard can or stockpot), fill it with water, and bring the water either just barely to the boiling point or to a simmer. Whether or not you wish to add a little flavoring to the water is a matter of personal preference; some cooks add some apple or pineapple juice, a couple of bay leaves, or a shot of Coca-Cola for extra flavoring. For either method, allow 20 minutes per pound cooking time. It's advisable to use a meat thermometer as a further gauge; the ham should simmer until it reaches 160°F. Then allow the ham to cool. There are two schools of thought about cooling: some

cooks remove the ham from the water to cool; others believe it should cool in the water. Either way, remove the ham from the water carefully. This is no easy feat, but if you've come this far, hey, you can do anything. (If you're so inclined, allow the water to cool completely, skim off the fat on top, and you'll find you've got yourself a good soup base.) Since the ham is still warm, this is a propitious time to debone it if you wish. Deboned hams are easier to slice than bone-in ones. Allow the ham to cool still further.

GLAZING, *THE FINAL STEP*

The glazing and "baking" steps are pretty much cosmetic. With a sharp knife, remove the skin and some of the fat from the ham. Score the remaining layer of fat diagonally in one direction, then diagonally in the other direction to form little diamond shapes. There are as many recipes for glazes as there are fleas on a dog in the summer. The simplest ones are best. A common one is to rub brown sugar over the ham and then sprinkle the surface with fine, dried bread crumbs; I like to make a paste of brown sugar moistened with a little apple cider. Sticking cloves all over is optional. Place the ham in a large roasting pan and set it in a preheated 375°F oven until the glaze melts and gets bubbly (around 30 minutes). Cool before slicing.

Broadbent's B&B Country Hams, Ham Hocks, and Ham Pieces

Broadbent's B&B Food Products, Inc.
6321 Hopkinsville Road
Cadiz, Kentucky 42211
(800) 841-2202; (502) 235-5294 (Monday to Friday, 7 A.M. to 5 P.M.; Saturday, 7 A.M. to noon, CST)

Free 15-page color catalog
VISA, MasterCard, American Express

The Broadbent family has run one of the best-known, large-scale country ham sources since the 1960s. Their specialty is an award-winning Trigg County ham that has taken the Kentucky State Fair's Grand Champion Country Ham Award five times and the same honor three times at the Mid-South State Fair in Memphis. These hams have also made bidding history at special auctions conducted for charity by setting records for the highest price per pound ($2,140) and for a whole ham ($35,150). And in 1985 the Broadbents made it into the Guinness Book of World Records by baking the world's largest biscuit with ham, a 10½-foot-diameter beauty that weighed over 400 pounds (15 hams were among the ingredients).

These are traditional country hams, dry-cured with a mixture of salt, sugar, and a pinch of sodium nitrate, smoked over a mixture of hickory and sassafras woods, and aged from nine months to a year. Weights range from 14 to 18 pounds and the prices include shipping based on UPS zone (there's a chart in the catalog). To simplify things, prices indicated here are for shipments made to the middle of the country. The hams are available cooked or uncooked. The regular country hams "have more age on them" (9 to 12 months) and are drier and saltier, with a more pronounced flavor than the "new" ones (aged around 6 months), which are less salty and less expensive. An uncooked 14-to-15-pound ham costs $49.90. A cooked and ready-to-eat, semi-boneless one weighing around 8 or 9 pounds is glazed with a honey/brown sugar/mustard mixture and shipped vacuum-sealed. It comes with a hock (for your bean soup) and costs $54.05. The milder, "new" country ham can be ordered uncooked (14-to-15-pounds, $45.65) or semiboneless, cooked (same size, $50.55).

One thing I like about the Broadbents' catalog

is that you can order ham in many variations. For example, if you can't use a whole ham there's the option of cooked country ham slices (3-pound vacuum-sealed package, $25.90) or nice, thick, uncooked ham steaks (6 pounds, $36.75). Ham hocks, ham pieces, and even ground cooked ham (use in omelettes and sandwich spreads) are also available. There's easy-to-slice, dry-cured, hickory-smoked slab bacon with the rind removed (4-to-5-pound slab, $16.10), bags of chunky bacon ends and pieces for use as seasoning (4-pound bag, $7.80), and excellent smoked country sausage (4.6 to 5 pounds, $19.10). If you've never tasted this style ham I highly recommend you consider ordering a combination called Kentucky Party Fare: 6 ounces of thin-sliced, cooked country ham with two dozen beaten biscuits for under $10. A good way to taste the Broadbents' three meats is with the Broadbent's Favorites: a couple of pounds each of uncooked country ham slices, bacon, and sausage, $30.60. Both are excellent values.

Carving a country ham is not the easist thing in the

world to do anyway, and trying to accomplish it with the ham skittering around on a platter is next to impossible. Yet the Broadbents are the only ham people I know of who are clever enough to include a ham rack in their catalog. This metal rack, which holds the ham firmly semi-upright at an angle, is designed to be used on a cutting board ($4.00).

VISITING THE SOURCE
— ❖ —

The B&B Country Store is part of an ambitious, prettily landscaped new tourist complex that lies a few miles east of Cadiz on Highway 68 at the I-24 junction (Exit 65) near Lake Barkley State Park. Open seven days a week, it sells the hams as well as sorghum, jams, Kentucky-made crafts, and gasoline. Hours are Sunday through Thursday, 8 A.M. to 5:30 P.M.; Friday and Saturday, 8 A.M. to 6 P.M.

— ❖ —

Clifty Farm Tennessee Country Hams

Clifty Farm Country Meats
P.O. Box 1146
Paris, Tennessee 38242

(800) 238-8239; (901) 642-9740 (January through mid-October, Monday to Friday, 7 A.M. to 4 P.M.; mid-October through the end of December, 7 A.M. to 10 P.M., CST)

Free 12-page color catalog
VISA, MasterCard

You'll find country hams cured throughout Tennessee, but it's said that those from the middle part of the state, where the temperature is predictable and there's plenty of hickory timber for curing, are the finest. Clifty Farm Tennessee Country Meats is one of the largest and most reliable of the commercial Tennessee ham curers, operating out of the area around the town of Paris. You'll want to be aware that Tennessee country hams are somewhat juicier and moister than the drier, saltier ones cured in Virginia and Kentucky, which are smoked a deeper, darker color. Nor is pepper used in the cure of Tennessee hams. So what do these differences really mean? Simply that Tennessee hams are a slightly different-style ham— not better, no less appealing, just different.

Company founders Truman Murphey and J. D. Murphree grew up together, and like most

farmer's sons they had a lot of hog-killing experience. In the mid-1950s the pair started curing hams as a business to supplement their farming incomes. Today their sons Dan Murphey and Terry Murphree run the operation and sell a phenomenal number of hams each year.

Even though J. D. has pointed out that "asking a man how he cures his hams is like asking him where his favorite fishing hole is," I can tell

THE HAM BOOK:
A COMPREHENSIVE GUIDE TO HAM COOKERY
— ❖ —

"Some folks consider the hambone to be the whole point of the ham."

A few years back Robert and Monette Harrell appeared on a couple of local Virginia TV programs discussing the ins and outs of dealing with country hams. Afterward they received so much mail pleading for the answer to "What do I do with all my leftover ham?" that they wrote *The Ham Book*. Robert's family has been in the Virginia ham business since 1898 and Monette is a home

economist and teacher, so they certainly know what they're talking about. Their 224-page book tells everything you need to know about "hamming it up," including an anecdotal history of ham and a description of the basic curing processes, along with clearly worded guides to ham selection, cooking, and carving. Though there is some information on other hams, the emphasis is on country ones. Most of the 350 or so recipes call for country ham as an ingredient (Country Ham Pie, Ham à la King), though there are some for complementary "country flavor" side dishes. The information on various ham glazes is particularly useful. *The Ham Book* is available for $9.95, postpaid, from Robert W. Harrell, Jr., P.O. Box 667, Suffolk, Virginia 23434.

Clifty Farm

you a little about these hams without betraying family secrets. The "salt rub" that each ham is smeared with is a mixture of salt, white sugar, and "secret" ingredients. For six to eight weeks the hams are left to "take the salt" before they're washed and hung in the smokehouse, where they're smoked continuously over hickory wood chips and dust until the meat takes on a thick, brown crust that seals in the natural juices.

The slick Clifty Farm catalog is filled with mouthwatering color photos, so don't try to browse through it when you're hungry. All ham shipments are accompanied by cooking, carving, and storing directions. Uncooked country hams weigh from 12 to 20 pounds and cost between $34.45 and $50.35 (postpaid, east of the Rockies; west of the Rockies, add an additional $4). People who plan to use the ham for frying only may request that it be presliced at an additional charge of $3.50 per ham. If you can't use the whole hog (as it were), there's a 2½-pound package of center slices, $16.95, for a smaller supply of breakfast or supper ham. Bone-in, fully cooked hams with the hock and skin removed weigh between 7 and 9 pounds and cost $47.95 (boneless, $56.95). These are not glazed, so you may want to cover the ham with a paste made of brown sugar moistened with vinegar and heat it in a hot oven until the sugar melts before slicing and serving.

Also featured in the catalog are slabs of dry-cured, hickory-smoked, rind-on bacon (8-to-10-pound slab, $23.31), cloth bags of medium-seasoned, hickory-smoked sausage (two 1-pound bags, $9.95), and 2-pound jars of Benton County sorghum from a farm a few miles down the road ($8.95). Various special gift assortments are available also. The Clifty Farm Sampler is a good way to try Clifty meats (a pound each of center ham slices, bacon slices, and smoked sausage, $19.95).

Colonel Bill Newsom's Kentucky Country Hams

**Colonel Bill Newsom's
Kentucky Country Hams
127 North Highland Avenue
Princeton, Kentucky 42445
(502) 365-2482 or 365-6311**

Free descriptive ordering
information
Prepaid orders only

Newsoms and their kin have been dry-curing hams in Kentucky and Virginia ever since the family first arrived from England in the mid-1600s. With a history like that it's really not surprising that the ones Bill Newsom and his daughter Nancy Mahaffey sell from their country store and by mail are so fine.

Back in the early 1930s, Newsom's father cured hams only for his own family's use; the ones he sold in his store came from the smokehouses of local farmers. But in the early 1960s, Bill Newsom began doing the curing for the store-sold hams himself. His output the first year was 25 hams; today he sells "thousands," though the exact number is "kind of like a military secret." These are top-notch hams that have won plaudits from countless food editors and authors, including Julia Child.

Newsom's fresh hams are massaged by hand

In the smokehouse are Colonel Bill Newsom and his daughter, Nancy Mahaffey.

with a mixture of only salt, sugar, and pepper—no nitrates, nitrites, preservatives, or additives are used. Covered with additional salt, the hams are set on low wooden platforms to cure for about a month in a temperature-controlled room. After a good hosing down, they're wrapped in stockinette bags and moved to the aging room, which also doubles as a smokeroom. The hams are smoked for around 30 days over a combination of hickory wood and sawdust that burns slowly in an old iron wash kettle. Newsom's hams then age, suspended hock-end down (he believes this makes for a thicker, meatier ham), at least 7 months and more often as long as 10 to 12 months. The hams weigh an average of between 13 and 17 pounds, though larger ones are sometimes available.

Miraculously, Newsom's prices have not changed in the past eight years for these delicious hams. They still sell for $2.69 per pound, plus shipping based on a flat rate for the UPS zone destination (for example, shipping would run around $9 to the West Coast; $5.50 to parts of the South). An excellent, detailed pamphlet with preparation instructions, ham tips, and recipes accompanies each shipment (they scribble the weight of your ham on the corner of the cover).

The late James Beard, who ordered from Newsom, once wrote, "To have an honest ham on hand is indeed a great culinary privilege." Order from the Colonel and you'll agree.

VISITING THE SOURCE

— ❖ —

You can drop by Newsom's Old Mill Store at 208 East Main Street and buy a ham in person. You can buy groceries, seeds, and garden supplies, too. It's located two doors away from the site of the original H. C. Newsom Store, which burned down several years ago. The store is open 8 A.M. to 5 P.M., Monday through Saturday; phone (502) 365-2482.

Doug Freeman's Country Ham

Doug Freeman's Country Ham
605 New Hope Road
Cadiz, Kentucky 42211
(502) 522-8900

No order form; write for current prices and availability
Prepaid orders only

Doug and Euneda Freeman with one of their award-winning hams.

Trigg County hams are well known among country ham fanciers. In the area around the small town of Cadiz you can buy lovely hams not only from Broadbent's, a big producer, but also from local farmers who still cure small numbers the slow, old-fashioned way. Farmer Doug Freeman, who only cures around 400 hams a year, has won the honor of Grand Champion Ham at the Trigg County Ham Festival, and his country hams are favored by John Egerton, the author of *Southern Food*. That's as fine a recommendation as you can get, since Egerton grew up eating hams from his grandfather's Trigg County smokehouse.

Four generations of Freemans have cured hams on their farm, but in the 30 years he's had his smokehouse Doug never really got involved in selling his hams until winning the grand championship. Now he can barely hang on to enough for his own use. Freeman raises some of his own hogs and buys the rest of the green (fresh) hams he needs locally, which means they're probably (though not necessarily) corn-fed. Each December he rubs the hams down with a saltpeter and salt mixture, covers them with salt, and leaves them to dry-cure for a month to six weeks. After washing and trimming, they're smoked for a month or longer over a mixture of hickory sawdust from a local sawmill and green sassafras from his farm. (Trigg County hams are characteristically slow-smoked a little longer than are Smithfields.) Then the hams hang aging in the darkness of Doug's two smokehouses until the following fall or early winter, when they've turned a deep mahogany color.

The average weight of one of Doug's hams is 16 pounds and the price is $2.75 per pound, plus shipping. But you'll have to hustle to order one, since the supply is very limited. Doug's wife Euneda, sends postcards out to regular customers sometime in August or September advising about current prices. New customers should send a stamped, self-addressed postcard along with their request for prices and availability; when the hams are ready in the late fall, she'll send a notification.

— ❖ —

Edwards Country Style Hickory Smoked Virginia Ham

S. Wallace Edwards & Sons
P.O. Box 25
Surry, Virginia 23883
(800) 222-4267; (804) 294-3121 (Monday to Friday, 9 A.M. to 5 P.M., EST)

Free 7-page color catalog
VISA, MasterCard, American Express

Some companies simply have nicer personalities than others. It comes through in the way they do business, create a catalog, and package their products. S. Wallace Edwards, Jr., and his son, Sam, have seen to it that their family business speaks to you on a deeper level than your credit card number. Their top-quality hams have been featured in the prestigious Williams-Sonoma catalog and named Grand Champion several times at the Virginia State Fair.

Back in 1926, S. Wallace Edwards, Sr., a captain on the Jamestown-Surry ferryboat, cured 25 hams on his farm and used them to make ham sandwiches for his hungry passengers. Later, as folks began asking to buy whole hams, the ferry became almost a "nautical butcher shop." By the 1930s Edwards had left life at sea to cure hams full-time. Today the company is run by his son and grandson with their wives, and the meats are cured in a Surry smokehouse located near the spot where, it is said, Indians first taught the secret of smoking to the colonists.

Edwards' Hickory Smoked Uncooked Virginia Ham is a short-cut one, meaning the hocks have been cut short (unlike a Smithfield ham) and the butt ends trimmed of their skin and some fat. The fresh hams are salt-cured and rubbed with coarse-ground black pepper. The smoking process lasts a week or so (a combination of hickory and apple woods are used) and the hams are aged from four to six months. Uncooked hams

weighing between 11 and 12 pounds sell for $44, postpaid, and arrive in a burlap sack or, for an additional $14, a handsome wooden gift box. The same ham, fully cooked (9 to 10 pounds) costs $55 (in a wooden box, $69). Edwards' ham has a deep reddish-pink color and a hickory underflavor that's milder and sweeter than a Smithfield. For a more pronounced-tasting, smokier ham, there's the Wigwam brand, which is aged 10 to 12 months (14 to 15 pounds, uncooked, $57; 10 to 11 pounds, cooked, $63).

For the person or small family not requiring a lifetime supply of ham, the Edwards have cleverly come up with a "petite ham" similar in flavor and texture to their larger ones but with an average weight of only 2 to 3 pounds, and I say "bless them" for thinking of this. It's the perfect size for effortless, modest-scale entertaining. Fully cooked and boneless, it should be sliced very thin before serving. The price of the petite is

GUIDELINES FOR CARVING A COUNTRY HAM
— ❖ —

1. A deboned ham is much easier to slice than a bone-in one. (Allow the ham to cool off just enough so you can handle it; it should still be quite warm so the meat will easily detach from the bone.) Don't throw the bones out—they can be used to season soups, beans (a cracked hambone is said to be the secret to the most flavorful red beans), and broth.

2. Always begin slicing at the hock end.

3. Cut a wedge-shaped piece out of the ham about 6 inches in from the end of the hock (or, if you sawed the hock off earlier, about 2 inches from the hock end).

4. Using a very sharp knife, begin slicing with a slant toward the hock end of the ham. Slice wafer-thin.

5. Work your way around the ham so slices are taken from the top and sides, too.

"It's the difference between extra-sharp Cheddar and American processed. A good country ham is like a fine cheese: the more you age it, the better it gets, like a country twang."

—Samuel Wallace Edwards III

$24.95, postpaid, and it comes in an attractive cloth gift bag and box.

I might have overlooked Edwards' smoked Virginia sausage if Camille Glenn, author of *The Heritage of Southern Cooking*, hadn't told me to be sure not to miss it. I'm glad I listened because these links of nicely seasoned, highly flavorful sausage are just great. Good browned for breakfast or in casseroles at suppertime, they contain no fillers, which you'll have to admit is something of a miracle these days. Long strings of links come tucked inside printed cloth bags, each containing 2 pounds of sausage. The bags must be ordered by the pair ($23.40, postpaid), or you may choose the more economical 5-pound box (no bags) for $19.95, postpaid. I highly recommend you try these.

The catalog also features Edwards' fine hickory-smoked slab bacon (4 to 5 pounds in a burlap bag, $18, postpaid), ready-for-the-skillet uncooked Virginia ham slices (eight 12-ounce vacuum packages, $39.90), and a Virginia Smokehouse Sampler with sausage, bacon, and slices of smoked ham ($24.95). The Edwards' packaging is especially attractive, not too slick yet not hokey, so all the products make wonderful-looking gifts. By the way, if you haven't been able to locate a lard can for boiling a country ham, you can order a big copper boiler with handles, just like the one Grandmother Edwards used, for $98.

VISITING THE SOURCE
— ❖ —

The Edwards family welcomes visitors to their famous smokehouse and retail store. The firm is located on Routes 10 and 31 on the west side of the village of Surry, which is a short ferry ride from the Jamestown/Williamsburg area. Tours of the smokehouse are conducted every hour on the half hour (9:30 A.M. to 11:30 A.M.; 1:30 P.M. to 4:30 P.M.), Monday through Friday

SMITHFIELD HAMS:
THE PINNACLE OF PORK
— ❖ —

Smithfield hams are the most famous type of Southern-style country ham. Thomas Jefferson served them at the White House and Queen Victoria is said to have ordered them for state occasions. These are by far the saltiest, driest, and most strongly flavored hams, so they're not for the faint-hearted or for people who have not tried country ham before.

These hams are in a class by themselves. A law literally governs what constitutes a genuine Smithfield ham, which can be cured only in the small town of Smithfield, Virginia. First established in 1926, the law states that the hams must be "cured by the long-cure, dry-salt method" and aged for six months or longer within the Smithfield town limits. Today only three commercial packing companies produce hams eligible to bear the Smithfield designation (The Smithfield Companies, Gwaltney of Smithfield, and Smithfield Packing Company). S. Wallace Edwards, for example, who prepares his hams the same way, is located in Surry, fifteen miles away, so his hams are not technically Smithfields.

The distinct differences between Smithfields and other country hams are the result of the Smithfield's longer smoking and aging times (which also make them more expensive). Although their officially mandated minimum aging time is 6 months, Smithfields are usually aged anywhere from 9 to 18 months. During curing and aging, a 25 to 30 percent moisture loss occurs, which means the percentage of salt increases. This is why Smithfields are much saltier and more strongly and pungently flavored than other country hams.

The steps in processing a Smithfield are similar to those for other country hams. Green (fresh) hams are hand-dredged with lots of salt, sprinkled with sodium nitrate (to preserve the color), and stacked in a cooling chamber, where they are repeatedly resalted (or "overhauled") for 30 to 45 days until the salt seeps through the meat all the way to the bone. Then they're rinsed and coated with coarse-ground black pepper. The pepper is a bow toward tradition rather than necessity; in the old days it warded off insects. The hams are hung from smokehouse beams, where they're smoked over hickory and aged.

As with other country hams, I recommend ordering one that is already cooked. The meat should be sliced wafer-thin and served at room temperature with beaten biscuits (see page 154).

from March 1 through September 30. The retail store is open January 1 through March 31, Monday through Saturday from 9 A.M. to 5 P.M.; April 1 through December 31 the store stays open an extra hour.

— ❖ —

Gwaltney Genuine Smithfield Ham

Gwaltney of Smithfield
P.O. Box 489
Smithfield, Virginia 23430

(800) 678-0770 (Monday to Friday, 8 A.M. to midnight; Saturday and Sunday, 8 A.M. to 4 P.M., EST)

Free 13-page color catalog
VISA, MasterCard, American Express

Back in 1870, P. D. Gwaltney, who was originally in the peanut business, cured his first hams. Later his son, P. D. Jr., who was more interested in hams than peanuts, operated a small ham business as a sideline to the family's general store until the late 1930s, when he and his two brothers closed the store and devoted themselves full-time to perfecting the Gwaltney cure. Although now a large-scale commercial meat packer, the company continues to cure and ship quite a few Smithfield hams. Edna Lewis, author of two marvelously evocative books on Southern cooking (*The Taste of Country Cooking* and *In Pursuit of Flavor*), feels that Gwaltney hams are the next best thing to a home-cured Virginia ham straight off the farm.

Gwaltney's uncooked Smithfield hams, which weigh from 13 to 15 pounds, cost $41.95, plus shipping. Fully cooked ones, weighing 10 to 12 pounds, cost $52.95. These hams, cured for six months, have aged anywhere from nine months to a year and a half. The "younger" Williamsburg hams, which are less salty than the Smithfield because they're cured for 90 days and aged between seven and nine months, weigh between 11 and 13 pounds and cost $34.95. A cooked Williamsburg, glazed with brown sugar and weighing 10 to 12 pounds, costs $44.95. The Williamsburg is best suited to frying, and the Gwaltney catalog also features a box of uncooked Williamsburg center cut and end ham slices ideal for country breakfasts. But be warned: this is quite a

BEATEN BISCUITS

— ❖ —

Beaten biscuits are the classic accompaniment for country ham. Small, dry, crisp, and as hard, some say, as hockey pucks, they're meant to be split open and filled with thin slivers of country ham. They date back to the plantation-era Old South, when plentiful labor was a given and no effort was spared in food preparation. Black cooks mixed up a simple, unleavened dough (flour, lard, water), which they took outside to a tree stump. There they pounded it vigorously with a heavy, flat object—a mallet, the side of an axe, a heavy skillet—flattening, folding, and turning the dough until it blistered, made popping and snapping noises, and eventually turned smooth, soft, and glossy. Since neither baking powder nor baking soda was yet available, the purpose of all this time-consuming pounding and thumping was to form tiny air pockets in the dough so it would rise. "Beat 500 times for company, 300 times for family" was the rule of thumb, though it is also claimed that 1,001 strokes were required for perfect beaten biscuits.

A labor-saving device called the biscuit brake was introduced in the late 1800s. It consisted of a pair of hand-cranked rollers mounted on a slab of marble. Dough was fed through it over and over again, sort of like clothes through a wringer. These intriguing-looking machines are much coveted family heirlooms today and some still in use have even been electrified.

These days hardly anyone bothers to make beaten biscuits, though a reasonable, less flaky facsimile can be achieved with a food processor (most new Southern cookbooks include a recipe). You're most likely to run across them served during festive seasons such as Christmas and Derby time, or at fancy affairs like wedding receptions and brunches, where they're piled high on elegant silver platters.

If you order a country ham, you owe it to yourself to taste it at least once served the traditional way. At the Cheddar Box, a specialty food store operated by Nancy Tarrant, beaten biscuits are made on the premises with an electrified antique biscuit brake. The biscuits cost $2.75 per dozen, plus $4.50 per dozen shipping and handling. Contact: Cheddar Box, 3909 Chenoweth Square, Louisville, Kentucky 40207; (502) 893-2324. Accepts VISA and MasterCard.

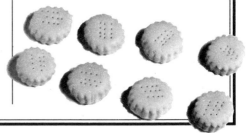

THE ULTIMATE AGED HAM

— ❖ —

Back in 1902 P. D. Gwaltney, Jr., cured a large Smithfield ham. It's still hanging, or rather lying, around, and it may well be the oldest piece of cured meat in existence. They even say it might still be edible, though the thought is not a particularly appetizing one. As the years marched on, the ham was given a name, Methuselah, and a brass collar inscribed with the words "Mr. Gwaltney's Pet Ham" was wrapped around the hock. At one time it resided in a case in Gwaltney's office, and he was even known to take it along with him occasionally on trips. Of course, it was insured, a fact reported in 1929 in Ripley's "Believe It Or Not."

hefty supply, as each box contains sixteen 12-ounce vacuum-sealed packages of slices ($39.95). There is a $4-per-item additional charge for shipping each of the products.

— ❖ —

Honey Baked Ham

The Honey Baked Ham Company
P.O. Box 370
Carrollton, Georgia 30177
(800) FOR-A-HAM

Free order form
VISA, MasterCard, American Express

Not every single ham from the South is a salty country one, even though at times it may seem that way. Honey Baked Hams are what I would characterize as "city" hams; they're closer to what most Northeners expect a ham to be like—mild in flavor, pinkish in color, and moist.

More than 40 years ago Harry J. Hoenselaar had a brilliantly practical, albeit somewhat strange, idea. He figured out a way to slice a ham in a single continuous spiral so that perfect slices of just the right thickness still clung to the bone. Harry's heirs are still using his patented machinery to radial-cut their hams.

These hams are sold in awesome quantities throughout the South and are available through the firm's own retail stores and by mail order. I first encountered the hams one Christmas when I realized several of my displaced Southern friends were placing orders just like their mothers had before them. These hams are a tradition in some families where "it just isn't Christmas without a Honey Baked Ham." The hams are mild-cured (nitrites and water are used) and baked with a tasty honey-and-sugar glaze. Fully cooked, they're shipped frozen and should be allowed to thaw in the refrigerator approximately two days before serving. Instructions are included on how to cut along the natural fat lines in the face of the ham to release the tidy, spiral-cut slices. I'd have to say this is an ideal ham for holiday buffets and snacking—it tastes delicious and you don't have to do a thing except pay the bill. There are half hams (7, 8, and 9 pounds, $39 to $45, postpaid) and whole hams (13, 14, and 15 pounds, $62 to $68, postpaid). Gift certificates are also available.

— ❖ —

Loveless Smoked Country Hams

Loveless Hams and Jams Catalog
Route 5, Highway 100
Nashville, Tennessee 37221
(615) 646-0067 (Monday to Friday, 8 A.M. to 3 P.M., CST)

Free color catalog
VISA, MasterCard, American Express

For years the superb home cooking and hospitality at the Loveless Motel & Cafe was one of middle Tennessee's best-kept secrets. Then Jane and Michael Stern, authors of *Goodfood* and *Roadfood*, ate there a few years ago and lauded the place as "one of the great undiscovered restaurants of the South," likening the food to a country song because it's so "honest and good." But even though the joys of eating the Loveless's legendary country breakfast have become an open secret, nothing has changed except you want to be darned sure to make a reservation because the cafe's 75 seats are always full. (If you have to wait awhile, you can amuse yourself looking at celebrity photos of Charley Pride, Jimmy Buffett, Minnie Pearl, Chet Atkins, and a host of other Loveless fans displayed in the screened-in porch.)

As with so many of the best places specializing in the food people were raised on, if you

didn't know better you might
drive right on by the simple clapboard-and-stone
building with its cheerily tacky pink and blue
neon signs and small cluster of motel cabins out
back. When the Lovelesses owned the business,
the motel was active; now it's not.

Donna McCabe and her late husband, Charlie, bought the business in 1973 and retained
not only the name but the services of Elizabeth
Roberts, the energetic cook whose biscuits and
preserves are the crowning touches of the hearty
breakfast served here all day. (There's a dinner
menu that includes fried chicken, chicken livers,
or gizzards, but most people like the breakfast so
much they simply never manage to venture further into the menu.) The huge slice of gently
fried country ham nestles on a platter with eggs
and is served accompanied by a bowl of red-eye
gravy and a supply of small, piping-hot biscuits.
On the red-and-white-checked tablecloths rest

bowls of Elizabeth's incredible preserves (see page 238) to slather on the biscuits, along with local honey and sorghum.

All the not-too-salty ham served here is specially cured for the Loveless by a secret source in West Tennessee. Cafe customers can buy hams at the register; armchair eaters can obtain them through the mail-order catalog run by George, Donna's son. The tasty, relatively mild, whole salt-cured, hickory-smoked hams have been aged around eight months and weigh between 14 and 21 pounds ($2.75 per pound, plus shipping). If you don't want to bother with a whole ham, there are vacuum-packed delicious center slices for $7.95. Remember that overcooking country ham toughens the meat; slices should just be heated through on both sides and removed from the frying pan when the fat along the edge turns translucent. The same hickory-smoked bacon (5-to-6-pound half-slab, $17.95; 1 pound sliced,

PORK, PEANUT, AND PINE FESTIVAL
SURRY COUNTY, VIRGINIA
— ❖ —

Surry County's principal industries are honored each year on the grounds of historic Chippokes Plantation State Park, home of the oldest continuously cultivated farm in America. Virginia's Pork Queen reigns supreme as the Virginia Porkettes frolic, Mr. Peanut and Little Miss Peanut work the crowd, and Smokey the Bear puts in a good word for the Surry lumber industry. Count on more than 200 craft exhibits and lots of food booths where you can pig out on pit-cooked barbecue, ham, and peanut soup and pies. Visitors are advised to "bring a lawn chair so they can sit in the shade." The festival is held the third weekend in July. Admission is free, but there's a small parking fee. For information, contact Chippokes Plantation State Park, Route 1, Box 213, Surry, Virginia 23883; or call (804) 294-3625.

$3.95) and perfectly seasoned hickory-smoked pork sausage (2-pound cloth bag, $7.95) served in the cafe can also be ordered. You could come pretty close to duplicating the Loveless breakfast experience (without the secret-recipe biscuits or Donna McCabe's friendly greeting, of course) by ordering a gift package called the Teaser. It includes all of the meats served at the cafe (bacon, sausage, and ham), along with 16-ounce jars of sorghum, honey, and two kinds of preserves ($36.75). Prices do not include shipping. Note that between May 1 and October 1 meats are shipped only via second-day air (these shipping charges run between $7.50 and $15).

VISITING THE SOURCE
— ❖ —

Reservations at the Loveless are recommended but not required; call (615) 646-9700. The cafe is located on Highway 100, about 16 miles southwest of Nashville. Hours are Tuesday through Saturday, 8 P.M. to 2 P.M. and 5 P.M. to 9 P.M.; Sunday, 8 A.M. to 9 P.M.; closed Monday.

— ❖ —

Robertson's All-Natural Sugar-Cured Country Hams

Robertson's Country Meats
P.O. Box 56
Finchville, Kentucky 40022
(800) 678-1521; (502) 834-7952 (Monday to Friday, 8 A.M. to 5 P.M., CST)

Free color brochure
VISA, MasterCard

Bill Robertson's hams are very good and very famous. They've been rated the number-one country hams by the *New York Times* food section, which crowned them "assertively flavored," and they come highly recommended by countless pleased customers I've spoken with. More important, they're among the only country hams available by mail order that do *not* contain nitrates or nitrites, the commonly used preservatives that also add color to hams.

This small regional company is operated by Robertson and his sister, Margaret Davis, who take pride in seeing to it that their hams are cured and aged with tender care. "We cure hams the way they did before this country was a country," says Robertson, whose family has run a

A NOTE FROM ROBERTSON'S

— ❖ —

One pound of cooked country ham will top 25 biscuits. If it's the only entrée, five pounds of cooked country ham will yield enough slices to serve 12 people; if it's combined with another entrée, 19.

country store in Finchville since around 1900. In the late 1940s Bill's father began curing hams as a sideline for the store, and today they're the main attraction.

Robertson and his small staff carefully trim fresh ("green") hams, which are then hand-rubbed with a mixture of salt, red and black pepper, and brown sugar, wrapped in butcher paper, and hung up to air-cure in net bags for a minimum of 10 months (and often up to 14 months) under natural conditions in an aging house. Unlike many other country hams, these are not smoked, a process that Robertson contends is a "cosmetic" treatment that adds color but no additional flavor. The flavor of a Robertson ham is salty but not overwhelmingly so: the flesh is somewhat dry (as it should be) and the lovely color of Italian prosciutto. All in all, Robertson cures a connoisseur's ham.

The hams can be ordered several ways. A basic uncooked, sugar-cured country ham weighing between 13 and 18 pounds costs $2.79 per pound, plus shipping (you may specify small, medium, or large; they'll fill your order accordingly). Clearly worded cooking and carving instructions accompany the ham, which does not require refrigeration before cooking (it will keep indefinitely if left in a cloth sack and hung in a dry place). Before cooking, you might want to cut off the hock for use later as bean-soup seasoning. When serving cooked country ham, remember that it's best sliced as thinly as possible, ideally up to 14 slices per inch, according to Robertson.

More than 65 percent of the hams Robertson ships are ready-to-eat, fully cooked, boneless ones—the same hams as the uncooked ones, but he has performed the drudgery of soaking, boiling, etc., for you, removed the fat and bone, and vacuum-packed the whole thing. The higher price of $7.29 per pound plus shipping is worth

every penny. These weigh between 6 and 8
pounds and may be ordered presliced, a major
convenience if you're going to serve the ham
at a party. This cooked ham will keep almost
indefinitely under refrigeration, thus guarantee-

A GOOD SOURCE FOR
HARD-TO-FIND SOUTHERN COOKBOOKS
— ❖ —

*"We Southerners talk about food
like we talk about the weather and
football—all the time."*
—Carol Daly
Proprietor of
The Everyday Gourmet

The Everyday Gourmet is a
food-lover's emporium lo-
cated just a few blocks from Mississippi's gold-domed state capitol.
In addition to all kinds of pots,
pans, and gadgets for cooks,
there's a huge selection of cookbooks with emphasis on difficult-
to-find Southern cookbooks compiled by Junior Leagues and other
groups. These lovingly written
volumes are a source of delightful, authentic (and sometimes
oddball) regional recipes you
won't find in other books. I'm
talking about titles like *Charleston
Receipts Repeats*, a sequel to the
oldest Junior League cookbook in
print; *I Promised a Cookbook*, by
Josephine Cannon, a popular
Mississippi Delta caterer who re-

veals at last the recipe for her Pie
in a Cloud; and *Standing Room
Only*, which includes recipes
from Eudora Welty and Beth
Henley, compiled by members of
Jackson's New Stage Theatre.
The shop is well known for its
cooking classes and also stocks
local specialty foods. For a free
catalog or to receive a copy of the
bimonthly newsletter, contact:
The Everyday Gourmet, 2905
Old Canton Road, Jackson,
Mississippi 39216; phone (601)
362-0723.

ing that you'll have months of carefree, effortless munching.

Robertson offers several country ham variety packs, which are an ideal way to sample this style of ham without committing to a whole one. For instance, for $30, postpaid, you can order two 1-pound packages each of uncooked sliced ham and of fully cooked sliced ham. This way you can stage your own mini ham tasting—bake a batch of biscuits to serve the cooked slices on and make a country breakfast of fried ham, red-eye gravy, and grits using the uncooked slices.

VISITING THE SOURCE

— ❖ —

Robertson's Country Meats Store is located off Interstate 64 (Taylorsville/Shelbyville exit) on Highway 55 South in Finchville, Kentucky. Store hours are Monday to Friday, 8 A.M. to 5 P.M.; Saturday, 8 A.M. to 5 P.M. between Thanksgiving and Christmas only.

s • Mrs. Fearnow's Delicious Brunswick Stew • Fuller's Mustard • Maunsel White's
e • Panola Pepper Sauce • Amber Brand Smithfield Ham • Billy Higdon's Happy Hol
try Hams • Colonel Bill Newsom's Kentucky Country Hams • Bucksnort Smoked Rain
• Callaway Gardens Speckled Heart Grits • White Lily Flour • Bailey's Homemade H

er Jelly   Sherardi   ansel's Rice • Garbe
Yams • Warrento   ssinger's Flying Pig
n Arrow Ranch Ax   ory-Smoked Sausag
• Golden Mill So   ms Sweet Vidalia O
of Luck Scottish S   ker Deluxe Moon Pi
s Kitchen Derby P   otato Chips • Char
s Rendezvous Ribs   Barq's Root Beer •
wine • Crickle •   ens Cut Leaf Poke S
s • Mrs. Fearnow   • Maunsel White's
e • Panola Pepper   Higdon's Happy Hol
try Hams • Colone   ksnort Smoked Rain

• Garber Farms Cajun Yams • Bland Farms Sweet Vidalia Onions • Callaway Garde
led Heart Grits • White Lily Flour • Bailey's Homemade Hot Pepper Jelly • Mayhaw
rdized Pecans • Virginia Diner Peanuts • Ellis Stansel's Rice • Ledford Mill Borrowe
ken Arrow Ranch Axis Venison • Comeaux's Boudin • Mayo's Hickory-Smoked Sausa
• Golden Mill Sorghum • Steen's Pure Cane Syrup • Best of Luck Scottish Shortbr
shoes and Nails • Double Decker Deluxe Moon Pies • Kern's Kitchen Derby Pie • L
n Orchard Cake • Warrenton Original Nashville Rum Cakes • Zapp's Potato Chips •
s Rendezvous Ribs • Maurice Bessinger's Flying Pig Barbeque • Barq's Root Beer •
wine • Crickle • Evelyn's Pralines • Goo Goo Clusters • The Allens Cut Leaf Poke S
s • Mrs. Fearnow's Delicious Brunswick Stew • Fuller's Mustard • Maunsel White's
e • Panola Pepper Sauce • Amber Brand Smithfield Ham • Billy Higdon's Happy Hol
try Hams • Colonel Bill Newsom's Kentucky Country Hams • Bucksnort Smoked Rain
• Garber Farms Cajun Yams • Bland Farms Sweet Vidalia Onions • Callaway Garde
led Heart Grits • White Lily Flour • Bailey's Homemade Hot Pepper Jelly • Mayhaw
rdized Pecans • Virginia Diner Peanuts • Ellis Stansel's Rice • Ledford Mill Borrowe
ken Arrow Ranch Axis Venison • Comeaux's Boudin • Mayo's Hickory-Smoked Sausa
• Golden Mill Sorghum • Steen's Pure Cane Syrup • Best of Luck Scottish Shortbr

Southerners are likely to go fishing whenever the pace of life gets too hectic. Harvesting the bounty of the sea, streams, and lakes is a way of making a leisurely private peace with nature. Of course, a little luck is always welcome—it can mean the difference between ending the day with a bunch of tall tales about the one that got away or enjoying day's end with a convivial fish fry. From the handful of folks in this section, you can order uncommonly good seafood delicacies that are a sure thing, like Pickwick Farm–raised Smoked Catfish and stone crabs from one of Florida's most famous restaurants.

Bucksnort Smoked Rainbow Trout

Bucksnort Trout Ranch
Route 1, Box 156
McEwen, Tennessee 37101
(615) 729-3162

Free order form
VISA, MasterCard

If you live in middle Tennessee you can buy Butch Imoberstag's sparkling fresh, preservative-free rainbow trout at the weekly Food Fairs held in the parking lots of a handful of local churches. (His customers claim the fish are so fresh they're almost swimming.) Or you can grab the kids and go spend a day catching your own at his trout ranch. But Butch only sells the delicious home-smoked version through the mail.

With his wife, Vicki, and their five children, Butch farms the trout on 33 acres, drawing springwater from the base of a nearby limestone bluff. While many trout farmers rely on antibiotics and chemicals, Butch is very proud he's never "used a lick of chemicals" in his aquaculture setup, where the fish grow in narrow, quarter-mile-long channels called "raceways" that ripple with a flow of crystal-clear springwater.

This simple but good-tasting trout is slowly smoked over hardwoods (which ones are Buck's

secret) right at the farm. No preservatives are used, though salt is (special requests for salt-free are accommodated). The flavor is clean, pure, and subtle, with just enough smokiness to add special interest to the moist, flaky meat. Whole fish are partially deboned before smoking. The head, backbone, and side rib cage are removed but the tail is left on, which means you'll encounter a few thin bones. They're smoked the same day they are shipped and arrive packed in a plastic container. The price is $8.50 per pound (two fish per pound), plus shipping. These succulent smoked rainbow trout make a lovely appetizer when served chilled, with a dab of horseradish.

VISITING THE SOURCE
— ❖ —

A visit to the Bucksnort Trout Ranch is a perfect family outing. The ranch is located an hour west of Nashville on I-40, five minutes off the Bucksnort exit (Exit 152), and is open seven days a week from 10 A.M. to 7:30 P.M. Adults and children can spend a lazy afternoon watching and feeding the trout or catching a mess of their own. No license is required for fishing, tackle and bait are provided free, and there is a nominal charge for deboning and dressing the family catch.

— ❖ —

Harold Ensley Fish Fry Coating Mix

c/o War Eagle Mill
Route 5, Box 411
Rogers, Arkansas 72756
(501) 789-5343

Free 16-page color catalog
VISA, MasterCard

For more than 35 years as television's popular "Sportsman's Friend," Harold Ensley has been sharing his enthusiasm and expertise on freshwater fishing with fishing buffs. Known as the most famous fisherman in America, Ensley created this fish fry mix for coating freshly caught fish about to go into the frying pan or onto a grill in the great outdoors, but it works well on store-bought fish and other foods.

The coating mix comes from War Eagle Mill, a historic Arkansas mill that specializes in healthy, stone-ground grains. The father of War

Eagle's miller, Zoe Medlin Caywood, used to go on fishing jaunts with Ensley, and he suggested Ensley ought to share his recipe with others. The fish fry mix is a fine powder composed of wheat flour, onion, garlic, white-pepper seasoning, plus a little paprika thrown in to add spice and color. Just dip your fish in plain water, roll or shake thoroughly in Harold's Fish Fry Coating Mix, then pan-fry to golden brown. The mix, which can also be used for coating baked foods, works nicely with chicken, rabbit, and vegetables such as okra and eggplant, as well. Any fisherman would appreciate having a bag of this tucked in his creel. A 2-pound bag of Harold Ensley Fish Fry Coating Mix costs $3.25, plus shipping charges of around $2, so you might want to stock up on some of War Eagle's other fine products (such as Yankee corn grits or white cornmeal) at the same time (see page 216).

War Eagle Mill's inventive, modestly priced gift assortments include the Fisherman's Gift Box ($14.50, plus shipping of around $3), with all the ingredients for a fish fry except the catch of the day—a 2-pound bag of Harold's Fish Fry Coating Mix and a 2½-pound calico sack of War Eagle Hush Puppy Mix, plus two Arkansas whetstones to throw in your tackle box. One is a soft oilstone for sharpening knives; the other is designed for sharpening fish hooks.

— ❖ —

Joe's Stone Crabs

The sweetly succulent meat of the stone crab must be counted among the truly great seafood delicacies. It's the specialty at Joe's, one of Florida's oldest and most famous restaurants, where nearly a ton of tricolored stone-crab claws are served each day.

Stone crabs were first popularized by the restaurant's late founder, Joe Weiss, back in the

Joe's Stone Crab Restaurant Take Away
227 Biscayne Street
Miami Beach, Florida
(800) 780-CRAB; (305) 673-4611

Free brochure (prices do *not* include air shipping charges); all orders shipped Monday through Friday via Federal Express overnight delivery; Saturday delivery available in most areas
VISA, MasterCard, American Express

1920s, when the crabs were in plentiful supply in Biscayne Bay. Since then, the crabs have grown scarcer locally, and now most come from the Gulf of Mexico, where Joe's operates its own fishery business to ensure that there's never a shortage. Only the claws of the crab are eaten—in fact, it is illegal to harvest the whole crab; by law fishermen may remove only the claws and must then return the crab to the water, where it eventually regenerates new ones. Although pretty-looking (a lovely coral pink with dark ebony tips), the shell is monumentally hard and takes determination and a mallet to crack. (Damon Runyon once described the shell as "harder than a landlord's heart.") Traditionally, the claws are boiled and served chilled and precracked on a platter along with a dipping sauce such as melted butter and lemon (or, at Joe's, with a special tangy mustard sauce, a heap of coleslaw, and some hash browns). You use a long fork to extract the chunks of delicious white meat, somewhat similar in flavor to lobster.

The claws, alas, don't come cheap and are relatively complicated to order by mail, but they're very special and worth splurging on the next time there's something special to celebrate. The restaurant has always packed crabs for visitors to take home, but filling mail orders was recently instituted by Jo-Ann Sawitz, Weiss's granddaughter, who now runs the business with her children.

Crab prices change each year. At this writing, an order of five large claws (total weight around a pound and half), the more popular size, accompanied by a container of the famous mustard sauce, costs $23.95. Air freight and packing, however, add enormously to the cost (roughly two or three times the cost of the claws). There's a $6 charge for packing each order in a leakproof box with real, not dry, ice, and shipments are made only via Federal Express overnight air.

JOE'S STONE CRAB RESTAURANT
MUSTARD SAUCE
— ❖ —

1 cup mayonnaise
3½ teaspoons Coleman's
    Dry English Mustard
2 teaspoons Lea & Perrins
    Worcestershire Sauce
1 teaspoon A-1 Sauce
⅛ cup light cream
Pinch of salt

Place the mayonnaise and mustard in a bowl and beat to combine for 1 minute. Add the remaining ingredients and beat until the mixture reaches a creamy consistency. Chill before serving.

Makes approximately 1 cup

The claws are shipped cooked and ready to eat, but uncracked. Use a regular old hammer for cracking them, or, for an additional $10, you can request a hefty wooden mallet with metal teeth that's identical to the ones used at Joe's. A bib and instructions on how to crack the crabs are included with each order.

VISITING THE SOURCE
— ❖ —

Joe's Stone Crab Restaurant is open only during crab season, from mid-October to mid-May. Lunch is served every day from 11:30 A.M. to 2 P.M.; dinner from 5 P.M. to 10 P.M. Reservations are not accepted, and although the place seats more than 400, there's usually a pretty long wait since Joe's is as popular with residents as it is with tourists.

— ❖ —

Pickwick
Farm-Raised
Smoked Catfish

Now, when most people think of catfish, they envision fresh-caught ones rolled in cornmeal, deep-fried, and served alongside a nice heap of freshly made coleslaw and a mess of piping-hot hush puppies. If you just happened to find yourself around Memphis and decided to head east about a hundred miles to the

**Pickwick Catfish Farm
Highway 57
Counce, Tennessee 38326
(901) 689-3805**

**Free descriptive price list
with serving instructions and
recipes
VISA, MasterCard**

resort area around Pickwick Dam, you could enjoy a fine and simple meal exactly like this at the Pickwick Catfish Restaurant, run by Betty and Quentin Knussmann. Back in the 1970s, Quentin ran a large New York corporation and counted himself a corporate climber. But when his best friend succumbed to the rat race, dying of a heart attack, it made Quentin step back and reevaluate his own life. Changes were called for. He and Betty narrowed the possibilities down to two: a tea plantation in Ceylon or a catfish farm in Hardin County, Tennessee. Catfish it was—and still is for the Knussmanns, who encourage visitors to eat them where they are grown.

As delicious as these catfish are, what the Knussmanns are really famous for are their spectacular-tasting smoked catfish. The smoked-catfish idea came up when Quentin remembered some he'd eaten in Alaska when he was in the service. He worked out a process in which the fish are marinated overnight in a mild brine,

WORLD'S BIGGEST FISH FRY
PARIS, TENNESSEE
— ❖ —

April in Paris—Tennessee, that is—is catfish time. At this mega–fish fry, a tradition since the early 1950s, 14,000 happy eaters head to the local fairgrounds for an all-you-can-eat traditional dinner of Kentucky Lake catfish and crusty hush puppies (fried in hundred-year-old wash tubs by the Lax family) accompanied by white beans, coleslaw, fries, and plenty of Pepsi. Other events include parades, a rodeo, an arts and crafts festival, jam sessions, catfish races (the fish speed down a 16-foot water-filled channel), the Catfish Cook-Off, and the Small Fry Parade for little kids. It's held for five days the last week in April. For information, contact Paris-Henry County Jaycees, P.O. Box 444, Paris, Tennessee 38242.

CHOPPED CATFISH SALAD
1 smoked catfish, flaked
1 red onion, chopped
mayonnaise or salad dressing
Remove all fish from bones. Mix well with equal amount of chopped red onion. Add just enough mayonnaise or salad dressing to hold together. Add salt & pepper to taste. Mix well. Mold in a bowl. Chill. Invert onto lettuce leaf when ready to serve. Serve with crackers.

then smoked over hickory dust. No chemical preservatives whatsoever are used.

Utterly sublime-tasting, each Pickwick Smoked Catfish weighs around a pound. Nothing namby-pamby about the way these taste—the outside is peppery and a little hot, while the flesh inside tastes smoky and salty. The fish are so rich that a little goes a long way, which is frustrating since you want to keep eating. One thing you've got to understand about this delicacy, however: a smoked catfish is not exactly a thing of beauty to look at before the flesh has been removed from the bone in strips or chunks (a surprisingly easy task). In all honesty, I'd have to say they're actually kind of off-putting (dark, dark brown and almost shriveled-looking), but under no circumstances should this prevent you from indulging in this superior treat. After all, beauty isn't everything, and once you've cut into the fish, you'll discover it's moist and creamy colored.

The fish may be eaten cold, at room temperature (best, I think), or briefly heated. Betty's recipe for Chopped Catfish Salad is handwritten on the order form, and it's delicious. Simply remove

WORLD CATFISH FESTIVAL
BELZONI, MISSISSIPPI
— ❖ —

The most intensive catfish raising is now done in the heart of the Mississippi Delta, in a section around the 3,000-person town of Belzoni. Just as cotton and soybeans were collapsing, many farmers were saved by the new catfish business. On the first Saturday in April (unless it falls on Easter weekend), they honor the creature with a day-long event held on the courthouse lawn. It draws nearly 40,000 visitors and features a Catfish Queen, plays for children, music groups, and, for a small fee, all the catfish and hush puppies you can eat. The health-minded enter a 10,000-meter run, while those with more sybaritic tastes vie with each other in the catfish-eating contest. Jugglers, acrobats, and arts and crafts booths all add to the celebratory aura with which Southerners surround food, and the fragrant smell of frying fish haunts the air and stirs the appetite. Tours of the local catfish ponds are conducted.

For information write: Belzoni–Humphreys County Industrial Development Foundation, Inc., 528 North Hayden Street, Belzoni, Mississippi; phone (601) 247-4238.

the fish from the bones and mix well with an equal amount of chopped red onion, moisten with mayonnaise to bind, and season with salt and pepper. Served on a lettuce leaf with crackers, it makes a most elegant dinner party hors d'oeuvre (if you can bring yourself to share it). The catfish, which are fully cooked, arrive wrapped in white paper and tucked inside a clear plastic bag. The cost is $7.50 each for 2 to 9 fish, postpaid; $6.50 each if you order 10 or more (no fish are shipped during June, July, or August).

VISITING THE SOURCE
— ❖ —

The restaurant is located on Highway 57, a few miles west of Pickwick, Tennessee, and is open Thursday through Saturday, 5 P.M. to

10 P.M.; Sunday, noon until around 8 P.M. The menu—fried or smoked catfish, barbecued ribs and chicken—is written on the wall. If you're lucky, Betty will also be serving some of the okra she grows out front.

— ❖ —

Soft Shell Crawfish

**Handy Soft Shell Crawfish
10557 Cherry Hill Avenue
Baton Rouge, Louisiana
70816
(504) 292-4552 (7 days a
week, 8 A.M. to 7 P.M.)
Fax (504) 292-5191**

**Free price list/order form
Prepaid orders only**

The latest seafood gem to emerge from the bountiful waters of Louisiana is an upscale aquaculture product, the soft-shell crawfish, also known as soft-shell *écrevisse* (French for crawfish). The initial research and "farming" of this succulent version of the hard-shell crawfish took place at Louisiana State University, and in the past several years hundreds of small-scale producers have entered the business to form a booming young industry. Baton Rouge–based entrepreneur Frank Eakin, who was among the first to see the potential for soft-shell crawfish, formed a partnership with the Handy Company of Maryland, the world's largest processor of soft-shell crabs, and these beauties come from their joint processing plant in the heart of Louisiana crawfish country.

The flavor of soft-shell crawfish is delicate, rich, and sweet, somewhere between a soft-shell crab and shrimp, and, like soft-shell crabs, they've shed their hard outer shell. These crawfish, which can be ordered fresh (live) or frozen, arrive in a Styrofoam container cooled with frozen gel packs. Live crawfish are packed under a layer of moistened sponges (be sure to ask for a recipe brochure); frozen ones are in Handypaks, handsome looking, four-color boxes printed with recipes and photos. The recommended methods of preparation include broiling, sautéeing in butter, and—best of all—gently dredging in tempura batter or fish fry mix and deep frying in vegetable oil. (Boiling, which toughens the delicate

meat, is not recommended.)

Handy sells mostly to fancy restaurants and gourmet stores but they're happy to ship to individuals. Two sizes of soft-shell crawfish are available by the dozen. Big Daddies, which measure 3 to 3½ inches from head to tail, cost $5.50 per dozen frozen, $6.25 fresh, plus overnight delivery via Delta Air Cargo (charges are collected from you at the time of delivery). Giants, measuring 3½ inches and up, cost $6.75 per dozen for frozen, $7.50 for fresh, plus freight. The company will ship as many or as few dozen as you wish, but be warned that the minimum freight charge on orders under a hundred pounds is $32. If you live in a big city and would like to circumvent the necessarily high air freight charges, the folks at Handy will also be happy to provide you with the name of a local distributor in your area if there is one.

CATFISH THE WAY GOD INTENDED

— ❖ —

"For catfish to be prepared the way God intended, it is a good idea to place it first in a buttermilk bath or, as a savory alternative, baste the catfish with a light coating of mustard.

Then, it must be dredged in seasoned cornmeal, preferably yellow and preferably coarse. The seasonings used may be fresh cracked black pepper, cayenne pepper, lemon pepper, and a little dried thyme.

Next the catfish must be deep fried in fresh oil—enough to amply cover—that has been heated to 375°F. A truly Southern method would be to use some bacon grease as part of the cooking medium. The amount depends on how reckless a person's abandon and the old Southern tradition of 'living to eat.'"

—Joe Middleton
Executive Chef to Ray Mabus,
Governor of Mississippi

s • Mrs. Fearnow's Delicious Brunswick Stew • Fuller's Mustard • Maunsel White's
• Panola Pepper Sauce • Amber Brand Smithfield Ham • Billy Higdon's Happy Holl
ry Hams • Colonel Bill Newsom's Kentucky Country Hams • Bucksnort Smoked Rain
• Callaway Gardens Speckled Heart Grits • White Lily Flour • Bailey's Homemade H
r Jelly   Sherardiz ... nsel's Rice • Garber
Yams • Warrento ... ssinger's Flying Pig
n Arrow Ranch Ax ... ory-Smoked Sausage
• Golden Mill So ... ms Sweet Vidalia On
f Luck Scottish S ... ker Deluxe Moon Pie
Kitchen Derby Pi ... otato Chips • Charli
Rendezvous Ribs ... Barq's Root Beer •
wine • Crickle • ... ens Cut Leaf Poke S
• Mrs. Fearnow' ... • Maunsel White's
• Panola Pepper ... Higdon's Happy Holl
ry Hams • Colone ... ksnort Smoked Rain

FROM THE FARM

• Garber Farms Cajun Yams • Bland Farms Sweet Vidalia Onions • Callaway Garden
ed Heart Grits • White Lily Flour • Bailey's Homemade Hot Pepper Jelly • Mayhaw
dized Pecans • Virginia Diner Peanuts • Ellis Stansel's Rice • Ledford Mill Borrowe
en Arrow Ranch Axis Venison • Comeaux's Boudin • Mayo's Hickory-Smoked Sausa
• Golden Mill Sorghum • Steen's Pure Cane Syrup • Best of Luck Scottish Shortbre
hoes and Nails • Double Decker Deluxe Moon Pies • Kern's Kitchen Derby Pie • Li
Orchard Cake • Warrenton Original Nashville Rum Cakes • Zapp's Potato Chips •
Rendezvous Ribs • Maurice Bessinger's Flying Pig Barbeque • Barq's Root Beer •
wine • Crickle • Evelyn's Pralines • Goo Goo Clusters • The Allens Cut Leaf Poke S
• Mrs. Fearnow's Delicious Brunswick Stew • Fuller's Mustard • Maunsel White's
• Panola Pepper Sauce • Amber Brand Smithfield Ham • Billy Higdon's Happy Holl
y Hams • Colonel Bill Newsom's Kentucky Country Hams • Bucksnort Smoked Rain
• Garber Farms Cajun Yams • Bland Farms Sweet Vidalia Onions • Callaway Garde
ed Heart Grits • White Lily Flour • Bailey's Homemade Hot Pepper Jelly • Mayhaw
dized Pecans • Virginia Diner Peanuts • Ellis Stansel's Rice • Ledford Mill Borrowe
en Arrow Ranch Axis Venison • Comeaux's Boudin • Mayo's Hickory-Smoked Sausa
• Golden Mill Sorghum • Steen's Pure Cane Syrup • Best of Luck Scottish Shortbre

Think of this section as your own family farm. It offers the joys of the real thing—the delicious anticipation of harvesttime, fresh seasonal things to eat—with none of the back-breaking work and worry that raising crops entails. You won't have to fret about the birds picking away at your newly planted seed or fear an early, unpredictable frost. You'll just have to decide whether you can bear to face another fall without tasting what makes the Garber family's South Louisiana yams taste so incredible or what it would be like to make onion rings using a unique sweet onion from Texas that's bigger than a softball but smaller than a bowling ball.

Bland Farms Sweet Vidalia Onions

Bland Farms
P.O. Box 506
Glennville, Georgia
30427-0506
(800) VIDALIA (Monday to
Friday, 8 A.M. to 8 P.M., EST)
Fax (912) 654-1330

Free 15-page color catalog
VISA, MasterCard, American
Express, Diners Club,
Discover

This is one of the largest growers and shippers of Vidalias. On the Blands' large, well-organized family farm, they plant about 500 acres of onions a year, in addition to other crops (including tobacco, corn, soybeans, and tomatoes) that are not shipped mail-order. Like most growers, the Blands ship three sizes of Vidalias, but they've also come up with the unique idea of harvesting "baby" Vidalias for fans who can't stand the agony of waiting for the first mature onions to emerge from the fields.

"Baby" Vidalias, as tender, sweet, and crisp as can be, are actually early spring Vidalias, and as far as I know, the Blands are the only growers who ship them. They look a bit like giant scallions, and every last morsel is edible, from the small white bulb at the end to the lovely, long green tops. Their taste is so fresh, if you close your eyes and munch one like a carrot you can pretend you just plucked it right from the field yourself. Delicious chopped in salads or casseroles, they're also very nice sautéed gently in a little butter and broth. The supply of these is much more limited than regular Vidalias, so placing an order well in advance is recommended. Availability dates vary somewhat from year to year, but generally the babies are shipped from late January through mid-April, and a box of 15 to 18 of them costs $17.95, including next-day air delivery. They should be refrigerated immediately upon arrival to maintain crispness and are best used within 14 days after they arrive. A Baby Vidalia Onion gift certificate is also available for $18.95.

The Blands' regular Sweet Vidalia Onions— jumbos, mediums, and pee-wees—are generally

VIDALIAS:
THE SWEETEST ONIONS
IN THE WORLD

— ❖ —

"A Vidalia onion is absolutely the most exquisite, delicate, succulent, scrumptious onion known to man . . . .It will not make your eyes water, your heart burn, or your sweetheart gag."

—Jody Powell

Imagine an onion so sweet, so delicately flavored, so unusually crisp and mild, that you could eat it raw like an apple if you had a mind to. It's not a dream. It won't give you dinosaur breath. And it won't sting your tastebuds to hell and gone. It's the Vidalia onion from Georgia. And it's so special that the farmers who grow it have to register with the state of Georgia to ensure that no counterfeit Vidalias escape into the markets. Many Vidalias even come labeled with a tiny sticker attesting to their authenticity.

There's something about the unique combination of the soil and climate in certain parts of south Georgia that magically transforms what might merely be an ordinary old strong-flavored hot onion into a subtle taste experience. An onion can only be called a Vidalia if it's grown from the yellow Granex or Granex hybrid and has been planted in a specific growing area of Georgia that's limited to 13 counties and parts of a handful of others. Pale yellow, thin-skinned, and exceptionally juicy, the Vidalia needs lots of special attention from farmers—it's planted and harvested entirely by hand. The harvest season is very short—generally from mid-May through July—so this is a once-a-year treat you've got to grab for fast.

You want to eat Vidalias up quickly, too, because with their high moisture content they don't keep well for very long. (To store for a week or so, most people drop them into the legs of an old pair of panty hose, tie a knot between each onion, and hang in a cool cellar or garage.) Delicious eaten hot or cold, Vidalias taste fabulous in salads and make perfect onion rings. I favor gently baking them in the oven with nothing more than a dot of butter on top.

Vidalias are one of a handful of so-called designer onions, a group of limited-crop specialties that includes Walla Wallas from Washington, the Maui from Hawaii, and the Texas 1015.

THE VIDALIA ONION FESTIVAL VIDALIA, GEORGIA

— ❖ —

Celebrate the Vidalia with the folks who grow it. Events include a Sweet Onion Cook-off, an Onion Eating Contest, and the "Little Miss Onion Pageant." The festival is held annually during the first weekend after Mother's Day. Contact the Vidalia Onion Festival, P.O. Box 1213, Vidalia, Georgia, 30474; phone (912) 537-4466.

shipped only from mid-May through late June, but some years they sell out of their harvest early, so advance orders are encouraged. Pee-wees, ideal for braising or serving as crudités, are sold only by the 10-pound box ($9.95). Jumbos, the most popular size, are shipped in three quantities: 10 pounds ($12.95), 25 pounds ($29.95), and 50 pounds ($56.95). Similar weights of mediums cost $11.95, $27.95, and $52.95. There is a $1.95 shipping charge on each box to each address. Gift certificates are also available.

Also featured in the Blands' catalog are various condiments made with Vidalias (including sweet-onion relish and pickled onions), jars of Georgia honey, and calico bags of onion-ring batter mix. You can also order lengths of red plastic netting for storing your Vidalias. Just drop an onion in, tie a knot, and drop in another onion. Enough netting to store 10 pounds of onions costs $3.95, plus shipping. And as you snip off that last from its netting, remember: these onions "only make you cry when they're gone."

— ❖ —

Cushman's HoneyBells

Cushman Fruit Company, Inc.
3325 Forest Hill Blvd.
West Palm Beach, Florida 33406-9998

(800) 776-7575 (Monday to Friday, 9 A.M. to 5 P.M., EST)
Fax (800) 776-4329

Free 24-page color catalog
VISA, MasterCard

Imagine citrus fruit so incredibly juicy that each shipment is packed with a plastic bib! It's no joke. There really is such a fruit: the trademarked Cushman HoneyBell, known as "the world's *only* limited-edition fruit" because it matures to perfect sweetness only four weeks each year. All I can say is you've got to order them to believe them—they are fabulous.

The HoneyBell, a bright reddish-orange fruit known among citrus growers as a Minneola tangelo, was developed back in 1931 by government researchers. It's a cross between the succulent Duncan grapefruit and the Dancy tangelo, a hybrid with the best of both. The late Ed Cushman, a citrus packer, more or less rescued the

Minneola tangelo from obscurity. One evening back in 1947 Cushman noticed that among the grapefruits being unloaded there were some odd, bell-shaped fruits (the stem end had a protrusion). Grabbing one for a closer look, Cushman peeled it and found that the juice that burst forth was as sweet as honey. He named the fruit HoneyBell and began combing the Indian River citrus area for growers. Although HoneyBells are not difficult to grow, the trees do not produce fruit consistently and it has taken the Cushmans 40 years to establish a reliable supply.

When Ed Cushman died in 1972 his sons began running the business, today Florida's second-largest gift-fruit shipper, and they market Honey-Bells with vigor and a sense of humor. Allen is in charge of marketing, Mike supervises harvesting and buying, and John runs the packing and shipping. The good news is they've got plenty of HoneyBells; the bad news is they're shipped only during January, when they mature. But they're worth the wait, I guarantee you.

HoneyBells are the size of a large orange. Heft one in the palm of your hand and you can actually *feel* how heavy with juice it is. Peeling and eating them is a messy but totally delightful activity; each segment fairly explodes with delicate honey-flavored juice when you bite into it. (Actually, I don't think it's possible to eat these with your mouth *closed*.) Hand-packed boxes of HoneyBells are shipped in five sizes: the 20-pound one is the most popular ($30.95, postpaid), but there are boxes ranging from 10 pounds ($20.95, postpaid) to 40 pounds ($41.95). And miniature HoneyBells shipped in a 20-pound box containing 60 or more fruits ($30.95,

postpaid) ought to be enough for a crowd of tasters. The fruits come packed in sturdy boxes accompanied by the bib and a silly cartoon booklet of testimonials from fans. Though they'll arrive in January, HoneyBells make a high-impact holiday gift, and the Cushmans will see to it that the "designated recipient" receives a special card announcing the forthcoming shipment. Also available is HoneyBell Marmalade, which is nice to have on hand while you're waiting for January to roll around again (11-ounce jar, $9.95).

Although HoneyBells represent well over half of the Cushmans' mail-order business, they ship other high-quality Indian River citrus fruits from November to June, including gift assortments.

Note: Due to state restrictions, no citrus shipments can be made to Arizona and only single-variety gift boxes can be shipped to California and Texas.

VISITING THE SOURCE
— ❖ —

The Cushmans' three retail stores, which are open from the last week of October through the end of May, sell fresh citrus fruit and local produce as well as tropical plants and cut flowers. The locations are: 3325 Forest Hill Boulevard in West Palm Beach (965-3535; open Monday to Saturday, 9 A.M. to 6 P.M.; Sunday 10 A.M. to 5 P.M.); 640 South Dixie Highway in Lantana (586-5925; open Monday to Saturday, 9 A.M. to 5:30 P.M.; closed Sunday); and 2815 Broadway in Riviera Beach (848-6686; open Monday to Saturday 9 A.M. to 5:30 P.M.; closed Sunday).

— ❖ —

Frank Lewis' Royal Ruby Red Grapefruit

They say the remarkable Ruby Red grapefruit was accidentally discovered in 1929 when a worker plucked six red-meated grapefruit from a tree in an orchard in the lower Rio Grande Valley. Unfortunately, he couldn't

Frank Lewis' Alamo Fruit
100 North Tower Road
Alamo, Texas 78516
(800) 477-4773 (Monday to
Friday, 8 A.M. to 6 P.M., CST)

Free color catalog; separate
brochure for cantaloupe upon
request
No credit cards; invoice
accompanies shipment

remember which tree it was exactly, and the impatient owner of the orchard had to wait another whole year until his grapefruit ripened again and the tree was found. Amazingly, the red grapefruit grew only on one limb—all the other branches grew the standard white grapefruit! Cuttings from the limb eventually produced whole orchards delivering the red grapefruit. Frank Lewis, a friend of the doctor who owned the original orchard, was among the first to ship these beauties through mail order.

Frank Lewis' Royal Ruby Red Grapefruit is a tradition in my family—I literally cannot recall a Christmas we haven't each received a shipment of these superlatively juicy, sweet fruits. The meat really is a lovely, deep red, and unlike ordinary pink grapefruit, which just look like white grapefruit from the outside, Royal Ruby Reds actually show a blush of pink through parts of the yellow skin. If you're in the habit of using sugar on grapefruit, you can forget it with these, because they're so naturally sweet it would only be gilding the lily. And they're big—each weighs a hefty pound or more.

These tree-ripened Royal Ruby Reds are not available in any store, so they make ideal presents. The grapefruits may be ordered in a number of ways and shipping charges are straightforward; there is a $3-per-package charge, regardless of weight or destination. The most popular gift box is called the Prince, which contains 16 to 20 grapefruits (weight about 20 pounds) and costs $21.98. Other boxes include the Royal Six (six grapefruits, weighing about 8 pounds, $14.98), the Duke (9 to 12 fruits, weighing about 12 pounds, $18.98), and the Monarch (27 to 32 fruits, weighing around 36 pounds, $29.98), which is a good buy. Smaller Royal Ruby Reds (less than a pound each) are available in the Family Pack of 21 fruits for $20.98.

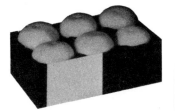

Once you've tasted a Royal Ruby Red it's pretty hard to work up any real enthusiasm toward grocery store grapefruit. I think having a regular supply of Royal Ruby Reds is the height of luxury. This is possible with Lewis's Winter Fruit Club. They'll send three separate quarter-bushel boxes containing 9 to 12 fruits to arrive at Christmas, Valentine's Day, and Easter ($18.98 per shipment), or you can go whole hog for five monthly shipments delivered December through April ($21.98 per shipment). The grapefruits, which keep well in the refrigerator up to three weeks, are available from about mid-November through April. For only three weeks in mid-July, Lewis also ships sweet field-fresh Royal Starr Cantaloupes, which grow in southwest Texas. Each melon weighs 2 pounds or more (box of six, $21.98, plus $3 shipping).

One thing that's strange and good-neighborly about this firm is its attitude toward holiday gift orders. Lewis does not take credit cards; however, you may place an order without advance payment and they'll send you an invoice, which you can pay when the packages have been received in good condition.

— ❖ —

Garber Farms Cajun Yams

Garber Farms
Route 1, Box 19
Iota, Louisiana 70543

(318) 824-7161; (318) 824-4953 (answering machine)

Free color brochure
Prepaid orders only

Whenever I see one of those utterly depressing news reports about the vanishing family-owned farm and the way of life that's disappearing with it, I remind myself that there is also good news. I think about the Garber family. And the outrageously delicious yams they grow. And I begin to cheer up. To my mind one of the purest eating pleasures a person can have is a baked yam. You can gussy up yams with orange juice and teeny-tiny marshmallows and brown sugar and all that stuff and they'll taste good, all right. You can bake yourself a nice

I YAM WHAT I YAM: HOW TO TELL A SWEET POTATO FROM A YAM

— ❖ —

This information is going to drive you crazy. Although the distinction between yams and sweet potatoes is an actual and botanical one, this fact is often obscured by the way Americans, particularly Southerners, refer to them. In common usage, the two names are used interchangeably. And in cooking the same holds true.

Strictly speaking, sweet potatoes (*Ipomoea batatas*), a relative of the morning glory, are widely grown in the United States. Most are somewhat dry-textured with pale yellowish flesh, and they are more likely to be grown by Northern rather than Southern farmers. Another type of sweeter, moister sweet potato with a characteristic dark orange flesh is commonly grown in the South, especially in Louisiana. It is this one that many Southerners consider the quintessential "yam." In part, this is the result of a highly successful marketing campaign begun in Louisiana in the 1930s to promote a scientifically developed "improved" sweet potato grown in that state. True yams, which superficially resemble sweet potatoes and also have whitish or yellowish flesh, are a member of the genus *Dioscorea* (a group of tropical and subtropical herbs and shrubs). They are not grown in the United States, but are a staple crop in places like West Africa, Indonesia, and the Caribbean.

What all this means is that Americans pretty much call sweet potatoes yams . . . except when we call them sweet potatoes, a semantic state of affairs that gives the word "confusion" deep meaning. Agreement seems to exist in one area—how we came to use the word "yam" itself. As in so many other realms of Southern food, the name came to this country via the slave trade. "Yam" comes from *nyami*, the Senegalese word meaning "to eat." And whether you call it a yam or a sweet potato, it's good eating.

sweet-potato pie that tastes great. But a plain baked yam is flat-out divine, especially if the yam was grown in Louisiana by these fine people.

Garbers have always farmed. In the 1880s, great-grandfather Garber left Switzerland and settled in Louisiana, where he grew vegetables. His son raised hot peppers for Trappeys (of hot sauce fame) and grew sugar cane. And *his* son, Walter, became a dairy farmer. In turn, Walter's sons Wayne and Earl grew up on the dairy farm but did not turn to farming right off the bat, though they did not stray far—Earl worked for the Soil Conservation Service and Wayne managed a sugar cooperative. And therein lines a tale.

In the late 1970s Walter and his wife, Eula, took stock of their lives. They had raised five kids on the farm and sent each through college, but their farm was so small that they could not offer their children the option of staying on the land if that was their choice. So the senior Gar-

SOUTHERN FRIED LOUISIANA YAM CHIPS
— ❖ —

4 medium Garber Farms
  Cajun Yams
Cold water
Solid vegetable
  shortening, for deep
  frying
Salt

Peel the yams and cut them crosswise into very thin slices. Cover the slices with water and refrigerate overnight. When you're ready to prepare the chips, drain the slices and dry them on paper towels. Heat the shortening to 365°F and fry about ⅓ of the potato slices at a time until golden brown, about 5 to 8 minutes. Drain them on paper towels. Sprinkle with salt to taste and serve. *Serves 4 to 6*

Variations: Omit the salt and sprinkle the yam chips with any of the following: celery, onion, or garlic salt; cinnamon sugar; confectioners' sugar; or a mixture of confectioners' sugar and orange extract.

bers did something so brave it almost takes your breath away. They made an even swap of their 80-acre family farm near Lafayette for 600 bare acres in bad shape a few miles away. There was no house, not even a barn on it. Wayne and Earl quit their jobs and moved their families onto the land, joining their parents to start a new Garber farm. "You have to have farming in your heart," explains Wayne, whose three teenage sons will no doubt be fifth-generation farmers.

These days the Garbers have expanded the farm to 1,300 acres, nestled on a sandy ridge that has the special South Louisiana soil that accounts for the extra-special flavor of their yams. Although the family plants 70 acres of Jewel variety yams (more than enough to sell to all the people

YAMBILEE
OPELOUSAS, LOUISIANA
— ❖ —

Almost 50 years ago the idea for this festival was born over a cup of coffee when Bill Low and his friend, yam shipper Felix Dezauche, decided it was high time to celebrate the yam, one of Louisiana's major crops. The event takes place each autumn during the last full weekend in October, right after the yam harvest. Pre-Yambilee activities are kicked off the week before with a thanksgiving mass in celebration of the crop. The festival begins the following week and has some pretty silly moments. There's a singing group of young ladies called Yamettes, a Yambilee Queen and King, the colorful Grand Louisyam Parade, and a goofy Yam-i-mals contest, in which contestants further embellish odd-shaped yams that already resemble animals. Fine cooks vie for honors in the Cooked Foods Contest and local growers from big producers to backyard gardeners display their yams for judging (later they're auctioned off as a fund-raiser). For more information, contact the Louisiana Yambilee, P.O. Box 444, Opelousas, Louisiana 70571-0444; phone (318) 948-8848.

Louisiana's Natural
Gourmet Gift!

who drop by the farm and drive home with 100 pounds of yams), the ones they ship via mail order represent the hand-selected very finest of the crop.

The yams are plump in the middle, with tapered ends, a bright coppery-colored skin, and a deep orange-colored, moist flesh that turns succulently soft and sweet when cooked (especially if baked). Opening the box is a treat—almost like getting a nest of eggs, because each yam, which has been tenderly hand-cleaned with a brush, is swathed in tissue paper and nestled in a bed of excelsior. A 5-pound Sampler box costs $9, postpaid; the 10-pound Family Favorite box costs $14, postpaid. Do note that these yams are shipped seasonally. Although orders may be placed anytime after September 1, actual shipments are made after the fall harvest and are shipped from October 15 through January 15, the peak of the season when yams are at their best. Once you've placed an order, Wayne adds your name to his special list; each fall you'll receive a letter from him sharing the year's events on the farm along with current pricing information and anticipated harvest dates.

— ❖ —

G&R Farms Vidalia Sweet Onions

**G&R Farms
Route 3, Box 35A
Glennville, Georgia 30427**

**(800) 522-0567 (Monday to Friday, 9 A.M. to 6 P.M., EST)
Fax (912) 654-3030**

**Free color brochure
VISA, MasterCard, American Express, Discover**

The Dasher family, owners of G&R Farms, was involved with Vidalias long before they became famous as "the caviar of onions." They've grown them since 1945 and claim to be the oldest and largest grower and distributor of these beauties. Brothers Gerald and Robert are fiends for detail and were among the first growers to develop and design, with the assistance of a University of Georgia extension food scientist, a special vented box for shipping and storing Vidalias. And they're still trying to find a way to send Vidalias to Japan.

Difficult as it may be to imagine, on this di-

versified 2,000-acre farm each tiny plant is individually hand planted and harvested. The onions are shipped only from May through July; the exact beginning and ending shipping dates change somewhat each year. Ten-pound bags of jumbos ($12.50, plus $3.95 shipping) or mediums ($11.50, plus $3.95 shipping) are available, as well as 25-pound bags ($29.50 and $27.50, plus $5.95 shipping).

OTHER MAIL-ORDER VIDALIA ONION SOURCES

— ❖ —

The entire annual Vidalia onion crop comes from only about 6,000 officially designated acres in Georgia. There is scant, if any, variation in pricing among shippers. Some years it seems like there just aren't enough Vidalias to go around and some large growers and shippers may sell out early in the brief season. If the two sources I've mentioned have run out, you might consider getting in touch with these other growers:

Atkinson's Plantation, Box 121, Garfield, Georgia 30425-0121; phone (800) 241-3408 (outside Georgia); (912) 763-2149 (inside Georgia). Ten- and 25-pound boxes of Vidalias. Accepts VISA, MasterCard, and American Express.

Grimes' Farms, Route 1, Helena, Georgia 31037; phone (800) 826-7376. Jumbo Vidalias shipped in 10-, 20-, 30-, and 50-pound boxes. Accepts VISA, MasterCard, and American Express.

VIDALIA SWEET-ONION PIE

— ❖ —

Pastry for 9-inch pie
3 cups sliced or cubed
   G&R Farms Vidalia
   Sweet Onions
3 tablespoons butter or
   margarine
2 eggs
½ cup evaporated milk,
   undiluted
1 teaspoon salt
⅛ teaspoon freshly
   ground black pepper

Line a 9-inch pie plate with the pastry. Sauté the onions in the butter or margarine until tender. Arrange the onions on the pastry. Beat the eggs slightly; add the evaporated milk and the salt and pepper. Pour the mixture over the onions. Bake the pie at 425°F until a metal knife inserted in the center comes out clean and the pie is well browned, 18 to 20 minutes.

Serves 4 to 6

Nellie & Joe's Famous Key West Lime Juice

Nellie & Joe's Inc.
P.O. Box 2368
Key West, Florida 33045
(305) 296-5566

Free order form
Prepaid orders only

When I was a child (and a "conch," which is what they call natives of Key West) my absolutely favorite dessert was Key lime pie, a Key West tradition and the unofficial state dessert of Florida. My grandmother's version, with its flaky pastry crust, soft, creamy-textured filling of hand-squeezed Key lime juice and beaten egg yolks, and crown of lofty meringue, was the traditional one served on the island. The nonsense of using a graham cracker crust and eliminating the meringue seems to have evolved during the 1950s. I don't care what anybody says, it is not the genuine article. Also, real Key lime pie is always made with sweetened condensed milk, a throwback to the early days when fresh milk was scarce in Key West and was brought over by boat from the mainland or milked from the island's handful of cows.

Introduced to the Florida Keys by Spanish settlers, the Key lime is a feisty little thing, smaller than the more common Persian or Tahiti lime, with a thin, yellowish skin and lots of tiny seeds. Its glory is that it bursts with a unique, vibrantly tangy, sweet-sour juice. Extremely sensitive to cold, the Key lime does not grow well in the usual mainland Florida citrus belt. These days, most Key limes are found only in home gardens or small, private orchards, and they're getting scarcer each year. In fact, whether *real* Key limes still exist is a hotly debated subject. Some conchs will tell you there is no longer any such thing, in part because the main orchards were virtually obliterated during the great hurricane of 1926. When the orchards were replanted afterward, it was with similar "crossbreed" limes.

For over 35 years Nellie and Joe Rodriguez sold their hand-squeezed, hand-bottled Key lime juice from the back of a truck to local residents and restaurants. Several years ago the elderly couple sold their business to another native Key

KEY WEST OLD SOUR

— ❖ —

Place two bird peppers (or other small hot peppers) in the bottom of a clean beer bottle. Strain a bottle of Key West lime juice through a clean T-shirt into the beer bottle. Add 1 teaspoon salt and a little freshly ground black pepper. Cork and let sit in a dark place for about two weeks; the brew will turn a clear, dark amber. Decant into a clean bottle and cap. Puncture little holes in the cap. Sprinkle on practically anything. This pungent flavoring is especially fine in fish stews and soups, on greens, or sprinkled over raw fish.

West family, the Kerrs. Greg Kerr kept the original company name but has semi-automated the bottling process and undertaken a campaign to introduce the juice outside Florida.

The juice in Nellie & Joe's is by no means solely from Key limes, though Greg swears a small percentage of it does come from limes grown around Key Largo. His juice is extracted from a mixture of commercial limes of the same species as the Key lime that are grown in the Bahamas, Mexico, and the Caribbean. The full-strength, pure juice contains no preservatives, and while it is not strictly speaking pure Key lime juice, it's a far cry from ordinary lime juice, and its distinctive flavor is delicious and different. Greg will ship two 16-ounce bottles for $10.95, postpaid; a better deal is a case of 12 bottles for $18.50, plus shipping. I have only one quibble with Greg and his juice: the recipe for Key lime pie on the back of the bottle uses cream cheese in the filling and calls for a graham cracker piecrust. For shame!

A bottle of tart and fruity Nellie & Joe's juice is terrifically useful to add a slightly tangy shot of character to many foods and drinks. It can be used in a refreshing limeade or daiquiri, cold mousse, as a marinade for seviche, or sprinkled over meats before they're barbecued. Mixed with melted butter and a splash of white wine, the juice becomes a fragrant sauce for fish.

— ❖ —

Royal Sugar Sweet Onions

Given the Texas penchant for hyperbole, it should come as no surprise that in the Lone Star State they're not shy about calling their 1015 SuperSweet onions "the million-dollar onion with a one-of-a-kind taste." It took researchers at Texas A&M University 14 years and a million bucks to come up with these

Royal International Ltd.
P.O. Box 125
San Juan, Texas 78589

(800) 331-7811; (512)
781-7511 (Monday to Friday,
8 A.M. to 5 P.M., CST)

Free 15-page color catalog
VISA, MasterCard, American
Express

agricultural beauties, which are mild and sweet, and they're not about to let you forget it. And, it almost goes without saying, since the onions are grown in Texas, they're big, very big—as in as big as one of those famed Ruby Red grapefruits.

So why is this the onion with a number instead of a normal-sounding name? The number 1015 is actually the suggested optimum planting date for growers, and it stands for October 15 as you might have guessed. The research team wrote the date on planting stakes while developing the onion, and the name just stuck.

These softball-size yellow onions first came on the market around 1984 and were an immediate hit. They're what's known as a "short-day" onion, meaning that they grow only during Texas's short winter days, and they're similar in many ways to Vidalia onions from Georgia. The bigger they grow, the sweeter they get, and the flavor is mild enough that you can eat them raw with impunity. Since they require fewer hours of sunshine than other onions do to mature, Texas 1015 SuperSweets contain less pyruvic acid, which is what gives most other onions that sharp pungency (and causes your eyes to water). On the downside, they're high in moisture (that's why they taste mild), which means they're unsuitable for long-term storage, period. You order 'em, you eat 'em up pretty quick—or else. Best of all, though, this special onion has more rings to the onion (and they separate easily), which means you can make lots of terrific onion rings.

The supply of the Texas 1015 SuperSweet remains fairly limited, with only a handful of mail-order specialists coping with the demand. Royal International, owned and operated by the LaMantia family, which also ships Ruby Red Grapefruit and Royal Bobwhite Quail (see page 309), is a reliable source. In their catalog the onions go by the name Royal Sugar Sweet Onions and are available mid-April through June. They ship two sizes of onions, jumbos (each onion weighs approximately a pound) and mediums (weight is approximately half a pound). A quarter bushel of jumbos or mediums costs $17.99, plus $2 shipping. Half bushels of either jumbos or mediums cost $22.99, plus $2 shipping. If you wish to receive a quarter bushel every month for April, May, and June, there's something called the Sugar Sweet 3-Month Onion Plan that costs $53.99 for jumbos and $49.99 for mediums (plus $2 shipping). Free recipes are enclosed with all onion shipments. Tony LaMantia says that in his family they cut the tops off the 1015s, slash an X in the bottom, and marinate them in big bottles of red-wine vinegar and olive oil seasoned with garlic, oregano, salt, and cracked black pepper.

Texas Agriculture Commissioner Jim Hightower says of the 1015: "This is to vegetables what a diamond is to jewels."

CRISPY TEXAS 1015 SUPERSWEET ONION RINGS

— ❖ —

3 or 4 large Texas 1015 SuperSweet Onions
2 to 3 cups buttermilk
1 cup all-purpose flour
1½ teaspoons baking powder
1 teaspoon salt
¼ teaspoon red pepper
⅔ cup water
1 beaten egg
1 tablespoon vegetable oil
1 tablespoon lemon juice
Vegetable oil, for deep frying
Salt, if desired

Peel and slice the onions and separate the slices into rings. Pour the buttermilk into a large shallow pan. Add the onion rings and soak 30 minutes. Combine the flour, baking powder, salt, red pepper, water, egg, 1 tablespoon oil, and the lemon juice; stir until smooth. Heat the oil for deep frying to 375°F. Remove the onion rings from the buttermilk and dip them into the batter. Fry in hot oil until golden brown. Drain on paper towels. Sprinkle with salt. *Serves 6*

TWO MORE SOURCES FOR
TEXAS 1015 SUPERSWEET ONIONS
— ❖ —

The shipping season for this onion is a short one, so the supply of field-fresh Texas 1015s is not endless. But if one source sells out early, you can always turn to another, such as:

Frank Lewis' Alamo Fruit, 100 North Tower Road, Alamo, Texas 78516; phone (800) 477-4773. Free color brochure features the onions under the name Colossal Rio Grande Gold Sweet Onions. Each shipment includes recipes and a handy expandable net tube in which to store the onions. A quarter bushel (about 13 pounds) costs $16.98, plus $3 shipping; a half bushel (about 18 pounds) costs $19.98, plus $3 shipping. Invoice sent with shipment; payment by check or money order only; no credit cards. No shipments to Alaska or Hawaii.

Pattison's Sunblest Farms of Texas, P.O. Box 547, Donna, Texas 78537; phone (800) 633-0572 or (512) 464-2294; fax (512) 464-2295. Free color catalog features Rio Grande Valley citrus as well as 1015 SuperSweets. Pack TOS weighs approximately 8 pounds and costs $12.95, postpaid; pack TOM weights approximately 14 pounds and costs $18.95; pack TOL weighs approximately 21 pounds and costs $24.95. They accept VISA, MasterCard, and Discover.

Wadmalaw Sweets

Most people by now have heard of Vidalia onions from Georgia. Some people know about the big 1015 onions grown in Texas. But practically nobody is aware—yet—of the Wadmalaw Sweet from South Carolina, which the Hanckel family swears is "the sweetest onion you'll ever eat."

Picturesque Wadmalaw Island, which lies off the southern coast of South Carolina, is a subtropical paradise where gentle ocean breezes whisper across bright, warm days and cool nights. The rich, black soil here is said to put a

Planters Three
P.O. Box 92
Wadmalaw Island
South Carolina 29487
(803) 559-5972 (no phone orders)

_____

Free descriptive order form
Prepaid orders only

little extra flavor into everything that grows in it, from asparagus and tomatoes to kiwi fruit, cantaloupes, and these Wadmalaw Sweets.

Wadmalaws are yellow, big-girthed jumbo onions with a thin skin and sweet, mild flavor. A slice from a jumbo, to put things in perspective, will more than cover a hamburger bun. Think of them as onions with good manners—a Wadmalaw won't give you smelly onion-breath, and you can cut and peel one without crying. They're grown from top-quality yellow Granex hybrid seed on nine or so of the 250 acres farmed by Paul and Rhett Hanckel along with their dad, "Sunny." Harvested by hand, each onion gets a signature sticker identifying it as a Wadmalaw Sweet before it goes into a mesh bag for shipping. The supply is limited, and shipments are made only at harvest time, which runs roughly from mid-April through late June and sometimes into July. (Once they arrive, store them in a cool, dry place arranged so they don't touch each

INTERNATIONAL BANANA FESTIVAL
FULTON, KENTUCKY
— ❖ —

Elvis Presley is known to have relished a big cozy serving of old-fashioned banana pudding now and then. Too bad he never made it to the week-long International Banana Festival held each September and sponsored by the twin cities of South Fulton, Tennessee, and Fulton, Kentucky (the "Banana Crossroads of the United States"). They don't grow bananas in either town, but for years their railroad facilities were a distribution center for banana shipments. Events include a Banana Bonnet Contest, the Banana Bake-off, a Banana Eating Contest, and the crowning of the Banana Princess. The top banana, however, is a one-ton banana pudding that's devoured by festival-goers right after the Grand Parade. Ingredients: 3,000 sliced bananas, 250 pounds of vanilla wafers, and 950 pounds of banana-cream pie filling! For information, contact P.O. Box 428, Fulton, Kentucky 42041-0428.

other and they'll keep nicely for quite a few months.) The onions are graded by size (jumbo, medium, and mini) and are shipped postpaid in 10-, 25-, and 50-pound bags. Ten pounds of jumbos cost $12.50; 25 pounds, $27.50; a 25-pound bag of mediums is $24.50; and 10 pounds of the minis costs $9.50. Like Vidalias, these are delicious eaten raw, but they also make good hefty onion rings and are very tasty grilled.

The Henckels also ship 5-pound gift packages ($20.25, postpaid) of tender asparagus from around the first of March through mid-May.

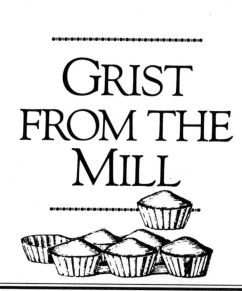

GRIST FROM THE MILL

• Mrs. Fearnow's Delicious Brunswick Stew • Fuller's Mustard • Maunsel White's
• Panola Pepper Sauce • Amber Brand Smithfield Ham • Billy Higdon's Happy Holl
y Hams • Colonel Bill Newsom's Kentucky Country Hams • Bucksnort Smoked Rainb
• Callaway Gardens Speckled Heart Grits • White Lily Flour • Bailey's Homemade H
• Jelly Sherardi   ansel's Rice • Garber
Yams • Warrento   ssinger's Flying Pig B
• Arrow Ranch Ax   ory-Smoked Sausage
• Golden Mill So   ms Sweet Vidalia Oni
• Luck Scottish S   ker Deluxe Moon Pies
• Kitchen Derby P   Potato Chips • Charli
• Rendezvous Ribs   Barq's Root Beer •
ine • Crickle •   ens Cut Leaf Poke Sa
• Mrs. Fearnow   • Maunsel White's 1
• Panola Pepper   Higdon's Happy Hollo
• Hams • Colone   ksnort Smoked Rainb
Garber Farms Cajun Yams • Bland Farms Sweet Vidalia Onions • Callaway Gardens
d Heart Grits • White Lily Flour • Bailey's Homemade Hot Pepper Jelly • Mayhaw Je
ized Pecans • Virginia Diner Peanuts • Ellis Stansel's Rice • Ledford Mill Borrowed
n Arrow Ranch Axis Venison • Comeaux's Boudin • Mayo's Hickory-Smoked Sausag
• Golden Mill Sorghum • Steen's Pure Cane Syrup • Best of Luck Scottish Shortbre
oes and Nails • Double Decker Deluxe Moon Pies • Kern's Kitchen Derby Pie • Lis
Orchard Cake • Warrenton Original Nashville Rum Cakes • Zapp's Potato Chips • C
Rendezvous Ribs • Maurice Bessinger's Flying Pig Barbeque • Barq's Root Beer • L
ine • Crickle • Evelyn's Pralines • Goo Goo Clusters • The Allens Cut Leaf Poke Sa
• Mrs. Fearnow's Delicious Brunswick Stew • Fuller's Mustard • Maunsel White's 1
Panola Pepper Sauce • Amber Brand Smithfield Ham • Billy Higdon's Happy Hollo
Hams • Colonel Bill Newsom's Kentucky Country Hams • Bucksnort Smoked Rainb
Garber Farms Cajun Yams • Bland Farms Sweet Vidalia Onions • Callaway Garden
d Heart Grits • White Lily Flour • Bailey's Homemade Hot Pepper Jelly • Mayhaw Je
ized Pecans • Virginia Diner Peanuts • Ellis Stansel's Rice • Ledford Mill Borrowed
n Arrow Ranch Axis Venison • Comeaux's Boudin • Mayo's Hickory-Smoked Sausage
Golden Mill Sorghum • Steen's Pure Cane Syrup • Best of Luck Scottish Shortbre

"Milly Amos used to say that when she died she wanted a hot biscuit carved on her tombstone."
—Anonymous

The ultimate Southern baked good is surely homemade biscuits—served hot and buttered at breakfast or supper, or used anytime to sop up a luscious load of sorghum or red-eye gravy. Regardless of which side of the Mason-Dixon line you live on, a light-crusted biscuit with a moist interior can be made anywhere, anytime—even by Yankees. You'll need two things: a supply of self-rising, low-gluten "soft" wheat flour (such as White Lily, the one found on most Southern grocery store shelves) and what Southern cooking authority Nathalie Dupree calls "a touch of grace." In this section you'll discover that White Lily can be shipped right to your kitchen door. As for the "touch of grace," well, it helps if you were born with it, but practice does make perfect.

Beyond that, Southern cooks are famous for breads and rolls too numerous to mention. Some of the best include the brioche-like Sally Lunn; the ice-box rolls that are brought by at least four people to any church picnic; the crusty, New Orleans–style French flutes you can't make a po' boy sandwich without; and those dainty, sweet-flavored muffins and savory cheese straws no hostess would fail to provide for a special occasion.

Adams Old-Fashioned Whole Heart Grits, Stone-ground Corn Meal, and Corn Dog Mix

**Adams Milling Company
Route 6, Box 148A
Napier Field Station
Dolthan, Alabama 36303**

(205) 983-4233 (Monday to Friday, 8 A.M. to 4 P.M., CST)

**Free price list
Orders shipped on the honor system (invoice accompanies shipment); check or money order**

You can't eat truer grits than the old-fashioned Whole Heart ones that come from sixth-generation miller Ted "Corky" Adams, whose mill rests on the banks of the Choctawhatchee River. The pride and care he takes in the mill founded by his grandfather, W.D., back in the 1930s shines right through the stone-ground grains he sells.

Adams's grits are treasured by the few people outside Alabama who know about them. If you've never tasted grits before, try these and you'll have experienced the best there are. Exceptionally fine-tasting, they are milled from whole-kernel corn grown primarily in the extreme northern part of Alabama and ground using the same eight French millstones that have been in place at the mill since it was built. Unlike mass-produced grits, these have not been stripped of the heart, or germ, of the corn, the part that's high in iron, niacin, and riboflavin. You can see for yourself that it's there—little dark speckles are the tipoff. These buff-colored grits have a rougher texture than fine-milled commercial grits; the flavor is straightforward, authentic, and full. When you're eating them you can really taste the corn, something that rarely comes through when you eat grits that are steel-ground. Cooked up, these will be homier-looking and -tasting and considerably thicker than commercial grits. These are a connoisseur's grits to be savored.

Adams grinds around 5,000 pounds of grits each month and has quite a following of mail-order customers. Two-pound bags cost $.74 each, plus shipping, and there is no minimum order quantity (a box quantity is 12 bags, if you're thinking about a big supply). If this sounds cheap, which it is, thank Corky Adams because somewhat miraculously he chooses to give mail-order customers the advantage of ordering at wholesale prices.

Be careful about storing these grits, though. Like all organic, stone-ground products, these absolutely *must* be stored in a cool or cold place. Ignore this advice at your peril, for room-temperature storage encourages pests. After each use, tightly reseal the bag and store in the refrigerator (no more than two to three months). Extra bags will keep in the freezer for up to a year.

Highest-quality stone-ground white and yellow corn meal in 2-, 5-, and 10-pound paper sacks can also be ordered from the mill. The white is available plain or self-rising; both white and yellow can be ordered ground medium (Corky says this has the most flavor), fine, or extra-fine (a very hard-to-find grind ideal for making spoonbread). Prices range from $.50 to $2.72 per bag, plus shipping.

Most of the corn dogs sold at fairs around the South are made using Adams Corn Dog Mix ("the eggs and milk are in it"), which comes in boxes complete with the essential wooden sticks. All you do is add water to the mix (14-ounce box, $.70). Boxes of Hush Puppy Mix (add water only) cost the same. Both mixes can also be used as a dry coating on fish and chicken to achieve a thin, crisp golden crust.

JUST PLAIN GRITS
— ❖ —

⅔ cup Adams Whole
    Heart Grits
3⅓ cup boiling
    water
¾ teaspoon salt

Stir the grits slowly into boiling, salted water in a heavy saucepan. Return to boil; reduce heat. Cover and cook slowly, stirring occasionally, until thick and cooked through, 10 to 15 minutes. Serve with butter, salt and pepper, or red-eye gravy.

Makes 4 servings

Boone Tavern Spoonbread Meal

**Berea College Crafts
College Post Office Box 2347
Berea, Kentucky 40404**

**(800) 824-4049; in Kentucky
(800) 432-1960 (Monday to
Friday, 8:00 A.M. to 5:00 P.M.,
EST)**

**Free 20-page color catalog
VISA, MasterCard, American
Express**

Spoonbread is without question one of the most elegant and classic Southern dishes. Blissfully creamy in texture, it is more akin to a custard or pudding than a bread. Think of it as a cornmeal soufflé. Moist and light, spoonbread puffs up (that's the beaten egg whites) and develops a lovely golden brown crust as it bakes. It's traditionally served piping hot from the oven, spooned family-style from the dish it was baked in, with each divine mound topped with a small knob of butter. According to John Mariani's *Dictionary of American Food & Drink*, its name probably comes from an Indian word for porridge, *suppon*, though spoonbread may also be named after the table implement it's most often served and eaten with. There are many variations, but spoonbread's basic ingredients are white or yellow cornmeal, a scalded liquid such as milk or water, eggs, a bit of butter, a dash of salt, and perhaps a little baking powder. It is the perfect side dish for braised ham or chicken, and all kinds of stews, especially rabbit.

But spoonbread is not just for supper. At Thomas Jefferson's Monticello it was served from early-morning breakfast right through light late-night suppers. Leftover spoonbread is out of this world for breakfast—just chill, slice, and brown in a skillet with a little butter. It's good by itself or with ham and eggs.

These days it's getting harder and harder to find spoonbread on restaurant menus, but in Virginia it is still served at the Boar's Head Inn in Charlottesville and at the dining room of the splendid Hotel Roanoke. And at Berea College, a small liberal arts college nestled in the foothills of Kentucky's Cumberland Mountains, they serve a spoonbread that's almost as famous as the school's student-made crafts. Berea's Boone Tavern, a student-staffed hotel and dining room located in the middle of the campus, opened its

doors in 1909. The tavern's reputation for superior Southern-style food (Jefferson Davis pie,
baked pork chops, chicken flakes in a bird's nest)
comes from the late Richard T. Hougen, who
managed the facility for 36 years and wrote three
cookbooks. Hougen's legendary spoonbread is
still served at the tavern, which is now managed
by J. B. Morgan, one of Hougen's former student
employees. "The spoonbread alone is enough to
justify a visit," says John Egerton in his book
Southern Food.

You can make spoonbread very close to Boone
Tavern's using their extra-finely-ground selected
white cornmeal, which can be ordered through
Berea's annually issued crafts catalog. A 2-pound
muslin sack of the meal with a recipe similar to
Hougen's printed on the label costs $5.95 and is
enough for at least four or five batches of spoonbread (each batch serves five or six people as a
side dish). There are also homey glazed-pottery
spoonbread baking dishes in two sizes ($12
and $24) handmade by Berea graduate Sarah
Culbreth. On orders up to $10.00, the shipping
charge is $3.00. You may want to look closely at
the catalog's many other items, all handcrafted
by Berea College students and craft professionals
(kitchen accessories such as rolling pins, cutting
boards, or cooling racks handcrafted from native
hardwoods; hand-thrown pie plates and jam jars;
and even furniture).

VISITING THE SOURCE

— ❖ —

Berea is located 42 miles south of Lexington,
Kentucky, just off Interstate 75. Boone Tavern, at the corner of Main and Prospect Streets,
serves breakfast, lunch, and dinner 365 days a
year. Guests are required to honor a dress code
(jackets for men, no denim or athletic-wear at
dinner). Madison County is dry; therefore the
tavern does not serve alcoholic beverages. Reservations are necessary; phone (606) 986-9358.

TRUE GRITS

— ❖ —

"True grits,
More grits,
Fish, grits and collards,
Life is good where grits are
swallered."

—*Roy Blount, Jr.*
One Fell Soup

Whether one is supposed to say "grits *is*" or "grits *are*" is a thorny semantic issue that may never be resolved. One thing is certain, however—whether pro or con, grits stir up strong and definite feelings. Grits have been described on the positive side as an "ambrosial comfort food" but they've also been somewhat rudely defined as "a Pat Boone of the palate." Still, no matter what, no matter how bland, white, and mushy they may be, grits are part of the Southern tradition that endures in hearts and stomachs from Alabama to Florida.

Grits, which take their name from the Middle English *gyrt*, for bran, are coarsely ground, hulled kernels of mature, dried corn. They're really just one small step removed from cornmeal, which is dried corn ground more finely. Along with other quintessentially Southern foods like sorghum and salty country ham, it helps if you grew up eating grits. Few people meet a pearly, farina-like mess of grits late in life and fall in love with their flavor (or lack of flavor).

More than 160 million pounds of stick-to-your-ribs grits are milled annually, most of them commercial grocery-store ones like Quaker Oats and Jim Dandy from Martha White, which cook up very smooth and snowy white. Less likely to go rancid on the shelf, such grits are okay, but they're no match for the earthier, more nutritious stone-ground types available from old-fashioned grist mills. Commercial grits come in three versions: regular (larger granules that cook in about 20 minutes), "quick" (smaller granules that cook in 3 to 5 minutes), and the atrocious, to be avoided at all costs, "instant" (precooked grits that have been dried before packaging and are "recooked" simply by adding boiling water).

You'll most often find grits keeping company with other more flavorful foods: grits and sausage, grits and fried fish. In New Orleans, you'll find grits and grillades served as a breakfast specialty but it makes a nice supper, too. Lean, thinly pounded strips of beef or veal are browned in hot fat, slow-cooked with onions and spices, and served with a thick blob of grits to soak up the flavorful juices. And when grits team up with eggs, biscuits, country ham, and red-eye gravy you've got the classic country breakfast.

Callaway Gardens Speckled Heart Grits

Callaway Gardens Country Store
Pine Mountain, Georgia 31822

(800) 262-8181 (October to December only, 7 days a week, 8 A.M. to 6 P.M., EST); (404) 663-5100 (year round, 7 days a week, 8 A.M. to 6 P.M., EST)

Free 12-page color catalog
VISA, MasterCard, American Express

If you don't like grits, you're not alone. Many Southerners profess to dislike them, too. But Callaway Gardens Speckled Heart Grits have been known to change minds. Stone-ground from whole-grain corn, they include the heart of the kernel, the most vitamin-rich part, and they take their name from the infinitesimal specks at the center of the grain. (You can see these tiny flecks, so don't go saying you weren't warned these grits have "funny dark things" in them.)

Callaway grits come with an impressive pedigree. Tucked away in the foothills of Georgia's Appalachian Mountains, Callaway Gardens is one of the South's most famous family-oriented vacation spots. It was founded specifically as a serene place where visitors could soothe their senses and refresh their souls in a natural setting. The food served at Callaway is famous, too, and that's where these grits enter the picture.

Speckled Heart Grits reward a half hour of your cooking time, I can promise you that. They're deeply satisfying, with a rich corn flavor. Unlike snowy-white grocery-store grits, these are more the color of muslin. And they're the same grits people line up for at breakfast time at the Callaway Country Store restaurant, where they're served along with Callaway's renowned country ham, biscuits, and muscadine preserves.

The grits come in 2-pound bags, and the minimum order is three bags for $10.95, plus around $3.50 shipping. This may sound like a lot of grits, but it's actually not if you eat them as often as many Southerners do, especially when you realize there are some pretty tasty ways of dressing up grits, including preparing them in a soufflé with cheese. Callaway's grits are also sold in combination with other edible specialties. For example, order Bacon 'n' Grits and they'll ship the grits along with a 2- to 3-pound slab of excellent Georgia-cured bacon for $17.50 (plus shipping)

CALLAWAY GARDENS CHEESE GRITS
— ❖ —

4 cups water
1 cup Speckled Heart
    Grits
1 teaspoon salt
2 cups grated sharp cheese
½ cup (1 stick) margarine,
    cut into pieces
Dash of Tabasco

You've got to handle grits with a little care so they don't turn out watery or dry and lumpy. The secret to making grits that are nice and creamy? Cook them slowly over low heat and stir frequently to avoid sticking. (Some people fix grits in a double boiler, which takes a bit longer but you don't have to bother stirring so much.) As you're patiently stirring, just remember that old saying: "Watery grits goes with sleazy ways."

Bring the water to a boil; stir in the grits and salt. Bring to a boil again, reduce the heat to medium, cover, and cook, stirring often to prevent sticking, until the grits are cooked through, 20 to 30 minutes. Combine the cooked grits with the remaining ingredients. Pour the mixture into a casserole dish, and bake at 325°F for 1 hour. *Serves 4 to 6*

or as part of a more lavish Southern Breakfast gift box, which includes grits and bacon, along with muscadine jelly, sauce, and syrup ($27.95; see page 234).

— ❖ —

Falls Mill Stone-Ground White Grits and White Corn Meal

Anyone who buys an old mill and puts it back into daily operation has to have a special passion. John and Jane Lovett, owners of Falls Mill, do. Several years ago, with money borrowed from relatives, they purchased Falls Mill, an east Tennessee mill located in lovely hill country and built in 1873 as a textile mill. Today the mill turns out stone-ground grits, meal, and flours. The sole power source for milling is a 32-foot overshot water-

Falls Mill and Country Store
Route 1, Box 44
Belvidere, Tennessee 37306
(615) 469-7161

Free non-illustrated black-and-white price list
VISA, MasterCard

wheel (installed when the mill operated as a cotton gin at the turn of the century), which moves the huge 1,500-pound, hand-quarried millstones. Only 15 miles away from the Jack Daniel's distillery, Falls Mill is listed on the National Register of Historic Places and attracts numerous visitors.

The Lovetts are particularly passionate about making sure that mill visitors get an accurate, eye-opening, historical view of the milling process. Detailed signs explain the creaking and groaning gears, belt, and levers that are driven by the waterwheel. And William Janey, the miller, stands ready to answer visitors' questions as they watch him at work.

No preservatives are used in Falls Mill's products. You can taste the freshness that comes from the slow stone-grinding necessary to ensure that the grains' nutrients are not lost through overheating. Prices, which do not include shipping charges, are astonishingly reasonable. Exact shipping charges are figured and billed at the time of shipment; you can figure roughly that it will cost $5 for shipping 6 pounds to the West Coast. A nice touch: the bags are tied with the traditional miller's knot. Falls Mill grinds excellent grits, which are available in several sizes: a 2-pound bag costs $1.20, 5 pounds, $2.05, and—in case you feel like staging a *really* big country breakfast for everyone you know—a 50-pound sack costs $16. High-quality White Corn Meal may be ordered bolted (sifted) or unbolted (contains more bran) in 2-pound bags, $1.20; 5-pound bags, $2.05; or a 50-pound sack, $16.00; or self-rising (baking powder and salt added), which costs a few cents more. The Lovetts also grind whole-wheat flour, buckwheat flour, and yellow cornmeal, in addition to limited quantities of harder-to-find things like oat flour, rye meal (for pumpernickel bread), and rice flour (believed by many bakers, including myself, to

VISITING THE SOURCE
— ❖ —

make the most meltingly tender shortbread). Prices on most of these grains are under $2 for a 2-pound sack, plus shipping. As with all stone-ground products, you should store them in the refrigerator or freezer upon receipt.

The Lovetts have been busily collecting artifacts, and on view are rare 19th-century woolen-textile machines and a 150-year-old log corncrib. John recently dismantled a log stagecoach inn dating from the 1800s, moving it log by log to the mill, where it's due to provide bed and breakfast accommodations in the future.

Falls Mill is located 12 miles west of Winchester, Tennessee, one mile north of U.S. Highway 64. It is open Monday to Saturday from 9 A.M. to 4 P.M., Sunday from 12:30 P.M. to 4 P.M. There is a small admission charge to tour the mill and view a slide presentation. The second floor houses a country store with local handcrafts and Falls Mill products displayed in turn-of-the-century surroundings. Picnicking is encouraged in the tranquil cove below the mill, and there are buckets to use for fetching cool water from the spring below the bluffs.

— ❖ —

Grady Brewer's Biscuit Bowls

Grady Brewer
Route 1
Toomsboro, Georgia 31090
(912) 933-5950

Send stamped, self-addressed envelope for free black-and-white illustrated price list
Prepaid orders only

If your grandmother was from the South, chances are she mixed her biscuit and bread doughs in a shallow wooden vessel known as a biscuit bowl, or doughbread tray. Grady Brewer learned how to carve these and other kitchen tools from his father, and today he's one of a handful of rural artisans still crafting these useful and nostalgic pieces.

A former pulpwooder and sawmill worker, Grady grew up in the swamps around the Oconee River near Toomsboro. Ten years ago, with the assistance and encouragement of his friend

A carved biscuit bowl.

"If the South had a coat
of arms, it might consist
of a corn pone rampant
on a field, or roasting
ears bordered by golden
brown corn muffins."
—The Southern
Heritage Breads
Cookbook

and onetime employer J. B. Jackson, who owned some of that swampland, Grady began turning his avocation into a full-time cottage industry. He does no advertising; he doesn't need to. Customers reach him through word of mouth. The pieces are simple and homey-looking, each entirely handcrafted; when not in use they look nice filled with fruit. A round bowl is for mixing "scratch" biscuits while the "trays" (actually tub-shaped ovals) do double duty with yeast doughs (kneading is easy within the bowl, then just cover for rising).

Not counting the time spent searching the swamps for tupelo gum, a wood that won't crack or chip, each bowl or tray takes Grady about 4½ hours to make. Once a tree is chosen and felled, the wood (preferably about 2 feet in diameter) is cut into 6-inch-thick chunks and hefted into his pickup. Back at the log cabin workshop near his house, Grady chain-saws a checkerboard pattern into the top of the wood, then hand-chisels the little squares up and out, forming a rough hollow. Further shaping is also accomplished with a chain saw, a tricky maneuver. Donna, Grady's wife, then sets the partially finished piece in her oven to bake for a few hours. This is the Brewers' quality control test; if the wood is ever going to crack, this is the time. Once it's passed the kitchen torture test, Donna sands it smooth by hand. If the piece will be used for mixing doughs, Grady recommends you season it so it will repel liquids. To do this, coat the inside with lard and place the bowl or tray in an oven for a few minutes until the lard melts and soaks into the wood, forming a seal. Although the pieces look very nice plain, some folks like to stain or varnish them if they don't plan on using them to mix dough.

The biscuit bowl, 12 inches in diameter and 3 inches deep, may be ordered with or without handles ($30, postpaid). The oval bread dough trays, also 3 inches deep, are made in four standard sizes with handles (22 inches long and 10 inches or 13 inches wide, for example) and cost $35, postpaid. Special orders for other sizes can be accommodated. Allow approximately 3 weeks for delivery.

— ❖ —

Ledford's Rock-Ground Corn Meal and Corn Grits

**Ledford Mill and Museum
Rural Route 2, Box 152
Wartrace, Tennessee 37183
(615) 455-1935 or 455-2546**

**Free 7-page color catalog
VISA, MasterCard, American
Express**

The century-old Ledford Mill is just a hop, skip, and a jump from Lynchburg, Tennessee, home of Miss Mary Bobo's Boarding House and the Jack Daniel's distillery. A picturesque structure, the mill nestles in a lush green hollow at the headwaters of Shippmans Creek. Water from the creek powers the turbine that turns the stones to grind Ledford's cornmeal, grits, and whole-wheat flour. In an earlier era, the mill ground grain not only for settlers but for several (legal) whisky stills nearby.

Owners Billy and Norma Rigler have spent the past 10 or so years working hard to restore and beautify the mill. Today it's not only as pretty as the proverbial postcard, it's also on the National Register of Historic Places. For a small fee, visitors can feast their eyes on Billy's large collection of antique woodworking tools and view a short slide presentation on the art of barrel making. On the second floor is a small country store stocked with Tennessee foods and handicrafts where visitors can purchase Ledford's stone-ground products packaged in muslin bags with a picture of the mill on the front.

The Riglers grind corn once a month, producing just enough unbolted grits and cornmeal to sell at their store and to a few other places, like Miss Mary Bobo's Boarding House and the Opryland Hotel. What's fun is that you can order by mail from them the very same cornmeal used

MISS MARY BOBO'S
BOARDING HOUSE
— ❖ —

For state-of-the-art Southern home cooking and hospitality, the legendary Miss Mary Bobo's just can't be beat. The boarding house, as popular an attraction in tiny Lynchburg, Tennessee, as the nearby Jack Daniel's distillery, opened its doors back in 1908 in an era when such establishments offered the comforts of home to strangers seeking a respectable, family-like atmosphere. Boarding houses eased the transition from farm to city life.

Miss Mary took pride in the delicious hot meals served family-style to her lodgers. When the bell rang at noon announcing the day's main meal (referred to as "dinner"), 10 or 12 happy folks sat down to heaping platters of Southern classics like country ham, creamed chicken on cornbread, pot roast with carrots, pork and gravy with buttermilk biscuits, and the like.

Miss Mary's place grew pretty famous, and although she stopped taking in boarders in the late 1930s, you can still enjoy the results of her famous recipes. In fact, Miss Mary planned the daily menus and supervised their preparation herself until a couple of years before she died in 1983, just shy of her 102nd birthday.

Today Miss Mary Bobo's Boarding House is presided over by Lynne Tolley, Jack Daniel's great-great-grandniece, and is open to the public Monday through Saturday (reservations required). At 1:00 sharp Lynne rings the brass dinner bell and guests join a Lynchburg hostess at each table for an unforgettable bounteous meal (adults, $8.50; children, $4) that includes a little local gossip along with vegetables grown in the garden out back and Miss Mary's original recipes, including cornbread made from locally ground meal.

Miss Mary Bobo's Boarding House is located off the Lynchburg Town Square, three doors west of the Moore County Jail. For information and reservations, contact Lynne Tolley at (615) 759-7394.

Ledford Mill

at Miss Mary Bobo's to make the famous crispy-crusted cornbread that pleases so many folks. A pair of 2-pound bags (specify white or yellow cornmeal) costs $7.50, postpaid. A couple of 2-pound bags of Ledford's comforting coarse-ground old-fashioned grits, white or yellow, cost $8.50; two bags of whole-wheat flour cost $8. A small recipe folder accompanies each product.

The Ledford Mill catalog offers other interesting things, including food assortments shipped in reusable bandana-lined baskets that make lovely gifts. For $18, postpaid, there's a Good Luck Feast to serve on New Year's Day; it includes a 2-pound bag of Ledford cornmeal and a 1-pound bag of black-eyed peas, along with onion relish and black walnut jelly. "Billy Bob" egg baskets and Shaker-style fruit baskets are woven by Billy Rigler himself from natural reeds and other local materials. Prices range from $9 for a small egg basket to $29.50 for a homey, handy pie carrier. And there are locally made wooden stirring and tasting spoons, signed and dated by the creator, that cost under $11. On shipments made west of the Rockies, there is an additional shipping charge of $1 per *package* (not per item).

VISITING THE SOURCE
— ❖ —

The Riglers welcome visitors Tuesday through Saturday from 9 A.M. to 5 P.M., Sunday from noon to 4 P.M., or "whenever the flag is flying." Winter hours (generally late December to mid-March) are 10 A.M. to 4 P.M. There's an admission charge of $1.50 for adults (kids under 12, free) for the mill and museum tour; visitors are presented with recipes and a 1-cup bag of cornmeal at the end of the tour. And there's more! On the ground floor of the mill there's a bed and breakfast hideaway—a small, cozy apartment, fully modernized (including a kitchenette), suitable for a couple or family of four. Advance arrangements required.

MISS MARY'S CORNMEAL WAFFLES
WITH SPIKED WAFFLE SYRUP
— ❖ —

Spiked Waffle Syrup
1 cup maple syrup
2 tablespoons butter
3 tablespoons Jack
   Daniel's Whiskey

Waffles
1 egg
1½ cups milk
1½ cups self-rising
   cornmeal
¼ cup vegetable oil

Butter for serving

Prepare the syrup: Combine all the ingredients and heat over medium-low heat until bubbly.

Preheat the waffle iron. Beat the egg, then add the remaining waffle ingredients. Stir vigorously until smooth. Ladle the batter onto the waffle iron and bake until golden brown. Serve hot with butter and Spiked Waffle Syrup.

Mississippi Hushpuppy Mix and Biscuit Mix

Crab Apple Pantry
205 Wensel Avenue
Natchez, Mississippi 39120
(601) 442-5751

Free price list
VISA, MasterCard, American Express

You don't eat fried catfish in the South without hush puppies, and no right-thinking person would even try. If you've never tasted hush puppies, this easy-to-use mix offers a chance to do something about it real quick, and the results will be better than most folks can make from scratch.

How these spicy little balls of fried cornmeal batter got their picturesque name is not certain. Some say it originated in Florida, where fishermen cooking the day's catch over a campfire also fried up dabs of cornbread batter, tossing them to their whining dogs with the admonishment, "Hush, puppy!" In another version of the tale, hush puppies first made their appearance during the hard, hungry post–Civil War years. When hungry dogs drawn by the tantalizing smells of cooking food got underfoot in the cooking quarters, harassed cooks fried up morsels of corn-

bread batter and . . . you can guess the rest.

Woodie Thomas and Miriam ("Mim") Moyer, co-owners of the Mississippi Hushpuppy Company, started their business a couple of years ago when they adapted Woodie's grandmother's hush puppy recipe into a handy mix "for people who don't like to cook, but who like to eat good food." Both women are home economists in the Brookhaven, Mississippi, school system, but even so, it took them a while to perfect their product. They just kept working on it until all the "tasters" in their hometown agreed on one version that tasted best.

I first met Woodie and Mim at a fish fry and picnic. It was a hot, sultry June day, and the sound of Delta blues drifted lazily through the air, mixing with the irresistible scent of frying catfish and hush puppies. Of all things, we were in New York City's Central Park, where a bunch of well-organized, expatriate Mississippians get together each year for an event known as "The Way Up North in Mississippi Picnic." The two had come up from Mississippi toting 75 pounds of hush puppy mix, and they were working like dogs frying up puppies for a thousand hungry people. I have to say they looked cute hooting and hollering and generally raising hell, all the while madly lobbing fresh, hot hush puppies onto paper plates. It was wild to watch.

I've always said good people make good products, and the two that Woodie and Mim produce prove my point. Mississippi Hushpuppy Mix, which comes in cotton bags stenciled with a jaunty, exceptionally attractive red logo, makes absolutely terrific-tasting, spicy hush puppies that are delicately seasoned with onion and have a good, honest cornmeal flavor. All you do is add water and an egg to the mix, then fry spoonfuls of the batter until golden brown. Each 1½-pound sack is enough for 50 to 60 hush puppies

A SOURCE FOR CAST-IRON CORNSTICK PANS, HAND-CRANK ICE CREAM FREEZERS, AND PICKLE CROCKS

— ❖ —

It's a known fact: Good corn-bread is made from fresh stone-ground cornmeal cooked in a well-seasoned cast-iron skillet or pan, preferably one handed down by a female relative. Should you lack this ancestral necessity, I'd like to refer you to the *Cumberland General Store Wish & Want Book*, an old-time mercan-tile and hardware catalog that's more like a 256-page book. Owner Ann Ebert stocks "goods in endless variety for man and beast," which means you can order honest kitchenware like cast-iron chicken fryers and cornstick pans, Patsy Prim Long-Handle Dustpans, home-dairy equipment, and even windmills and horse-drawn buggies. The catalog is a delicious time warp. Revised annually, it'll take you an hour (at least) to read. Send $3 to: Cumberland General Store, Route 3, Crossville, Tennessee 38555. Or visit the store in person; it's located in Homesteads, Tennessee, four miles south of Crossville on Highway 127.

(figure on 18 puppies per 1½ cups of mix) and costs $4.95, plus shipping. Their other product is handy if you don't have the gift of making good biscuits from scratch. Add water and a few minutes of your time to Mississippi Biscuit Mix and you'll have a batch of light, fluffy biscuits that'll do you proud. A 1½-pound sack of biscuit mix makes 16 biscuits and costs $4.95, plus shipping. The products are preservative-free. Orders for the mixes are filled through a friend, Bettie Ellard, who owns a shop that features Mississippi and Louisiana food specialties.

New Orleans French Bread

Gazin's
P.O. Box 19221
New Orleans, Louisiana
70179-0221

(800) 262-6410; (504)
482-0302 (Monday to Friday,
9:30 A.M. to 4:30 P.M., CST)

34-page color catalog, $1
(applied to first order)
VISA, MasterCard, American
Express

Two of New Orleans's most famous eating treats are the oyster loaf and the po' boy (or poor boy). Each sandwich is based on New Orleans's distinctive, crispy-crust version of French bread. The boat-like oyster loaf is a hollowed-out flute slathered with spicy tartar sauce, heaped with crisp, hot fried oysters (rolled in cornmeal or corn flour and fried in lard), and dressed with some shredded lettuce and maybe a few tomato slices. Errant 19th-century husbands, skulking home in the wee hours after a night in the bars of the French Quarter, often arrived back home with an oyster loaf known as *la médiatrice*, or "peacemaker," a toothsome peace offering to placate angry wives.

The po' boy is the Southern equivalent of the North's hoagie, submarine, hero, or grinder. Said to have originated at a workingman's bar near the Mississippi River front during the Depression to satisfy big appetites for small change (they cost 20 cents back then), today's po' boy is often piled with thinly sliced roast beef and bathed with a rich gravy (underneath it all, of course, the shredded lettuce, mayo, and tomatoes). Other versions include catfish or ham and Swiss cheese.

Gazin's will ship New Orleans–style French bread

Alois J. Binder's Bakery
French Bread by

(each about 10 inches long), fresh from one of the city's leading bakeries, double-wrapped, ready to be heated and gobbled up immediately or frozen for the future. Twelve loaves cost $7.99, plus shipping; 24 loaves, $14.50. (West Coast orders are shipped by Second Day Air only; the charge is $6 for 12 loaves, $4 for each additional dozen.) Because the bread is highly perishable, during the summer months shipments are made only to: East Texas, Oklahoma, Arkansas, Tennessee, North Carolina, South Carolina, Mississippi, Alabama, Georgia, and Northern Florida. If you live outside these areas, the company suggests that you order extra and freeze for summer sandwiches. Want a regular supply? Place an order for the "Staff of Life" and Gazin's will ship 10 loaves each month for four months (around $34.95, postpaid). Or there's the "Bountiful Bread," 20 loaves each month for four months (about $57.50, postpaid). West Coast orders don't include postage.

— ❖ —

War Eagle Mill Stone-Buhr-Ground Cornmeal and Yankee Corn (Yellow) Grits

War Eagle Mill
Route 5, Box 411
Rogers, Arkansas 72756
(501) 789-5343

Free 16-page color catalog
VISA, MasterCard

The historic water-powered War Eagle Mill, a great place to visit, is located along a scenic rural Arkansas highway with a wonderful creaky old bridge (the War Eagle River runs underneath, and there's fine summertime fishing and swimming). The three-story red mill has the distinction of being run by Zoe Medlin Caywood, possibly the only female miller in America and a woman dedicated to promoting the benefits of whole-grain meals and flours. The miller directs and runs the process by which —at War Eagle—a large redwood waterwheel captures the energy flow of the nearby river to turn three large stone "buhrs" (sets of discs that crush the corn or wheat grains fed into them).

In healthful contrast to modern roller milling,

in War Eagle's stone-buhr milling method nothing is separated or added to the natural grain, and the slow grinding speed that Zoe maintains ensures that no extra heat destroys the grain. The wheat germ, oil, vitamins, and bran are left intact in all the mill's meals, cereal, and flour.

The structure's first floor is the mill itself. On the second floor is the War Eagle Mercantile, which is stocked with Arkansas-made baskets and wooden toys, and handmade knives, dolls, and Arkansas honey. On the third floor is the Bean Palace lunchroom, which serves tasty meals using War Eagle whole-grain products. Throughout the mill are displays of tools used in everyday life in the 1800s, including gourds once used to store cornmeal.

All this emphasis on history comes honestly

HOW TO SEASON CAST-IRON COOKWARE

— ❖ —

Cast iron is cornbread's best friend. You won't get that hallmark golden brown crust without it, in part because no other cookware material is so good at evenly distributing heat. Cast iron gets better with age. "Seasoned" with use, these pieces are treasured by Southern cooks, who likely will pass them on in the family. If you didn't inherit pieces, you'll have to carefully season the new ones you buy before using them. To do this, rub the inside and outside evenly and thoroughly with lard or vegetable oil (avoid safflower or corn oils, which leave a sticky residue) and place the pan upside down in a 350°F oven for an hour or so. Allow to cool. Repeat the process two or three more times over several days. After use, aim to keep the surface clean but not necessarily spotless. Scrubbing too hard with detergents and abrasives will undo the "seasoning," so either scrub the pan out by rubbing it with a handful of cornmeal or—if you *must*—clean it with hot, soapy water. And make sure it's perfectly dry by popping it briefly into a warm oven for a few minutes.

THERE'S NO SUCH THING AS LEFTOVER CORNBREAD

— ❖ —

Grab yourself a nice, big iced tea glass. Split the alleged "leftover" cornbread and toast it. Now crumble it into largish chunks and drop them into the depths of the glass. Pour in enough buttermilk to cover the cornbread. Give the bread a minute or so to soak up the buttermilk. Some people call this treat "Muddle Up." No matter what you call it, it's easier to eat with an iced tea spoon.

to Zoe and her husband, Charles, who serves as millwright. This mill was founded in the 1830s by Sylvanus Blackburn. Shortly before the Civil War, the mill washed away during a flood; it was rebuilt, only to have a Confederate officer order its destruction during the Civil War to prevent the Yankees from using it. In those early days, War Eagle Mill was the center of small community social life. Folks who had come long distances bringing their corn crops to be milled could gather to horse trade, hear gossip, and even enjoy a square dance. Blackburn's son rebuilt the mill once again on the same spot but it burned to the foundations in 1924. The present mill, its fourth incarnation, is the dream come true of Zoe's father, Jewell, whose childhood memories of taking corn to a mill inspired him to rebuild an authentic reproduction of the original War Eagle Mill sixteen years ago.

War Eagle Mill's excellent products are very modestly priced (but remember, shipping is extra and grains and flours are heavy) and come in attractive bags or sacks bearing a color drawing of the Mill done by Zoe's sister Phyllis. Yellow Cornmeal, White Cornmeal, and Whole-Wheat Flour are sold in 2-pound ($2) or 5-pound ($3.15) paper bags and 10-pound ($7) and 25-pound ($13) cloth sacks. Buckwheat or rye flour costs a dollar more. North of the Mason-Dixon line some folks eat yellow grits, which most Southerners, says Zoe, "wouldn't be caught dead eating." Nevertheless, she mills these hard-to-find coarse-ground "Yankee" yellow grits, which are made from whole cracked corn; they do have a "cornier" flavor than white grits (5-pound bag, $6.50). Zoe's three whole-grain cookbooks are featured in the catalog as well as an array of gift boxes at reasonable prices (nine War Eagle products along with a cookbook and a jar of honey are charmingly packed in an Arkansas-made half-bushel basket for $33.50, plus shipping). War Eagle Mill is also the source for Harold Ensley Fish Fry Coating Mix, described on page 166.

VISITING THE SOURCE

— ❖ —

War Eagle Mill is open seven days a week from 8:30 A.M. to 5:00 P.M., except during January and February, when it is open only on weekends (from 8:30 A.M. to 5:00 P.M.). The Bean Palace is open every day from March 15 through January 1, serving hearty breakfasts from 9 A.M. to 10:30 A.M. and lunch from 11 A.M. to 4:30 P.M. The mill is located 13 miles east of Rogers, Arkansas, on Highway 98, a mile and a half off Highway 12.

— ❖ —

Weisenberger's White Flours and Southern Specialty Mixes

Weisenberger Flour Mills
Box 215
Midway, Kentucky 40347
(606) 254-5282

Free brochure and price list
Invoice accompanies
shipment; pay by check or
money order upon receipt

After five generations, the Weisenberger Mill, a three-story structure on the banks of South Elkhorn Creek, is still grinding away. Founded in 1863 by German immigrant Augustus Weisenberger, it is run today by Phil Weisenberger and his son, Mac. This mill is something of a rarity, a small commercial one that grinds about 750 pounds each of Kentucky-grown wheat and corn daily (in contrast to the 10,000 pounds a day the big commercial guys grind). Although most of their business comes from local restaurants, hotels, and small grocery stores, residents of this part of central Kentucky are in the habit of dropping by Phil's office to pick up flours, grains, and mixes for home use. "I don't have a desire to get a lot bigger. We've found our niche," says Phil, who took over the mill from his father in the mid-1950s. Once powered by a waterwheel, today the mill's roller grinders and sifters use electricity, some of which is generated by the dual turbines powered by water from the creek out back.

The Weisenbergers' prices are incredibly rea-

WEISENBERGER

sonable, but remember, the products may weigh a lot, so freight charges often exceed the cost of what you're ordering. The prices indicated here do not include shipping; shipping charges on a 5-pound bag of flour to Chicago would cost around $3, for example. The Soft Wheat Unbleached White Flour is pure and simple. It is ground only from the endosperm of the degerminated wheat berry with nothing added. The flour's texture may seem strange if you've never baked with this type before—it's very much like talcum powder. In Kentucky they say this is the only flour to use for making beaten biscuits and it also turns out the finest regular biscuits and piecrust. The flour comes in a comforting-looking hand-packed, 5-pound brown paper bag with a drawing of the mill on the front and recipes on the back ($1.20). Bags of unbolted white cornmeal (plain or self-rising), soft whole-wheat pastry flour, and hard white flour for breadmaking are similarly priced. And speaking of breadmaking, Red Star Yeast, the brand Southern bakers are accustomed to, is often difficult to find in other parts of the country. The Weisenbergers sell 2-pound packages for $5 (freeze and use a little at a time).

For busy cooks the Weisenbergs have developed a number of very tasty mixes for Southern specialties like spoonbread, hush puppies, and biscuits that can be made lickety-split—all you add is water or milk. They come in convenient 5½-ounce paper packets with just enough for one meal, contain only natural ingredients, and are preservative-free. The most popular is a spicy Fish Batter Mix, which does double duty as a fish coating (dip fish in warm beer, roll in dry mix, and fry) and as a really delicious batter for deep-fried vegetables. The mixes are shipped only by the 12-package case (all one kind or mixed) for $4.95.

I highly recommend *The Weisenberger Cookbook* (210 pages, $8.50, postpaid), a collection of recipes Phil has accumulated over the years. There are directions for Russ Hauck's small-batch biscuits and Buena Bond's Corn Bread Supreme (so good it'll make you "so fat and pudgy that you won't be able to stand yourself").

SARAH FRITSCHNER'S TOMATO COBBLER WITH CORN-BISCUIT TOPPING
— ❖ —

Tomato Filling
4 tablespoons (½ stick) butter
¼ cup chopped onion
1 rib celery, minced
2 pounds fresh tomatoes
1 teaspoon sugar
¼ teaspoon salt
Dash black pepper

Biscuit Topping
½ cup Weisenberger cornmeal
1½ cups Weisenberger Unbleached White All-Purpose Flour
2½ teaspoons baking powder
½ teaspoon baking soda
½ teaspoon salt
3 tablespoons butter
3 tablespoons shortening
¾ cup buttermilk

Serve this with baked chicken or ham and cooked leafy greens.

Make the Tomato Filling: Melt the butter in a large skillet over medium heat. Add the onion and celery and cook until the celery is tender. Meanwhile, dip the tomatoes into boiling water for 15 seconds. Remove, drain, peel, and core. Quarter the tomatoes (or cut them in eighths if they are large) and stir them into the celery mixture along with the sugar, salt, and pepper. Transfer to an ovenproof casserole.

Make the Biscuit Topping: Combine the cornmeal, flour, baking powder, baking soda, and salt in a bowl. Cut in the butter and shortening until the largest bits are the size of small peas. Add the buttermilk, stirring until the mixture holds together. Knead the dough briefly until it is smooth, then roll it out to ½-inch thickness. Cut the dough into 2-inch rounds and place them on top of the tomatoes.

Bake the casserole at 400°F for 20 minutes or until the topping is browned.   *Serves 6 to 8*

White Lily Flours

The White Lily Foods Company
P.O. Box 871
Knoxville, Tennessee 37901
(615) 546-5511 (no phone orders)

Free order and information sheet
Prepaid orders only

If there's any doubt in your mind that hot, light, fluffy biscuits are important in the South, just remember that a duel was once fought between two families over the relative merits of their biscuit recipes.

White Lily is *the* flour of the South, a regional grocery store staple that cooks don't think twice about . . . until they move up North where it's virtually unobtainable. Luckily, the folks at White Lily understand how frustrating this can be and are willing to make shipments to individuals. Not everybody who misses White Lily seems to be aware of this, though, and it's a long-standing joke at major Southern airports that whenever an exceptionally heavy suitcase is checked in, it's probably loaded with bags of White Lily headed North with some displaced Southerner.

There is a built-in lightness factor in White Lily Flour, which is milled from soft red winter wheat (in contrast to the hard summer wheat used in Northern products). Soft wheat absorbs approximately 7 percent less liquid than hard wheat and is low in gluten, thus ensuring a more tender, lighter result. White Lily flour *is* different, and this may explain why your biscuits or other baked goods did not turn out quite as light as expected if you used a Southern recipe that *assumed* you'd be using White Lily. You'll find White Lily is less dense than most flours you may be accustomed to—1 cup plus 2 tablespoons equals a single cup of other brands. White Lily's finer granulation, which comes from extra milling steps, makes it so fine and light, it can be successfully substituted for cake flour in any recipe and it never needs sifting.

Today White Lily Foods Company is part of the Memphis-based Holly Farms Corporation, but its history goes back more than 100 years to J. Allen Smith, a young Georgian who may have chosen his brand name because the purity of a

The Light Baking Flour

white lily symbolized the purity of the flour he produced. In 1885 Smith opened an expanded mill with a special roller-mill system that ground his grain finer than ever. On the first day of operation his foreman is said to have walked into Smith's office clutching a small cloth sack. Sprinkling some of the flour out, he announced: "Mr. Smith, for years you've been wanting a flour whiter than snow and smoother than silk. I think you've finally got it!"

Six items from White Lily's product line are available by mail, each shipped postpaid in 5-pound bags. The cost is $2.50 per bag for shipments east of Mississippi, and $3.50 per bag for shipments west of Mississippi. Use White Lily

WHITE LILY "LIGHT" BISCUITS
— ❖ —

2 cups White Lily
   Self-Rising Flour
¼ cup shortening, chilled
⅔ to ¾ cup milk, chilled

For tender biscuits, always handle dough gently and use as little extra flour for kneading and rolling as possible.

Preheat the oven to 500°F. Measure the flour into a bowl by spooning it into a measuring cup and leveling it off. Cut in the shortening until the mixture is like coarse crumbs. Blend in just enough milk with a fork until the dough leaves the sides of the bowl. (Too much milk makes the dough too sticky to handle; not enough milk makes the biscuits dry.) Knead the dough gently on a lightly floured surface 10 to 12 strokes. Roll out the dough to about ½ inch thick. Cut biscuits with a 2-inch cutter, without twisting the cutter. Place the biscuits on an ungreased baking sheet spaced 1 inch apart for crusty biscuits, almost touching for soft sides, and bake for 8 to 10 minutes. Serve at once. *Makes about 12 biscuits*

AN OLD-FASHIONED COUNTRY WOOD STOVE FOR MODERN COOKS

— ❖ —

Do you love the look of those wonderful old iron wood stoves that cooks once used to turn out mouth-watering fried chicken, oven-smothered pork chops, and hot, fluffly biscuits? Do you also remember the hours those cooks spent on their knees building a wood or coal fire? The House of Webster, one of the South's oldest mail-order firms, has combined the appeal of the old with the convenience of the new. Their Country Charm Electric Range (just like the one in Evelyn Webster's kitchen) contains the innards of a modern electric range inside a line-for-line replica of a cast-iron stove made over a hundred years ago in Sheffield, Alabama.

This is a real beauty, scaled to fit modern range areas, with lovely decorative old-time scrolling wrought in the black enamel. The price is $1,425 (plus freight) if you want standard coil electric cooking elements, or $1,524 if you demand authenticity down to the last detail and opt for solid cast-iron cooking elements.

If you love your microwave oven but aren't thrilled with the way it looks, then you might like to know about the Webster's model that fits into the wall. It's camouflaged in a beautifully embossed cast-iron frame ($950).

And that's not all. The Websters make a conventional electric wall oven with an embossed door ($595), as well as two smaller appliances. The electric cast-iron skillet with lid is perfect for frying chicken (12 inches in diameter, $99.95), and for beans and greens there's a lidded cast-iron pot (5 quarts, $99.95).

For information, contact The House of Webster, P.O. Box 488, Rogers, Arkansas 72757-0488, or call (501) 636-4640.

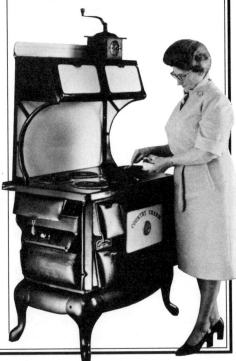

Self-Rising Flour (or White Lily Unbleached Self-Rising Flour) for perfect biscuits, muffins, shortcake, corn fritters, or quick breads. (A cup of self-rising flour already contains the equivalent of 1½ teaspoons baking powder and ½ teaspoon salt.) White Lily Plain All-Purpose Flour is for making cakes, cookies, and piecrust. It does not require sifting and can be successfully substituted for an equivalent amount of cake flour. White Lily Unbleached Bromated Bread Flour, a blend of hard spring and winter wheats with a higher protein content, was developed for making tender yeast-raised baked goods such as a delicious North Carolina Sally Lunn (serve toasted, buttered slices as a delightful accompaniment to a cup of American Classic Tea; see page 46). And for cornbread or corn muffins there's White Lily Self-Rising Cornmeal Mix or Buttermilk Cornmeal Mix (both with leavening and salt added).

— ❖ —

Woodson's Mill Old-Fashioned Grits Country Style, White Cornmeal, and Whole Wheat Flour

Woodson's Mill
Lowesville, Virginia 22951
(800) 446-8555;
(804) 622-2224 (in Virginia, call collect)

Free price list
Invoice sent with shipment; payment by check or money order

More than a hundred years ago in Nelson County, Virginia, a white-corn hybrid was developed. It had a special flavor and such sweetness that farmers still grow it. Just around the bend from Nelson County today is Woodson's Mill, a water-powered gristmill dating back to the 1790s. And Woodson's turns this fine local corn into delicious Old-Fashioned Grits Country Style and White Cornmeal.

The owner and spirit behind Woodson's Mill is a man with unusual experience in the business of delivering fine food. Gill Brockenbrough, proprietor of the mill, also happens to be president of First Colony Coffee & Tea Company, a name associated with fine gourmet coffees and teas from around the world. The fourth generation of his family in the business, Gill personally tastes

WOODSON'S MILL WHOLE-WHEAT BREAD

— ❖ —

1 cup cold water
¼ cup molasses
1 cup cold milk
1½ teaspoons salt
2 packages yeast
2 tablespoons butter, at
    room temperature
6 cups Woodson's Mill
    Whole-Wheat Flour

Mix together the water, molasses, milk, and salt. Stir until the molasses is dissolved. Add the yeast slowly to the molasses mixture. Stir well. Add the butter. Gradually add the flour. Stir until all ingredients are thoroughly mixed. Knead by hand for 4 to 5 minutes. Place the dough in a greased bowl, cover, and let it rise in a warm place (80°F) for 1½ hours. After the dough has risen, punch it down, divide it in half, shape each half into a loaf, and place them in greased loaf pans. Let rise again for 1 hour. Bake in a 400°F oven for 35 minutes.

Makes 2 loaves

Woodson's Mill, lovingly restored by Gill Brockenbrough.

and blends the coffees that First Colony sells to gourmet stores.

When he bought the sadly run-down mill in Lowesville in the early 1980s, Gill didn't intend to launch a major restoration. He simply hired mill enthusiast Steve Roberts to paint the roof and one thing led to another. Almost before they knew it, says Gill, they were knee-deep in a major restoration that experts said would take 10 years to complete. It took only three. Today, the four-story mill rises in newly restored neatness just across the Piney River from Lowesville in a beautiful mountain setting, and Steve Roberts is the miller. Five days a week, the restored water-wheel turns, and the milling that went on for 200 years continues.

Woodson's Old-Fashioned Grits Country Style are a considerably coarser grind than most other grits. The resulting cooked grits—very thick and muslin-colored, dotted with small, dark flecks of the heart of the corn—are probably pretty close to what people ate 50 years ago, before

most grits lost their character. Like all the Woodson's Mill products, they come in an appealing buff-colored drawstring cloth bag imprinted with a picture of the mill (a recipe is enclosed in each bag). The grits are $2.45 for a 2-pound bag.

Woodson's excellent white cornmeal costs $2.45 for a 2-pound bag. The mill also sells whole-wheat flour, johnnycake mix, and a three-grain pancake mix made from corn, wheat, and buckwheat (a 2-pound bag is $2.75). Gill believes in the honor system of ordering. Customers place an order using Woodson's price list (which shows only product prices, not UPS charges), and shipment is made accompanied by an invoice payable upon receipt.

The mill office features a wood stove and photographs from the mill's bustling past. The name comes not from the original builder in the 1790s, but from an energetic doctor named Julian B. Woodson, who acquired the place at the turn of the century. In his office in the mill, Woodson doctored both people and animals, and he added a 3,000-tree apple orchard as well as a machine shop. In his spare time he was a state senator!

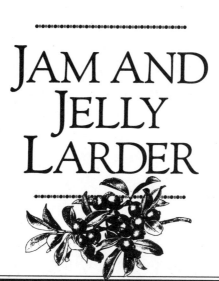

JAM AND JELLY LARDER

The sweet seduction of Southern jams, jellies, and preserves is unrivaled. For every hot buttered biscuit there is a correspondingly delicious topping, and some of the finest you're ever likely to taste—such as Bailey's Homemade Hot Pepper Jelly and Callaway Gardens' Muscadine Preserves—are right here in this section. Most are still made the time-honored way, in small batches by hand, and they feature fruits of the tree, bush, and trailing vine that are unique to the South, such as the wild mustang grape from Texas, Georgia's sweetly delicate mayhaw, and the earthy-tasting muscadine from Mississippi and Georgia.

In the past, the domestic ritual of putting up fruits and vegetables ensured there would always be a little something on hand to add sparkle and interest to the plain, boring meals of winter. Pantry shelves held a profusion of glass jars with the gemlike contents meticulously noted on hand-scrawled labels. Then as now, glistening sun-kissed preserves spooned from a wide-mouth mason jar were a guarantee that the memories and smells of spring and summer would flood back into one's consciousness on even the coldest, most barren days.

Bailey's Homemade Hot Pepper Jelly

Mrs. H. A. Bailey
400 South Commerce Street
Natchez, Mississippi 39120
(601) 445-8452

Free illustrated order form
Prepaid orders only

It's just really hard to say which is more delightful, Aunt Freddie Bailey herself or the widely heralded hot-pepper jelly made out in back of her huge Victorian home in a cozy jelly kitchen cooled by breezes from the nearby Mississippi River. I *do* know each is one of a kind.

Mrs. H. A. Bailey, or "Aunt Freddie" as everyone calls her, may already be familiar to you through her charming, anecdotal little cookbook *Aunt Freddie's Pantry* (regrettably out of print), which was published a few years back. ("In this house," she wrote, "we have good food and lots of fun.") The book was a project instigated by her nephew Lee Bailey, a well-known designer and himself the author of several exceptionally stylish cookbooks that reflect Southern roots. In fact, 20 years ago it was Lee who first urged Aunt Freddie to begin selling jelly through the mail. Up until that time, you had to be a lucky local resident who could visit her shop called Tot & Teen & Mom to pick up a few jars. Aunt Freddie still has the shop—it's located on the ground floor of her picturesque four-story, turreted, pale yellow Victorian home—where clothes, antiques, and the jelly share selling space.

The jelly recipe is the one that was handed down to Aunt Freddie by her grandmother. Every Friday she and an assistant get busy making about 200 jars of this sweet hot stuff in small 50-jar batches. It's a moderately pepper-hot yet sweet concoction made from the simplest ingredients: peppers, sugar, vinegar, pectin, and a dash of red or green food coloring for eye-appeal (nothing fake-looking or aggressively bright; the colors are muted and kind of sophisticated, actually). When you unscrew the lid and sniff, the vinegar makes your salivary glands jump up and down. Pretty little flecks of pepper are visible as you spoon the jelly from its simple glass jar. The first taste is sweet, then it slides toward tartness, and

It is a fetish in the South that the sun shines just a little brighter, the moon rays are just a little softer, the breezes blow just a little gentler, the birds sing just a little sweeter, the flowers are just a little prettier, and its climate just a little more salubrious.

—Mrs. S. R. Dull
Southern Cooking

finally the pepper sets off a little bang in the back of your mouth—a completely satisfying experience. The jelly is typically served with cream cheese on crackers, though Aunt Freddie likes it by itself on Ritz crackers or combined with peanut butter. But it is also an excellent glaze for a ready-to-eat smokehouse ham.

The minimum order is four 5-ounce jars (two of each color, $9, postpaid), but other quantities are also shipped (6 jars, $12.50; 8 jars, $16; 12 jars, $22). The label is no-frills black and white, made more interesting by a drawing of Aunt Freddie's famous house. Add a dollar to your order during the holidays and receive the jelly wrapped in glossy gift paper with a big cotton-bearded Santa cut-out, packed in cellophane with red and green bows.

Although her other book is no longer available, you can still order *Freddie Bailey's "Favorite" Southern Recipes*, a homegrown-looking spiral volume that includes recipes for smothered doves, Jezebel sauce, and even gumbo (Aunt Freddie was born and raised in Louisiana). The book is $3 when shipped with jelly and was designed to fit nicely inside the top of the jelly cartons.

Freddie Bailey once told a TV interviewer that she only thought of happy things while making her jelly and that she hoped it went into happy homes. I know that things cheered up around my place when the first jelly shipment arrived. I hope yours will do the same for you.

HOT-PEPPER FRUIT SALAD
— ❖ —

1 package lime Jell-O
1 jar Bailey's Homemade
   Hot Pepper Jelly
1 cup canned fruit salad

Dissolve the Jell-O in 1 cup of boiling water. Add the pepper jelly and the fruit salad. Pour into molds and allow it to solidify. Serve on lettuce with mayonnaise.   *Serves 6 to 8*

Branch Ranch Strawberry Preserves and Orange Marmalade

The Branch Ranch Dining Room
P.O. Box 2012
Plant City, Florida 33566
(813) 752-1957

Free black-and-white illustrated order form
VISA, MasterCard, Diners Club

I t's not widely known, but the famous Branch Ranch Dining Room will ship some of the homemade specialties that are served in its rustic dining rooms—and they beat store-bought versions by a mile.

Simple food honestly prepared from scratch is the hallmark of a great country meal. Food this good is usually found only at home, rarely in restaurants. Since the 1950s the family-owned and -operated Branch Ranch Dining Room, located a bit east of Tampa in the midst of orange groves, vegetable fields, and placidly grazing cattle, has been regarded as one of this country's premier outposts of groaning-board farm fare. What draws folks in are slabs of country ham and crispy fried chicken, piping-hot biscuits with plenty of homemade preserves, marmalade, and orange blossom honey, and old-fashioned relish and salad trays heaped with pickled beets and thick-sliced spiced pickles. Long after they've returned to their microwave ovens, visitors dream about the so-called "side dishes," a meal in themselves, that waitresses bring to each table in a towering stack. Diners serve themselves family-style, dishing up whole baked yellow squash, ham-flavored pole beans, baked yams, scalloped eggplant, and a remarkable chicken potpie topped with the same biscuits that also accompany all entrées.

Much of the food that's served in the three huge Branch Ranch dining rooms is actually grown on the family's nearby farmland and citrus groves, including the fruits used in these terrific preserves. The recipes are the same ones Mrs. Mary Branch served Sunday dinner guests in her own home over 30 years ago. It was because those guests enjoyed themselves so much and wanted to bring along friends that Mrs. Branch found herself in business, serving paying guests in the family's converted TV room.

The Branch Ranch's mail-order goodies are all superior. Superb strawberry preserves made from locally grown berries are fragrant, not overly sweet, and contain whole berries. You could pay twice as much for fancy imported preserves that don't hold a candle to these. The orange marmalade with bits of pineapple has character and substance as well as a slightly bitter edge that comes from chewy little chunks of orange rind. It's good enough to eat from the jar with a spoon. There are also the same small pickled beets, spicy and homey, that appear on the Ranch's relish tray, and which would be equally good tucked into a picnic basket. The thick-cut cucumber pickles are old-fashioned sweet ones with garlic and spices. A six-item sampler gift pack containing one of each of the above, plus a jar of Orange Blossom Honey and a 12-ounce bag of Homemade Biscuit Mix, costs $21.50. (Prices are postpaid to states east of the Mississippi; add 15 percent delivery to states west of the Mississippi.) Or you can order by the case choosing your favorites, either 6 jars, one flavor or assorted ($21.50) or 12 jars ($39). All these items are also sold at the Branch Ranch's gift shop.

VISITING THE SOURCE
— ❖ —

The Branch Ranch Dining Room, located off the Branch-Forbes exit off I-4 (about 15 miles east of Tampa), is open Tuesday through Sunday from 11:30 A.M. to 9:30 P.M., including holidays. Reservations are recommended.

— ❖ —

Callaway Gardens Muscadine Jelly, Preserves, and Sauce

The taste of muscadines is a special Southern pleasure. These grapes have an unforgettable sweet yet tart flavor that has long made them popular for jellies and jams. Generations of adventurous little kids plucked wild muscadines right off the vine, savoring their pleasant

**Callaway Gardens Country Store
Pine Mountain, Georgia 31822**

(800) 282-8181 (October to December only, 7 days a week, 8 A.M. to 6 P.M., EST); (404) 663-5100 (year round, 7 days a week, 8 A.M. to 6 P.M., EST)

**Free 12-page color catalog
VISA, MasterCard, American Express**

slipperiness. Best of all, though, was when the vines grew twined through tree branches, forming natural ropes for precariously swinging from one tree to the next.

Callaway Gardens has been selling its special—and famous—muscadine sweets ever since founder Cason Callaway planted his own vines back in the 1940s. It was Virginia, Cason's wife, who suggested that he adapt his mother's treasured wild plum sauce recipe to muscadines.

The rich, clear, claret-colored Muscadine Jelly is marvelous on hot biscuits and muffins. The Muscadine Preserves, thick with bits of fruit, are every bit as good. The country breakfasts served at the Callaway Gardens restaurant always arrive at the table accompanied by biscuits and these preserves. Callaway is the only place you can order Muscadine Sauce, a specialty topping that's scrumptious over vanilla ice cream. It also makes an unusual condiment for chicken, pork, and wild game. A set of three 12-ounce jars (1 jar each of preserves, jelly, and sauce) costs $16.95 (plus $3.50 shipping), or for the same price you can order three of one muscadine product.

CALLAWAY GARDENS MUSCADINE BREAD
— ❖ —

½ cup (1 stick) butter
1 cup sugar
2 eggs
2 cups all-purpose flour
1½ teaspoons baking powder
½ cup milk
1 cup Callaway Gardens Muscadine Sauce
½ cup chopped pecans

Cream the butter and sugar together until light and fluffy. Add the eggs, beating in one at a time. Sift the dry ingredients together and add to the butter mixture alternately with the milk and muscadine sauce. Stir in the nuts. Bake in a greased and floured loaf pan at 325°F until a toothpick inserted in the center comes out clean, 50 to 60 minutes.

Makes 1 loaf

VISITING THE SOURCE
— ❖ —

Callaway Gardens is an extremely popular, breathtakingly beautiful resort covering 2,500 acres of woodlands and flowers. Visitors can watch wildlife, hike nature trails, visit spectacular flower displays, or eat to their hearts' content at the restaurant. Callaway Gardens is located on U.S. Highway 27, seventy miles south of Atlanta. For visiting information call (404) 663-2281.

— ❖ —

Fischer and Wieser Old-Fashioned Peach Preserves, Butter, and Honey

Das Peach Haus, Inc.
Route 3, Box 118
Fredericksburg, Texas
78624-9301

(800) 369-9257; (512)
997-7194, (7 days a week,
9 A.M. to 5 P.M., CST)

Free order form
VISA, MasterCard, American
Express

In the heart of Texas's hill country lies Fredericksburg, a unique and historic German community dotted with lovely gingerbread buildings. Just a little way from Main Street is a restored log cabin, the scenic headquarters of Das Peach Haus, makers of the most outrageously delicious jams, jellies, and preserves you'll ever have the pleasure of spreading all over a hot biscuit or piece of toast.

Das Peach Haus was started in the late 1960s by Mark Wieser, a former teacher and now the county judge of Gillespie County. The area around Fredericksburg is peach country, and Mark's father, like lots of other folks nearby, grew peaches. As a child, Mark ran an informal peach stand by the side of the road. Later, as an adult, he dreamed of setting up a permanent roadside market featuring the succulent Gillespie County peaches. Now, while this may sound like an obvious idea, the reality is that no one else in Fredericksburg had thought of it, so when Mark opened the stand in the late 1960s it attracted a lot of attention. Today scores of fruit stands dot the highway, but Das Peach Haus was the first. It wasn't long before Mark asked his mother, who lived next door to the stand, if she'd make up some of her preserves to sell along with the peaches. Eventually the preserves and jellies out-

sold the fresh fruit and sort of took over the stand. A few years ago one of Mark's former students, Case Fischer, joined him as a partner and together they've been expanding the business. But don't get the wrong idea. Das Peach Haus jams, jellies, and preserves are still made like they were when Mrs. Wieser was alive—by hand, using local fruits.

It's difficult to single out favorites. Not surprisingly, the peach products, made from home-grown fruits, are superior. Best are the unthickened (no pectin) Old Fashioned Peach Preserves, which are chunkier and tastier than a version called Texas Peach Preserves. Without the cloying sweetness of many other preserves, the clean, fresh, pure taste of the fruit comes right through. The Peach Butter is dark and spicy, and the best-selling Peach Honey, a delicious, thinnish fruit syrup originated by Mark's aunt, is just plain terrific dribbled over ice cream, used as a ham glaze, or spread on biscuits. There are a number of exceptionally good-tasting nonpeach products, too (among them are the Green Grape Preserves). They're extra-special over ice cream but also make a lovely condiment with turkey. Also of note are sublime, limited-edition Fig Preserves made from fresh figs, Dewberry Preserves, marmalade-like Winter Melon Preserves, golden-red Texas Agarita Jelly, Texas Cactus Jelly, and an excellent version of the inevitable Texas Jalapeño Jelly.

All of the more than 50 flavors of jams, jellies, preserves, and honeys made by Das Peach Haus come in 9-ounce Kerr canning jars ($4.25 each, plus shipping) and some are also available in 5.5-ounce mini-jar tasting sizes ($3.25 each, plus shipping). Gift crates and boxes are also available: three 9-ounce jars of the same or assorted flavors in an attractive cardboard box will run $12.74, plus around $3.25 shipping, or you can order

three minis packed in a wooden crate for $9.75, plus around $2.75 shipping.

VISITING THE SOURCE
— ❖ —

Das Peach Haus's retail store is located on Main Street in Fredericksburg, 1.5 miles from the Nimitz Center, on Highway 87 South. Open seven days a week from 9 A.M. to 5 P.M., it sells all the delicious jams and jellies, as well as fresh peaches when they're in season, and Texas wines.

— ❖ —

Loveless Old Fashion Peach and Blackberry Preserves

Loveless Hams and Jams Catalog
Route 5, Highway 100
Nashville, Tennessee 37221
(615) 646-0067 (Monday to Friday, 8 A.M. to 3 P.M., CST)

Free color catalog
VISA, MasterCard, American Express

The pink and blue neon sign outside the legendary Loveless Motel & Cafe reads HOT BISCUITS COUNTRY HAM. The small, state-of-the-art hot biscuits and home-made preserves served with every meal here are an important element of the cafe's claim to fame. And on hectic Sundays, when 500 or more of the Loveless's famous country breakfasts are served, happy eaters work their way through 3,500 or more biscuits. The biscuit dough is mixed up in large buckets and the recipe is the secret of Elizabeth Roberts, now in her seventies, who's been a waitress and cook at the Loveless for 28 years.

When you pull at a Loveless biscuit, it comes apart in three pieces. The soft, fluffy middle is for sopping up the red-eye gravy that comes to the table with your slice of country ham and eggs. And the crusty top and bottom are vehicles for Roberts's other culinary masterpiece, absolutely incredible peach and blackberry preserves, which are set on the checked tablecloths in small dishes alongside Benton County sorghum and clover honey from Early, Tennessee.

Once you've tasted these extraordinary preserves, which are simplicity itself (they contain only fruit and sugar), you may find yourself eating them the way I do: by the spoonful, straight

from the Kerr canning jar they come in. It's true—I don't even bother with a biscuit. They're that special. Donna McCabe, who owns the Loveless, has never offered dessert on the menu because she says most people eat so many biscuits slathered with preserves that they never have room for dessert.

The preserves are made fresh each morning by Elizabeth Roberts, who begins the day in the cafe's kitchen at 6:00 A.M. by heaping the fruits into a huge braising skillet along with some water and sugar. Then she allows the mixture to ever so gently slow-cook for around five or six hours. According to Donna McCabe, the secret to the preserves' succulence rests "all in knowing how long to cook them." The peach preserves, dotted with chunky bits of fruit, are a lovely deep-golden color. McCabe and Roberts searched a long time to find just the right type of black-berry for the other preserves. They found it in the Marion blackberry, which has a rich, full, slightly tart taste. Both of the preserves are so nice and thick that they can also be used as a sumptuous ice-cream topping. The preserves come in big 16-ounce Kerr canning jars (peach, $5.45 per jar, plus shipping; blackberry, $5.95). They're also included in some of the gift pack-ages shown in the Loveless catalog. A jar each of the preserves can be ordered along with sorghum and honey ($16.95) or with a pound of the same sliced country ham served at the cafe ($18.95). For more details about Loveless Smoked Country Hams and visiting the source, see page 156.

— ❖ —

Mayhaw Jelly and Southern Specialties

Up until 1983, about the only way you could get your hands on a jar of lovely coral-hued mayhaw jelly was to sweet-talk your way into your great-aunt's pantry on a

The Mayhaw Tree
P.O. Box 144
Colquitt, Georgia 31737

(800) 677-3227 (Monday to
Friday, 8:30 A.M. to 5:30 P.M.,
EST)

Free color brochure
VISA, MasterCard

day she was feeling especially kindly toward blood relatives. Most people in the South grew up with mayhaws, a tart red berry that thrives in swamps and marshes, but like many other casually growing, distinctively Southern crops, in recent years the mayhaw has been pretty much ignored. Its revival is a tale of civic pride. And a tribute to the true grit of four Southern women determined to help their small town out of the economic doldrums.

Colquitt, population 2,000, lies in southwest Georgia. As in many rural farming communities, its economy is in tough shape. There's little industry—two peanut plants and a ladies' underwear factory—and farming gets harder each year. Discussing the state of Colquitt's economy at a party one night, Joy Jinks, Dot Wainright, Betty Jo Toole, and Pat Bush vowed to do something about providing employment for the community, especially for women. Meeting weekly to explore ideas, they kept returning to the mayhaw, "the only thing we had that was unique." On almost every farm in Miller County mayhaws were growing wild and going to waste. Renting an empty house for storage, the women spread the word that they'd pay $5 a gallon in crisp, new

MAYHAW JELLY COOKIES
— ❖ —

¾ pound butter or
  margarine
¼ cup sugar
2 egg yolks
4 cups all-purpose flour,
  sifted
1 teaspoon vanilla extract
Mayhaw Tree Mayhaw
  Jelly

Cream the butter and sugar together. Add the egg yolks and mix well. Add the flour and vanilla. Chill the dough until it is stiff enough to handle. Shape it into balls the size of marbles; make a dent in the top of each ball with a thimble. Place a small amount of jelly in each dent. Bake at 450°F until slightly browned, about 10 minutes.

Makes about 24 cookies

bills for berries—and mayhaws came pouring in. At night in the borrowed deli kitchen of the local IGA grocery, they made their first batches of mayhaw jelly. Today the Mayhaw Tree employs 11 full-time people in a 2,000-square-foot plant, and its cheerful, hardworking founders are always easy to spot at food trade shows—they're wearing the brightest green outfits you ever laid eyes on, and they're each wearing a golden mayhaw tree pendant.

The Mayhaw Tree makes eleven products now, each with a perky bright green and white label showing a mayhaw tree. The products are shipped postpaid in a number of boxed assortments or by the case, single or mixed. Classic Mayhaw Jelly is the main product. "The recipe's

Under The Mayhaw Tree with the company's four founders.

The Mayhaw Tree

no secret," Joy Jinks likes to point out. "It's the basic ingredient that's hard to find!" A romantic, wistful, very beautiful pale coral color, the jelly has a mild sweet-tart flavor. Best on hot biscuits, it also makes a nice hors d'oeuvre spread combined with cream cheese. The minimum order is three 11-ounce jars ($17.95, postpaid; in the catalog it's called "Mayhaw Lovers Box"). Other specialties include Deep South Salad Dressing, a sweet dressing made with mayhaw jelly, Vidalia onions, tomatoes, herbs, and spices that I find irresistible splashed on home-grown sliced tomatoes or steamed broccoli; Plantation Sauce, a mayhaw base combined with raisins and spices; Light Mayhaw Jelly, made with half the sugar; Mayhaw Wine Jelly, a deep-flavored blend of port and mayhaw jelly; Mayhaw Syrup (great on French toast with a dollop of sour cream); Vidalia Onion Jelly; Pepper Jelly; and Cucumber Jelly. There are two good ways to try the products: the Southern Sampler (ten 2-ounce bottles

THE MAYHAW
— ❖ —

Mayhaws are known regionally as berries, but they're actually members of the rose family (along with peaches, pears, and apples). Bright red and about the size of a cranberry, they grow wild rather than cultivated, on bushy, thorny trees. The supply of mayhaws is highly variable; bumper crops may be followed by poor harvests. Mayhaws ripen in May and the harvest season is very short, usually only about three weeks. Nature helps with the harvest. Ripened berries fall to the ground (where they are retrieved by hand) or drop into creeks and ponds (where they are scooped up with nets). While they're edible right from the tree, mayhaws are not really a pick-and-eat crop since they're extremely tart and have very little meat. For jelly and wine making, the berries are boiled and squeezed for their juice.

of the jellies and syrup, $23.95) or the Southern Savory Box (10- to-16-ounce sizes of the whole shooting match, $38.50, postpaid).

VISITING THE SOURCE
— ❖ —

The Mayhaw Tree production facility and homey retail store are located at 560 East Main Street in Colquitt, which is about 50 miles southwest of Albany, on U.S. Highway 27 and State Route 91. The shop is open Monday through Friday from 8:30 A.M. to 5 P.M.

— ❖ —

Miriam's Texas Original Mesquite Jelly

Miriam's Texas Original Mesquite Jelly Inc.
313 East Main Street
Port Lavaca, Texas 77979
(512) 552-5295

Free descriptive price list
Prepaid orders only

As long as anyone can remember, Texas cattle ranchers have cursed the low-growing mesquite shrubs that dot more than 60 million acres of Texas and other parts of the Southwest. They're scraggly devils with cruel thorns and an unquenchable thirst for the precious water cattle need. Ranchers have pulled pesky mesquite up by the roots, sprayed, burned, bulldozed, and hollered at it, but it just lives on. Despite mesquite's bad reputation in some circles, it's valued in others. Barbecue fanatics prize mesquite wood for its ability to provide intense, sustained heat and subtle, delicious flavor (also, a few mesquite beans thrown on the fire impart a bit of sweet flavor to meats). And the long narrow bean pods that grow clustered on mesquite were a source of nutrition for Indians and early Lone Star settlers.

When Jim Chatelle was a little boy, he used to grab sweet mesquite beans right off the trees and chew on them as if they were candy. Today Jim has turned the beans into a golden-colored jelly just right for spreading on biscuits. The jelly recipe originated with his mother, Miriam, who passed it down with tips on foraging for the beans (they're difficult and time-consuming to harvest, plus not all trees yield usable ones).

Miriam's
Texas Original
Mesquite
Jelly Inc.

Mesquite jelly might have remained simply a family tradition if Jim had not been left jobless when the local chemical plant folded. But Jim's daughters Melody and Trudy proposed a jelly-making business as a new career. The Chatelles figured they had nothing to lose and took a few jars of "the family jelly" to a Taste of Texas marketing show in San Antonio, where it was a big hit. Today the Chatelles are a small family corporation operating out of their own store on Main Street (and Jim is an active member of Los Amigos de Mesquite, a worldwide nonprofit organization that promotes mesquite's virtues).

The flavor of mesquite jelly is somewhat difficult to describe—it tastes most like a cross between honey and apple jelly with faint coconut undertones. It is *very* sweet and subtle. Jelly is made in the store year round, but the beans are harvested during a very short 45-day season that begins around the end of July and ends in early September. At harvest time the Chatelles and their assistants snap beans at a worktable in the store and then slowly boil them to extract the bean essence that is the basis for the jelly (extra bean liquor is frozen for future jelly making). Jim says Texans have found a number of ways to use his unique jelly other than on a morning English muffin; some people use a couple of tablespoons in barbecue sauce when they want to sweeten it up a bit, others say it's good as a ham glaze.

Miriam's Texas Original Mesquite Jelly is available in 2-ounce ($1.50), 4-ounce ($2.95), and 8-ounce ($4.95) jars. Postage is extra; there is no minimum order (shipping will cost around $2 on orders of $10 or under). Jim plans to add another product, mesquite bean syrup, in the future.

VISITING THE SOURCE
— ❖ —

Port Lavaca lies halfway between Houston and Corpus Christi on Highway 35. Miriam's Texas Original Mesquite Jelly Shop is located at

313 East Main Street and is open Monday through Friday from 8 A.M. to 5 P.M. Drop by for a visit with the Chatelle family, sample their jelly, and—if you're there at the right time—watch the Chatelles and their helpers make jelly.

— ❖ —

Serendipity of the Valley Wild Orange, Jalapeño, Orange Jalapeño, and Ruby Red Grapefruit Jellies

Marty & Harley, Inc.
P.O. Box 787
Lake Jackson, Texas 77566
(409) 297-2367 (Monday to Friday, 9 A.M. to 5 P.M., CST)

Free order form
Prepaid orders only

For those of us used to getting our morning citrus from half a grapefruit or a glass of juice, here's a new twist. Marty and Harley Tyson specialize in unique jellies made from the finest citrus from the Rio Grande Valley.

Marty's sister, Mary, who lives in the Valley, originally founded the business, naming it after the "delightful adventure" and "unexpected discoveries" she had while experimenting with the jelly recipes. When she sold the company to the Tysons for a dollar back in the mid-1970s, they kept the name because it's such a conversation starter. The Tysons do everything themselves, purposely remaining a small business. "We aren't in this to get rich," says Marty, who gave up organ playing at the church because of time demands. "We just enjoy what we do."

The Tysons travel to the Rio Grande Valley each December and January—the height of the citrus season—to personally select ingredients. Finding growers willing to sell the sourish, wild oranges used in their Wild Orange and Orange Jalapeño jellies is the hardest part. Citrus growers plant these not as a crop but as hardy hedges and windbreaks in their orchards. "We have to convince them to sell the oranges to us," Marty notes. Their unusual flavor is worth the effort; the Tysons' Wild Orange Jelly is tart and fresh-tasting, with a purer, more pronounced orange flavor than any jelly made from regular oranges.

The same wild oranges lend a mellowing fruit flavor to the punch of the fiery jalapeños used in their Orange Jalapeño Jelly. This is not something you'll want to spread on breakfast toast; try it instead as a relish with meats, as a glaze for a pork roast or ham, or to make "gringo nachos" (top a corn chip or cracker with cheese and a dab of jelly). Jalapeño jelly without the sharp, interesting wild-orange touch is also available in hot and mild versions. The Texas Ruby Red Grapefruit Jelly, which is a pretty pink, is very sweet, with a mildish grapefruit flavor; it's nice for something like tea sandwiches.

Made in small batches, the Tysons' serendipitous sweets come in 8-ounce old-fashioned jelly jars, which are shipped in various flavor combinations in 6- ($22.95) and 12-jar packs ($34.95). Prices include shipping.

— ❖ —

TexasFresh Blackberry Jam, Blueberry Jam, and TexasGem Pepper Jelly

Brockett-Tyree Farms
P.O. Box 1088
Royse City, Texas 75089
(214) 635-9222 (Monday to Friday, 8 A.M. to 5 P.M., CST)

Free order form
Prepaid orders only

On a crisp December morning you can hear the crunch of horses' hooves, the giggling of little kids, and the happy jingle of bells as wagons full of families make their way deep into the heart of the piney woods of Brockett-Tyree Farms to cut their own fragrant Christmas trees. The scene looks and smells like something right out of an old-fashioned Christmas card. After the perfect tree has been chosen and cut, the families usually hang out awhile, mesmerized by Doug Belzer making cane syrup back at the syrup mill or watching the cows being milked. And they'll definitely pick up a jar of succulent blackberry or blueberry jam made from Brockett-Tyree's homegrown berries.

Today Brockett-Tyree Farms is one of the largest cut-your-own Christmas tree farms in Texas, but back in the 1960s it existed only in the imagination of accountant Jerry Brockett and mechanical engineer Daryl Tyree, Dallas neighbors who'd had enough of big-city life. Their escape plan succeeded, and today the two families work in partnership providing rural entertainment and a taste of their own hardworking country life-style to scores of urban families who make the pilgrimage to visit from the Dallas/Fort Worth area. Over the years, the tree farm has expanded to include a dairy farm, an authentic old-time working syrup mill, and acres of berries.

The farms' very reasonably priced products, sold under the brand name TexasFresh, are put up in a new plant, where a family member supervises each batch. Handpicked blueberries and blackberries are plucked at just the right moment of ripeness, which is why these thick jams are so pure-tasting and satisfying. The blackberry jam (10-ounce jar, $2, plus shipping) is especially nice on biscuits or toast, and the blueberry (8-ounce jar, $2, plus shipping) can be heated as a topping for ice cream or cheese cake. Square, 11-ounce glass bottles of berry syrups ($2.12, plus shipping) are made by cooking and crushing the whole berries and bottling the juice while it's still hot. These are additionally sweetened with small amounts of corn syrup; a touch of vanilla is added to the blueberry and a dash of cinnamon to the blackberry.

Brockett-Tyree's version of pepper jelly is unusual both in taste and appearance. Most versions of pepper jelly are brightly colored, usu-

ally as green as grass, but this one is a lovely clear amber color with gay, confetti-like bits of homegrown red and jalapeño peppers suspended throughout the jelly. When you hold a jar up to the light, it's like looking through a stained-glass window. Flavorwise, it's sort of sneaky—the first taste is sweet yet tart and rather mild, but after a few seconds the heat of the jalapeño hits the roof of your mouth and you'll feel and taste their fire. I found this to be the most sophisticated and complex-tasting of the countless pepper jellies I tried, and it's good not only as an hors d'oeuvre with cream cheese, but as a meat glaze as well. A chubby 9-ounce jar of TexasGem Pepper Jelly costs $2, plus shipping.

Since many visitors buy Brockett-Tyree Farms' products at Christmastime for gifts, these can all be ordered in a variety of special gift packaging that ranges from simple wooden crates (2 jars of jam, $6.50, plus shipping) to more elaborate containers such as wooden boots (a jar each of jam and syrup, $7.80) and even wooden cows, geese, and wagons. One reason the prices are so low is that credit cards are not accepted. It is recommended that you call the office, tell them what you want, and they'll quote the total (including shipping) so you can send a check.

VISITING THE SOURCE
— ❖ —

Brockett-Tyree Farms is located in Winnsboro, nine miles east of Quitman on Highway 2088. The Christmas tree farm, syrup mill, blacksmith shop, and smokehouse are on an area of the farm known as Turkey Creek Village, which is open to visitors from the middle of November through December 23 daily from 9 A.M. until "dark" (usually around 6 P.M.).

• Mrs. Fearnow's Delicious Brunswick Stew • Fuller's Mustard • Maunsel White's
• Panola Pepper Sauce • Amber Brand Smithfield Ham • Billy Higdon's Happy Holl
y Hams • Colonel Bill Newsom's Kentucky Country Hams • Bucksnort Smoked Rain
• Callaway Gardens Speckled Heart Grits • White Lily Flour • Bailey's Homemade H
Jelly Sherardi   ansel's Rice • Garber
Yams • Warrento   ssinger's Flying Pig B
Arrow Ranch Ax   ory-Smoked Sausage
• Golden Mill So   ms Sweet Vidalia Oni
f Luck Scottish S   ker Deluxe Moon Pie
Kitchen Derby Pi   otato Chips • Charli
Rendezvous Ribs   Barq's Root Beer •
ine • Crickle •   ns Cut Leaf Poke Sa
• Mrs. Fearnow'   • Maunsel White's
• Panola Pepper   Higdon's Happy Holl
y Hams • Colone   ksnort Smoked Rain

• Garber Farms Cajun Yams • Bland Farms Sweet Vidalia Onions • Callaway Garden
ed Heart Grits • White Lily Flour • Bailey's Homemade Hot Pepper Jelly • Mayhaw
dized Pecans • Virginia Diner Peanuts • Ellis Stansel's Rice • Ledford Mill Borrowe
en Arrow Ranch Axis Venison • Comeaux's Boudin • Mayo's Hickory-Smoked Sausa
• Golden Mill Sorghum • Steen's Pure Cane Syrup • Best of Luck Scottish Shortbr
hoes and Nails • Double Decker Deluxe Moon Pies • Kern's Kitchen Derby Pie • Li
Orchard Cake • Warrenton Original Nashville Rum Cakes • Zapp's Potato Chips •
Rendezvous Ribs • Maurice Bessinger's Flying Pig Barbeque • Barq's Root Beer •
ine • Crickle • Evelyn's Pralines • Goo Goo Clusters • The Allens Cut Leaf Poke S
• Mrs. Fearnow's Delicious Brunswick Stew • Fuller's Mustard • Maunsel White's
• Panola Pepper Sauce • Amber Brand Smithfield Ham • Billy Higdon's Happy Holl
y Hams • Colonel Bill Newsom's Kentucky Country Hams • Bucksnort Smoked Rain
• Garber Farms Cajun Yams • Bland Farms Sweet Vidalia Onions • Callaway Garde
ed Heart Grits • White Lily Flour • Bailey's Homemade Hot Pepper Jelly • Mayhaw
dized Pecans • Virginia Diner Peanuts • Ellis Stansel's Rice • Ledford Mill Borrowe
en Arrow Ranch Axis Venison • Comeaux's Boudin • Mayo's Hickory-Smoked Sausa
• Golden Mill Sorghum • Steen's Pure Cane Syrup • Best of Luck Scottish Shortbr

Whether you're throwing a handful of salted peanuts down into the depths of an icy bottle of RC, Pepsi, or Coke, or gearing up to make a nut pie, you'll find that the finest nuts are grown in the South. In this section you'll learn how to order the largest, sweetest, best-of-the-crop pecans from the groves of a Mississippi Delta plantation, discover the almost extinct pleasures of the Roddenbery's boiled green peanuts, and make the acquaintance of the absolutely crunchiest, most delectable roasted peanuts on the face of the earth from the Virginia Diner.

Koinonia Partners Spiced Pecan Halves

Koinonia Partners, Inc.
Route 2
Americus, Georgia
31709-9986
No phone orders

Free color catalog
Prepaid orders only; $10
minimum order

Koinonia Partners is more than just a mail-order business in rural southwest Georgia—it's a community ministry devoted to a simple yet physically rigorous lifestyle of service, work, and worship (*Koinonia* is a Greek word that means "communion" or "fellowship"). The community was founded in 1942 by Clarence Jordan as "a demonstration plot, an experiment designed to show the power of the Gospel in changing human lives." Today around 30 permanent members, known as Resident Partners, assisted by volunteers who join the community for three-month visits, live and work on a bustling 1,500-acre farm where pecans, peaches, and vegetables are grown. The Partners run a nursery and preschool center, youth after-school, summer, and tutoring programs, and a food co-op.

The mail-order business makes it possible for Koinonia to remain financially self-sufficient (thus freeing its residents to do non-income-producing good works) and to provide employment for around 60 of its neighbors, many of whom have no other employment. All items in the catalog are prepared on the premises, and some, like the pecans, are grown right on the farm. Spiced Pecan Halves are Koinonia's most well known product. The nuts are smothered in a sugary cinnamon-flavored candy coating that makes them look a little like moon rocks ($3.75 for an 8-ounce box; 1-pound bag, $6.95). Also available are Spiced Peanuts with the same coating as the pecans (1-pound bag, $2.95) and Hickory Smoked Pecan Halves actually smoked over a fire (8-ounce box, $4.25; 1½-pound tin, $13.95).

From Koinonia's own kitchens there's a modestly priced fruitcake (1-pound 5-ounce boxed loaf, $6.95; 2-pound 4-ounce round in a tin, $14.45) flavored with big chunks of candied and dried fruit and sweetened with honey, and a Honey-Nut Peachcake (same price as the fruit-

cake) made with Georgia pecans, dried peaches, carrots, raisins, dates, and honey (no white sugar). Seven gift packs are also offered (example: the #3 pack includes a 1-pound 5-ounce Honey-Nut Peachcake along with an 8-ounce box each of Spiced Pecan Halves and Hickory Smoked Pecan Halves for $12.75). Shipping is included for orders east of Denver; west of Denver you must add 10 percent of the order total for shipping. (Koinonia doesn't ship between May 20 and September 20.)

— ❖ —

Missouri Dandy Black Walnuts

**Missouri Dandy Pantry
212 Hammons Drive East
Stockton, Missouri 65785**

**(800) 872-6879; (800) 872-6880, in Missouri
(Monday to Saturday, 9 A.M. to 5 P.M., CST)**

**Free 20-page color catalog
VISA, MasterCard, American Express**

Finding a recipe that calls for black walnuts is easy. Most Southern cookbooks contain at least one, usually a cake, calling for these distinctive, strong-flavored nuts. But the nuts can be difficult to find, which is why it's good to know about this source, the mail-order division of Hammons Products Company, the world's largest processor of eastern black walnuts.

Black walnuts grow wild in the Ozarks and throughout the central and eastern parts of the country and are generally gathered on a small scale. The trees are prized for their beautiful wood and the nuts have an aggressive, rather exotic, almost fermented flavor quite unlike the more familiar, subtler-tasting English walnut. A main reason shelled black walnuts are on the expensive side and not readily available is that they're a real pain in the neck to remove from the intricately chambered, hard-as-a-rock shell.

The nuts, which retain their distinctive flavor during baking, are used to flavor everything from cakes and cookies to candies and ice cream and are a delicious addition to stuffing for strong-flavored birds such as wild duck. They are best ordered in small quantities, as their oil has a

BLACK WALNUT BARGE BARS
— ❖ —

⅓ cup butter
1 ounce unsweetened
    chocolate
1 cup sugar
¾ cup all-purpose flour
½ teaspoon salt
½ teaspoon baking powder
2 eggs
1 teaspoon vanilla extract
1 cup chopped Missouri
    Dandy Black Walnuts
10 large marshmallows,
    halved

Melt the butter and chocolate together over low heat. Remove from the heat and stir in the sugar. Sift together the flour, salt, and baking powder, and add it to the chocolate mixture. Beat in the eggs, vanilla, and black walnuts. Pour the batter into a greased 11- x 7-inch pan. Bake at 350°F for 35 minutes. Remove the pan from the oven and immediately top the bars with the marshmallows. Return the pan to the oven to soften the marshmallows and make them spreadable, 3 minutes. Remove the pan from the oven and gently spread the marshmallows over the top. Cool and cut into bars.
Makes twenty-two 3½ - x 1-inch bars

tendency to turn rancid more quickly than other nuts (store in the refrigerator).

Recipe-ready, coarsely chopped shelled black walnuts come in 1-pound ($6.65, postpaid), 2-pound ($12.75), and 3-pound ($18.45) bags. Slightly larger pieces, called "Fancy Large," run just a few cents more. A crunchy, translucent Black Walnut Brittle dotted with the nuts is sold in 2-pound tins ($17.50); Missouri Dandies, a candy along the lines of Turtles, come in a 14-ounce metal gift tin ($14.75); and there are also unusual Dandy Nuggets (chocolate-covered black walnut pieces), which come in a 1-pound 2-ounce clear plastic container ($11.75). Candy prices include postage; no shipments May through September.

Nuts D'Vine Home Style Peanuts

**Nuts D'Vine
P.O. Box 589
Edenton, North Carolina
27932**

**(800) 334-0492; (919)
482-2222 (Monday to Friday,
8 A.M. to 5 P.M., EST)**

**Free 16-page color catalog
VISA, MasterCard, American
Express**

Nuts D'Vine, the mail-order branch of a 40-year-old wholesale peanut company, is run with care and a lot of personal attention. And the company's name is true to itself—not only do peanuts grow on vines, the peanuts and peanut products from this source really do taste divine. Think of Nuts D'Vine as the Rolls-Royce of peanut shippers.

North Carolina ranks third in the nation in peanut production, and its specialty is the Virginia-type peanut, a large, meaty peanut with a lower fat content and more pronounced flavor than some other types. Many people don't realize that there are grades of peanuts just as there are grades of meats. U.S. Jumbos are the biggest and best in-the-shell, while U.S. Extra Large are considered the best shelled ones. At Nuts D'Vine they're very persnickety about quality, and you'll find only these two top grades in their catalog.

Nuts D'Vine ships peanuts in every imaginable permutation. The Jumbo roasted-in-the shell ones make a fun gift because of their packaging. You can order these in an enormous 4-gallon jar ($39.95) or in a rustic half-bushel basket loaded with 10 pounds of peanuts for $19.95. If you like to roast your own peanuts (worth it for the aroma alone), there are plastic mesh sacks bursting with 5-pounds of raw in-the-shell Jumbos ($7.95).

For snacking that doesn't require shelling, there are tins of crispy, really delicious home-style peanuts prepared the traditional North Carolina way: the raw peanuts are soaked first in water, then small batches are cooked over extremely high heat in cold-pressed peanut oil. Little blisters dotting the peanuts' surface occur as the steam that builds up inside them during cooking tries to escape. Home Style Peanuts are available lightly salted or unsalted (1-pound can, $4.95, or $94.80 for a case of 24; 3½-pound can, $14.95, or $79.95 for a case of 6). And then there are the

Perpetual Peanuts: for $39 you can order a big 5-pound red can of roasted-in-the-shell Jumbos with three refills shipped at various times during the year (if it's a gift, a personalized letter will explain your generosity).

For people who believe peanut butter is the staff of life, Nuts D'Vine's Natural Old Fashioned Peanut Butter will be a connoisseur's treat. It's literally custom-made. When someone orders it, an employee grabs an empty jar and grinds fresh-roasted peanuts—no salt, no sugar, no perservatives—directly into the jar, screws on the lid, and ships it right out the same day. The peanut butter costs $3.50 per 1-pound jar (or you can order it in a red and gold gift box for $4.50).

NUTS D'VINE VIRGIN COLD PRESSED PEANUT OIL

— ❖ —

Most peanut oil is just not in the same league as the version from Nuts D'Vine. Ordinary, run-of-the-mill peanut oil is made from lower-grade peanuts and has been filtered and heated in processing, so it is flavorless and characterless. But Nuts D'Vine's Virgin Cold Pressed Peanut Oil, which has been available for only a few years, is cold-pressed from high-quality peanuts just like the finest olive oils are pressed from the finest olives. You can taste the olives in top-grade olive oils, you can taste the peanuts in Nuts D'Vine's peanut oil, which has a slightly nutty flavor and a delicate bouquet. Use it for frying chicken or in salad dressings. It contains no preservatives, additives, or chemicals. Nuts D'Vine's Virgin Cold Pressed Peanut Oil comes in 16-ounce bottles ($3.95 a bottle, or two bottles for $7, plus postage).

Another way to try the oil is to order Nuts D'Vine's Cookin' Sampler, a colorful gift box packed with a bottle of the oil, a 12-ounce bag of Extra Large water-blanched peanuts, and a recipe pamphlet ($5.95, plus shipping).

HOMEMADE PARCHED (ROASTED) PEANUTS

— ❖ —

Roasting in a Conventional Oven: Place raw peanuts, in-the-shell or shelled, 1 layer deep in a shallow baking pan. Roast in a 350°F oven 20 to 25 minutes for in-the-shell and 15 to 20 minutes for shelled. Remove just short of doneness as peanuts continue to cook as they cool.

Microwave Oven Roasting: Place 2 cups raw shelled peanuts in a 10- x 6-inch glass or other microwave container. Dot with butter or margarine. Microwave on high for 2 minutes. Stir the peanuts. Continue to microwave 2 minutes at a time followed by stirring until the peanuts have been microwaved 10 minutes for lightly roasted and 12 minutes for regular roast. Remove the peanuts from the microwave. Season to taste.

Note: Cooking time may vary with different ovens.

Nuts D'Vine's peanuts are very special indeed, but the firm's attention to detail also sets it apart. If you order a gift, the recipient will get a gift card enclosure that is *handwritten*! And the gift selection known as the Snackin' Box ($29.95) doesn't merely come in a printed carton—an assortment of peanut goodies (24 ounces of brittle, a tin of home-style peanuts, and a burlap bag of raw shelled peanuts) comes packed in a smart-looking, reusable pine box made locally by hand ("something that looks like your granddaddy sat down and made for you for Christmas," say the folks at Nuts D'Vine). Best of all, the items are nestled in a bed of *real* roasted-in-the-shell peanuts, so you can even eat the packing material!

— ❖ —

Roddenbery's Peanut Patch Green Boiled Peanuts

It has been noted on more than one occasion that boiled peanuts just may be one of the few remaining true cultural differences between Northerners and Southerners. This has the ring of truth about it. Most Northerners have never

MIXED NUTS 257

W. B. Roddenbery Co., Inc.
P.O. Box 60
Cairo, Georgia 31728
(912) 377-1431

No order form; call or write to
confirm price and shipping
charges
Prepaid orders only

heard of them, much less tasted them, and even Southerners will be the first to say that "you have to have eaten them since you were a kid."

No one is sure how or when the notion of taking freshly harvested in-the-shell green peanuts and boiling them in a stupendously salty brine first came about. In the early part of this century, little boys growing up on Georgia peanut farms used to boil them up at home and sell them in town for pin money. Former president Jimmy Carter remembers that as a six-year-old boiled-goober salesman in Plains he "was able to distinguish very clearly between the good people and the bad people of Plains. The good people . . . bought boiled peanuts from me!"

Canned boiled peanuts bear only a passing resemblance to peanuts as most people know them. The shell is still there (a somewhat sodden, salty, juice-filled version of its former self), and once it's opened you can see the kernels inside, looking gray and amorphous. Their flavor is the essence of gooberness. Each firm kernel is slightly gelatinous in texture, very moist and incredibly salty (next to a country ham, probably the saltiest thing you're likely to ever run across). They taste nutty, though not especially *peanutty*—more like a butter bean or a pea, which is in the same legume family peanuts originate from. Most people just dump them from the can into a saucepan, heat them briefly, then dip their hands into the warm brine and grab at the peanuts. After a while your fingers begin to shrivel up from shelling them, but you probably won't care.

The century-old W. B. Roddenbery Company of Cairo, Georgia, which first started selling boiled peanuts in the 1960s, produces well over a million bright yellow cans of them a year. The Roddenbery name is famous in Southeastern grocery stores for a line that includes Cane Patch Syrup, more than 60 varieties of pickles, and 4 styles of peanut butter. The company's roots go back to Dr. Seaborn Anderson Roddenbery, a horse-and-buggy country doctor who took his homemade open-kettle sugarcane syrup along with him on his rounds. Today five generations of Roddenbery's run the family-owned company, including the venerable 96-year-old "Mr. Julien," who dispensed his family's cane syrup from a miniature log cabin at the St. Louis World's Fair.

Though the Roddenbery's run a very large wholesale manufacturing operation, they understand that for the few diehards who miss them, a can of boiled peanuts is a gift from the gods. Although they don't have an official mail-order setup, they will ship cases of boiled peanuts to persevering individuals. Be warned, however, that since canned goods weigh a lot the cost of the shipping and handling will run you quite a bit more than the price of the goodies themselves. You'll pay $9.10 for a 24-can case of Peanut Patch Green Boiled Peanuts, but shipping and handling are extra and vary according to destination (count on paying around $15 per case in shipping on top of the $9.10 for the peanuts).

— ❖ —

Sherardized Pecans

Sherard Plantation
Sherard, Mississippi 38669
(800) 647-5518; (601)
627-7211 (Mississippi
residents call collect)

Free color brochure
VISA, MasterCard

The Sherard Plantation was established in 1874 when John Holmes Sherard arrived from Alabama with six mule wagons to claim a jungle area of the Mississippi Delta smack alongside the Mississippi River. Today the plantation is run by a fourth-generation Sherard, Dick Sherard IV. Pecans from the Sherard orchard—of the highest quality and nourished on the rich Delta topsoil—are treasured by customers not only for their taste but for the sense of tradition behind them. In-the-shell pecans come in a bag you won't want to miss—it's a collector's item in itself. Made of a sturdy white sizing cloth, it's splashed with bold red and blue lettering and imprinted with a scattering of big brown pecans. No one throws this bag away. Customers have written that they've turned a Sherardized Pecans bag into everything from wall hangings and dish towels to throw pillows.

Though the pecans have been grown in the groves stretching along the Mississippi since the 1890s, the shipping of nuts didn't start until the 1930s, when a Sherard began a bold marketing ploy: he offered every depot agent of the Illinois Central Railroad, which runs through the Delta, a free bag of pecans—provided the agent responded with the names of 10 interested customers who had sampled a free pecan or two from the bag. And that's the closest to advertising a Sherard pecan has ever been; the company has never run an ad, relying on word of mouth.

Today the business is run in the same family tradition of enterprise, operated in the same brick country building sitting on a bend of the road that curves to run along the river. Inside Dick Sherard IV runs the business in an office filled with antiques, family photographs, and an IBM PC. Though his enterprises now stretch from international agribusiness to a Southern fast-food chain, his heart remains close to the annual pecan shipment. "You're never in danger of getting a shipment of last year's pecans from us," he says proudly, "because there are never any left!"

The pecans are not shipped until late November, after the fall harvesting, but they'll still arrive in plenty of time for the holiday baking and cooking they're so prized for. (The Cook's Special, 1 pound of pecan halves and two 1-

Sherardized PECANS

EST. 1874

pound bags of chopped pieces, is $21, postpaid.) There are two pecan varieties to choose from. The Schley is the thinnest-skinned of pecans, a smallish, rich, oily nut that is difficult to grow. The more familiar Select is large and moist.

In-the-shell pecans, available in that great cotton bag, range from a 4½-pound bag ($15.95, postpaid) to a giant 49-pound size ($99, postpaid). All bags come with a small, handsome recipe booklet of nine pecan recipes. Both varieties of pecans are also available shelled in cello bags or reusable vinyl buckets (1-pound bag of halves is $10, postpaid; 2¼-pound bucket of large pieces runs $16, postpaid). But Sherard warns that "storage is important for shelled nuts. They should be refrigerated as soon as possible and then will keep up to nine months. Unshelled nuts can be kept in any cool, dry place for up to two months. After that they, too, should be refrigerated."

— ❖ —

Sunnyland Farms Pecans

Jane and Harry Willson
Sunnyland Farms, Inc.
P.O. Box 8200
Albany, Georgia 31706-8200
(912) 883-3085 (Monday to Friday, 8:30 A.M. to 5 P.M., EST; also evenings and weekends in November and December)

Free 36-page color catalog
VISA, MasterCard ($30 minimum on credit card orders)

Sunnyland Farms' catalog of pecans and other nuts is one of the most down-to-earth and delightfully browsable to hit my mailbox. Unlike many catalogs that have been slicked up to resemble gourmet food magazines (with sunlight glinting off the cornbread!), Sunnyland still preserves an old Sears, Roebuck catalog feeling—big, floppy pages crammed to their very edges with bright color photographs and ordering choices. There are running photo essays on past and present pecan-growing seasons at Sunnyland and chatty news not only about owners Jane and Harry Willson, their family, and employees (more than half have worked at Sunnyland 10 or more years), but about longtime customers, too (Gene Autry has been ordering

from Sunnyland for years).

My favorite way to order pecans from Sunnyland is in-the-shell; however the Willsons ship both the smallish, thin-shelled Schleys and the bigger, thicker-shelled Stuarts in an almost inexhaustible number of ways: toasted or natural, salted or not, in or out of the shell, gift or plain packaged. For example: a 2-pound 1-ounce gift tin of shelled Extra-Fancy Mammoth Halves ($18.75); a 3-pound plain box of in-the-shell Schleys ($15.15); and a 10-pound plain box packed with natural, untoasted halves—between 200 and 250 halves per pound ($57.40; they'll stay fresh for months in the freezer). Note that due to state laws, in-the-shell pecans cannot be shipped to California or Arizona.

People who like to bake will be thrilled that the Willsons devote two catalog pages to economically priced pecan selections in plain boxes, in-

"BEST EVER" PECAN PIE

— ❖ —

1 cup sugar
1 teaspoon ground
   cinnamon
1 teaspoon ground cloves
2 eggs, separated
½ cup large Sunnyland
   Farms pecan pieces
½ cup seedless raisins
4 tablespoons (½ stick)
   butter, melted
2 tablespoons vinegar
1 8-inch pastry shell,
   unbaked
Unsweetened whipped
   cream

Mix together the sugar, cinnamon, and cloves. Beat the egg yolks and add them to the sugar mixture. Then, add the pecans, raisins, and butter, and stir to blend. Beat the egg whites until stiff. Fold them gently into the mixture (do not beat), adding the vinegar as you fold. Pour the batter into the pastry shell and bake at 400°F for 10 minutes. Reduce the oven temperature to 350°F and bake for 25 minutes more. Cool and serve with unsweetened whipped cream.

Makes one 8-inch pie

cluding broken pecan meats. A 3-pound 4-ounce "home box" of Extra-Fancy small pieces (just right for granola or salads) costs $20.70. Pecan meal, ground so fine it looks sort of like buckwheat flour, costs $14.20 for 5 pounds (use this in bread recipes or piecrusts).

Sunnyland's authenticity stems from the fact that it is one of the oldest mail-order purveyors of pecans around. Harry Willson inherited his pecan groves in Pecan City, Georgia, and the mail-order business began in 1948 when Jane's Wellesley College alumni group asked if the couple could provide pecans for a fund-raising effort. It set the Willsons off into a business that has doubled again and again. Jane is still in charge of the mail-order division, their son Larry runs the pecan-growing side of things, his wife, Beverly, oversees the catalog, and Harry does "whatever's left over."

Also included in the catalog are candies (pecan brittle and bark, chocolate clusters, etc.) and cakes made from recipes developed at Sunnyland. Catalog prices are postpaid.

— ❖ —

Tracy Deluxe Hand-Packed Cellos

Fran's Pecans
110 North Hicks Street
P.O. Box 188
Harlem, Georgia 30814

(800) 476-6887; (404) 556-9172 (Monday to Friday, 8:30 A.M. to 5:30 P.M., EST)

Free color brochure
VISA, MasterCard

For the most gorgeously packed gift of top-grade nuts imaginable, Fran's Pecans win hands down. They're so beautiful you feel almost guilty destroying their exquisite hand-packed symmetry. Perfectly formed, premium-quality pecan halves without the tiniest nick or chip are arranged by hand in circular patterns inside round, see-through cellophane containers. Each box, truly an object of beauty, is elegantly decorated with a red and green tartan ribbon. The dexterous arrangement of the nuts approaches folk art, right up there in a league with fine needlework. Every November and December, when the Thanksgiving and Christmas gift-giving season heats up, women from the area devote themselves to this delicate work.

Fran's Pecans is the gift division of an old-line commercial pecan processor. The parent company was founded in a home garage during the peak of the Depression by the late Arthur and Ruth Tracy and their son, Frank, who still runs things. Back in the early 1970s, it was Fran, Frank's daughter, who came up with the idea of launching a separate gift line of the family's pecans.

The hand-packed "cellos" (short for cellophanes) were a special gift idea in response to a customer's appeal for "a fine, all-natural gift." Because they are so special-looking, the Deluxe Cellos are a very hot gift item in corporate circles as well as among individual customers. They contain only top-grade Select pecans and come in three sizes: 1 pound, $18.50, postpaid; 2 pounds, $24.50; and 3 pounds, $29.50. Cellos are available November and December only, although orders may be placed in advance.

Year round, Fran's plump, golden pecan halves, natural ($17.95) or roasted and salted ($18.95), are shipped postpaid in 2-pound gift tins or simple attractive bright red boxes (natural, $15.95; roasted and salted, $16.95). In less-fancy bags shipped year round, you can order plain (for cooking) or roasted and salted (for nibbling) Mammoth Halves in any assortment: a pair of 1-pound bags costs $14.95, postpaid; three bags cost around $19.50, postpaid.

Fran's Pecans are guaranteed to arrive in peak condition. Leslie Lambert, who runs the day to day operation of Fran's Pecans, likes to say, "Our pecans are so fresh, we practically ship them before they're harvested."

Virginia Diner Peanuts

Virginia Diner
P.O. Box 310
Wakefield, Virginia
23888-0310

(800) 642-NUTS (7 days a week, 9 A.M. to 5 P.M., EST)
Fax (804) 899-2281

Free 12-page color catalog
VISA, MasterCard

I would definitely advise any peanut fiend who doesn't know about Virginia Diner peanuts to rush an order immediately to "the Peanut Capital of the World." One taste will make you a customer for life.

Since 1929 the Virginia Diner, situated on U.S. 460 in the tiny hamlet of Wakefield, has served up classic Southern fare like new-cured Virginia ham, crispy fried chicken, freshly baked peanut pies, and banana pudding to hungry travelers. You can hardly get near the place during peak summer tourist season (many make a special trip just for the food). Right next to the cash register is a bowl filled with samples of the diner's famous water-blanched Virginia-style, top-grade peanuts, and nearby, the diner's gift shop is bursting with cans of the nuts along with "peanutwear" fashion statements bearing the diner's emblem (a peanut in overalls), and the slogan "The World's No. 1 Nut." Out back, in the minimally mechanized cookery, peanuts are

THE ADULTS-ONLY
PEANUT BUTTER LOVERS FAN CLUB
— ❖ —

It's true. Even though the average child who graduates from high school will have eaten 1,500 peanut butter and jelly sandwiches, adults are the greatest consumers of peanut butter, especially in the South. Several years ago the Peanut Advisory Board, a promotional group made up of Georgia, Florida, and Alabama peanut-grower organizations, established the Peanut Butter Lovers Fan Club. They had envisioned it as a fun thing for kids, but when it turned out that more adults than children joined, the name was changed to include adults. Today the club has more than 60,000 grown-up participants. For a $3 membership fee, you'll receive a membership card, recipe booklet, refrigerator magnet, a "Peanut Butter Lover On Board" bumper sticker, and a year's subscription to *Spread the News!*, the official quarterly newsletter. To join, write: Distribution Center, Adults-Only Peanut Butter Lovers Fan Club, P.O. Box 7528, Tifton, Georgia 31793.

hand-cooked in vegetable oil by strong-armed experts who don't need a timer—they "just know" when it's time to flip a basket of peanuts out of a huge vat onto a table for light salting.

These peanuts are a rich, golden color, very brittle, with tiny blisters on the surface—definitely peanuts of a higher order. Their flavor is unmatched for pure nuttiness, and the very essence of peanut taste emerges as you bite through one. The blisters come from a special water-blanching process in which the peanuts are soaked in artesian-well water. "You have to have good water," says owner Bill Galloway, who feels this is the real difference between his peanuts and anybody else's. It's this soaking that allows the "secret oil blend" they're cooked in to provide flavor without creeping into the peanut and interfering with its natural good taste.

The Virginia Diner's proud claim.

Try the Virginia Diner's sensational crispy peanuts with the Gourmet Peanut Trio, which includes a huge 2½-pound can of lightly salted peanuts, a 1½-pound can of unsalted ones, and a 1½-pound can of Butter Toasted Peanuts ($21.15). The Butter-Toasted peanuts (each nut encased in an incredible crunchy sugar-butter coating) are so good there should probably be a law against them. Unless noted otherwise, the nuts are vacuum-packed in plug-lid cans with a foil lining. Once opened, the nuts should be stored in the freezer (best eaten directly from there, or you can warm them in the oven for a few minutes). Individual cans of each style peanut are also available (1½-pound can, salted or unsalted, $6.40; 2½-pound can, $8.45; Butter-Toasted in same sizes, $6.80 and $8.75). Cans with a cheery Christmas label are available during the holiday season at the same prices. A plain old 1-pound cellophane bag of nuts runs $3.20. For those who like to roast their own, the diner offers shelled or unshelled raw peanuts in burlap or cloth bags (5-pound burlap bag, red skin, shelled, $8.70; 2-pound cloth bag, in shell, $4.25). Roasted-in-the-shell Virginia Diner peanuts (salted or unsalted) would make a very splashy-looking present because they're packed in old-fashioned wooden bushel- or peck-size baskets (bushel, $34.95; peck, $10.95).

Also in the catalog: Virginia Diner Gourmet Peanut Oil in tall wine bottles with a peanut in the bottom of each (a pair of 13-ounce bottles, $7.95), an old-fashioned bright red gumball machine shipped with 2½ pounds of the peanuts of your choice ($29.95), and bright gold T-shirts with the peanut logo (kids' sizes, $5.95; adult sizes, $7.95). Shipping charges for all items are based on the dollar total of your order (for example, east of the Mississippi, $20–35 order, $4; west of the Mississippi, $6.50).

VISITING THE SOURCE

— ❖ —

The Virginia Diner is located on Highway 460, between Richmond and Virginia Beach, a short distance from Richmond, Petersburg, and Hampton Roads. It is open seven days a week, from 6 A.M. to 8 P.M., and serves everything from peanut-shaped peanut butter and jelly sandwiches to old-fashioned Virginia ham country dinners topped off with a slice of freshly baked peanut pie (see page 357). The diner's famous peanuts are sold at the gift shop along with a variety of silly peanut-logo souvenirs.

— ❖ —

Williamsburg Home Style Peanuts

The Peanut Shop of Williamsburg
P.O. Box GN
Williamsburg, Virginia 23187
(804) 253-0060

Free brochure
VISA, MasterCard

The Peanut Shop of Williamsburg is a tiny, charming, brick shop tucked between Duke of Gloucester and Prince George streets on Merchants Square in Colonial Williamsburg. Festooned at one end with a hanging rack of Smithfield hams and barrels filled with packages of slab bacon for sale, the little shop actually does its biggest business in Virginia extra-large Jumbo peanuts. The shop's managers say they follow the tradition of Colonial Virginians, who slowly roasted small quantities in their ovens to produce an evenly toasty taste. Still not mass-produced today, Williamsburg Home Style Peanuts are cooked in peanut oil in small batches daily and quickly shipped out to customers.

The plump, wonderfully crunchy peanuts (salted or unsalted) are shipped in attractive beige-wrapped tins decorated in flowery script. Prices include shipping, unless you live west of the Mississippi, in which case there is an additional $1 per item shipping charge. Sizes range from a 1-pound 6-ounce tin for $9.95, to a 2½-pound tin for $12.95, to a duo package of two 1-pound 6-ounce tins for $16.95. A 5-pound bag of raw (uncooked) peanuts accompanied by do-it-yourself recipes costs $11.95, or you can get a

2-pound burlap bag of roasted-in-the-shell "ballpark type" peanuts for $7.95.

The creamy, preservative- and additive-free Williamsburg Peanut Butter is rated excellent by peanut butter fans. Like the peanuts, it comes either salted or salt-free, and three 18-ounce jars cost $12.95. Slather it on a slice of Wonder Bread, top with a layer of sliced bananas, and you've got an old Southern standard to munch on. (This was one of Elvis Presley's favorite snacks.) Also available are jars of Williamsburg Peanut Soup (three 15-ounce jars, $9.95). A thick, creamy, traditional soup made from peanut butter and chicken broth with a bit of extra flavoring from onions, this is a house specialty in many Virginia inns. But be warned, it sounds a bit more interesting than it tastes unless you're a true peanut fan. If you do try it, don't forget to sprinkle a few ground roasted peanuts on top as a garnish.

DIXIE PEANUT BRITTLE
— ❖ —

2 cups sugar
1 cup light corn syrup
½ cup water
½ teaspoon salt
4 cups raw shelled peanuts, skins on
2 tablespoons butter or margarine
2 teaspoons baking soda

Heat the sugar, syrup, water, and salt to a rolling boil in a heavy saucepan. Add the peanuts. Reduce the heat to medium and cook, stirring constantly, until the syrup reaches 293°F on a candy thermometer or spins a thread. Stir in the butter. Add the baking soda and beat rapidly. Pour out the syrup onto a buttered surface (baking sheet, marble slab, or large casserole dish), spreading it to approximately ¼ inch thick. When cool, break the brittle into pieces and store in an airtight container. *Makes 2½ pounds*

RICE AND BEANS

"People who were raised on this basic food develop a craving for it that persists no matter to what dizzying heights they rise in business and commerce. All the way from South America to the Mason-Dixon line, variations of rice and beans are a way of life."

—Miriam Ungerer

Rice and beans are mainstay ingredients for some of the South's tastiest specialties such as the curried chicken dish known as country captain; the Carolina favorite, purloo; and that Monday night Louisiana supper tradition, red beans and rice. The South has long been a major rice growing region and today rice fields still ripple in the breeze across parts of Arkansas, Texas, and Louisiana. On the following pages, you'll discover some intriguing, little-known strains of rice such as an aromatic, popcorn-like one grown by Ellis Stansel in Louisiana as well as a source for the best red beans.

Rice

Della Gourmet White Rice and Organic Brown Rice

Southern Rice Marketing
P.O. Box 880
Brinkley, Arkansas 72021
(501) 734-1233

Free order form
Prepaid orders only

It takes a special combination of climate and terrain to grow top-quality rice in America. That's why it's grown in only a handful of states, including Louisiana, Alabama, Mississippi, and Texas, and in the fertile soil of Arkansas, where this delectable rice comes from.

Arkansas native Lehman Fowler, who established Southern Rice Marketing in the early 1980s, has been involved in one way or another in the rice business for 40 years, and his company is the fulfillment of a lifelong dream. Fowler's long-grain rice is a basmati-type hybrid called Della. In his highly informative book *The Grains Cookbook*, Bert Greene described Della as the "daddy of all scented U.S. varieties." It's in a small category of very special American aromatic rices based on a variety originating in Indochina and first introduced into this country at the beginning of the century. The Della strain and other aromatics (including Ellis Stansel's Rice and Konriko Wild Pecan Rice, also described in this section) were developed after many years of experimentation by Southern farmers and the U.S. Department of Agriculture's Rice Experiment Stations. Believe me, it was worth the wait.

Della Gourmet White Rice is sort of the best of two worlds because it combines the characteristics of conventional American long-grain rice with Asian basmati. Della cooks up into distinct, fluffy separate grains with a smooth, even texture. And both the cooking aroma and the taste are kind of milky and subtly nutty. The flavor also has a rich undertone of the most fragrant

AN EXQUISITE GRAIN

popcorn. Sound intriguing and good? Well, it truly is, so if you always thought of rice as bland, you're in for a very happy surprise.

Della Gourmet Organic Brown Rice, a Della strain grown in the Arkansas River Valley area without chemical pesticides or weird fertilizers, is also available. A nice golden-tan color, it has the same pleasing nutty flavor. Only the hull has been removed in milling, so you get all the benefits of the bran's high-fiber content.

Both types of Della Gourmet Rice are pretty hard to get your hands on unless you live in Arkansas, but you can order them by the case in smart-looking cloth bags (nice for gifts) or in paper boxes or bags. Prices are the same for both rices; shipping and handling are extra and you may order small quantities or by the case. A case of fifteen 2-pound cloth bags costs $26.80 (or $1.79 per bag). A case of twelve 14-ounce boxes costs $15.10 ($1.26 per box); a case of fifteen 2-pound paper bags, $23.30 ($1.55 per bag).

COMPANY RICE CUSTARD
— ❖ —

½ cup Della Gourmet
　Rice
1 quart milk
4 tablespoons (½ stick)
　butter
3 eggs
¾ cup sugar
1 teaspoon vanilla extract
¼ teaspoon salt
½ teaspoon ground
　nutmeg

Cook the rice in 2 cups of the milk in the top of a double boiler placed over simmering water. When the rice is tender, add the butter. Beat the eggs, sugar, vanilla, salt, and the remaining 2 cups milk together. Add the hot rice mixture and stir well. Pour the custard into a greased 2-quart casserole. Sprinkle with the nutmeg. Bake in a 350°F oven for 50 minutes.

Serves 6

•:•

Ellis Stansel's Rice

Ellis Stansel
P.O. Box 206
Gueydan, Louisiana 70542
(318) 536-6140

No order form; call Ellis or Melinda to find out postpaid prices
Invoice accompanies shipment (it's called the honor system); payment by check or money order

E llis Stansel likes to describe himself as "a crazy old rice farmer in South Louisiana," and I sure wouldn't want to be the one to disagree. You see, one of the joys of mail-ordering Southern food specialties is that some company owners are such flat-out colorful characters that simply talking with them and placing an order is half the fun. I'd have to say that even if Ellis Stansel were selling quart jars of mud for outrageous sums I'd get a kick out of doing business with him. Luckily Ellis, a second-generation rice farmer, happens to grow and sell an absolutely superb-tasting special rice that ought to be a staple in every household. It's a long-grain, hybrid strain with the smell and flavor of popping-corn.

If you were to visit Ellis's two-story house you'd find the structure looming gently above a sea of rice fields stretching almost as far as the eye can see. For most of his 77 years Ellis grew "conventional" rice on 1,250 acres of Louisiana's lowlands, but he always planted some "special" rice for family use. Back in the 1920s, Bert, Ellis's father, had been among the first local farmers to plant a special hybrid strain of rice from seed offered by the U.S. Department of Agriculture Experiment Station in nearby Crowley. The experimental rice took many years to perfect, but in the end elaborate hybridization resulted in a rice so reminiscent of popped corn that locally it became known as "popcorn rice."

Twenty years ago, when the incorrigible Ellis "retired" from farming, he decided to concentrate exclusively on the "special" rice, which he grows today on 179 acres. The yearly crop is a modest 25,000 pounds or so.

Ellis's order-filling is the epitome of personal service. There is no catalog or price list because he *wants* you to have to give him a call so he

I do not have a Catalogue or any printed material, just the best rice -

Sincerely
Ellis Stansel

can get to know you. Still, if you're compelled to write for postpaid prices, you'll get back a hand-written postcard. And I'm here to tell you Ellis has got the prettiest handwriting you've seen in many a year. Orders are filled from the backyard "rice house"—a concrete garage that serves as a refrigerated warehouse—where his daughter-in-law Melinda bags and wraps the day's orders (never shipped later than the day after they're placed).

From the minute you receive the hand-addressed box that arrives via parcel post—Ellis enjoys going to the post office, you see, because it's a livelier spot than UPS—you're in for a treat. As you rip open the package, the aroma of freshly popped corn is released. Inside, the rice sits in plump, old-fashioned white cloth bags with blue lettering. The 10-pound bag is the best

CALAS TOUT CHAUD
(SPICY DEEP-FRIED RICE BALLS)
— ❖ —

⅔ cup long-grain rice
1½ cups boiling water
1½ cups all-purpose flour
1½ teaspoons baking
  powder
1 teaspoon ground
  cinnamon
½ teaspoon ground
  nutmeg
2 eggs
1½ tablespoons sugar
½ teaspoon vanilla extract
Oil for frying
Confectioners' sugar
Maple or other syrup, or
  honey

Cook the rice in boiling water according to the manufacturer's directions. Drain if necessary, and cool to room temperature. Mix together the flour, baking powder, cinnamon, and nut-meg. Beat the eggs in a separate bowl; beat in the sugar, then the vanilla. Stir the rice into the egg mixture. Gradually stir in the flour mixture. Make 12 small rice balls by wetting your hands and forming them by squeezing and shaping the mixture. Fry them in deep fat at 350°F until golden and crunchy. Sprinkle with confectioners' sugar. Serve with syrup.

Makes 12 balls

bet for a first-time order; it costs $8, plus parcel post and 50 cents handling (to Omaha, for instance, the shipping would run around $5.90). As you'll see, the more you order, the less costly the shipping charges. Two-pound bags are sold only in larger quantities starting with a minimum of 10 bags ($22.50 for 10; shipping to Omaha would be an additional $7.99). I'll just point out that the 2-pound bags make terrific gifts, so the only problem you might have is deciding who you are *not* going to share them with. Five-pound bags are shipped only by the 12-bag case ($54, plus around $12.09 shipping). Ellis recommends storing rice in the refrigerator or freezer (frozen, it'll keep up to two years at *least*); no need to defrost or return to room temperature before cooking.

No cooking instructions are on the bags; cook as you would any long-grain rice using two cups water to one cup rice. It's almost a crime to put anything, even butter, on this rice. The rice stands alone, unusual and full of character. Like Ellis Stansel.

Konriko Wild Pecan Rice

Konriko Company Store
P.O. Box 10640
New Iberia, Louisiana
70562-0640

(800) 551-3245 (Monday to Saturday, 9 A.M. to 5 P.M., CST)

Free color catalog
VISA, MasterCard, American Express

The heart of southern Lousiana Cajun country, around New Iberia, is the home of some of Louisiana's most famous products, including Tabasco sauce, Trappey's Red Devil Louisiana Hot Sauce, and Konriko Wild Pecan Rice. The Conrad Rice Mill, near the banks of Bayou Teche, is America's oldest operating rice mill (it's even on the National Register of Historic Places). The specialty here is a remarkably flavorful long-grain rice with the nutty aroma and flavor of wild pecans.

Louisiana is one of a handful of states with the special combination of climate and terrain needed to produce top quality rice. As far back

as 1912, P. A. Conrad was growing rice in the moist soil of Iberia Parish, hand-cutting it, and setting it out to dry in the sun on the levees. But until Conrad opened his own mill, the sacks of rice were taken by boat all the way to New Orleans for milling. By the 1950s Conrad had developed the Konriko trademark (from KONrad RIce KOmpany) and was selling small sacks of rice to consumers. However, in the years following P. A.'s retirement, the mill became increasingly inactive, and by the time young Mike Davis, a former teacher and farmer, bought the mill in 1975, it had been idle for several years.

Mike Davis has turned the once sleepy Conrad Rice Mill into a thriving specialty-rice business. The most unique offering is called Wild Pecan Rice, a long-grain rice that contains neither wild rice (which is actually a grass seed) nor pecans, but which gives off a unique aroma while cooking and has a subtle pecan-like flavor. (Because it's incredibly tasty even without butter or additional flavorings, it's a civilized diet food!) Davis chose the name because the flavor "just reminded me of the small native pecans of Iberia Parish." The rice, a botanical hybrid developed during experiments at Louisiana State University, is the result of crossbreeding Louisiana long-grain rice with several species of aromatic rices imported from Indochina.

Conrad's original "slow and gentle" three-step milling process (it keeps the rice cool, which results in fewer broken grains) is still used. And since only about 10 percent of the bran layers are removed during milling, the rice's cooking time of around 20 minutes is somewhat shorter than usual. Grains stay nicely fluffy and separate.

The 7-ounce boxes of Wild Pecan Rice are readily available in many grocery stores, but fans who indulge regularly can order it postpaid direct from the source in larger quantities (a case of twelve 7-ounce boxes, $24.75; a 2-pound burlap sack, $9.50; or a 10-pound burlap sack, $25). Other Konriko products available from the catalog include 5-pound bags of excellent long- or medium-grain white rice (usually sold only in stores along the Gulf Coast; $8.75 and $8.25), cases of Hot 'N Spicy Creole Seasoning "to put on everything but dessert" (twelve 8-ounce cans, $25.95), cases of Original Brown Rice Cakes (twelve 5¼-ounce packages, $21.35), and a line of specialty mixes for dishes like gumbo and jamba-

ARKANSAS RICE FESTIVAL
WEINER, ARKANSAS
— ❖ —

Arkansas is rice country, and there are some West Poinsett County women who've been doing everything in their power since 1975 to make sure you don't forget it. "We didn't want the recipes to get away from us," say the volunteers, who began this festival as a get-together aimed at preserving and celebrating old farm recipes, especially those using rice, the area's main crop. Tiny Weiner, an old German settlement and farming community in northeastern Arkansas, now hosts up to 20,000 visitors annually. The festival highlight is the Rice Tasting Center, where there are free tastes of over 500 rice dishes prepared by the farm women of West Poinsett County using family recipes. The beauty pageant presents an array of local beauties, culminating in the selection of Miss Arkansas Rice Festival, and there's the Riceland Foods Riceriffic Rice Cook-Off recipe contest sponsored by a local grower. The two-day celebration also includes a parade, nonstop live music, a rice-sack sewing contest, demonstrations of the latest advances in rice farming, a rice-eating contest, and a harvest service of thanks. The festival is held the second weekend of October, after the harvest. For information, call or write Weiner City Hall, Weiner, Arkansas 72479; phone (501) 684-2284.

laya (around $30 per case of 12). There is a minimum of $15 on all orders. Mike Davis loves to promote tourism, so the entire back of his catalog highlights things to do and see in the Iberia Parish area.

VISITING THE SOURCE
— ❖ —

The Conrad Rice Mill and the adjacent Konriko Company Store are located at 307 Ann Street. Tours of the mill, which include a short film and a brief introduction to Cajun culture, are conducted every hour Monday through Friday, from 10 A.M. to 3 P.M. ($2.75 charge for adults, $2.25 for senior citizens, $1.25 for children under 12; group rates available). The Company Store, a cheery pale yellow wooden building, was built in 1971, and its design is based on the company stores once located on sugarcane plantations. Inside it's crammed with Konriko's own products as well as a wide variety of Acadian food specialties and handicrafts.

Beans

Camellia Brand
Red Kidney Beans

A not-to-be-denied, deep-from-the-pit-of-your-stomach-and-the-depths-of-your-soul craving for a specific thing to eat is an irresistible and inexplicable force. When it hits, nothing else on earth will do. That's how I feel about red beans and rice. Jazz musician Louis Armstrong had some pretty strong feelings about it too—he used to sign his letters "Red beans and ricely yours." As a young musician Armstrong gobbled up plates of red beans and rice prepared by Buster Holmes, who operated out of a wagon on New Orleans's Congo Square

Gazin's
P.O. Box 19221
New Orleans, Louisiana
70179-0221

(800) 262-6410; (504)
482-0302 (Monday to Friday,
9:30 A.M. to 4:30 P.M., CST)

34-page color catalog, $1
(applied to first order)
VISA, MasterCard, American
Express

(jazz bands played this spot). Much later Buster opened a bustling joint in the heart of the French Quarter, and his way with this traditional dish became even more famous. The cafe is closed now, but when it was still hopping, Jane and Michael Stern, the authors of *Roadfood* and other guides to simple, good eating, pronounced Buster's beans "legumes transcendent."

In New Orleans and other parts of Louisiana, red beans and rice is a traditional Monday meal that harks back to the days when Monday was washday. Too busy to fuss much over the Monday evening meal, women often just took the ham bone left over from Sunday's dinner, threw it in a big pot with beans and seasonings such as thyme and garlic, and let them slowly simmer all day on the back burner until the wash had dried and the beans had grown rich and creamy. Ladled over a fluffy mound of rice, the beans made a cheap, nutritious meal. Today you'll still find this dish on the Monday menus of most Louisiana restaurants.

While it's true you could use pretty much any red kidney beans, the brand sold in every Louisiana grocery store is Camellia, from L. H. Hayward & Company, a family-owned firm in business since 1923 that sells more than seven million pounds of U.S. #1 Grade beans annually. Camellia beans, with their bright red camellia logo, still come in old-fashioned cellophane packages rather than the usual plastic sacks because, they say, this keeps the beans fresher longer. The Haywards do not ship to individuals, but their beans can be ordered through Gazin's, a mail-order specialist in Creole and Cajun foods. Gazin's sells the beans two ways. Featured in their catalog is a red beans and rice "package" that includes a 2-pound bag of Camellia beans, a 7-ounce bag of Konriko long-grain rice, a 7-ounce "Smokey Jo" sausage, along with a recipe for rice and beans ($8.95, plus shipping). Not always mentioned in the catalog is the fact that Gazin's will also ship a case of twelve 2-pound packages of the beans for around $22.40, plus shipping, which is very good news indeed.

A CULINARY PAMPHLET ON RICE AND BEANS
— ❖ —

"Few dishes offer so much for so little, and fewer yet have wended their way through our culinary history to the present remaining so redolent of their heritage, so aware of their origins."

—John Thorne

Rice and beans join each other in a felicitous union of taste in almost endless variation across many cultures and times. For a fascinating look at this combination, from the red beans and rice of New Orleans to the black beans and rice of Cuba, I recommend that you order yourself a copy of *Rice & Beans: The Itinerary of a Recipe*, a 24-page booklet written by John Thorne. Thorne's lyrical and opinionated writing about food (he also wrote a book called *Simple Cooking*) is a joy to read, always informative and larded with historical background and recipes that help cooks (and even the merely curious) get to the heart and soul of a dish. So if you want to get some insight into how to pickle pork like they do in New Orleans (some folks prefer it to a cracked ham bone for red beans), or gain a little insight into things like butterbeans and South Carolina Hopping John, and the real truth behind soaking beans, this'll tell you. The pamphlet costs only $3, postpaid, from: The Jackdaw Press, P.O. Box 58, Castine, Maine 04421.

Ledford's Borrowed Beans

**Ledford Mill and Museum
Rural Route 2, Box 152
Wartrace, Tennessee 37183
(615) 455-1935 or 455-2546**

**Free 7-page color catalog
VISA, MasterCard, American
Express**

In Tennessee, as in other parts of the country, when times were tough—during the Great Depression, for instance—families often survived on soup. A hearty, nourishing bean soup could always be counted on to fill the aching void in hungry stomachs. But sometimes households ran short of even these simple, inexpensive makings. Maybe mother had only a handful of dried kidney beans or cowpeas. So she'd go around to the neighbors, borrowing a cup of beans here and there until she had enough beans and peas to fill the pot. The warm and wonderful supper dish she then made was known as borrowed bean soup.

The historic Ledford Mill in Moore County, Tennessee (see page 209), sells more than stone-ground cornmeal and old-fashioned grits. From them you can order calico bags of borrowed beans (two 1-pound sacks, $8.25, postpaid). Each sack contains a colorful mixture of 12 kinds of beans plus barley. You won't have to run around the neighborhood knocking on doors with a cup in your hand, but you will have to wash and soak the beans before adding a few touches of your own (like whatever is hanging around in the vegetable bin) for a little extra flavor. While the beans are simmering, make up a nice batch of cornsticks. Then dish up, dig in, and enjoy.

THE SMOKEHOUSE

• Mrs. Fearnow's Delicious Brunswick Stew • Fuller's Mustard • Maunsel White's
• Panola Pepper Sauce • Amber Brand Smithfield Ham • Billy Higdon's Happy Hol
ry Hams • Colonel Bill Newsom's Kentucky Country Hams • Bucksnort Smoked Rai
• Callaway Gardens Speckled Heart Grits • White Lily Flour • Bailey's Homemade
r Jelly   Sherardiz... ...nsel's Rice • Garbe
Yams • Warrento... ...singer's Flying Pig
n Arrow Ranch Ax... ...ory-Smoked Sausag
• Golden Mill So... ...ms Sweet Vidalia Or
f Luck Scottish S... ...ker Deluxe Moon Pie
Kitchen Derby Pi... ...otato Chips • Charl
Rendezvous Ribs... ...Barq's Root Beer •
vine • Crickle • E... ...ens Cut Leaf Poke S
• Mrs. Fearnow'... ...• Maunsel White's
• Panola Pepper... ...Higdon's Happy Holl
ry Hams • Colone... ...ksnort Smoked Rain
• Garber Farms Cajun Yams • Bland Farms Sweet Vidalia Onions • Callaway Garde
ed Heart Grits • White Lily Flour • Bailey's Homemade Hot Pepper Jelly • Mayhaw
dized Pecans • Virginia Diner Peanuts • Ellis Stansel's Rice • Ledford Mill Borrowe
en Arrow Ranch Axis Venison • Comeaux's Boudin • Mayo's Hickory-Smoked Sausa
• Golden Mill Sorghum • Steen's Pure Cane Syrup • Best of Luck Scottish Shortbr
hoes and Nails • Double Decker Deluxe Moon Pies • Kern's Kitchen Derby Pie • Li
Orchard Cake • Warrenton Original Nashville Rum Cakes • Zapp's Potato Chips •
Rendezvous Ribs • Maurice Bessinger's Flying Pig Barbeque • Barq's Root Beer •
vine • Crickle • Evelyn's Pralines • Goo Goo Clusters • The Allens Cut Leaf Poke S.
• Mrs. Fearnow's Delicious Brunswick Stew • Fuller's Mustard • Maunsel White's
• Panola Pepper Sauce • Amber Brand Smithfield Ham • Billy Higdon's Happy Holl
y Hams • Colonel Bill Newsom's Kentucky Country Hams • Bucksnort Smoked Rain
Garber Farms Cajun Yams • Bland Farms Sweet Vidalia Onions • Callaway Garde
ed Heart Grits • White Lily Flour • Bailey's Homemade Hot Pepper Jelly • Mayhaw
dized Pecans • Virginia Diner Peanuts • Ellis Stansel's Rice • Ledford Mill Borrowe
en Arrow Ranch Axis Venison • Comeaux's Boudin • Mayo's Hickory-Smoked Sausa
• Golden Mill Sorghum • Steen's Pure Cane Syrup • Best of Luck Scottish Shortbr

"In the morning they rose in a house pungent with breakfast cookery, and they sat at a smoking table loaded with . . . eggs, ham, hot biscuit, fried apples seething in their gummed syrups, honey, golden butter, fried steak, scalding coffee. Or there were stacked batter-cakes, rum-colored molasses, fragrant brown sausages, a bowl of wet cherries, plums, fat juicy bacon, jam."

—Thomas Wolfe
Look Homeward, Angel

The cornerstone of old-time Southern cookery was a supply of home-cured, slowly smoked country meats. The smokehouse supply of sausage, hams, and slabs of bacon was a delicious promise of plenty, a hedge against hunger and hard times in the days before refrigeration. The crisp, cold weather kicked off not only the annual hog butchering, but hunting season as well. Hound and hunter set off in quest of squirrel or rabbit for the burgoo pot, and quail to pan-fry as a crispy breakfast treat. Even in these modern times, there is a security that can't be denied when you have a nice big slab of Early's hickory-smoked bacon on hand, or a poke (slender cotton bag) of Mayo's ambrosial country sausage for a city/ country breakfast.

Bates Hickory-Smoked Fully Cooked Turkey

**Bates Turkey Farm
Route 1, Box 138
Fort Deposit, Alabama 36032**
**(205) 227-4505 or 227-4386
(Monday to Friday, 8 A.M. to
5 P.M., CST)**

**Free color brochure
VISA, MasterCard**

Bill Bates with an unsmoked turkey.

If you've driven through Alabama, chances are you've eaten at one of the three Bates House of Turkey restaurants, where—what else?—a turkey-only menu is featured that includes everything from an old-fashioned roast turkey dinner served with two veggies and Teresa Bates's cornbread dressing to simple, home-style roast turkey sandwiches. Every morsel of turkey served comes from the Bateses' farm and at each restaurant plain and smoked turkeys are sold to take back home (but only smoked ones are available by mail order).

Bill Bates first began smoking turkeys in the 1960s, giving them as Christmas gifts to his commercial customers. When people began trying to order them, he began selling a few at the farm's retail shop. Smoked turkey was something of a novelty in those days, but soon the Bateses were serving turkey sandwiches, and that inspired their first restaurant in the late 1960s.

A Bates Hickory-Smoked Fully Cooked Turkey has integrity. Sweet and full-flavored, the meat's subtle smokiness comes from curing in a secret mixture of spices and herbs and 8 to 12 hours smoking over a combination of green hickory and pecan wood from trees located right on the farm. A purist, Bill is adamant about not using liquid smoke or preservatives and in recent years has cut back on salt as much as is feasible. The birds are "grown natural, as nature intended," which means they wander around in stress-free surroundings under the shade of pecan trees and dine on a mixture of corn, soybeans, oats, and vitamins (no growth hormones, no antibiotics, no feed additives). Although the turkeys are shipped frozen, this does not seem to affect their good taste or texture.

Fully cooked, ready-to-eat smoked turkeys are shipped frozen directly from the farm via UPS and prices noted here include delivery to most

Bates' birds arrive in a neat-looking treasure chest.

states. West Coast shipments are sent only via air at an additional $12 charge. Shipments are made only on Monday, Tuesday, and Wednesday. A full-breasted, medium-size whole turkey weighing 8 to 9½ pounds costs $31; a slightly larger one weighing 10 to 12 pounds costs $33.50; or for $37.50 you can order a 6-to-8-pound smoked turkey breast. The birds are shipped in Styrofoam "treasure chests" that can do duty later as a child's toy chest. The meat is best savored in wafer-thin slices and tastes nice cold or heated. Once thawed, carefully wrapped meat can be kept in the refrigerator for as long as two weeks.

Bill's father started the farm more than 60 years ago when his sister gave him nine turkey eggs as a wedding present, and it's still a family affair. Sons Pete and Thomas work on the farm with Bill and his wife, Teresa, and another son and daughter each manage one of the restaurants. The sign in Bill Bates's office appropriately reads: "It's difficult to soar with eagles when you work with turkeys."

VISITING THE SOURCE
— ❖ —

There are Bates House of Turkey restaurants located near Greenville on Interstate 65 (Exit 130), near Montgomery on Interstate 85 (Exit 6), and near Spanish Fort on Interstate 10 (Exit 35). Hours vary from location to location but each is open every day except December 25 and 26 and Thanksgiving Day and the day after.

— ❖ —

Broken Arrow Ranch Axis Venison

You can turn to Broken Arrow Ranch for one of the rarest commodities by mail in America: wild venison, USDA inspected and approved. Native wildlife, like the American

Texas Wild Game Cooperative
P.O. Box 530
Ingram, Texas 78025

(800) 962-4263 (Monday to
Friday, 8 A.M. to 5 P.M., CST)

Free descriptive brochure
VISA, MasterCard

white-tailed deer, are considered public property under the law and cannot be raised for profit. But nonnative game is regarded as private property and can, therefore, be raised to be sold. That's just what the Texas Wild Game Cooperative sells—axis deer, blackbuck antelope, and other exotic game (such as the wild boar), which were introduced into Central Texas some 30 years ago by game hunters.

The man behind this nearly one-of-a-kind venture is Mike Hughes. Since he started the cooperative in the mid-1970s, the company has grown to include game on a hundred Central Texas ranches. Venison is increasingly being used by innovative American chefs, and Broken Arrow has become the trusted supplier of venison for fancy restaurants ranging from New York City's Windows on the World to Houston's The Mansion on Turtle Creek.

This is pure, unadulterated venison, with no artificial hormones, steroids, antibiotics, or chemicals of any kind. Consumers will also be interested to know that since 1987, the game has fallen under USDA jurisdiction as well as state inspection and receives stamps of approval from both.

Hughes likes to point out that axis venison has one-third the calories of beef and one-eighth the fat content. And it is lower in calories than chicken; a 3½-ounce uncooked piece has about 126 calories. The meat has a milder, less gamey taste than native deer, and its texture is similar to veal. Though the minimum order is $30, Broken Arrow's prices are actually quite reasonable. For only $59.95 (plus $15 shipping or 15 percent

BROKEN ARROW RANCH SAVORY VENISON STEW
— ❖ —

Vegetable cooking spray
1 pound Broken Arrow Ranch venison chunks, cut into bite-size pieces
1 tablespoon pickling spice
1 bay leaf
1 cup coarsely chopped onion
⅛ teaspoon garlic powder
2 carrots, cut into ½-inch pieces
2 celery ribs, cut into ½-cubes
2 red potatoes, cut into ½-inch cubes
2 chicken bouillon cubes
2 cups water
1 teaspoon red wine vinegar
¼ teaspoon freshly ground black pepper
1 can (8 ounces) tomato sauce

Spray a nonstick skillet with vegetable cooking spray. Place the skillet over medium-high heat, add the venison, and brown quickly on all sides. Wrap the pickling spice in cheesecloth and tie with a string. Put the venison, spices, and the remaining ingredients in a pot and simmer until the venison is tender and the vegetables are cooked, 1½ hours. Remove the spice bag before serving.   *Serves 6*

of billing, whichever is greater; in Texas the fee is a flat $10), the Complete Sampler includes two venison rolled shoulder roasts, 2 pounds each of venison cubes for stews, ground venison, and venison chili (coarse ground) meat, along with two ¾-pound rings of mildly seasoned smoked venison sausage and ¾ pound of venison salami. The vacuum-packed sausage and salami are cured and come fresh (the other meats are frozen). Accompanying the shipment is the Ranch's excellent recipe booklet (Venison à la Bourguignonne, Elizabeth's Ranch Chili), which includes tips on cooking this low-fat meat so it doesn't dry out. Each venison specialty may also be ordered individually by the pound at prices ranging from $4.98 per pound for cubed venison to $5.98 per pound for the salami. Broken Arrow also ships two other exotic treats: cured and smoked wild boar hams ($39.98, plus shipping) and rings of smoked wild boar sausage ($3.28 each, plus shipping).

A final note, if you call the 800 number and get put on hold, a music box will tinkle "Home on the Range" while you wait.

— ❖ —

Comeaux's Boudin

Comeaux's Grocery
1000 Lamar Street
Lafayette, Louisiana 70501
(800) 323-2492; (800) 737-2666 (Monday to Saturday, 7 A.M. to 7 P.M., CST)
Fax (318) 232-4853

Free order form (prices by phone only)
VISA, MasterCard, American Express

Most of the people who drop by Ray Comeaux's store aren't there for the coconut balls, pickled quail eggs, pigs' feet and lips, or even the homemade sweet dough pies. They make a beeline for the red glass-fronted meat case that contains the big, plump, spicy links of Comeaux's famous Cajun sausage, boudin. You won't find a version of boudin finer than Ray Comeaux's. His father Frank's boudin was legendary, and Ray still follows the same tried-and-true recipe. The only difference is that Frank Comeaux made 15-pound batches of sausage, while his son makes 1,200 pounds at a time.

Boudin, along with andouille and tasso, is part of a triumvirate of Cajun meat specialties that are pretty hard to lay your hands on except in the heart of Acadia. There are two types: red boudin, made with pork blood (not available for shipment), and the more common white boudin, usually referred to simply as boudin. Along with tasso and andouille, this sausage was one of the meats customarily made in the course of a *boucherie*, the communal hog butchering event that was a festive, neighborly marking of midwinter. Although *boucheries* are held less commonly now than in the past, boudin is still made in South Louisiana, where it's most likely sold at a Mom and Pop grocery store like Comeaux's or at the boisterous Cajun dance halls and nightclubs dotted along the highway from Lafayette to Shreveport. At Comeaux's Grocery you can buy a freshly made boudin po' boy or packages of the links to take home and fix yourself.

Comeaux's boudin is prepared in a USDA-approved plant located near the store. The links, which are an uninspiring pallid white, taste infinitely better than they look. They're made from a mixture of pork shoulder, pork liver, and rice seasoned with vegetables like onions, celery, and bell pepper and spiced with cayenne and paprika (there is also some MSG). Only natural casings are used, as it's important for the sausage to be able to expand and contract as it steams. The links are shipped frozen and with gel packs in 1-pound vacuum-packs via next-day air. As with most mail-order specialty meats, the price of the goody you're ordering is very reasonable—it's the shipping that adds up. Currently the boudin is $2.60 per pound, plus next-day-air shipping charges. The links can be kept refrigerated for about a week or frozen almost indefinitely.

Boudin is usually eaten in a po' boy. To serve, steam (do not boil) the boudin for about 10 minutes. The trick is to heat the links until the skin shrinks and the rice expands; you can tell it's ready if the sausage springs back when you touch it. Split open a warmed crusty French roll or 10-inch length of French bread, spread it with a layer of tart (not sweet) barbecue sauce, and arrange a few slices of diagonally cut andouille (kielbasa can be substituted) on top of the sauce. Now split open the sausage casing and dump the steaming spiced contents onto the bread.

Ray Comeaux also ships other things like andouille ($4.49 per pound), tasso ($4.49 per pound), and an unusual crawfish boudin ($4.79

TWO CAJUN SPECIALTIES
— ❖ —

Andouille ("ahn-DOO-ee") and tasso ("TAH-so") are two important, hard-to-find regional Louisiana ingredients that Cajun cooks rely on for some of the unique flavor characteristic of their special cooking. Both are seasoning meats, but andouille, a hearty, spicy, smoky sausage, can also be served grilled as a breakfast sausage or main dish. The origins of these meats lie in a Cajun custom that has almost vanished today, the *boucherie*. When the fall pig-slaughtering season came around, it was marked by gatherings of friends and family communally toiling to prepare meat for the months ahead. The men butchered and cleaned the animals; the women processed the meat and rendered pork lard, transforming them into delicacies such as andouille, tasso, boudin, hogshead cheese, cracklins, and chitterlings. *Laissez les bon temps rouler* ("Let the good times roll") is not a famous Cajun saying for nothing—a *boucherie* was also a rollicking good social occasion that might span a week to 10 days. There was plenty of good food, and after everyone had feasted, the evening ended with a *fais-do-do*, music and dancing that often lasted all night.

per pound). The prices vary based on the seasonal cost of ingredients, so it's best to call for up-to-the-minute prices. Ray's got a fancy computer operation, so order-filling runs smoothly.

VISITING THE SOURCE
— ❖ —

Comeaux's Grocery is located at 1000 Lamar Street, at the corner of General Mouton. Hours are 7 A.M. to 6 P.M., Monday to Friday; 8 A.M. to 5 P.M. on Saturday.

— ❖ —

Early's Old-Fashioned Hickory Smoked Pork Sausage

Early's Honey Stand
P.O. Box K
Spring Hill, Tennessee
37174-0911

(800) 523-2015 (Monday to Saturday, 9 A.M. to 5:30 P.M., CST)

Free 32-page color catalog
VISA, MasterCard, American Express, Diners Club

Early's name is something of a misnomer. It's been some time since honey was the mainstay of this very famous mail-order concern, one of the largest and oldest in the South. Early's began 60 years ago as a roadside stand when Erskine Early and his mother set some barrels out under a big shade tree and posted a hand-lettered sign announcing HONEY FOR SALE. If no family member was on hand to watch the stand, customers just dropped their money in a tin can nailed nearby. Erskine's dad, who had a local reputation for making the tastiest, lip-smacking sausage you ever ate, soon began setting out a few pokes of his home-smoked Tennessee hill country pork sausage and some hams alongside the canning jars of honey. One thing led to another and the Early family found themselves filling mail-order requests out of their kitchen. Erskine retired recently, and I'm told he's off doing important things like hunting, fishing, and spinning tall tales for his grandson. The business remains in good hands, however.

The Old-Fashioned Hickory Smoked Pork Sausage from Early's is legendary (in the last 60 years or so they've sold maybe 2 million pokes). This is the genuine article—no tacky fillers or unappetizing mystery cereals are allowed to diminish the secret blend of red pepper, sage, and

spices that characterize this truly superior treat. Ground, seasoned pork is sewn into pokes (slender cotton bags) and lingeringly smoked over green hickory wood until the meat turns a golden brown. This is what good sausage is all about—an unadulterated, hunger-stanching meat that was farmer's fare when eggs were eggs and breakfast was meant to get you through the chores. Each 2-pound poke costs $12.95, postpaid (April through October meat shipments are made by air only at an additional charge of $3).

Great old-fashioned bacon is also available—hand-massaged with spices and Early's honey, the slabs are smoked slowly over hickory wood embers and yield nice, lean slices that don't shrink up into mere scraps like supermarket bacon. It is available vacuum-packed, thick- or thin-sliced with the rind removed (3 pounds of thick-sliced costs $16.20, postpaid; 2 pounds of thin-sliced, $12.95, postpaid). For those who prefer to wield the knife themselves, 9-pound slabs of bacon cost $39.95, postpaid.

Early's sells yummy aged Tennessee Country Ham (dry salt-cured, and smoked over green hickory) in a variety of ways: whole 14-pound ham ($51.95); country ham squares cut just right for setting atop a biscuit (2 pounds, $19.95; 4 pounds, $16.95). And, yes, there's still honey, hefty 2½-pound jars of White Clover ($9.25) or Sourwood ($10.25), as well as local sorghum and bags of grits and seasoned flour.

I highly recommend the selection of reasonably priced gift boxes. The Sampler Box (a 2-pound poke of sausage, 1 pound of thick- or thin-sliced bacon, 1 pound of center-sliced country ham, and an 8-ounce jar of honey) at $27.50 is the ideal way to get acquainted with Early's.

VISITING THE SOURCE
— ❖ —

Early's retail store is located about 40 miles south of Nashville. Take I-65 South to Exit

61 and go out about four miles to the Goose Creek bypass at U.S. 31, then bear left and continue another four or five miles until you see Early's Honey Stand on the right side of the road. The store is open Monday through Saturday from 9 A.M. to 5:30 P.M. When you get there, someone is bound to pour you a nice, cold cup of cider.

— ❖ —

Filé Powder: Yogi Brand and Zatarain

FILE POWDER
— ❖ —

There is a trick to using filé powder: It must *never* be allowed to boil (or even cook), as this will make a gumbo too gummy or "ropey." The powder should be sprinkled into the hot liquid immediately after the pot has been removed from the heat. After adding the powder, cover the pot and allow the gumbo to sit undisturbed for five minutes or so. Then give it a couple of good stirs to blend and ladle it over piping-hot rice.

Gumbo. The word alone conjures up the pleasurable piquancy of Cajun and Creole cooking. It is the classic, hearty Louisiana soup, just this side of a stew, meant to be poured over a steaming heap of fluffy long-grain rice. The first gumbos were concocted by early South Louisiana settlers to take advantage of the abundant local seafood, and came to be known as "the bouillabaisse of Louisiana." But other versions evolved, and today there is a wide range of gumbos based on everything from smoked meats and/or chicken to duck and wild game.

All gumbos begin with a roux, the mixture of flour and oil combined over high heat that Paul Prudhomme only half-jokingly defines as "Cajun napalm." Most gumbos require a thickening agent—either filé powder or glutinous pods of okra. Gumbo is said to take its name from the Bantu for okra, *gombo*. And versions made with filé powder became known as gumbo filé, to distinguish them from those with okra.

Filé powder's role in gumbo is to add a bit of thickening and additional subtle flavor. It is made from young sassafras leaves that are picked just before reaching the shade of green that signals maturity, then dried and pulverized into a fine powder. Once the Choctaw Indians used the leaves medicinally, and in the early days of New Orleans's French Market, Choctaw women sold the leaves from wide, shallow baskets.

**Louisiana General Store
The Jackson Brewery
620 Decatur Street
New Orleans, Louisiana 70130**

**(800) 237-4841; (504)
947-0293 (Monday to Friday,
8 A.M. to 4 P.M., CST)**

Free 39-page color catalog
VISA, MasterCard, American
Express

Two popular Louisiana brands (and sizes) of filé powder are available from the Louisiana General Store. A 1½-ounce bottle of Yogi Brand Gumbo Filé costs $1.35, plus shipping. Or if you're interested in ordering a large enough supply to hand down to your children, ask about the 2-pound jar of Zatarain Brand Pure Ground Gumbo Filé for $12.50, plus shipping, which is not usually mentioned in the catalog. It's useful to know that most gumbo recipes call for ¼ to ½ teaspoon of filé powder. Shipping charges will be high if you're only ordering a little bottle of the powder, but the Louisiana General Store's wonderful catalog contains many additional Cajun and Creole cooking ingredients of interest.

— ❖ —

K-Paul's Louisiana Kitchen Cajun Andouille and Tasso

**K-Paul's Louisiana Mail Order
P.O. Box 770034
New Orleans, Louisiana
70177-0034**

**(800) 4KPAULS; (504)
947-6712 (Louisiana
residents call collect; Monday
to Friday, 8 A.M. to 5 P.M., CST)**

Free 15-page color catalog
VISA, MasterCard, American
Express

"When the taste changes with every bite and the last bite is as good as the first, that's Cajun!" says Paul Prudhomme, Louisiana's premier Cajun chef. If it hadn't been for him, who knows how long it might have taken for those of us outside Louisiana to discover the delights of Cajun and Creole cooking? As the youngest of 13 children, Prudhomme began cooking alongside his mother, Hazel, when he was only seven, and the rest is pretty much history by now—the blackened redfish, the famous K-Paul's Louisiana Kitchen Restaurant in New Orleans (where the lines stretch for blocks), his exceptional ability to communicate flavor and the nuances of working with fresh ingredients the Cajun way.

The K-Paul meats are carefully produced in a smokehouse in St. Martinville, Louisiana, under the supervision of Paul's brother Abel. Prudhomme's andouille is a combination of ground, seasoned prime pork Boston butt, potato, and onion that has been smoked for many hours. Use

it as a flavoring in red beans and rice, gumbo, and jambalaya. I prefer the more traditional hot version, but Prudhomme also ships a milder "regular" andouille. The tasso, sometimes called "Cajun ham," is big meaty chunks of the same prime pork rolled in brown sugar, salt, and peppery spices before it is hot- and cold-smoked. The result is an intensely smoky, interesting flavor. Diced or julienned, tasso traditionally appears in jambalaya and bean dishes, but it'll add zest to almost anything, including soups, casseroles, and scrambled eggs. A few hearty Louisiana souls swear that thinly sliced it makes a great sandwich but most of us would find the flavor too strong. Once you've had the opportunity to cook with these meats, you'll surely wonder why you didn't try them earlier. They are shipped two ways: a single meat in a 5-pound, vacuum-packed bulk package ($39.95, including second-day air charges); and 12-ounce pack-

Chef Paul Prudhomme with a selection of andouille and tasso.

ages, with a minimum order of five packages in any combination of andouille or tasso ($7.50 per package, including second-day air charges).

The colorful K-Paul catalog is lots of fun. In addition to the meats, it features Sweet-Potato

PAUL PRUDHOMME'S CHICKEN, ANDOUILLE, AND TASSO JAMBALAYA
— ❖ —

3 tablespoons unsalted butter
½ pound tasso, diced (about 2 cups)
½ pound andouille smoked sausage, cut into ¼-inch slices (about 1½ cups)
¾ pound boneless chicken, cut into bite-size pieces (about 2 cups)
2 bay leaves
2 tablespoons plus ¾ teaspoon Cajun Magic Poultry Magic
1 tablespoon minced garlic
1 cup chopped onions
1 cup chopped celery
1 cup chopped green bell peppers
½ cup canned tomato sauce
1 cup peeled and chopped tomatoes
2½ cups chicken stock
1½ cups uncooked rice (preferably converted)

Melt the butter in a 4-quart saucepan over high heat. Add the tasso and andouille; cook, stirring frequently and scraping the pan bottom well, until the meat starts to brown, about 4 minutes. Add the chicken and continue cooking, stirring frequently and scraping the pan bottom as needed, until the chicken is brown, about 4 minutes. Stir in the bay leaves, Cajun Magic, garlic, and ½ cup each of the onions, celery, and bell peppers. Cook until the vegetables start to soften, stirring and scraping the pan bottom frequently, 6 to 8 minutes. Add the tomato sauce and cook, stirring often, 1 minute. Stir in the tomatoes and the remaining ½ cup each of the onions, celery, and bell peppers. Stir in the stock and rice, mixing well. Bring the mixture to a boil, stirring occasionally. Reduce the heat to very low, cover the pan, and simmer the jambalaya until the rice is tender but still a bit crunchy, about 30 minutes. Stir well and remove the bay leaves. Let sit, uncovered, for 5 minutes before serving. To serve, arrange two heaping ½-cup mounds of jambalaya on each serving plate for a main course; allow one heaping ½-cup mound for an appetizer.

Serves 6

> *Trouble always sets heavy on an empty stomach.*
>
> —*Alice Hegan Rice*

Pecan Pie, jars of hot-pickled quail eggs, and bottles of Al's South Louisiana Chow Chow. There are also some very nifty nonfood items—things like copies of the *Chef Paul Prudhomme's Louisiana Kitchen* cookbook and *The Prudhomme Family Cookbook* (specify a first name and the book or books will arrive autographed; $19.95 per book, plus $2.80 shipping); a 2-quart cast-iron roux pot ($13.95, plus $5 shipping); Cajun music tapes ($8.95 each, plus $1.80 shipping); and a Video Magic Gift Package, which consists of nine bottles of Prudhomme's various Cajun Magic seasoning blends shipped along with two 32-minute how-to videos featuring Chef Paul ($47.50, plus $4 shipping).

— ❖ —

Kary's Gumbo Roux

Gazin's
P.O. Box 19221
New Orleans, Louisiana
70179-0221

(800) 262-6410; (504)
482-0302 (Monday to Friday,
9:30 A.M. to 4:30 P.M., CST)

34-page color catalog, $1
(applied to first order)
VISA, MasterCard, American
Express

If you've ever used cookbooks by Paul Prudhomme, the master chef of Cajun cooking, you may already know that roux is that rich brown mixture—a combination of flour and oil browned until it has thickened—valued by Cajun cooks for the distinctive taste and texture it lends many Louisiana specialties, especially gumbo. Sounds straightforward enough, until you realize that even if you follow Prudhomme's meticulous directions, roux can be a pain in the neck to make from scratch. It requires great concentration on the part of the cook, and there is some potential danger involved since the oil must be heated to an extremely high temperature. Kary's Gumbo Roux, however, is ready to use straight from the jar, and it's an excellent alternative to making roux yourself.

The late Archange LaFleur ran the Pig Stand Restaurant in Ville Platte, Louisiana, which was noted for its delicious gumbo and barbecue. Over the years, customers got into the habit of asking Archange to measure out a little of his

roux so they could take home a supply. When Archange's son, Kary, returned home from college, the two men began working on a way to bottle the roux commercially. After Archange died in 1980, Kary and his mother, Annie, sold their interest in the restaurant and built Kary's Roux Kitchen, a small factory where the roux is made today in small batches.

Kary's Gumbo Roux is made the traditional way, from flour and vegetable oil stirred constantly over high heat in huge roux kettles. A deep chocolatey brown, the mixture contains salt and a minute amount of preservative to guard against rancidity. It takes about five tablespoons of the roux to make a batch of gumbo, and it's a good flavoring and thickener for stews, gravies, and soups, too. There are recipes printed on the label, including a tasty one for crawfish or

GUMBO FESTIVAL
BRIDGE CITY, LOUISIANA
— ❖ —

Celebrating one of the most delectable of Louisiana's signature dishes, the Gumbo Festival began in 1973 when then-governor Edwin W. Edwards proclaimed Bridge City "the Gumbo Capital of the World." It's staged by the parishioners of the Holy Guardian Angels Church on the second weekend in October. The good times begin rolling with the crowning of King Creole Gumbo and Miss Creole Gumbo at a formal ball known as the Champagne Coronation held the weekend before the festival. Gumbo eating, beer drinking, and beautiful child contests follow the next week, along with good eats that include jambalaya, red beans and rice, and the festival's two famous gumbos—a chicken-andouille one and a seafood version—which are prepared in huge vats at the local fairgrounds. Hot sauce is provided, but bring along your own bottle of filé powder. For more information, write P.O. Box 9069, Bridge City, Louisiana 70094.

shrimp bisque. Gazin's will ship three 16-ounce bottles for $8.99, plus shipping.

— ❖ —

Mayo's Hickory-Smoked Sausage and Bacon

**Baltz Brothers
1612 Elm Hill Pike
Nashville, Tennessee 37210**

(615) 360-3100 (Monday to Friday, 8 A.M. to 4:30 P.M., CST)

**Free illustrated brochure
VISA, MasterCard, American Express**

There's no doubt about it—some of the most delicious country sausage comes from Tennessee. Nashville in particular has often been called the "sausage capital of the world," and part of the reason is the Mayo Sausage Company.

In the early 1930s, as fewer and fewer folks were making their own sausage at hog-killing time, L. M. Mayo decided there would be a market for his homemade hickory-smoked sausages. He packed the seasoned meat in cloth bags sewed by his wife, Lillie, and took them over to his mother's smokehouse for slow curing. Retail grocery stores like Piggly Wiggly were quick to realize L. M. was making the real thing and began placing orders, which he delivered in a Model A Ford. Today Mayo Sausages are carried in most leading supermarkets in the area. But don't, for heaven's sake, assume that since supermarkets carry Mayo products they're only fair in the taste department, because it simply isn't true. They're good eating through and through.

L. M. Mayo's son, Frank, and grandson David ran the family business until recently, when they decided to sell it to Baltz Brothers, another well-known Nashville meat company with a good reputation. So far nothing has changed except the address for orders— the Mayo meats are as wonderful-tasting as ever.

Mayo Hickory-Smoked Sausages are made from premium-cut boneless pork shoulder that's 70 percent lean, and there are no added fillers or water. Unlike many so-called country sausages, whose hickory flavor comes via the miracle of modern chemistry, Mayo's marvelous meat-and-sage mixture, which is packed into 100-percent cotton bags called pokes, gets its flavor the old-fashioned way—hand-hung like stalactites in the plant smokehouse and slowly smoked over hickory for 18 hours. This is good, honest sausage that's as tasty eaten at supper with a mound of mashed potatoes as it is at breakfast with some grits and fried apple slices. A word of caution: It's easy to overcook country sausage, so don't ruin a good thing. Three pokes of sausage, weighing a pound each, cost $12.95, postpaid (six cost $24.90).

Good bacon that doesn't "fry away in your skillet" is almost as hard to find as good sausage, and you can count on the Mayos for this, too. Slabs of Mayo's Hickory-Smoked Bacon are smoked over hickory and dry-cured (no water added) after being hand-rubbed with a mixture containing honey and a touch of sodium nitrite. Three 1-pound packages of thick-cut bacon cost $14.95, postpaid (six 1-pound packages cost $26.95).

A good way to taste Mayo products is by ordering one of their reasonably priced gift packs. Mayo's Choice includes 2 pounds of the sausage, two 1-pound packages of the bacon, and two slices (about a pound) of their center-cut, not-too-salty country ham for $27.95, postpaid.

— ❖ —

Oak Grove Smokehouse Andouille, Tasso, and Creole Jambalaya and Gumbo Mixes

Oak Grove Smokehouse is a family-owned business run by Robert and Babette Schexnailder along with their children Robert Jr. and Yvette. Like most good Cajuns, Robert used to smoke his own meats out in the backyard for the family table (he used an old refrigerator). But in the early 1970s Robert left behind his career in agricultural research at

Oak Grove Smokehouse
17618 Old Jefferson Highway
Prairieville, Louisiana 70769

(504) 673-6857 (Monday to
Friday, 8 A.M. 4:30 P.M., CST)
Fax (504) 673-5757

Free descriptive brochure and
price list
Prepaid orders only

Louisiana State University to turn his hobby into a business, establishing a smokehouse near Bayou Manchac below Baton Rouge. Here the Schexnailders and a small staff smoke a variety of meats, including two regional Louisiana specialties available by mail order: andouille, the Cajun smoked pork sausage called for in many variations of gumbo and jambalaya, and tasso, which is chunks of smoked ham used primarily as a seasoning. Mail-order prices for the meats are reasonable at $2.99 per pound, plus shipping; there is a $15 order minimum. Shipping charges for second-day air are $1.25 per pound to most states west of the Rockies, 50 cents per pound ground shipping to Southern states.

Although the andouille and tasso are tasty, it's an excellent line of packaged mixes for Louisiana dishes that has brought fame to Oak Grove Smokehouse. About 15 years ago the Schexnailders noticed that a lot of their out-of-state mail-order customers really weren't too clear about how to use the meats they'd ordered. So Robert began fiddling around with various blends of seasonings and spices, perfecting jambalaya and gumbo mixes that turned out dishes

so close to "from scratch" that even locals accustomed to making their own started buying them. At the annual Jambalaya Festival in Gonzales, Louisiana, Oak Grove Smokehouse Creole Jambalaya Mix is so highly regarded that it's sold as an official souvenir of the event, and I know for a fact some big restaurants use these mixes, too.

Each mix comes in a cellophane bag, will feed four to six people, and is a snap to use (even the rice is included). Your task is merely to add browned meat and water or lightly seasoned stock, and cook it all for less than a half hour on

top of the stove. The flavor of both dishes is undeniably authentic, with the hearty spiciness characteristic of Cajun cooking (be warned, however, some of this good flavor is because MSG is in the mix). The jambalaya mix, usually prepared with chicken and/or andouille, is close to fabulous when crawfish or crabmeat is added instead. Once the jambalaya and gumbo mixes caught on, the Schexnailders came up with nine others, some for main dishes, others for coatings and desserts. These include a gumbo base without rice, fish fry with creole seasonings, seafood boil, and even a beignet mix. To test the waters, you could order the Taste of Louisiana gift box sampler of six mixes (two each of Creole Gumbo, Creole Jambalaya, and Beignet mixes, one each of Chicken Fry, Fish Fry and Hush Puppy) for only $4.50, plus $2.50 shipping. Or you can order a minimum of 15 bags, one kind or assorted, or buy a case of 24 bags. Main dish mixes cost $11.25 (15 bags), $18 per case, plus shipping. Coating mixes and the beignet or hushpuppy mix are less expensive; 15 bags for $6, $9.60 per case, plus shipping. All shipments include a 15-page recipe booklet enumerating many ways to use the mixes, which are surprisingly versatile.

VISITING THE SOURCE
— ❖ —

If you find yourself in Louisiana, visit the Oak Grove Smokehouse retail store, open Monday through Friday, 9 A.M. to 4:30 P.M. It's located 10 miles southeast of Baton Rouge near the intersection of Old Jefferson Highway and Highway 42.

— ❖ —

Palmetto Pigeons

The Palmetto Pigeon Plant, despite a rather industrial-strength-sounding name, devotes itself to raising and processing that posh poultry known as squab. Pharaohs once feasted on these tender morsels, and

Palmetto Pigeon Plant
P.O. Drawer 8060
333 Broad Street
Sumter, South Carolina 29151

(803) 775-1204 (Monday to
Thursday, 8 A.M. to 5 P.M.;
Friday, 7:30 A.M. to 4:30 P.M.,
EST)

Free nondescriptive price list
Prepaid orders only (call for
estimate of cooler and freight
charges)

during the Middle Ages squab was known as "the meat of kings." FDR served King George VI Palmetto's squabs at an elegant White House dinner in his honor and every president since has ordered from the Palmetto Pigeon Plant.

So what exactly *is* a squab? It's a young, fledgling pigeon prepared for market when it is about four weeks old and weighs around one pound (it has never reached flying age, which is 60 days). This pricy connoisseur's treat is not common; though Palmetto is the world's largest pigeon plant under one roof (shipping around 150,000 birds annually), it is one of only four in the U.S.

Now in its 66th year, the firm was founded in 1923 by Wendell M. Levi, who raised pigeons as a boy in Sumter, South Carolina, and his buddy Harold Moise. Today the 13-acre plant is in the center of Sumter's bustling commercial district. But once (before the town grew up around it) the plant lay so far outside the city limits that Levi and Moise used to hand-pump and carry water to their birds. The late Wendell Levi was and still is regarded as the world's foremost authority on pigeons, having written two books on the subject in addition to the Boy Scout handbook on pigeon breeding. (His *Encyclopedia of Pigeon Breeds*, considered the bible of the pigeon world and still in print, is widely consulted.) Now Patty Barnett, Levi's daughter, operates the plant, which was completely modernized and automated after a 1980 fire consumed the original buildings.

The flavor of squab is unique. Slightly gamey, a little reminiscent of duck and dove, the meat is dark, tender, and succulent (also very low in cholesterol). Barnett, who believes "you can do anything with a squab that you can with a chicken," says the best way to enjoy the flavor is to bake the bird stuffed with a wild rice and mushroom mixture (allow one 13-to-16-ounce squab per person). She suggests a peach and grape salad as an

PALMETTO PIGEON PLANT

accompaniment (her husband, Henry, is a peach grower!). Barnett concurs with other squab raisers that while most cookbooks suggest roasting at 350°F, better results are achieved at 400°F, or even 450°F, though care must be taken not to overcook (Southerners like theirs "cooked through"). At South Carolina's Pawleys Island Inn, chef-owner Louis Osteen serves grilled squab accompanied by sage-and-thyme-flavored cornmeal dressing.

Palmetto pigeons, white-feathered Kings and Carneaus, are meticulously raised on whole grains and pure spring water and range in weight from 9 to 17 ounces. Most of the plant's sales are to fancy big-city "white tablecloth" restaurants or to wholesale suppliers, but Palmetto honors its motto "Quality squabs, one or a thousand," and also ships to individuals. The squabs are available frozen (most popular, with each bird individually sealed in a Cryovac bag) or fresh (costs around 10 percent more), and shipments are certified by the South Carolina Meat and Poultry Inspection Service. The price list can be a bit confusing at first; printed prices do *not* include the thick-walled insulated Styrofoam cooler and next-day air freight charges, but Palmetto is happy to figure charges on the phone once you've decided what to order. A dozen frozen, oven-dressed, 16-ounce squabs with giblets cost around $62.30 (plus second-day air shipping); a dozen frozen, partially boned (breast plate, rib cage, and thigh bones removed) squabs of similar weight cost around $76.50 (plus second-day air shipping); frozen boneless breasts cost around $26.75 per pound (plus second-day air shipping). Half-dozens can be shipped upon request—just ask. Patty Barnett says the latest hit on the Southern cocktail party hors d'oeuvre circuit is squab wings (sprinkle with soy and Worcestershire sauce, flavor with ginger, and roast); a 50-

count bag costs around $6.50 (plus second-day air shipping). "New York dressed" squabs are shipped with head and feet still on at prices similar to oven-dressed.

So what do they do with the feathers plucked from those 150,000 birds? They're marketed to milliners, toy makers, and people who make fishing flies. Then there was the time a movie producer ordered enough feathers to turn his actors into bird people...

— ❖ —

Poche's Cracklins, Boudin, and Churice

Poche's Meat Market and Restaurant
Route 2, Box 415
Breaux Bridge, Louisiana 70517
(318) 332-2108 (7 days a week, 6 A.M. to 9 P.M., CST)

Free price list
VISA, MasterCard

The Poches (pronounced poe-chez) are famous for their freshly made boudin and cracklins and they're the only mail-order source I'm aware of for churice, a Cajun sausage less well-known than andouille.

The restaurant and meat market were founded over 30 years ago by Lug Poche, whose seven children grew up working with him. In the mid-1970s Lug's son Floyd took over the business and we have him to thank for expanding into mail-order. Assisted by his brother Sidney, Lloyd and his helpers produce all of Poche's Cajun meat specialties on the premises. To make the cracklins they cut 1-inch pieces of pork skin with a layer of fat and a little bit of meat, frying the bits for an hour or so in huge black-iron Cajun kettles until the fat is rendered and crispy bits of skin remain. The resulting flavorful, crunchy snack, which is also good crushed and added to cornbread batter, comes in red and white paper sacks and costs $4.50 per pound, plus shipping.

Poche's boudin, that delicious white sausage, is still made according to Lug's original recipe and the filling ingredients include fatty pieces of pork combined with pork liver, green onions, jalapeños, and rice. Although this is a cooked sausage, it's customary to heat boudin briefly before eating. After heating, you can remove the tasty filling from its casing, spread it on a saltine, and you've got a nice snack, especially when accompanied by an icy cold beer. The boudin is $2.09 per pound, plus shipping.

Churice (sometimes spelled chaurice) is a garlicky, unsmoked coil of marinated Cajun pork sausage that, like andouille, is used mainly as a gumbo seasoning. The Poches make theirs year round using pork meat and stomach, green onion tops, and bell peppers, with red and black pepper for seasoning. Churice can be delicious barbecued on a grill; it costs $1.95 per pound. The two smoked Cajun meat specialties andouille and tasso are both $2.95 per pound. The tasso, nice and spicy, marinates for several days before it is taken to the smokehouse behind the restaurant, where it is smoked for eight hours over green pecan wood.

Sunday is bar-b-que dinner day at Poche's restaurant and you can mail-order the same highly satisfying sauce that's ladled over their chicken and pork. The color of old bricks, Poche's Bar-B-Que Sauce is thick with bits of onions and bell pepper. The full, interesting flavor comes from a long list of seasonings that include garlic, lemon, tomato paste, Worcestershire sauce, chili powder, brown sugar, cayenne, and a tiny shot of liquid smoke. There are no preservatives. This sauce kind of grows on you. It's not fancy or sophisticated; it's good and simple, and for some untold reason it reminds me of circa-1950s home cooking. A quart glass jar sells for $1.95, plus shipping. Nonperishable items such as the cracklins

and barbecue sauce are shipped via UPS. Perishables are sent second-day air packed in specially insulated boxes.

VISITING THE SOURCE
— ❖ —

If you ever get to Louisiana, you'll definitely want to cat at Poche's. It's located on Highway 31 about four miles north of Breaux Bridge. Plate lunches (including smothered pork chops, meatball fricassee, or backbone stew) are served daily from 10:30 A.M. to 1:30 P.M., and on Sunday they serve bar-b-que dinners.

— ❖ —

Ranch House Mesquite-Smoked Beef Brisket, Peppered Bacon, and Beef Jerky

Mesquite-smoked meats are part of the Texas mystique, and in tiny Menard, Texas, Max and Marsha Stabel keep mesquite embers burning almost day and night in their smokehouse. Max, who once taught meat science at Texas Tech, and Marsha, a former county extension agent with a degree in animal science, decided to give the free enterprise system a whirl about 10 years ago, when they bought and renovated an old meat processing plant on the edge of Texas Hill Country. From them you can order some of the finest smoked meats you ever lapped a lip over.

As if they weren't busy enough, the Stabels have rigged up a traveling road show for their meats. Max roams all over the Southwest to state fairs and livestock events, hauling with him a rustic cedarwood cabin along with a big barbecue pit, automated rotisserie, and wood-burning grills for preparing mesquite-flavored hot, cured turkey drumsticks and spicy sausage-on-a-stick for ravenous fairgoers. So if you're planning to attend the San Angelo Livestock Show and Rodeo, follow the aroma of smoldering mesquite and you'll likely meet up with Max.

Ranch House meats are vacuum-packed and

Ranch House Mesquite Smoked Meats
303 San Saba
Menard, Texas 76859

(915) 396-4536 (Monday to Friday, 8 A.M. to 5 P.M., CST)

16-page color catalog
VISA, MasterCard, American Express

shipped frozen, which means they'll keep unopened in the refrigerator for up to two weeks, or frozen for three or four months. All of the meats are smoked over mesquite embers (and sodium nitrite is used). The very reasonable prices include shipping. The Stables' mesquite-smoked beef brisket is a hand-trimmed hunk of the Lonestar State's favorite cut, rubbed with spices and freshly cracked pepper, then smoked for 12 to 15 hours (4 to 5 pounds, $34.95, postpaid). This is good reheated and served with a tomato-based barbecue sauce on the side. For lovers of lamb, there's a cured, smoked, boneless leg that's fully cooked, weighing about 5 pounds ($38.95).

For snacks and lunchboxes there's the cowboy's saddlebag staple: chewy beef jerky made from real lean strips of beef with lots of black pepper (½ pound in a burlap bag, $15.25; 1-pound box, $21.95). Also available is salty, highly flavorful smoked dried beef, made from less tender beef round, which is handy to have on hand for use chopped as a seasoning in gravies, sauces, and casseroles (3 pounds, $25.95). My favorite Ranch House meat is the thick-cut, meaty slices of hearty-tasting peppered bacon. The exterior is rubbed with brown sugar, spices, and lots of cracked peppercorns that give the meat a deep, distinctive flavor set off by the pungent mesquite it's smoked over (3-pound package, $14.75, postpaid). Other mesquite-smoked products include turkeys, chickens, hams, Canadian bacon, beef or pork tenderloin, and sausage.

— ❖ —

Royal Bobwhite Quail

Tasty game birds have long been a Southern treat. These days, though, it's less likely their presence on the table is the result of a jovial harvesttime hunting trip in the

Royal International Ltd.
P.O. Box 125
San Juan, Texas 78589
(800) 331-7811; (512)
781-7511 (Monday to Friday,
8 A.M. to 5 P.M., CST)

Free 15-page color catalog
VISA, MasterCard, American
Express

crisp fall air accompanied by man's best friend. The LaMantia family, which owns a large mail-order food company that ships Texas citrus fruits and Royal Sugar Sweet Onions (see page 191), began farm-raising bobwhite quail for their own use about seven years ago. The hobby eventually turned into a business when friends and relatives who had received the birds as gifts expressed interest in buying more. Today the LaMantias ship almost a million bobwhites a year to individuals and fancy restaurants.

The bobwhite is native to the South, and it's distinguished from other, lesser quail by the fact that it's all succulent white meat that has a mild, sweet taste. Although there are many other species, including the much more common Pharaoh, which is smaller-breasted with darker meat, the bobwhite is considered the best. The bobwhite's charming name stems from its call, which is said to sound as if it's warbling "ah, bobwhite." Quail, incidentally, has virtually no fat and (without skin) about half the calories of chicken. However, the lack of fat means care should be exercised in cooking, as it has a tendency to dry out if not properly prepared. Quail tastes best roasted or grilled and accompanied by a nutty-flavored side dish like wild rice or one of the aromatic Southern rices such as Ellis Stansel's Rice or Konriko Wild Pecan Rice (see pages 273 and 275).

Royal Bobwhite Quail are raised on the La-Mantia family's Crystal City farm just south of San Antonio. Royal ships plump-breasted raw or fully cooked, mesquite-smoked bobwhite quail, which are vacuum-packed, then frozen and shipped in a reusable Styrofoam chest; recipes are included (10 quail, approximately 6 to 7 ounces each $53.98, plus $6 shipping). These are very nice for a sophisticated picnic or buffet. The company also ships uncooked, frozen Royal

Semi-Deboned Bobwhite Quail Breasts and Quail Drum Petites, both of which make nice appetizers or would add a special touch to holiday breakfasts. The breasts are completely deboned except for the wing bone, which is left on for appearance. A combination package, with recipes, contains 8 pairs of breasts and 40 Drum Petites ($55.98, plus $6 shipping).

— ❖ —

Shuckman's Old Louisville Sausage

Shuckman's Meat Company, Inc.
3001 West Main Street
Louisville, Kentucky 40212
(502) 775-6478 (Monday to Friday, 8 A.M. to 5 P.M., EST)

Free computer printout of current prices
Prepaid orders only; check or money order (just give a call and they'll quote a postpaid price)

Former residents of Louisville back for a visit have been known to bring along a cooler specifically so they could stock up on Shuckman's sausages to take home. These are not the customary Southern smokehouse country sausages, but rather European-style ones that people around Louisville are used to buying to throw on the grill in the backyard for a summertime cookout.

The Shuckman family pork specialties hark back to Russian immigrants Isia and Sarah, who started the business as a butcher shop back in 1919. Today their son A.J. and his son, the irrepressible Lewis, who has been spotted on more than one occasion wearing a tie with pigs on it, run the small company using old family recipes.

In Louisville, the sausages are carried in local grocery stores, but the Shuckmans have been getting mail-order requests from former residents often enough that they've recently started filling orders from their wholesale headquarters. Shuckman's Old Louisville Sausages are hickory- or mesquite-smoked and are made in three versions: mild (seasoned with mustard seed and ground nutmeg), hot, and super-hot (the pretty serious lingering heat in these comes from crushed red peppers). You may choose between natural (they cook up crisper) and artificial casings (said to be a bit more tender). Spicy, chubby Italian-style

Shuckman's old louisville™ sausage

sausages (either sweet or mild) and old-world bratwurst are also available. The company buys only Kentucky-grown hogs, and although the government minimum standard for pork sausages is 50 percent lean, Shuckman's sausages are at least 70 percent lean (they do, however, contain MSG). A newer product is the tasty pork dinner frank introduced at the Kentucky State Fair a couple of years ago. These are mellow in flavor with hints of garlic and onion. The best way to fix any of the meats is on a grill outdoors; second-best is to broil them. The sausages cost $4 per pound, plus shipping (approximately four links per pound), and arrive packed with "blue" or dry ice in a reusable Styrofoam cooler. There is a 5-pound minimum order (mixed or same sausage) and shipment is via UPS second-day air. If you like lamb, it may interest you to know that the Shuckman's are busy perfecting a new lamb sausage.

RAISING CANE

"When I die, you can bury me deep
Put a jug o' molasses at my feet,
Put nine biscuits in each hand,
And I'll sop my way to the Promised Land."
—Governor Ross Barnett
A Cook's Tour of Mississippi

Until refined sweeteners came on the scene, sorghum and cane syrup were basics in the Southern kitchen. Their strong, full-bodied taste is still favored over refined sugar in many homes today. In times of plenty, the syrups were liberally used in everything from the cookies in the cookie jar to grandmother's gingerbread. When times were lean, you could pour a thick, glossy stream of syrup over a biscuit or wedge of cornbread and call it dessert. Today, pure versions of these syrups are pretty hard to find unless you get lucky and drive by a farmstand with a few jars for sale, or unless you turn to the following pages and meet people like the Steens of Louisiana and the Ecks in Kansas, folks who still make syrup the old-fashioned way.

Golden Kentucky Sorghum and Sorghum Praline Topping with Kentucky Bourbon

Golden Kentucky Products
P.O. Box 246
Livingston, Kentucky 40445
(606) 453-9800

Free descriptive order form
Prepaid orders only

When the going gets tough, the tough seek alternatives, especially if they're small farmers. A few years ago in eastern Kentucky a bunch of hardworking tobacco farmers, discouraged by their waning profits, started raising cane. Sorghum cane, that is, and with the help of Earl Baker, a tobacco farmer with years of experience as a sorghum maker, they're turning out 100 percent pure sorghum just like their grandparents enjoyed.

Golden Kentucky Products reflects a community fighting back against changing times on the farm. The organizing spirit is the Livingston Economic Alternatives in Progress Program (LEAP), a community organization working to create jobs and new opportunities for the residents of Rockcastle County. The enterprise is very much a community affair. Mr. Baker, for example, is passing along his sorghum-making skills to Carol Blackburn, who's working the second shift (sorghum making requires grueling 14-to-16-hour days). Carol, the mother of five, also farms with her husband, Russell. And, it's generally acknowledged around town that Carol is *the* person to go to if you want the natural cure for anything.

Each fall, farmers bring their fresh-cut sorghum cane to the cooperative mill, where the pure juice is pressed from it and made into sorghum, using the open-pan method. The women of Golden Kentucky Products market and develop the cooperative's specialty foods products, which are sold by mail and to specialty stores. They've developed a prettily packaged jar and label for the sorghum, which can be ordered in calico-capped pints ($4.65) and half-pints ($3). A free brochure of recipes from the National Sorghum Association comes with each shipment.

Unlike some other so-called sorghums, this is the real thing, as pure as can be, no preservatives or corn syrup added. Use it as an overall sweet-

ener or in baked goods like cakes, cookies, and breads. Do be aware, however, that the sweet, almost metallic flavor of sorghum makes it one of those Southern foods that your tastebuds may have to tune in to early in childhood; the flavor is not universally loved.

Sorghum Praline Topping with Kentucky Bourbon is sorghum with a kick, a *big* kick. The topping is made of sorghum, walnuts, cream, honey, butter, and a jolt of good old Kentucky bourbon. Heated, it gently caramelizes over ice cream, pound cake, or baked apples. Each 9-ounce jar costs only $4.35. Two other modestly priced offerings from the co-op are pure cold-filtered honeys. One comes from a delicate tall wild clover that grows locally ($4 per pint) and the other is a darker colored wildflower honey that includes nectar from blackberry and persimmon blossoms as well as tulips ($3.75 per pint). Add 25 percent of the value of your order (mini-

Cutting sorghum cane in Livingston, Kentucky.

OLD-FASHIONED SORGHUM COOKIES

— ❖ —

½ cup sugar
½ cup solid shortening
½ cup sorghum
1 egg
3 cups sifted all-purpose
  flour
¼ teaspoon salt
1 teaspoon baking soda
1 teaspoon ground
  cinnamon
1 teaspoon ground ginger
  (optional)
¼ teaspoon ground cloves
  (optional)
⅓ cup sour milk

Cream the sugar and shortening together. Add the sorghum and the egg; beat well. Sift together the dry ingredients and add them to the sorghum mixture in thirds alternating with the sour milk. Beat smooth after each addition. Chill the dough before rolling. On a well-floured surface, roll the dough out to ¼ inch thick. Cut out 4-inch cookies with a cookie cutter and place them on a greased baking sheet. Bake at 400°F for 8 to 10 minutes.

Makes about 24 cookies

mum of $2) to all prices for postage and handling. Orders over $20 are accompanied by a free copy of a 20-page handwritten booklet of sorghum history and recipes detailing how to use the syrup in everything from baked beans and divinity to ham glaze and Indian pudding. Sorghum was the principal sweetening used by the colonists and Golden Kentucky enables us to share this old favorite in pure, unfancied-up form.

— ❖ —

Golden Mill Sorghum

Before our collective sweet tooth was seduced by refined sugar, sorghum was a basic sweetener of the South. These days sorghum-making is a gastronomic folk art, a fragment of culinary heritage kept alive by a handful of widely scattered small concerns producing limited quantities.

Eck & Sons is run communally by two gener-

Eck & Sons
Route 1, Box 29
Bartlett, Kansas 67332
(316) 226-3368 (don't call on Sunday)

Prepaid orders only
Send a stamped, self-addressed, business-size envelope for recipe pamphlet and order form with current prices to the attention of Marilyn Eck

ations of the Eck family on their southeast Kansas dairy farm ("one mile north of the Mason-Dixon line"). Although the Ecks are now the third-largest sorghum producers in the country, sorghum making was originally a family hobby inspired by Donald Eck's desire to share with his children a vanishing treat from his childhood. The family's first less-than-perfect batches were made outdoors in copper kettles in 1972, but in the early 1980s, after much trial and error and consultation with experienced old-time sorghum makers, the Ecks perfected their sorghum skills and their hobby became a business. Sorghum season is short—generally from mid-September to the first hard freeze—and unpredictable. According to Marilyn Eck, the family cane crop is "totally dependent on the weather and the Good Lord." Around August each year the Ecks know if they'll be able to make sorghum.

The season is hectic, with Donald and Marilyn, their three children and their spouses, and even nieces and grandchildren pressed into service from daybreak to dusk to meet the 400-gallon-a-day goal. Donald and sons Herschel and Ivan harvest the cane from the family's 95 acres. The mill is fired up to squeeze the brilliant green juice from the cut and trimmed cane stalks. Then juice is strained into a holding tank, where it is slowly brought to a boil, and the foam that rises to the top is skimmed off with long, boxy wooden shovels. The juice then moves through an agitating tank, where it is filtered 36 times before it is siphoned into 20-foot-long cooking pans, where a sticky fog rises upward as the juice boils until thickened to a dark, golden syrup. When the syrup reaches 78 percent sugar it is drawn off into a vacuum cooker to reach a final sugar content of 80 percent (much sweeter than molasses). The sorghum is then hand-bottled in jars and plastic buckets.

Sorghum fanciers who live in Kansas, Arkansas, and Tennessee may get lucky and find Golden Mill Sorghum in local stores. The rest of us can order directly from the Ecks, who will ship a 4-pound plastic tub of sorghum ($5.25, plus about $5 shipping) or a gallon-size plastic container ($14, plus about $6 shipping) to mail-order customers. Glass jars of sorghum are available only by the case (twelve 2-pound jars, $34, plus shipping).

Contact the Ecks to make certain there is sorghum available. A pamphlet of sorghum-based family recipes, including the Brown Stew the Ecks stoke up on while they're raising cane, is available.

VISITING THE SOURCE
— ❖ —

Golden Mill Sorghum is also sold right at the farm and the Ecks welcome visitors year round. No appointment is necessary but you should call ahead just to confirm someone will be home. Sorghum-making time, of course, is the most exciting season to pay a visit (generally from mid-September through the end of October). Bartlett, Kansas, doesn't appear on most maps but Chetopa does and the farm is located about ten miles west of Chetopa, off Highway 166. You'll see the Eck's yellow sign along the road.

— ❖ —

Steen's Pure Cane Syrup

C. S. Steen Syrup Mill, Inc.
P.O. Box 339
Abbeville, Louisiana 70510
(318) 893-1654 (Monday to Friday, 8 A.M. to 5 P.M., CST)

Free color brochure
VISA, MasterCard

For four generations the Steen family has had a way of pinpointing fall that's different from yours or mine. They like to say that when the first ripe pecan falls in Abbeville, it's time to light the boilers at the mill. You can smell fall in Abbeville all right—the sweet perfume of Steen's "soppin' good" cane syrup burbling away in brass kettles pervades the air.

Mother nature pulled a nasty trick on C. S. Steen in 1911—a heavy early freeze left him with

600 tons of frozen cane standing in the fields and the nearest refinery too far away to reach in time. Steen quickly erected a little mill with equipment purchased from a local hardware store and ground some of the cane. The first barrels of syrup were thick and sour. But soon Steen was grinding his cane at precisely the right stage, and the result was the same "nothing added, nothing extracted, open-kettle" syrup made of the juice of 100 percent sugarcane that his heirs make today on three acres on the shaded banks of Bayou Vermilion. The mill is run by Albert C. Steen, grandson of C.S., and his son, energetic and friendly Charley, a beared guy in a dashing Panama hat who says that even as a kid he used to live for grinding season.

While molasses and cane syrup are both made from sugarcane, most of the sugar is removed when molasses is processed; with Steen's Pure Cane Syrup nothing is removed and its thick golden-brown goodness is naturally high in iron and calcium. Charley will tell you that the Steens make "the best syrup humanly possible depending on Mother Nature," pointing out that each year's production is slightly different. "Like a wine, you have vintage years," he notes.

The syrup is heaven for soppin' with biscuits or drenching a chunk of cornbread, and first-rate in cookies. Try the tasty, cakey gingerbread recipe printed on the back of each can, or a sugarless cake called Masse Pain. (This and other family recipes are in "The Story of Steen's Syrup and Its Famous Recipes," compiled and edited by Mrs. J. Wesley Steen, $2.50.) The syrup adds something extra to baked beans and fruit cakes and is perfect for glazing some of Wayne Garber's Cajun Yams (see page 183).

An Economy Pak of four 12-ounce distinctive Steen-yellow cans costs $7.50, plus shipping; a pack of four pudgy 25-ounce cans costs $12, plus shipping. You should note that since the syrup weighs a lot, shipping costs are a little high in comparison to the syrup's price. These, along with other less well-known Steen products, including light and dark molasses as well as the company's newest product, cane vinegar, are detailed in a colorful brochure.

The Steens' most unusual and interesting product does not appear in the brochure, so you'll have to ask about La Cuite, an orgy of sweetness dating from plantation days, when children globbed the sugary base onto a stick and dipped it in chopped pecans. The French translation of the name is literally "the last of the cooking," and so it is—pure cane syrup cooked in small, open stainless-steel kettles almost to the point of no return, until the consistency turns so thick and taffy-like it can only be spooned from

MASSE PAIN
(SYRUP CAKE)
— ❖ —

½ cup vegetable oil
1½ cups Steen's Cane Syrup
1 egg, beaten
2½ cups sifted all-purpose flour
1 teaspoon ground cinnamon
1 teaspoon ground ginger
½ teaspoon ground cloves
½ teaspoon salt
1½ teaspoons baking soda
¾ cup hot water
Chopped pecans (optional)
Raisins (optional)

Combine the oil, syrup, and egg, stirring until well blended. Mix and resift the dry ingredients, except the baking soda. Dissolve the baking soda in the hot water. Add the dry ingredients to the syrup mixture in thirds alternating with the soda-water. Begin and end with the dry ingredients. Add the pecans and raisins if desired. Pour the batter into a greased 9-inch-square pan (or a 13½- x 8½-inch pan). Bake in a 350°F oven for 45 minutes.

Serves 8

the jar. La Cuite is available in 11½-ounce jars ($4.75 each; four-jar minimum order; ask about shipping charges).

VISITING THE SOURCE

— ❖ —

Visitors are always welcome at the mill (119 North Main Street), especially between October and December, which is "grinding" season. "Just let the good smells direct you," say the Steens. Mill hours are Monday through Friday, from 8 A.M. to 5 P.M.

— ❖ —

TexasFresh Ribbon Cane Syrup and Sorghum

Brockett-Tyree Farms
P.O. Box 1088
Royse City, Texas 75089
(214) 635-9222 (Monday to
Friday, 8 A.M. to 5 P.M., CST)

Free order form
Prepaid orders only

In East Texas if you want to choose and cut your own Christmas tree, the place to head is Brockett-Tyree Farms, where you can pick the tree of your dreams from 250 acres of Virginia pines grown by the Brockett and Tyree families. Each year more than 40,000 people indulge in this holiday ritual, leaving their cars (and cares) behind and clippity-clopping into the forest via horse-drawn wagons. Co-owner Daryl Tyree has a practical, if somewhat indelicate, way of measuring success each year: it's based on the number of Porta-Pottis he sets out for the crowds. Last count, it was up to 40.

Once the main event, the tree, is taken care of, there's still lots to see and do on the farm in a wooded visitors' area known as Turkey Creek Village. There's a working smokehouse and a blacksmith operation where "Goose" Michaels and his son make miniature horseshoes to pass out to the children. But visitors seem to have the most fun lining up at the restored circa-1901 syrup mill, where they can watch ribbon cane syrup and sorghum being made in open kettles from cane and sorghum grown right on the farm. The Brockett and Tyree families are proud that they have Texas's first licensed syrup mill (other syrup making in the area is done on a more casual basis).

Knowing just when the syrup is ready is either an art form or a science, depending on who you speak with. Tyree claims it's "all black magic." Either way, Doug Belzer, the man at the cooking vat, waits for the "frog eye" bubble to break and stay open, a signal that the syrup is just right. He makes around 40 gallons a day, and most days visitors buy almost all of it, so there's a limited supply available for mail orders.

City folks like the ribbon cane syrup because it's gentler-tasting and sweeter than the sorghum that most East Texas old-timers grew up with. Either can be mixed with butter before using or even combined with a bit of white corn syrup for a less pronounced flavor. The prices are very low. Pretty square 11-ounce bottles of each syrup cost $1.50; 15-ounce round jars cost $1.57, plus shipping. You can also order the syrups in wooden gift crates or fancier gift packages such as wooden cowboy boots, which are listed on an order form that also includes some lovely jams and

a terrific pepper jelly made from farm-grown ingredients (see page 246).

Brockett-Tyree Farms has been shipping their products for only a few years, mostly to visitors who wanted more of the goodies they bought during Christmas-tree outings. As a result, this is not yet a highly sophisticated mail-order operation and they do not accept credit cards. It is recommended that you call the office, tell them what you wish to order, and someone will calculate a total (including shipping) while you're on the phone so you know how much to send.

Desserts

"Desserts should be like the end of a sermon. Heavy enough to stick with you, but light enough to remember the main scriptures."
—LaMont Burns, author of
Down Home Southern Cooking,
sharing the culinary wisdom
of Ausiebelle, his grandmother

Nowhere is the South's fabled sweet tooth more in evidence than in the delectable profusion of cakes and pies, both plain and fancy, that have pleased generations of eaters. No family member or guest is ever too full for that final mealtime indulgence of a generous wedge of flaky-crusted pie, a towering hunk of feather-light cake, or a warm, spicy square of gingerbread. In the pages that follow are fine sources for special occasion confections (timeless fruitcakes, colorful Mardi Gras King Cake, a Derby-time pie as famous as the race itself) along with classic pies and honest, old-time sideboard dessert staples such as Virginia Diner Peanutty Pie and Tennessee Jam Cake blanketed with caramel icing.

Benne Wafers and Benne Bits

Byrd Cookie Company
P.O. Box 13086
Savannah, Georgia
31406-0086

(912) 355-1716
(Monday to Friday, 8 A.M. to
5 P.M., EST)

Free illustrated color brochure
with price list
Prepaid orders only

Slaves arriving in the coastal regions of Georgia and South Carolina brought with them a tiny edible treasure they believed would ensure health and good luck. In West Africa these flat honey-colored seeds had been called bĕne; in the South they became known as benne. Planted near the slave quarters, the benne seed grew, becoming an integral part of the South's culinary heritage, an often-used ingredient in cakes, cookies, and even some breads. Yankees call them sesame seeds and they are what makes Byrd's Benne Wafers and Benne Bits so wildly delicious.

The Byrd Cookie Company's origins date back to 1924, when founder Benjamin T. Byrd, Sr., slid a few batches of sugar cookies out of the oven, hopped into his Model T, and delivered them to small local grocery stores. By 1927 he had moved the business into one of the first sites in the area to have electricity, a telephone, *and* running water! His son, Benjamin, Jr. (nicknamed—surprise, surprise!—"Cookie"), grew up making cookies in his father's plant. After a stint as a World War II pilot airlifting supplies over the Himalayas to General Claire Chennault's famed Flying Tigers, Cookie joined the business and ran it until he sold it not long ago to his daughter and son-in-law, the Benny Curls of Atlanta.

Though all Byrd products are of high quality and none contain preservatives, those made with benne seeds are the most special. Twice a year tractor-trailer loads containing 10,000 pounds of the triple-washed seeds unload their cargo at the automated cookie factory next to Byrd's retail shop, the small wooden Cookie Shanty. Inside the factory are ovens that can bake up to 40,000 cookies per hour. Peak baking time runs from September 15 until the week before Christmas.

Although a few varieties of sweet cookies are still made, Byrd's best-seller is the Benne Wafers,

which are very small, crisp, lacy, tan-colored cookies dotted with benne seeds and made delicately flavorful with brown sugar, maple flavoring, and whole-wheat flour. Just sweet enough, they are tasty served with after-dinner coffee or tea. Totally irresistible are Benne Bits, thickish savory rounds about the size of a dime that are also made with whole-wheat flour. The bits are more of a cocktail munchie, tangy and zingy (from a combination of Tabasco, cayenne, and Wisconsin Cheddar cheese). I can tell you, there's not a person alive with enough restraint to eat only a few. Both benne specialties come packed in Byrd's distinctive square 8-ounce tin decorated with a *white* mammy figure (she changed during the 1960s). All Byrd products cost about $8 per 8-ounce tin, and most are shipped in sturdy, attractive mailing cartons. A Twin Pack (one each Benne Wafers and Benne Bits) costs $14, and there's also a Quad Gift Pack for $22.50 that allows you to choose any four Byrd products. (All products are postpaid in the continental U.S.; in Alaska and Hawaii, add on another $2.50.) Other benne products include hard Benne Candy, Benne Straws (cocktail straws with cheese and poppy seeds), and Confederate Cannonballs (flavorful pellets seasoned with onion and garlic). Benne Bits fans who want to go on a binge will be relieved to know that they can order a 72-ounce bulk party-size supply in a plain plastic bucket for $21, postpaid.

VISITING THE SOURCE
— ❖ —

Byrd's Cookie Shanty, with U.S. and Confederate flags waving from the porch, is located at 2233 Norwood Avenue, right next to the factory. Here Byrd goodies are sold in a country store atmosphere complete with old cracker barrels and aged soda-pop bottles on the fireplace mantel. It's on tour bus routes so it gets crowded. Hours are Monday through Friday, 9 A.M. to 5 P.M.

Best of Luck Scottish Shortbread Horseshoes and Nails

Hunt Country Foods, Inc.
P.O. Box 876
Middleburg, Virginia 22117
(703) 364-2622

Free brochure
VISA, MasterCard

Life is filled with gift-giving quandries. Who hasn't wracked his brain over how to wish a friend, relative, or business associate the best of luck? Worry no more. From the heart of Virginia's hunt country, where they've always known horseshoes ensure good luck, there are gift-boxed, absolutely realistic, life-size shortbread horseshoes, complete with "nails."

The cookies are the brainchild of former photographer Maggi Castelloe and her husband, writer Barnard Collier, who got the idea during family baking sessions with their two children. Casting about for an interesting shape, someone took a horseshoe off the wall, set it on the cookie dough, and cut around it. For the next five years Maggi researched and tested shortbread recipes, developing her own rich, buttery version that contains Chinese rice flour, wheat flour, butter, and a blend of orange-flavored sugars. In a sunny kitchen on the family farm in Fauquier County that overlooks the Shenandoah hills, the cookie dough is hand-stamped with custom-made cutters from Switzerland and slowly baked for two hours at a low temperature in small batches in convection ovens until the horseshoes and nails are golden and nicely chewy. Best of Luck horseshoes are popular gifts among the horsey set—often given with the pur-

Kate Collier, Maggi Castelloe's daughter, stamps out life-size shortbread horseshoes.

chase of a horse at horse sales, as party favors during Kentucky Derby and Preakness time, or as Christmas gifts from stables to their riders. One Kentucky breeder always takes a supply on his trips to Japan to use as gifts.

The packaging, of course, is half the fun. The horseshoes come nestled in an exceptionally attractive hunter green and red box with the distinctive Best of Luck logo. A 12-ounce box contains 4 horseshoes with about 40 equally edible nails ($13, postpaid); the 6-ounce version contains 2 shoes and about 20 nails (this size is popular as a favor at fancy parties; $8, postpaid).

— ❖ —

Claxton Fruit Cake

Claxton Bakery, Inc.
P.O. Box 367
Claxton, Georgia 30417-9990
(912) 739-3441

Free color order form
VISA, MasterCard

The city water tower looming against the sky announces in bold lettering: CLAXTON, FRUITCAKE CAPITAL OF THE WORLD. And some staggering statistics suggest the city fathers aren't just whistling Dixie. The Claxton Bakery, owned and operated by Albert Parker, his daughter, and three sons, annually bakes more than six million pounds of fruitcake.

Around 1928 twelve-year-old Albert Parker began sweeping the floors, helping make ice cream, and preparing dough for Italian immigrant Savino Tos, owner of a general store and bakery. When Mr. Tos retired in 1945, a now grown-up Albert acquired the bakery and focused his sights on fruitcake, a favorite of local residents. Fifteen thousand pounds of fruitcake were sold that first year, much of it personally peddled by Albert to grocery stores in neighboring Savannah.

A quirk of fate pushed Claxton into the big time in 1952. A Tampa man installing refrigeration equipment across the way wandered in to buy a little something as a lunchtime dessert. The fruitcake set him thinking. It was so good,

he told Albert, that the Civitan Club, a philanthropic volunteer group he belonged to in Florida, should sell it as a fund-raiser. Soon after that the organization adopted the cake as a nationwide project, and today Civitan Clubs sell almost half of all Claxton Fruit Cakes.

Peak baking time in Claxton's seven huge ovens runs from the day after Labor Day until the first week of December, but cakes may be ordered year round. This is a commercial-tasting, 80 percent fruit and nut blend, a spicy, moist poundcake batter dotted with good-size chunks of pineapple and cherries, along with pecans, almonds, walnuts, and California raisins, and flavored with citrus peel. There are light and dark (molasses) versions. The recipe has changed little over the years, and the batter is still mixed in a Rube Goldberg-like cement-mixer-type contraption that was masterminded by a longtime employee.

The fruitcake comes cellophane-wrapped, in 3- ($11) or 5-pound ($15) versions, available either as individually wrapped 1-pound cakes or a solid loaf. Prices are postpaid east of the Mississippi; add 75¢ for shipments west of the Mississippi. Orders are shipped in sturdy red, white, and black boxes bearing Claxton's famous logo of an old-fashioned Savannah buggy.

VISITING THE SOURCE
— ❖ —

Visitors are most welcome at the bakery, which is located at 203 Main Street. Guided tours are conducted Monday through Saturday from 8 A.M. to 6 P.M.

— ❖ —

Double Decker Deluxe Moon Pies

For seven generations the classic Southern quick lunch consumed along dusty roadsides, in front of ramshackle country stores, and in modern offices has been a Moon Pie and an RC. Fried chicken, cornbread, grits,

THE MOON PIE
CULTURAL CLUB
— ❖ —

The Moon Pie Cultural Club, with its "world headquarters" in Charlotte, North Carolina, is a zany organization devoted to spreading the story of the Moon Pie and to establishing club chapters throughout "the civilized world." Ron Dickson, the executive director, who even flies a Moon Pie flag on his boat, is a very amusing guy obsessed with immortalizing his favorite snack. The club is a loose-knit body of fanatics scattered around the country. Activities include "a campaign to have the Moon Pie Logo attached to some Rest Stop signs on interstate highways" and a campaign to have the Moon Pie declared "the Official Snack of all states in which it is sold." From the club's small mail-order department fans can obtain authorized clothing and accessories imprinted with the Moon Pie logo. Items include T-shirts ($6), adjustable baseball caps ($4.50), and embroidered emblems ($1.50) to sew on your jacket or shirt.

The Moon Pie is probably the only snack on earth that has its own guide. *The Great American Moon Pie Handbook*, written by Ron Dickson and illustrated by cartoonist Sam C. Rawls, authoritatively and humorously covers Moon Pie history, folklore, and protocol. There are chapters on unacceptable manners and uses of Moon Pies, a "pilgrim's" visit to the Chattanooga Bakery, and detailed guidance on how to eat a Moon Pie. Order it from the club for $7.45.

When ordering, add $1.50 postage for the first item and $1 for each additional. Orders are shipped postpaid. For information about how to start your own chapter of the club, or to order something silly to wear or read, contact: The Moon Pie Cultural Club, 11706 Musket Lane, Charlotte, North Carolina 28217. As "president for life" of the club's New York chapter, I encourage that state's interested residents to write me: (no phone calls, please) Joni Miller, New York Chapter of the Moon Pie Cultural Club, c/o Workman Publishing, 708 Broadway, New York, NY 10003.

Chattanooga Bakery, Inc.
P.O. Box 111
Chattanooga, Tennessee
37401

(800) 251-3404 (Monday to
Friday, 8 A.M. to 5 P.M., EST)

Free order form
VISA, MasterCard

and barbecue may be the icons of Southern home cooking, but the commercially made Moon Pie is the ultimate morsel in Southern food folklore. This snack is so firmly entrenched in the gastronomic tradition of rural America that it's got an official fan club (The Moon Pie Cultural Club) a guide (*The Great American Moon Pie Handbook*), and, due to relentless lobbying on the part of concerned citizens, a governmentally proclaimed day of its own: October 8, which is Moon Pie Day in Alabama, Arkansas, Georgia, Mississippi, and Tennessee.

The Moon Pie is a 4-inch-round snack cake made of three secret-recipe, graham-cracker-like cookies layered together with marshmallow and dipped in a flavored frosting. Most purists wouldn't dream of eating anything but a chocolate one, though they do come in other, color-coded flavors: pale yellow banana, creamy white vanilla, and off-white coconut. There are imitators on the market (tsk, tsk) but the Moon Pie brand, "the Original Marshmallow Sandwich," is easily identified by the grinning yellow half-moon trademark printed on the clear cellophane wrapper. It is manufactured solely by the Chattanooga Bakery.

Back when I was a little kid, we ate the "original" version made only with two cookies. But in 1969, the Double Decker Deluxe Moon Pie everyone eats today was introduced. Oddly enough, Moon Pies are better-tasting now than they were when I was growing up. Back then they were kind of dryish and crunchy, probably because they were almost always stale. Today they're much softer, the result, I assume, of modern shipping and inventory controls.

The origins of the name remain shrouded in mystery. But according to Sam H. Campbell IV, vice-president of the bakery and the founder's grandson, the Moon Pie was the inspiration of

THE ANNUAL WORLD CHAMPIONSHIP MOON PIE EATING CONTEST

— ❖ —

E ach October 8, Moon Pie Day, the Wal-Mart discount market out on Highway 75 in Oneonta, Alabama, sponsors the Annual World Championship Moon Pie Eating Contest. The contest began by accident in 1985 when assistant manager John Love and two other employees simultaneously ordered shipments of Moon Pies from the Chattanooga Bakery. When 21,000 Moon Pies arrived, John Love was inspired to initiate the contest and the rest . . . well, it's a combination of history and indigestion as contestants see how many they can eat in 10 minutes. Recent winners include Rodney Frazer, known locally as "the Rambo of Moon Pie Eaters," who won the 1987 adult division crown by gobbling down 15 pies ("Anyone who can eat that many has got to be a boy at heart," says John Love). A stockman at Wal-Mart, Rodney is admiringly described by Love as "270 pounds of rompin', stompin' Alabama boy who loves his Moon Pies like a hog loves slop." For the 1988 contest, big Rodney, who likes the banana ones best, arrived by limousine nattily decked out in a tuxedo and a Moon Pie T-shirt but only managed to eat 11 pies. The 1988 champion was David Dunn of Arab, Alabama, who wolfed down 15 and waddled off with the $100 prize.

The 1989 champion, North Carolinian Mort Hurst, who arrived at Wal-Mart with his own cheerleading squad, wolfed down 16½ banana-flavored Moon Pies in 10 minutes. "I went to win," boasted the six foot two, 215-pound "Godzilla of Gluttony." Hurst took up speed eating as a hobby in 1983 and claims to have consumed 750 shrimp, 8 pounds of steak, 7½ pounds of collards, 6 whole chickens, 6 pounds of trout, 54 scrambled eggs, 52 deviled crabs, 19 catfish, and 21 hot dogs at other events. He plans to have "One bite too many" inscribed on his tombstone when the time comes. You bet!

one of the bakery's traveling salesmen. After a hard day of selling, this hero (whose name is lost to us) walked into the offices and said, "You know what you need? You need two big round cookies. You need some marshmallow filling in between, and you need chocolate icing on the outside. And it's got to be as big as the moon."

The Chattanooga Bakery sells more than 50 million Moon Pies each year, with quite a few of them shipped right to people's doors. A case containing 6 boxes of 12 Moon Pies each costs $25.20 (plus $3 shipping for the first case, $2 for each additional case). Only chocolate, vanilla, and banana flavors are available through mail order (no coconut), and you cannot mix flavors in a case. When your shipment arrives, keep a grip on yourself. According to Ron Dickson of The Moon Pie Cultural Club, "It is considered extremely bad manners to rip open the wrapper in an uneven, boorish way."

— ❖ —

Dutch-Maid Old-Fashioned Applesauce Fruit Cake

Dutch Maid Bakery
P.O. Box 487
Tracy City, Tennessee
37387-0487

(615) 592-3171 (Monday to Saturday, 8 A.M. to 5 P.M., CST)

Free brochure and order form
VISA, MasterCard

High on southeast Tennessee's Cumberland Plateau in the little town of Tracy City is the state's oldest family-owned-and-operated bakery. It's the sweet-smelling bakery of our childhoods—bustling, warm, friendly, filled with good cheer and good things to eat, including a famous applesauce fruitcake based on a recipe brought from the old country by Swiss immigrant and master baker John Baggenstoss. According to his son Herman, the bakery is called "Dutch" even though the family is Swiss because people were always confusing the Swiss, Germans, and Dutch. "I got tired of trying to correct folks and the name stuck," he says.

Today two of the six Baggenstoss sons are still active in the business: 76-year-old Albert, young-

Albert Baggenstoss, the official Dutch Maid Baker.

est son and now the official Dutch Maid Baker, and 85-year-old Herman, the business manager. Their late father opened the bakery in 1902, using his $100 savings to buy a small open-hearth oven. Back then local coal miners were the main customers, deliveries were made in a basket (you can see the very one in the bakery window today) or wheelbarrow, and the growing family lived above the bakery.

Although the bakery's daily bounty includes everything from potato rolls and pudgy loaves of salt-rising bread to angel food cakes and doughnuts, it's the fruitcakes shipped around the world that are most sought-after. There's a standard citrus-fruit version, but the applesauce one is the most popular. Last year 7,000 pounds of fruit-

FAMOUS

cakes were shipped. Both are mixed in small batches and contain imported fruits that are soaked overnight in a secret concoction that's said to seal in moisture during baking. After baking at low heat for several hours, the cakes cool on racks for a day before packing. The Applesauce Fruitcake is made of a tasty, light brown, almost stodgy batter dotted with raisins and chunks of pineapple, cherries, dates, and Georgia pecans. Additional flavoring comes from honey, applesauce, and spices. It grows better with age (Herman points out that you can easily stash one of his cakes in the basement and forget about it until the following holiday season). Post-paid prices are the same for both types of fruit-cake, which come packed in a round tin (2-pound cake, $15.40; 3-pound cake, $20.70; 5-pound cake, $31.50). For a more impressive presentation they may be ordered in a sturdy, handcrafted Tennessee-made wooden box (you can store keepsakes in it later) with the bakery's logo silk-screened on the sliding top. (The box adds approximately $5.50 to the cost of the cake.)

Other Dutch Maid Bakery specialties available by mail include a Sugar Plum Cake (a Swiss recipe made with buttermilk and spices, offered as an alternative to fruitcake; 2-pound cake, $11.60, postpaid) and a bread sampler of four round loaves (a loaf each of sourdough and pumpernickel and two of salt-rising bread, so named because the batter is left to warm overnight in a rock-salt-filled bucket; $14.70, postpaid).

VISITING THE SOURCE

— ❖ —

The bakery, always filled with local residents and tourists, is a charming place to visit. It is located six miles off Interstate 24. The exit number is 134 onto U.S. Highway 41, near the center of Tracy City. Hours are Monday through Saturday, 8 A.M. to 5 P.M.; Sunday, 1 P.M. to 5 P.M. Amidst the baked goods there's a vast array of locally produced mountain crafts, such as bird feeders and child-size rockers, as well as honey, hams, and sorghum. Lucky children have been known to get a tour of the bakery with Albert.

— ❖ —

Eilenberger's Pecan Cake

Eilenberger's Butter Nut
Baking Company
P.O. Box 710
Palestine, Texas 75801
(214) SAY-CAKE (729-2253)

Free color brochure
VISA, MasterCard, American
Express, Diners Club

Eilenberger's Pecan Cake may resemble fruitcake, but don't confuse the two. This East Texas confection is rich with sweet Texas pecans—nearly one third of the cake, in fact, is pecans. Blended in are dates, pineapple, and cherries, bound by a small amount of delicious honey-sweetened batter. The resulting hand-decorated cake is wonderfully chewy, a dense, sticky nut-fruit blend that's a welcome alternative to standard fruitcakes. Indeed, this pecan cake is the most popular cake at Eilenberger's Butter Nut Baking Company, and it sells well all year round. Along with the firm's traditional fruitcake, the Pecan Cake has won the Monde Selection Award in Vienna, Austria.

Eilenberger's is thought to be the oldest working bakery in Texas, and a Texas state historical marker commemorates its history. Two years before the 20th century began, a young Leipzig baker, F. H. Eilenberger, settled in Palestine, Texas, among the Belhlers, Dietzes, Vogels, and other Germans who had made East Texas their home. Eilenberger, a fine baker, made his butternut bread popular throughout the region and created the recipes for the cakes the firm still sells. His tradition of baking is carried on today by his son, Fred, the company's master baker, who oversees the baking of every cake.

The Butter Nut Baking Company's cakes still carry a very personal touch. Letters to the company are individually answered by the principals of the firm. The 2-pound and 3-pound loaf-style pecan cakes ($11.95 and $16.00, postpaid) come

in a pretty white box decorated with dogwood blossoms. Tucked inside the packages are instructions for slicing and storing. A thoughtful extra—a Zip-loc bag of matching size—is also provided. Once unwrapped, the cake can be stored in the bag in the refrigerator, where it will stay fresh, moist, and tasty literally for months. The 5-pound version is round and arrives in a dogwood-splashed tin ($26.50 postpaid). Eilenberger's also ships two newer cakes: Chocolate Amaretto Cake made with fruits, and a yellow-batter Australian Apricot Cake made with a splash of apricot brandy.

VISITING THE SOURCE
— ❖ —

If you find yourself in Palestine, stop by the Eilenberger's Bake Shop, a warm place with flower-sprigged wallpaper, old-style tables and chairs, and a counter of cookies and cakes. At least one recent visitor felt comfortable enough as he munched on a platter of Eilenberger treats to keep his Stetson on. The Bake Shop is located at 512 North John Street and is open Monday through Friday from 7:30 A.M. to 5:30 P.M., Saturdays 7:30 A.M. to 4 P.M.

— ❖ —

Gethsemani Trappist Bourbon-Flavored Fruit Cake

**Gethsemani Farms
Trappist, Kentucky 40051
No phone orders
Fax (502) 549-8281**

Free color brochure with
order form
VISA, MasterCard

The handmade fruitcake infused with Kentucky bourbon made by the Trappist monks of the Abbey of Gethsemani always gets raves in those rating roundups of mail-order fruitcakes we read each year in food magazines and local newspapers. I can guarantee you that the raves are totally justified; no other fruitcake I've encountered smells *and* tastes this good.

Head baker Brother Simeon supervises the preparation of around 50,000 cakes each year, following a recipe the monks perfected more than 30 years ago. Ingredients include plenty of chunky mixed fruits, pecans, English walnuts,

pineapple, fresh orange and lemon peel, honey, a healthy shot of Italian table wine, raisins, traditional spices, and margarine as well as butter. The four monks who bake the cakes for year-round shipment hand-mix the batter, carefully smooth it into tube pans, and top each cake with four pecan halves and four cherries before baking. Once the cakes are baked, a clever machine shoots aged Kentucky bourbon into seven areas of each one, thus ensuring every bite you take will be as mellow as can be. The cakes age for 10 or 11 months, which is why they're so marvelously moist-textured and dark brown in color and don't have the cloyingly stark sugariness of some fruitcakes. Two sizes of cakes are shipped in simple red and white tins: a 2½-pound one, $14.50, postpaid, and a 5-pound one for $26.25. These very special fruitcakes may also be ordered together with Gethsemani Farms cheeses (see page 363) in a variety of combinations (for example, a 2½-pound cake with a half-wheel of cheese for $22.75, postpaid). I wish I could be there to see your face when you take the lid off a tin and get a whiff of this fine cake.

— ❖ —

Haydel's Bakery Traditional King Cake Package

In the period from Twelfth Night until Fat Tuesday, the last day before Lent, literally hundreds of thousands of king cakes are shipped each year from New Orleans to the far reaches of other cities. Many wend their way to California and New York, which are known as king cake "concentration areas." A few years ago David and Gary Haydel of Haydel's Bakery began shipping this edible carnival tradition from their family-owned bakery. And the inventive way they package the cake makes receiving it almost as festive as Mardi Gras itself.

The Haydels' king cake is the usual cinnamon-

MARDI GRAS
KING CAKE

— ❖ —

Everything is special in New Orleans during the hectic hoopla surrounding Mardi Gras—even the cake. King cake (*Gateau de Roi*, or Twelfth Night Cake) is churned out in phenomenal quantities at local bakeries during the season which starts after Christmas on Twelfth Night and goes until Mardi Gras Day (Shrove Tuesday). And *everyone* throws a king cake party. Mostly store-bought cakes are served since only a very few ambitious traditionalists take the time and trouble to bake their own.

The king cake's origins lie in the medieval celebration of Epiphany, which commemorates, among other things, the visiting of the infant Jesus by three kings bearing gifts. French settlers are said to have introduced the custom of the cake to New Orleans. Early cakes were nothing more than French-style bread made festive with a scattering of sugar on top and a small surprise—such as a large bean, a ring, a coin, or a shelled pecan—baked inside. Fancified braids evolved over time and at one point the surprise was a tiny porcelain bisque doll.

Today king cakes are usually made of a cinnamon-flavored brioche-like dough, similar to coffee cake, that's braided into a thick, crown-like oval. The surface is drizzled with thin white frosting and decorated with sugar in official Mardi Gras colors: purple for justice, green for faith, and gold for power. The surprise representing the Holy Infant is now a small, pink, soft-plastic baby doll that won't break teeth (by law this is described on packaging as "foreign matter"). The person who ends up with the slice containing the doll becomes king or queen and must throw the next year's king cake party. At least, that's the theory. In reality, it's a more piggy proposition. During this period, New Orleans residents have a king cake party every week (in many offices and schools they have one every *day*). Nobody gets bored since the bakeries cleverly vary the fillings (blueberry, pineapple, cherry, apple, or cream cheese, which is the most popular alternative).

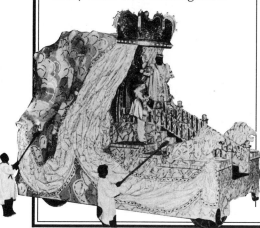

Haydel's Bakery
4037 Jefferson Highway
New Orleans, Louisiana 70121

(800) 442-1342; (504)
837-0190 (Tuesday to
Saturday, 8 A.M. to 6 P.M., CST)

Free illustrated color brochure
VISA, MasterCard

flavored coffee-cake-like braid decorated with colored sugar, but what's so great about it is that it comes with lots of other goodies to help duplicate Mardi Gras no matter where you live. Each freshly baked 15-x-11-inch braided oval arrives in a specially imprinted Federal Express box decorated in Mardi Gras colors. The large king cake, which serves at least 20 revelers, is accompanied by a scroll detailing its history, along with a few strands of splendidly sleazy, brightly colored plastic carnival beads and three doubloons (these are customarily tossed at bystanders from floats in the Mardi Gras parade). Best of all, a copy of the official "Mardi Gras Guide" is enclosed. In it you'll find Mardi Gras trivia and history as well as practical information, such as the routes and times of the countless extravagant float parades that sparkle through New Orleans and its suburbs during the carnival season. All this fun is called the Traditional King Cake Package and costs a modest $19.99, including overnight shipping via Federal Express.

The Haydels also ship the Complete Mardi Gras Package, which contains all of the above

BINDER'S BAKERY MARDI GRAS KING CAKE
— ❖ —

Gazin's, a well-established Cajun-Creole gourmet catalog loaded with food specialties, always features a king cake in the Mardi Gras issue of the catalog. It is a large, cinnamon-flavored, brioche-type cake decorated with colored sugar in Mardi Gras colors. The cakes are made by the Alois J. Binder Bakery and come in three sizes: regular ($9.94; serves ten), large ($20.95; serves twenty), and giant ($29.95; serves forty people). Shipping and handling, will probably cost under $5.

To order the cake write Gazin's at P.O. Box 19221, New Orleans, Louisiana 70179; phone (800) 262-6410 or in Louisiana (504) 482-0302. Their 34-page color catalog is available for $1 (credited to first order). Gazin's accepts VISA, MasterCard, and American Express.

plus a fun, informative 30-minute VHS videocassette about Mardi Gras narrated by Arthur Hardy, a well-known Mardi Gras historian. The package costs $29.95, including overnight shipping via Federal Express. The videocassette may also be ordered separately for $15.99, postpaid.

And since partygoers can't live on cake alone, you might plan on following another Mardi Gras food tradition and serve red beans and rice before the king cake is cut.

— ❖ —

Kern's Kitchen Derby-Pie®

Derby-Pie is a registered trademark of Kern's Kitchen Inc.

The thing about Kentucky Derby time is you have to put it in perspective—it's as much about food as it is horse racing. The Derby is actually one long party with lots of eating and drinking followed by "the greatest two minutes in sports." The traditional dessert served at everything from brunch to supper, in homes as well as restaurants, is a madly delicious

**Mousetrap Cheese
P.O. Box 43307
Middletown, Kentucky 40243**

**(502) 245-9197 (24 hours,
7 days a week)**

**Free 16-page color catalog
VISA, MasterCard, American
Express**

chocolate-nut concoction called Derby-Pie, which is made from a recipe so zealously guarded that it's been protected by a registered trademark since 1968.

Derby-Pie was created in the 1950s by George Kern and his parents, Walter and Leaudra, as a specialty item on the menu of the famous Melrose Inn, which they managed in Prospect, Kentucky. When the family couldn't agree on a name for their creation, they threw all the suggestions into a hat and drew out Derby-Pie. By the time the Kerns retired from innkeeping in the 1960s, the pie was so famous they continued baking it in their own home right out on a government-inspected carpeted patio. When the Kerns died, their grandson Alan Rupp and his wife, Sheila, continued the pie-baking in their home. Today the company is called Kern's Kitchen and the pies are still made mostly by hand, baked 24 at a time in a sparkling clean little bakery on the outskirts of Louisville. Last year, the Kerns made more than 100,000 of the pies. Only four people know the secret recipe (Alan shared it with Sheila on their wedding day, and even their lawyer doesn't know precisely how it's made).

All it takes is one taste to instantly understand why this rich "slice of Kentucky history" is such a big deal. The pie's filling tastes like a sublime cross between a chocolate chip cookie and a pecan pie, although no description can truly do it justice. The pie is shallow, about an inch or so high, with a good-tasting flaky crust. Nestlé's chocolate chips are scattered on the bottom, and then the secret filling, which includes eggs, sugar, and California light walnuts, is carefully poured in circles over the chips so as not to disturb them. Part of the secret seems to lie in what happens once the pie is baked: it somehow transforms into three distinct layers. The very sweet

Chocolate Nut Pie

bottom layer is gooey, the middle layer is the walnuts, and the top layer turns into a pale tan, thin crackly topping. Whatever goes on, the end result is just terrific. Alan Rupp advises that his Derby-Pie is at its best warmed all the way through so the nuts and chocolate blend together just right. Top with a dollop of fresh whipped cream or serve with vanilla ice cream. As a Louisville chef once summed it up, "Your body almost crystallizes as you eat it."

Kern's Kitchen does not ship its own pies but rather directs mail orders to Mousetrap Cheese, a Kentucky catalog that specializes in mail-order foods for gifts. A regular-size 20-ounce Derby-Pie costs $12.95 plus shipping charges which vary based on destination. All pies are shipped frozen and two-day air is recommended. Individual serving 2¾-ounce Derby-Pie tarts are $9.50 for 4, plus two-day air-shipping charges.

— ❖ —

Lisenby's Lemon Orchard Cake

Jefferson Farm Foods
Route 3, Box 234
Jefferson, Georgia 30549
(404) 367-8407 (Monday to
Saturday, 3 P.M. to 7 P.M., EST)

Free descriptive brochure
with color photo of cake
Prepaid orders only

I make just one special cake, one way," Barbara Lisenby Jackson says modestly. In a remodeled equipment shed on her farm, Barbara, a librarian, bakes small batches of a spectacularly flavorful lemon cake that is without peer. Searching for a recipe she and her daughters could use for holiday gift-baking, Barbara cannily recognized that many of us could exist quite happily if we never faced another traditional dark fruitcake with dates and citron. So she adapted her cousin Bonnie Goolsby's recipe, creating a light, exquisitely lemony dense-textured loaf that actually does melt in the mouth.

The cake was first baked as gifts for friends. Then in 1984 the principal of the school Barbara works for needed a faculty present. A taste of her cake convinced him to order 80. "I got so many compliments that I thought that if I ever needed

LISENBY'S

Lemon Orchard Cake

some extra money, it was the logical place to turn." The following year, confronted with the possibility of losing her farm, Barbara began her small business, investing in a convection oven and Hobart mixer, and baking at night with her mother's help. These days Barbara ships around 100 cakes a month, mostly to people whose friends raved about it.

A thin slice of Lisenby Lemon Orchard Cake is delicious anytime, not just around the holidays. Made with butter and pure lemon extract, it's closer to a lemon pound cake with a well-balanced scattering of candied pineapple, raisins, and Georgia pecans. No preservatives, no fakery. Though splendid-tasting on arrival, the longer it is kept in the refrigerator, the mellower it gets (it also freezes admirably). A 2-pound Lisenby Orchard Cake in a sturdy box costs $14.95 plus $3.45 shipping. A small, elegant printed card is enclosed. On the back, in tiny print, there is a quotation from the Bible that concludes, "For he satisfieth the longing soul and filleth the hungry soul with goodness."

— ❖ —

Mrs. Travis F. Hanes's Moravian Cookies

Moravian Sugar Crisp Co., Inc.
Route 2, Box 431
Friedberg Road
Clemmons, North Carolina
27012
(919) 764-1402

Free black-and-white brochure
and order form
Prepaid orders only

Imagine a cookie so wafer-thin that you can hold it up to the light and see the shadow of your finger through it. You can't make a cookie that thin with a machine, and Evva Hanes and the 35 strong-armed women who work with her wouldn't even try. "Elbow grease" is the secret ingredient at this Moravian community bakery where the recipes are a legacy from the past. Moravians were a sect of persecuted Protestants from Moravia (once part of Czechoslovakia) who fled first to Germany and then to the United States before the Revolutionary War. Today there are settlements in Pennsylvania and Florida as well as North Carolina.

The cheerful bright blue bakery is located on the land that was once Evva's father's dairy farm. To supplement the farm's income in the 1950s, Bertha Foltz, Evva's mother, baked and sold a special Moravian sugar crisp made from an old family recipe. Area residents could just drive on over to the farm and buy a batch. When old age slowed her mother down, Evva began to help with the baking. Demand increased, and by 1970 Evva and her husband, Travis, who is in charge of production, moved the baking out of the family kitchen and into its own quarters right next door. Today their son Mike mixes ingredients and oversees shipping while daughter Mona Templin handles orders.

The scent of baking cookies permeates the air for miles. Beginning around six o'clock each morning, the delicate, fragrant doughs are hand-rolled on specially constructed muslin-covered tables crafted by Mona's husband (a variation on your grandmother's trick of covering a rolling pin with stockinette to keep the dough from sticking). Then each cookie is hand-cut using special cutters from Old Salem, North Carolina—hearts, and plain and scalloped rounds. Too fragile for machine packing, short stacks of the cookies are hand-wrapped—Ginger Crisps in slick white deli paper, Sugar Crisps in homey, plain white napkins—and carefully nestled into tins or tall, slender cardboard tubes.

The remarkably thin, crispy cookies come in five flavors and contain no preservatives. The most popular—and a traditional Moravian Christmas treat—are the mild, delicately spicy Ginger Crisps, flavored with molasses and a traditional Moravian mixture of cinnamon, nutmeg, ginger, and cloves (two 8-ounce tubes of the round shape, $13, postpaid; assorted shapes in a 1-pound tin, $13, or a 2-pound tin, $21.50, postpaid). These are terrific with ice cream. Crunchy Sugar Crisps, the understated, vanilla-flavored cookie Bertha began the business with, are comforting and delicate, an ideal accompaniment for a cup of tea (two 7-ounce tubes of rounds, $12.50, postpaid; assorted shapes in a 1-pound tin, $12.50, or a 2-pound tin, $21, postpaid). Lemon, chocolate, and butterscotch versions are also available in assorted shapes at the same prices as the Sugar Crisps. Combinations of the crisps can be ordered in five special gift packs (a tube each of Ginger and Sugar Crisps, $13, postpaid; a 1-pound tin of each flavor, $53, postpaid).

— ❖ —

Original Deluxe Fruitcake

Think of it. The small East Texas town of Corsicana, population 21,712, is the fruitcake capital of the world. (In all fairness, it must be pointed out that Corsicana is not the only claimant to the fruitcake capital of the world title; there are a number of other contenders, including Claxton, Georgia.) This fact is so globally well known that orders simply addressed Fruit Cake, Texas, reach their destina-

Collin Street Bakery
401 West Seventh Avenue
Corsicana, Texas 75110

(800) 248-3366 (October to
December); (214) 872-8111
(January to September)
Fax (214) 872-6879

Free color brochure
VISA, MasterCard, American
Express, Diners Club

tion: the Collin Street Bakery, an officially designated historical landmark and home of the famous Original DeLuxe Fruitcake. "We really do exist for one day: December twenty-fifth," says co-owner John Crawford, who enjoys pointing out that the bakery has "never been bought up, absorbed, spun-off, or been part of a hostile takeover."

In 1896, Gus Weidmann, a young German baker with an Old World recipe, went into partnership with flamboyant Tom McElwee, a wealthy local entrepreneur. Gus's fruitcakes sold so well in the oil-boom town that in 1906 the pair built a bigger bakery. Tom, something of a celebrity worshiper, also owned the Corsicana Opera House, which brought touring opera, vaudeville, theater, and sports stars to town. He transformed the second floor of the big bakery into a fancy hotel that welcomed famous guests including Enrico Caruso, Will Rogers, Tom Mix (with Tony, the Wonder Horse), and performers from the John Ringling Circus. Departing guests invariably left with several of Gus's famous fruitcakes to munch on the road. Soon the Ringling Circus troopers began asking Gus to mail the fruitcakes around the world to their friends and families. The rest, as they say, is history.

Today, Collin Street Bakery Original DeLuxe Fruitcakes, which are available *only* by mail, are shipped to 194 countries and every state in the U. S. They go to ordinary mortals like you and me and (Tom McElwee would be pleased to know) countless celebrities, including Gene Autry, Lawrence Welk, and Estée Lauder. Although the cakes are freshly baked and available all year round, from June 1 through the end of December, "every waking and sleeping moment" is devoted solely to fruitcake making. The staff balloons from 50 to 550 employees. Gus's original recipe hangs on a weatherbeaten clipboard in the

kitchen, and it's still followed. Each fruitcake is chock-full of Southern Mammoth pecans (27 percent of the weight of each fruitcake is pecans), laden with fancy fruits from around the world, and meticulously hand-decorated on top with pecans and glacéed fruit—an "honest culinary beauty," as John Crawford puts it. The hokey decorative holiday tin the fruitcakes are shipped in is part of the Collin Bakery mystique. It's downright, irretrievably ugly, but an attempt to change the design in the late 1940s met with such an outraged public hue and cry that the bakery quickly reinstated the original.

Modestly priced, Collin Street Bakery Original DeLuxe Fruitcakes are baked in three sizes: regular, about 2 pounds ($11.25, postpaid); medium, about 3 pounds ($16.30, postpaid); and large, about 5 pounds ($26.70, postpaid). Christmas orders are shipped in *that* tin; at other times of the year orders are shipped in one that has an inoffensive needlepoint design. The bakery does a substantial international business (they're a favorite of American embassies and homesick Americans, and sales to Japan border on the incredible). As John Crawford once observed, "We've sent the fruitcakes to places where you couldn't pronounce the name even if you were looking at it."

— ❖ —

The Original Texas YA-HOO! Cake

There are darned near as many Texas-baked cakes available by mail as there are Texans in Texas. Of course, not all of them are baked in the shape of Texas like this one, and they don't all contain rich, big chocolate chips either.

Like all things Lone Star there's a tall tale about the Ya-Hoo Cake. Seems three cowpokes met on the Chisholm Trail. One carried cherries

The Original Texas Ya-Hoo! Cake Co.
5302 Texoma Parkway
Sherman, Texas 75090-2112
(800) 683-7234; (214)
868-9665 (Monday to Friday,
9 A.M. to 5 P.M., CST)
Fax (214) 893-5036

Free color brochure
VISA, MasterCard, American
Express

and sugar stashed in his saddlebags. Another had picked up some chocolate in Mexico. The third, a camp cook low on supplies, was waiting for ranch hands to bring provisions from up north. Luckily, he still had a few Texas native pecans on hand. It was the holiday season. Campfire conversation turned to fruitcakes. There was agreement that they were passable, but these old-timers hankered for something better. Next thing you know, the cook whipped up a special cake. The cowboys gave it a taste test. Better than fruitcake, they agreed, and let out a whoop: *Yahoo!* They say the recipe and the legend were found written on a piece of boot-sole leather stuffed under the chuck wagon floorboards. If you believe in Santa Claus, you'll fall for that.

Ya-Hoo! Cake is baked in the shape of the state of Texas and comes nestled in a glossy red box branded in gold with the Ya-Hoo lasso logo. Glazed cherries and jumbo Guittard semisweet chocolate chips are the primary ingredients, along with plenty of Texas pecans. The top is covered with plump pecans halves, and a single cherry is situated right where you'd find Sherman, Texas, on the map. Ya-Hoo! The cake is baked in a 1½-pound ($15.95, plus about $3 postage) and a 3-pound size ($23.95). And there is a round 2-pound version called the Wagon Wheel ($16.50, plus about $3 postage). Like fruitcake, the taste gets more interesting if you pour a jigger or two of spirits over it, wrap it tightly, and let it sit about a week.

— ❖ —

The Original Volunteer Jam Cake and Fruit Jams

Succulent jam cake is a traditional "once-a-year" Southern holiday dessert that you don't usually find offered by mail. People who grew up in Tennessee or Kentucky probably remember it as a special treat baked by an el-

Volunteer Ventures, Inc.
P.O. Box 159009
Nashville, Tennessee 37215
(615) 385-4508 or 747-4060

Free illustrated catalog
VISA, MasterCard

FRUIT JAMS
— ❖ —

derly relative who also made wonderful jam. The finest preserves of the canning season were held back until Thanksgiving, when they were used to create a spicy, rich cake that grew mellower and more complex in flavor as it aged. The trick was to bake it in November, store it in an airtight tin, and keep it under the bed in a cool room until Christmas came.

Strawberry Volunteer Jam Cake, dense and finely-textured, is made from a highly spiced batter that contains little bits of pecans and is sweetened with Volunteer's excellent jam. (When you lift the lid from the tin there's a nice smell of cinnamon, nutmeg, and allspice). While the smallish round cake is still hot from the oven, a thick glaze of jam is slathered over it instead of icing and, as the cake ages, this strawberry flavor slowly insinuates itself throughout. Nearly a full pound of jam is used for each cake! Blackberry Volunteer Jam Cake, closer to the recipes found in old Southern cookbooks because of its penuche-like icing, is similarly made but with blackberry jam. While it's still hot, a delicious caramel icing is slathered all over the top and sides. Each handmade 24-ounce cake comes packed in a tin ($22.95, plus $3 postage). No preservatives are used; the cakes will keep in the freezer for up to six months.

The jam used in the cakes was the company's first product and therein lies a tale. For founders Jim and Emmie Thomas, Volunteer Ventures is a food marketing company with a mission. Several years ago while figuring out a way to help provide local food banks with consistent funding, the couple, inspired by actor Paul Newman's food line, hit on the idea of selling jam with a clever name. Each year country-rock star Charlie Daniels holds a music extravaganza known as Charlie Daniels' Volunteer Jam

and proceeds are turned over to charity. The Thomases arranged to use the name for the jams they sell and a percentage of their profits are pledged to Nashville's Second Harvest food bank.

The preservative-free jams are made in small batches and flavors include the strawberry and blackberry jams uses in the cakes, plus peach (16-ounce jar, $4.50, plus postage) as well as blackberry and raspberry (16-ounce jar, $4.95). For Tennessee football fans, Volunteer makes Big Orange Marmalade ("the winning point spread," 16-ounce jar, $4.50) with a label listing all SEC and Bowl Game Championships (profits benefit University of Tennessee athletics). Their catalog also offers a good-value Tennessee Breakfast Sampler box that would make a terrific gift: a jar each of peach and strawberry Volunteer Jam, Martha White biscuit mix, along with Mayo's (see page 300) famous hickory-smoked sausage and dry-cured bacon ($25.95, plus postage).

— ❖ —

Rowena's Wonderful Almond Pound Cake

**Rowena's & Captain Jaap's Jam and Jelly Factory
758 West 22nd Street
Norfolk, Virginia 23517**

(800) 627-8699 (Monday to Friday, 9 A.M. to 5 P.M., EST)

**Free illustrated color catalog
VISA, MasterCard**

The first time I tasted Rowena Jaap's Wonderful Almond Pound Cake I almost gave up baking. It was that good. In fact, it's so delicious that when my friend Gloria from Mississippi bit into a slice, she said something that'll probably get her disinherited. "Good grief," she exclaimed, "this is better than my mama makes—and she makes the best pound cake in Holcomb!" So as you can see, this cake comes highly recommended.

The cake is carefully baked in small batches at Rowena's & Captain Jaap's Jam and Jelly Factory from a recipe that originated with Rowena's former mother-in-law. The cake, along with preserves made from the Jaaps' own backyard fruit trees, was given as a gift to family and neighbors. A few years back, when their trees yielded a

bumper crop, the Jaaps began canning extra jars of jams and jellies to sell. Then Rowena baked a few extra cakes to help raise funds for the schools and organizations she was involved with as a volunteer. Pretty soon they were operating a business out of a renovated warehouse. Rowena and Joseph Jaap (a former naval officer known as the Captain) have parted, but the factory they started is going great guns, with 16 employees, 2 sparkling kitchens, and a devoted mail-order following (the products are also available in some specialty stores).

Rowena's Wonderful Almond Pound Cake tastes so rich and good because it contains only fresh ingredients and the texture is perfection. Each is attractively swathed in clear cellophane, tied with a perky red-and-white polka-dot bow, and packed in a glossy white box. Very moist and almondy, the cake stays wonderfully fresh a week or more at room temperature if tightly wrapped (it gets even mellower), or it can be frozen for up to a year for future use. It's wonderful thinly sliced with a cup of tea, toasted for breakfast, or served in thick slices topped with ice cream. A round cake, weighing 2¾ pounds, costs $15.50 plus postage; a loaf cake, weighing 1¾ pounds, costs $12. Rowena's Lemon or Pineapple Curd ($5 per 9-ounce jar) is tasty on the cake, too. Either size cake may be ordered gift-boxed with a jar of curd ($17 to $20.50).

Rowena's real-life jam factory adventures were the inspiration for her illustrated story/cookbook for little kids, *The Adventures of Rowena and the Wonderful Jam and Jelly Factory* (40 pages of text with color illustrations, $12.95). Shipping is extra; for example, $2.75 for orders under $20.

VISITING THE SOURCE
— ❖ —

There are no formal tours of the jam and jelly factory, but visitors are invited to drop by the retail store in front of the factory, where Rowena's & Captain Jaap's complete line of specialties is for sale. The shop is open Monday through Friday 9 A.M. to 5 P.M.

— ❖ —

Texas-shaped Czech Fruitcake and Texas-size Cookies

Gladys' Cookie Shop
Cistern Community
Route 1, Box 281-A
Flatonia, Texas 78941
(512) 865-3682

Free color order form
VISA, MasterCard

You probably never realized that a 150-pound Texas-shaped fruitcake cut into bite-size pieces will feed 7,000 guests. This very cake, baked by Gladys Farek and measuring six feet from the Panhandle to McAllen and five feet from El Paso to Texarkana, is listed in *The Guinness Book of World Records*. It took six strong people to heft it into the oven where it was baked for about three hours. Almost unbelievably, you can actually order one of your very own through the mail from Gladys' famous cookie shop for $998 (plus $75 shipping). But you shouldn't wait until your guest list hits 7,000. For those of us with a few less friends, she offers sizes that are much more manageable (more about this later).

Sheer boredom is what led Gladys Farek to become a professional baker about 15 years ago. And boredom made Gladys, in her words, very nervous. Other, less energetic, people would have found that raising six children on a 188-acre farm was enough to keep them busy, but Gladys is sort of a cheerful workaholic and a terrific baker (the youngest of nine children, she began cooking when she was five). She started baking tasty "Texas-size" cookies, selling them to local restaurants and shops. Soon she had helpers and an ever-expanding line of homemade goods from country-style bread to noodles. But Gladys got bored again in 1975 during the slack winter months when cookie sales slow down. She began thinking about fruitcake, developing a recipe by trial and error ("our hogs got fat and sassy on my mistakes").

"We bake the cake that takes the cake," Gladys likes to say, and she's right. It's actually more of a pecan cake than a fruitcake, since it's 50 percent or more pecans combined with candied pineapple and cherries and just enough flour and egg batter to hold the ingredients together. There is no citron ("People think it tastes bitter"), no raisins ("So many people don't care for them"), and no spices (because Gladys doesn't think they're needed—though there *is* a touch of rum flavoring). For the second year of baking Gladys went down to Montgomery Ward, bought herself a cement mixer, and painted it red. With the blades removed the mixer holds 190 pounds of batter, which is briefly tumbled until the ingredients are blended. The top of each fruitcake is hand-decorated with rows of the freshest, fattest Texas pecan

Gladys Farek uses a cement mixer to toss batter for her Texas-shaped fruitcakes.

halves and the highest-quality candied cherries from France. The Texas-shaped cakes come in a variety of sizes (2-pound, $19.95, postpaid; 3-pound, $26.45; 5-pound, $43.45; 10-pound, $84.90; 25-pound, $195). The smaller versions are available in tins for a few extra dollars.

Gladys still makes the Texas-size cookies she began with. They come in oatmeal, sugar, chocolate chip, and molasses (one dozen 5-inch cookies, $7.50, postpaid). Cakes and cookies are available all year round.

— ❖ —

Virginia Diner Peanutty Pie

Virginia Diner
P.O. Box 310
Wakefield, Virginia
23888-0310

(800) 642-NUTS (7 days a week, 9 A.M. to 5 P.M., EST)
Fax (804) 899-2281

Free 12-page color catalog
VISA, MasterCard

Every day is Peanut Pie Day at the famous Wakefield Diner ("the Peanut Capital of the World") where freshly baked pies have been tempting eaters since 1929. Virginia Diner Peanuts, the diner's mail-order division, has shipped incredibly delicious peanuts by mail for years (see page 264) but it wasn't until recently that you could order the equally famous, much-praised peanut pie by mail.

The Virginia Diner was originally housed in a railroad paymaster's car when it first opened in 1929. And although the diner has expanded several times, owner Bill Galloway is very proud of the fact that the old car remains part of the actual restaurant building today (there's even a drawing of it on the menus). The diner is packed to the rafters most of the time (it's a hot spot for tourists) but Galloway says the goal has never changed: "to achieve the highest quality possible in down-home country cooking and traditional hospitality." The bill of fare ranges from sublime fried chicken and Virginia ham to zany peanut-shaped peanut butter and jelly sandwiches with a side of peanuts. Not many visitors escape without having a wedge of peanut pie for dessert, a pie judged "a class act" and "a doozy" by Jane

and Michael Stern when they included the diner in their book *Road Food and Good Food*.

Peanut pie is, of course, an old Southern dessert classic. In the 1900s, when Dr. George Washington Carver was trying to convince everyone how great peanuts were by listing 105 ways to prepare them, you can bet peanut pie was on the list. It's very similar to pecan pie, with the obvious exception of the nuts. The Virginia Diner version is gooey and good. Literally hundreds of peanut halves and pieces cover every millimeter of the top; underneath there's a thick layer of gooey sweet brown filling that's a blend of eggs, sugar, dark corn syrup, butter, and vanilla (the crust is nothing to write home about but with all those peanuts, who cares?). The pie is available two ways: shipped in a tin ($12.95, plus postage) or in an 8½-inch reusable white ceramic microwave-safe pie dish ($19.95, plus postage). One of these pies might make a funny birthday "cake" for a peanut lover. The pie tastes nicest warmed and served with a scoop of vanilla ice cream just like they serve it at the diner.

— ❖ —

Warrenton Old English Plum Pudding, Original Nashville Rum Cakes, and Golden Fruit Cake

Some folks have been on Warrenton's customer list for three generations or longer and they wouldn't think of getting through the holidays without a Warrenton's Old English Plum Pudding. "The fifty-three-year-old recipe hasn't been changed one bit," proudly notes Rosie Brown, one of the four owners.

Back in the 1930s, Nancy Warren DeLuca was considered one of Nashville's best cooks, a gracious hostess presiding over countless entertainments sponsored by her husband, head of the local music conservatory (where Dinah Shore was a student). The social elite of Nashville counted themselves lucky if Mrs. DeLuca gave

Warrenton, Ltd.
P.O. Box 40019
Nashville, Tennessee 37204

(615) 297-8070 (Monday to
Friday, 9 A.M. to 5 P.M., CST)

Free postcard-size descriptive
order form
VISA, MasterCard, American
Express

them one of her famous plum puddings at Christmastime. Later, as a young widow, Mrs. DeLuca supported her children by selling the puddings to a select mailing list of friends. She named the company after Warrenton, Virginia, where her family had been early settlers. In 1956 Rosie Brown, a second generation customer, and her friends Elaine Goetz, Margie Overton, and Jayne Hagan bought the small company.

The puddings are still made by hand. From August to December each year the partners and a small family of helpers chop and mix ingredients. The tubby puddings contain pineapple, raisins, currants, bread crumbs, suet, milk, eggs, sugar, flour, brandy, and spices. They steam the rich mixture for six hours, then dry the puddings on racks for several weeks before packing them in bright red cardboard holiday boxes bearing the Warrenton logo. Marvelously moist, aromatic, and spicy, the puddings put to shame the common commercial vacuum-packed ones that are dry and crumbly. Warrenton Old English Plum Puddings come in three sizes (1 pound, $14.95, postpaid; 2 pounds, $21.50, postpaid; and 3 pounds, $27.95, postpaid). Each pound of pudding will serve five or six people. A pound of Warrenton's hard sauce can be ordered for $7.25, postpaid.

The recipe for Warrenton's Original Nashville Rum Cakes originated with Mrs. Ruth Haury, co-owner Jayne Hagan's mother. These heavenly tidbits, baked only from October through mid-December, sell out earlier each year, so timing your order can be tricky. These are two-bite-size, one-inch squares of homemade angel food cake that are hand-iced with scrumptious real rum frosting on all six sides. They're rolled in finely ground pecans until there's not a speck of frosting visible, arranged in miniature white paper muffin cups, and packed in a decorative white

SOUTHERN BOILED CUSTARD
— ❖ —

3 egg yolks
¼ cup sugar
Pinch of salt
2 cups milk, scalded
½ teaspoon vanilla

Southern boiled custard, although a liquid, is often served as a winter holiday dessert. It is served in an old-fashioned or stem glass, topped with whipped cream and nutmeg, and accompanied by a rum cake, fruit cake, or crisp Christmas cookie. It is served cold, and usually a small pitcher of bourbon is passed to the adults.

Beat the egg yolks slightly, and add the sugar and salt to them. Gradually stir in the milk. Place the mixture in the top of a double boiler over simmering water. Stir constantly until the mixture thickens and coats a spoon. Allow it to cool, then add the vanilla. If the custard separates or becomes lumpy, put the pan in cold water and beat with a rotary beater until smooth. *Approximately 2 cups*

tin with the Warrenton logo on the lid (2-pound tin with 28 cakes, $19.95, postpaid). Rosie Brown advises these are "absolutely lip-smacking" served alongside boiled custard.

Less well known than the other two products is the round Warrenton Golden Fruit Cake made from Mrs. DeLuca's recipe (2-pound cake in a red tin, $18, postpaid). Pale rather than dark, delicate rather than spicy, it's made like traditional Virginia white fruitcakes from a butter and whole-egg batter lightly flavored with lemon, sherry, and brandy, with flecks of coconut, cherries, pineapple, raisins, and almonds.

Nashville residents can place orders by phone and pick them up in person at Warrenton's kitchens, located at One Buchi Court. All other orders are shipped UPS. "I'm an absolute authority on zip codes," laughs Rosie Brown.

SNACKS

• Mrs. Fearnow's Delicious Brunswick Stew • Fuller's Mustard • Maunsel White's
• Panola Pepper Sauce • Amber Brand Smithfield Ham • Billy Higdon's Happy Holle
Hams • Colonel Bill Newsom's Kentucky Country Hams • Bucksnort Smoked Rainb
Garber Farms Cajun Yams • Bland Farms Sweet Vidalia Onions • Callaway Garden
d Heart Grits • White Lily Flour • Bailey's Homemade Hot Pepper Jelly • Mayhaw J
ized Pecans • Virginia Diner Peanuts • Ellis Stansel's Rice • Ledford Mill Borrowe
n Arrow Ranch Axis Venison • Comeaux's Boudin • Mayo's Hickory-Smoked Sausa
• Golden Mill Sorghum • Steen's Pure Cane Syrup • Best of Luck Scottish Shortbr
oes and Nails • Double Decker Deluxe Moon Pies • Kern's Kitchen Derby Pie • Lis
Orchard Cake • Warrenton Original Nashville Rum Cakes • Zapp's Potato Chips •
Rendezvous Ribs • Maurice Bessinger's Flying Pig Barbeque • Barq's Root Beer •
ine • Crickle • Evelyn's Pralines • Goo Goo Clusters • The Allens Cut Leaf Poke S
• Mrs. Fearnow's Delicious Brunswick Stew • Fuller's Mustard • Maunsel White's
Panola Pepper Sauce • Amber Brand Smithfield Ham • Billy Higdon's Happy Holl
Hams • Colonel Bill Newsom's Kentucky Country Hams • Bucksnort Smoked Rainb
Garber Farms Cajun Yams • Bland Farms Sweet Vidalia Onions • Callaway Garde
d Heart Grits • White Lily Flour • Bailey's Homemade Hot Pepper Jelly • Mayhaw J
ized Pecans • Virginia Diner Peanuts • Ellis Stansel's Rice • Ledford Mill Borrowe
n Arrow Ranch Axis Venison • Comeaux's Boudin • Mayo's Hickory-Smoked Sausa
• Golden Mill Sorghum • Steen's Pure Cane Syrup • Best of Luck Scottish Shortbr

"You can't be lonesome when you're eating."
—Anonymous

The only thing a true Southerner loves more than eating is. . . snacking. When breakfast, lunch, or supper have turned into distant memories, when that hollow feeling rears its head and you're seized up by a craving, you'll wish you'd ordered a thing or two from the following pages. Oh, sure, you could probably get by without a few bags of Zapp's Potato Chips (the best in the universe) or some of Kim's Fried Pork Rinds sprinkled with hot sauce. You might even be able to face a late afternoon sinking spell without a handful of crackers spread with Hot Dang Cheese. But why should you?

Gethsemani Trappist Semi-Soft Cheeses

Gethsemani Farms
Trappist, Kentucky 40051
No phone orders
Fax (502) 549-8281

Free color brochure with order form
VISA, MasterCard

While we're all still snug in bed dreaming, the 80 or so Trappist monks of the Abbey of Gethsemani in central Kentucky, whose day begins at 3 A.M., have been up for hours in harmonious pursuit of a unique contemplative religious life based on silence, solitude, simplicity, and hard manual labor. To support the abbey, the monks make and sell delicious semisoft cheeses aged in their curing cellar and a wonderful, moist fruitcake that's too good to order only during the holidays (see page 339).

According to Brother Raphael, a former Marine pilot who joined the order in the mid 1950s and who manages Gethsemani Farms, cheese has been made here practically since the monastery was founded in 1848. This is a natural, creamy semisoft cheese made using the same old-world formula followed for hundreds of years by European Trappist monasteries. The flavor is superb, quite strong and full of character, tasting similar to a Port Salut. Three versions, each excellent, are available: mild, aged (real sharp), and smoked over hickory chips (my favorite). The cheeses come vacuum-sealed and may be ordered in a variety of ways. A whole wheel of mild or aged cheese weighing about 3 pounds costs $18, postpaid; half-wheels cost around $9.50; or you may order a combination of three quarter-wheels, one of each type, for $14.25. For gift-giving the monks offer a quarter-wheel of each cheese nicely packaged in one of their round, handmade poplar-wood boxes with a drawing of the monastery on the lid ($16.50, postpaid). Unwrapped, the pale, buttery-colored wedges look like something from a Brueghel painting, so it's no surprise they make a lovely, scenic dessert when set out on a board accompanied by bunches of grapes and some crisp apples. Be aware: When these natural cheeses are subjected to warm temperatures during shipping, they sometimes release a strong-smelling gas that may puff up their plastic wrappings. But don't worry, this is *not* an indication of spoilage.

— ❖ —

Hot Dang and Hot Damn Old Kentucky Beer Cheese

Here's a little something tasty to spread on crackers at your next poker party. Beer cheese is a savory, old-time Kentucky cheese spread that most Northerners are not familiar with, though a version of it is also made in Wisconsin, where it was introduced by German settlers. According to Camille Glenn, author of *The Heritage of Southern Cooking*, Kentucky beer cheese was first concocted at the turn of the century by a German saloon keeper in Frankfort, Kentucky. This was the age when saloons served free food in abundance to their customers and the beer cheese was set out on the

Party Kits Unlimited
3730 Lexington Road
Louisville, Kentucky
40207-3000

(502) 896-0400 and
896-6236 (Monday to Friday,
9 A.M. to 7 P.M., EST)

Free 20-page color catalog
VISA, MasterCard, American
Express

counter in large crocks so drinkers could slather it on crackers and get even more thirsty.

This commercial but tasty version of beer cheese is the brainchild of Tillie Moore, who got the recipe from a friend about 35 years ago. Tillie and her husband, Cleo, always served it at their poker parties. It is marketed by her small company, Moorethings, and is available only through local Kentucky shops and a couple of catalogs.

Tillie's Old Kentucky Beer Cheese is a sort of jazzed-up pasteurized cheese spread, a kissing cousin of Cheez-Whiz but with a lot more character. It comes in two "strengths," both guaranteed to be "knee-slapping good." Hot Dang, with a little zing, is the milder one; from Hot Damn (which I like best) you get a serious jolt of heat from cayenne and hot sauce. When you open a jar, you'll get a brisk whiff of beer, one of the main flavorings. The spread is based on a combination of Cheddar and Colby cheeses, along with a liberal dose of beer and some other flavorings. To manufacture her product, Tillie turned to Fresh Approach, a local food-service training center for disabled adults that prepares and bottles the beer cheeses in its commercial kitchens.

Hot Dang and Hot Damn Old Kentucky Beer Cheese come in 11-ounce jars ($4.95 each, plus shipping) and may be ordered through Party Kits Unlimited, a firm that specializes in mail-ordering Kentucky Derby–related merchandise.

This firm's shipping charges are high ($4 is the minimum shipping charge). However, several pages of the catalog are devoted to Kentucky specialty foods and related items, among them the deliciously fruity- spicy Maker's Mark Bourbon Gourmet Sauce (see page 118) and Charles Patteson's excellent book *Kentucky Cooking*, which is filled with elegant, delicious recipes.

Kim's Fried Pork Rinds and Cracklings

Kim's Processing Plant
417 Third Street
Clarksdale, Mississippi
38614
(601) 627-2389

Free order form
Prepaid orders only

President George Bush's favorite snack is a handful of crispy pork rinds splashed with hot sauce. His fondness for this good old Southern treat has not surprisingly lead to his administration being dubbed "the pork-rind presidency." There's even an unconfirmed rumor that soon they'll be stocking bags of pork rinds in White House vending machines. And I know for a fact (although presidents don't generally like these things to be known) that George Bush has actually tasted Kim's Fried Pork Rinds and pronounced them "delicious."

Pork rinds are crispy, sinfully salty, fried curls of pigskin that taste best accompanied by big gulps of RC, Coke, or a cold long-neck beer. They're definitely not for faint-hearted eaters, since they are what they are—pigs' skin—and that's that. Some folks like them plain, while others think they're best when sprinkled with some hot sauce like Tabasco for zing. Cracklins are the crunchy bits of pork and fat that remain behind after lard has been rendered from pork. For many Southerners, both pork rinds and cracklins bring back memories of the fall pig-slaughtering time that once took place on every Southern farm in this land of hog and hominy. When the work was done and the meat laid by, there were always leftover bits of skin to fry up for snacking. Today pork rinds are still essential munchies, and literally millions of bags are sold throughout the South.

Kim Wong is a second-generation Mississippian

whose rinds reflect the zany borrowings and culinary swappings that have taken place in much delta cooking. For generations, the Chinese, Lebanese, and countless other ethnic groups flocked to the Mississippi Delta in search of new lives. They settled right in, which meant learning to cook Southern—but without losing their own cuisines. The upshot had been a culinary melting pot that produces things like Abe's famous Southern barbecue with a Lebanese twist and baklava on a menu that also features red beans and rice. Kim's business is another example of this cross-cultural blending of good eats.

For many years Kim Wong and his wife, Jean, ran the most popular Chinese restaurant in Clarksdale, Mississippi. From his post at the cash register, Kim noticed that the little bags of pork cracklins he sold could hardly be kept in stock. Cautiously, back in his own kitchen, he experimented with making his own. Kim's Cracklings turned out just a little different from other people's because he adds some secret Chinese spices that make them taste a bit more interesting. At first he simply gave them away to customers to see how they stacked up against commercial ones, but the public quickly proved willing to buy his cracklins instead of other brands, and before long the Wongs were out of the restaurant business and into full-time cracklin production. A little while later the Wongs began making fried pork rinds as well (without Chinese spices), and now their firm processes up to 42,000 pounds of meat a month. Both the pork rinds and the cracklins carry with them the fragrant, mouthwatering odor of fried bacon along with a deeply satisfying crunchiness. Kim himself designed the bold bright yellow and black design of the cellophane bags.

While Kim is mostly set up to sell to grocery stores and other commercial outlets, he'll gladly

ship a supply of either product to individuals. He says folks in beer-drinking states like Wisconsin and Michigan are especially avid customers. But be warned: You can't get a small supply. The minimum order for fried pork rinds is a case of twelve 4-ounce bags (these are about the size of your average potato-chip bag) for $10.80, plus UPS charges. Kim's Cracklings are shipped eighteen 8-ounce packages to a case for $27.90, plus UPS. The cracklins, which should be refrigerated upon arrival, are good whirled briefly in a food processor and used like bacon bits for salad flavoring, with green vegetables, or on baked potatoes—anything you might sprinkle with bits of bacon. And, of course, you can use them in that classic Southern hot treat, cracklin bread.

— ❖ —

Zapp's Potato Chips

Z app's Potato Chips are hands down the best chips I've ever eaten, and I'll bet if you give them a try, you'll agree with me 100 percent... and then some. No kidding. These chips have become so popular in Louisiana that Mardi Gras parade participants are even dressing up as bags of Zapp's.

Founder Ron Zappe (rhymes with *happy*) is what you'd have to call a potato chip king now, but he hasn't let it go to his head. He's still hanging out in jeans and a baseball cap and is quick to remind you he went "from crude oil to peanut oil" when he began his company in the summer of 1985. Zappe used to run an oil-field equipment business but got out during the hard times of the oil crunch. One day his wife, Anne, returned from a visit to Texas with a bag of jalapeño-flavored potato chips so unusually tasty that Zappe called up the company that made them and asked them to teach him the chip business. "I just followed them around and asked

Zapp's Potato Chips
P.O. Box 1533
Gramercy, Louisiana
70052-1533
(800) HOT-CHIP; (800)
826-4253; (Monday to Friday,
8 A.M. to 6 P.M., CST)

Free order form
VISA, MasterCard

Zapp's

"a lot of questions," says Zappe. Five months later he established his "little chippery in Gramercy" in a former Chevrolet dealership located on a two-lane highway midway between New Orleans and Baton Rouge (if you drive by you can see chips being packaged through the showroom windows). The chips sold like crazy almost from the beginning, but when *People* magazine published the HOT-CHIP ordering number in an article on the zany Zappe, sales skyrocketed and have never slowed down.

Zapp's Potato Chips are thick, incredibly crunchy, and taste better because they're made better and with more care than other chips (they even throw a few extra chips in each bag after they're weighed). Zappe goes out of his way to use Louisiana products whenever possible (everything from the potatoes to the bags) and pays attention to the little things. For example, once potatoes arrive direct from farmers, they're placed for a while in a "cooling room." This allows the sugar content in the potatoes to drop, which is important because high sugar content can make chips turn too brown when they're fried. And after the potatoes are cleaned and sliced, they're washed again to remove excess starch. Then they're fried in "Cajun frying kettles" filled with 100 percent pure Louisiana peanut oil, which is much more expensive than other oils but makes a crisper, fresher-tasting chip. Kettle-cooked chips are fried in

DEAR ZAPP'S

— ❖ —

Zapp's gets fan mail like you wouldn't believe. Among the letters I've seen was one signed by a "potato eatin' fool" (actually, a guy in the Air Force stationed in Greenland 900 miles from the North Pole) who swore the chips brought warmth in minus-47-degree weather and another from a group of homesick Southern seminarians studying at the Vatican's North American College in Rome who sent their blessings with a check for chips. But my favorite fans were the two guys who went scuba diving off of Grand Cayman Island and fed crushed chips to the fish as snacks.

batches rather than the usual continuous assembly-line process used by most companies and the result is a "hard-bite" chip that's slightly greasy, thicker, and infinitely crunchier than other chips.

The chips come in a variety of flavors, including lightly salted, unseasoned regular, and no-salt. Spices are added to the chips only seconds before they're sealed in bags, which is one reason they're so highly flavorful. The best-seller by far is Cajun Craw-Tators, which are very spicy and a little hot from a secret mixture of red pepper, garlic, and onions. The flavor is similar to that of crab boil and they're utterly addictive. (I'm not proud of it, but I have eaten an entire 7-ounce bag at one sitting.) Other flavors include a fresh-tasting Jalapeño (you can *see* the little green flecks), Mesquite BBQ (fabulous), and dill-speckled Cajun Dill Gator-Tators, which taste exactly like a hot dill pickle. Deciding what new flavors to add to the line is a fairly casual proposition. "Our research and development department consists of our friends and two fifths of scotch," Zapp explains. "We try things out on them, and if they like it we go with it." All prices include postage. You can order a 4 Bagger Box sampler of 7-ounce bags, your choice of flavors, for $9.96; a case of twelve 7-ounce bags, all one flavor, $25.96 (mixed, add $2); or a 3-pound bulk box of any flavor for $9.50 (good for parties). Little 1⅛-ounce bags for lunchboxes are shipped 36 to a case (all one flavor) for $22.96 or 13 bags (mixed flavors) for $9.96. You've got to taste them to believe them, so don't delay.

Index

Recipe Index

> *As God is my
> witness, as God is
> my witness . . . I'm
> never going to be
> hungry again. No,
> nor any of my folks.
> If I have to steal or
> kill—as God is my
> witness, I'm never
> going to be hungry
> again.*
>
> —*Scarlett O'Hara*
> in Gone with
> the Wind
> *by Margaret
> Mitchell*

Recipe Credits

Thank you to the following people and companies for the use of their recipes in *True Grits*: page 25: John Wills's Watermelon Ice courtesy of John Mills; page 56: Cheerwine Carolina Cooler courtesy of Carolina Beverage Corporation; page 58: Café Brûlot courtesy of Community Coffee Company; page 61: Mint Julep courtesy of Tillie Moore; page 62: Martinez courtesy of Sazerac Company, Inc.; page 101: Famous Ro★Tel Cheese Dip courtesy of Knapp-Sherrill Co.; page 103: Trappey's Sweet Potato-Pecan Pie courtesy of Trappey's Fine Foods, Inc.; page 121: Bubber's Bloodys courtesy of Panola Pepper Corporation; page 126: Grits and Grillades from *The Land of TABASCO® Sauce*, courtesy of the McIlhenny Company; page 169: Joe's Stone Crab Restaurant Mustard Sauce courtesy of Joe's Stone Crab Restaurant; page 184: Southern Fried Louisiana Yam Chips courtesy of Garber Farms; page 189: Vidalia Sweet-Onion Pie courtesy of G&R Farms; page 193: Crispy Texas 1015 Supersweet Onion Rings

courtesy of Royal International Ltd.; page 205: Callaway Gardens Cheese Grits courtesy of Callaway Gardens Country Store; page 212: Miss Mary's Cornmeal Waffles with Spiked Waffle Syrup courtesy of Lynne Tolley, Miss Mary Bobo's Boarding House; page 221: Sarah Fritschner's Tomato Cobbler with Corn-Biscuit Topping, from *The Weisenberger Cookbook*, courtesy of Weisenberger Flour Mills; page 223: White Lily "Light" Biscuits courtesy of The White Lily Foods Company; page 226: Woodson's Mill Whole-Wheat Bread courtesy of Woodson's Mill; page 232: Hot-Pepper Fruit Salad courtesy of Aunt Freddie Bailey; page 235: Callaway Gardens Muscadine Bread courtesy of Callaway Gardens Country Store; page 240: Mayhaw Jelly Cookies courtesy of The Mayhaw Tree, Inc.; page 253: Black Walnut Bars courtesy of Missouri Dandy Pantry; page 256: Homemade Parched (Roasted) Peanuts courtesy of Growers Peanut Food Promotions; page 261: "Best Ever"

Pecan Pie courtesy of Sunnyland Farms; page 268: Dixie Peanut Brittle courtesy of Growers' Peanut Food Promotions; page 272: Company Rice Custard courtesy of Southern Rice Marketing; page 274: Calas Tout Chaud, from *Great Desserts of the South* by Mary Leigh Furrh and Jo Barksdale, courtesy of Pelican Publishing Company, Gretna, LA; page 288: Broken Arrow Ranch Savory Venison Stew courtesy of Texas Wild Game Cooperative; page 297: Paul Prudhomme's Chicken, Andouille, and Tasso Jambalaya copyright © 1988 by Paul Prudhomme; page 317: Old-Fashioned Sorghum Cookies courtesy of National Sweet Sorghum Producers and Processors Association; page 321: Masse Pain, from *The Story of Steen's Syrup and Its Famous Recipes*, courtesy of C.S. Steen Syrup Mill; page 360: Mrs. A. Arthur Halle's Southern Boiled Custard, from *The Memphis Cookbook*, courtesy of the Junior League of Memphis.

Photography Credits

Page 24: Courtesy of John Wills Bar-B-Que Pit; page 52: Courtesy of Barq's, Inc.; page 82: Courtesy of Lammes Candies; page 88: Both photos courtesy of Rebecca-Ruth Candies; pages 96 and 97: Courtesy of Piggly Wiggly Corporation; page 104: Courtesy of Trappey's Fine Foods, Inc.; page 135: Courtesy of The Smithfield Companies; page 137: Courtesy of Higdon's Foodtown; page 141: Courtesy of Broadbent's B&B Food Products, Inc.; page 144: Courtesy of Clifty Farm Country Meats; page 147: Courtesy of Colonel Bill Newsom; page 148: Courtesy of Doug Freeman; page 149: Courtesy of S. Wallace Edwards

& Sons; page 153: Courtesy of Gwaltney of Smithfield; page 154: Courtesy of The Honey Baked Ham Company; page 157: Courtesy of Loveless Hams and Jams Catalog; page 170: Courtesy of *The Courier*, Savannah, TN; page 177: Courtesy of Bland Farms; page 180: Courtesy of Cushman Fruit Company, Inc.; pages 182 and 183: Courtesy of Frank Lewis' Alamo Fruit; pages 188 and 189: Courtesy of G&R Farms; page 193: Courtesy of Planters Three; page 201: Courtesy of Berea College Public Relations, New Bureau (photographed by Kara Beth Brunner); page 210: Courtesy of Jack Daniel Distil-

lery; page 224: Courtesy of House of Webster; page 264: Courtesy of the Virginia Diner; page 285: Courtesy of Bates Turkey Farm; page 296: Courtesy of K-Paul's Louisiana Enterprises (photographed by Tom Jimison); page 304: Courtesy of Palmetto Pigeon Plant; page 316: Courtesy of Golden Kentucky Products; page 329: Photo by Maggi Castelloe; page 336: Courtesy of Dutch Maid Bakery; page 341: The Historic New Orleans Collection, Museum/Research Center; page 356: Courtesy of Gladys' Cookie Shop; page 357 and 358: Courtesy of the Virginia Diner.